WINDS OF HISTORY

WINDS

John H. Backer

OF HISTORY

THE GERMAN YEARS of
Lucius DuBignon Clay

VAN NOSTRAND REINHOLD COMPANY
New York   Cincinnati   Toronto   London   Melbourne

Acknowledgments

The following are excerpted and used by special permission:

From "Uncommon Clay," by Drew Middleton. Copyright 1945, The New York Times Company.

From "Soldier in Mufti," by E.J. Kahn, January 13, 1951. Copyright 1951, 1979, The New Yorker Magazine Inc.

From "An American Viceroy in Germany," by Demaree Bess, in *The Saturday Evening Post*. Copyright 1947, The Curtis Publishing Company.

From "General Clay—On His Own," by William H. Hale. Copyright 1948 by *Harper's Magazine*, reprinted from the October 1948 issue. All rights reserved.

From the interviews of Dr. Jean E. Smith with General Lucius D. Clay. Copyright by The Trustees of Columbia University in the City of New York, 1976.

Library of Congress Catalog Card Number 82-13574

ISBN 0-442-21382-4

Printed in the United States of America
Designed by Kenneth Milford

Published by Van Nostrand Reinhold Company Inc.
135 West 50th Street
New York, New York 10020

Van Nostrand Reinhold Publishers
1410 Birchmount Road
Scarborough, Ontario M1P 2E7, Canada

Van Nostrand Reinhold Australia Pty. Ltd.
480 Latrobe Street
Melbourne, Victoria 3000, Australia

Van Nostrand Reinhold Company Limited
Molly Millars Lane
Wokingham, Berkshire RG11 2PY, England

16   15   14   13   12   11   10   9   8   7   6   5   4   3   2   1

Library of Congress Cataloging in Publication Data

Backer, John H., 1902–
  Winds of history.

  Bibliography: p. 294
  Includes index.
  1. Clay, Lucius D. (Lucius DuBignon), 1897–1978.
2. Germany—History—Allied occupation, 1945.
3. Generals—United States—Biography.   4. United
States. Army—Biography. I. Title.
E745.C47B3 1983   940.53′144′0924   82-13574
ISBN 0-442-21382-4

Contents

FOREWORD / *John J. McCloy*   vii

Introduction   1

One / Taking the Reins   3

Two / The Setting   31

Three / Bad Orders   44

Four / The Power of the Purse Strings   76

Five / A General Sets Policy   103

Six / A Temporary Expedient   128

Seven / The President Sets Policy   155

Eight / Falling in Line   181

Nine / Fate Intervenes Again   206

Ten / Defending Berlin   233

Eleven / And Engineering the Ramparts   255

Twelve / An End and a Beginning   281

EPILOGUE / *Don D. Humphrey*   292

BIBLIOGRAPHY   294

INDEX   315

★

Foreword

DURING THE COURSE OF WORLD WAR II, IN WHICH I SERVED AS THE ASSISTANT
Secretary of War, I heard intermittently of the effective service in the War
Department of one of General Brehon Somervell's chief assistants, named
Lucius Clay. Somervell, an outstanding figure in the war, was the chief
supply and procurement officer of the War Department under Secretary
Robert Patterson. It seemed that whenever a difficult problem arose, particularly in the international area, General Clay was called upon to solve
it, and this reputation as a performer frequently came to the attention of
the Secretary of War's office. These reports were sometimes accompanied
by vivid accounts of his somewhat arbitrary or brusque methods of
operating.

Clay was a distinguished product of West Point and the Corps of
Engineers. He was deeply imbued with the traditions of both these institutions. In addition, in the course of his experience in and out of the army,
he seemed to have a real knowledge of how our civilian governmental and
particularly the federal legislative and executive systems worked. It was the
image of him in this capacity which stayed in the back of my mind, as well
as the fact that he was a regular and most proficient army officer.

When the close of the German war seemed to be in sight, I received
an abrupt summons to come to the White House and report to the President.
I had participated in a number of conferences and meetings where political
and military aspects of the war were discussed and at which President
Roosevelt was present, but I had never had an individual meeting with him.
He greeted me in the debonair manner described to in this book, from
which I gleaned that he wished me to be the United States High Commissioner for Germany in the postwar period. Recovering from my surprise
at the form of his greeting, I promptly and strongly urged on the President
the unwisdom of appointing a civilian to be in charge of the postwar administration of Germany at the outset. I maintained that, at least in the
beginning, the situation would demand a military figure and a military
governor. The civilian Commissioner could come later. I put forward my
reasons as rapidly and vigorously as I could. The President stated that he
knew of no military figure who could fill the difficult and complex role that
the German situation would immediately require. I was well aware of the

exacting difficulties of the job, but I have often since been surprised at how promptly the name of General Clay came to my mind when the President first spoke to me about the postwar occupation of Germany. I immediately suggested his name as a regular military officer who came as close as anyone I knew, civilian or soldier, to possessing the capacity to deal with the difficult problems that the German occupation would entail. I told the President that Senator James Byrnes knew Clay well and that Clay's father had long been a distinguished senator from Georgia. I think the President was intrigued when I also mentioned that Clay had once been a page boy in Congress. The President asked me to talk the matter over with Senator Byrnes. Byrnes turned out to be most enthusiastic in regard to Clay.

There were others who, unlike Clay, really aspired to the job of directing the occupation of Germany, but none, in my judgment, could meet the challenge of such a mission as well as he. By suggesting him, I felt the ground was being laid for an intelligent, well-sustained direction of Germany's postwar occupation. In spite of many changes in policy and at times of a lack of clear instructions from Washington, the fact that there eventually emerged the highly creditable and well-motivated western democratic state in the form of the Federal Republic is, in my judgment, largely due to the effective administration of General Clay.

Mr. Backer's account of General Clay's administration as the U.S. Military Governor of Germany is a comprehensive and detailed record of how the General came to be the center of the formative period of the German occupation as well as of many later phases of its development. The author's account brings up many memories and tempts one who followed the course of the occupation closely to dwell on them. But this is not the place to discuss or comment upon the success or failure of the policies of the then U.S. Administration or of those for which General Clay was perhaps chiefly responsible.

In spite of many disappointments, Clay adjusted to the changes in policy induced by Washington and Moscow intelligently and constructively. He was a powerful factor in the creation of the Federal Republic of Germany and in the establishment of a viable German state in the community of the democratic nations of the West. This was achieved without generating the traditional enmities and prejudices that plagued other attempts to create peace and stability in Europe following the wars of 1870 and 1914.

Throughout his administration it was General Clay's wisdom, persistence, courage, drive, devotion to duty, and knowledge of governmental practices that marked him as the one above all others who could meet the exacting needs of his mission. It required a man of such qualities to carry an Administration past the influences of the negative Morgenthau/Churchill policies of the early days and the collapse of sincere efforts to unify the policies of both the Eastern and Western zones in Germany. Such a man also enabled the Administration to pass successfully from the period of denazification, decartelization, and dismantling to the currency reform, the rehabilitation program, the maintenance of our Berlin rights through the airlift, and the other developments that directly led to the political and economic strength of the new Federal Republic.

In short, the Federal Republic is largely the story of the courage and persistence of this remarkable man; that truly should constitute both the foreword and the epilogue of any account of General Clay's career.

General Clay never wished to become the U.S. Military Governor of Germany. He always wanted combat duty with troops. He constantly sought assignment to active duty in the Pacific, but he was never able to effect it. Yet, there are few army officers whose military careers had a more direct bearing on the course of this country's history than did that of General Lucius Clay.

John J. McCloy
May 24, 1982

★

Introduction

WINDS OF HISTORY IS A SEQUEL TO TWO EARLIER BOOKS ON THE OCCUPATION of Germany, *Priming the German Economy* and *The Decision to Divide Germany*, published by Duke University Press, Durham, North Carolina, in 1971 and 1978 respectively.

The writer served with the 82nd Airborne Division from the Normandy landings and through the European campaigns, reaching Berlin in July 1945. Following the Japanese surrender and subsequent demobilization of the American army, the 82nd returned to the States, but he transferred to the economic division of military government, a challenging assignment in itself. Moreover, it led to an enduring academic interest in Soviet studies and a career in the American Foreign Service, with duties in the Federal Republic of Germany and in the Soviet Union. Much later, after his retirement from the army, the writer's experiences with the revival of German export trade combined with research in military government files by then declassified, provided the material for his *Priming*.

The work with German industry was not directly affected by the contemplated dismantlement. But research, and the thereby opened new vista, provided insight into the highly complex reparations problem, whose roots go back to the Twenties. The political impact of unpaid Allied war debts, the controversy over the Reich's capacity to pay, the speculative promotion of German bonds, the international economic crisis, and the severe losses of German-bond holders merged in the public mind into one chaotic picture. This image greatly influenced America's economic policies toward Germany after the Second World War and—as the author's *The Decision to Divide Germany* shows—accelerated a division of the defeated country.

Research for these two books and a personal involvement in the economic problems of occupied Germany have convinced the writer that General Lucius D. Clay's critical role in the framework of his country's postwar policies is not well known. He is often seen as a leading cold warrior, and "Operation Vittles," the code name for the Berlin airlift, is considered the most important accomplishment in the General's military career. But this interpretation fails to do justice to one of the outstanding personalities of his period.

As General Clay's public papers show, there was probably no political leader in the United States at that time who stood more consistently and more vigorously for a continuation of the wartime alliance and friendly cooperation with the Soviet Union. Many of his memoranda cited here reveal a rare sense of history and an almost prophetic political vision.

Lucius Clay's political posture changed only when he was made aware that the winds of history had shifted and he was officially told that the noble experiment of Roosevelt's policy had to be abandoned. It was not surprising to anybody who knew this fighting Georgian that he was soon again in the lead, stressing the necessity for a healthy and strong German economy. Working tenaciously toward this goal, he became the architect of a democratic West German republic. His inspiring stand during the blockade of Berlin captured worldwide headlines that overshadowed his far more difficult, political achievements in the public mind. It is the writer's hope that *Winds of History* will help in establishing a much-needed balance.

In this endeavor, the gracious assistance of Mrs. Lucius D. Clay, the General's "best soldier," as he was wont to say, is particularly appreciated. She not only made herself available for several interviews, but also gave access to a collection of family photographs as well as to the General's efficiency reports covering his army career. Two friends read the entire manuscript. Paul A. Smith, Jr., editor of *Problems of Communism*, offered many good suggestions and an occasional but always appropriate reminder that a biographer must let the reader make his own value judgements. Robert T. Tims, a colleague from foreign service days, with his fine sense of style, gave good editorial advice. William I. Parker, and Karl and Martha Mautner also read parts of the manuscript, pointing out sections which had to be clarified and strengthened. Charles A. W. Kraft used his long professional experience in the selection of effective photographs. Nancy Roberts, who typed the manuscript, excelled in her dependability and accuracy. Finally, the writer wants to express his gratitude to his wife, Evelyn, for her interest, judgment and encouragement through many years of travail.

JOHN H. BACKER

CHAPTER ONE

Taking the Reins

ON AN EARLY SPRING DAY IN 1945, THIRTY-ODD SENIOR OFFICERS OF THE U.S. Group Control Council, the American planning staff for a future Allied government of Germany, were assembled in a spacious salon of the once-elegant Trianon Hotel, in Versailles. Their eyes were on the aquiline features of a three-star general who had just entered the room. Slightly built, of less than medium height, with no combat decorations on his tunic, Lucius DuBignon Clay might have attracted little attention at this military gathering had not the White House announced his appointment as deputy to Dwight Eisenhower for military government, and had not his reputation preceded him. Those in the know had told others of his great accomplishments as General Brehon Somervell's Director of Matériel of the Armed Service Forces, and later as Justice J. Byrnes' deputy at the Office of War Mobilization and Reconversion. The Cherbourg supply bottleneck that he had speedily broken also was mentioned. He was a brilliant administrator and leader, a sparking, always tuned-up dynamo, it was said, and therefore the War Department's choice. Working incredibly long hours, with a retentive mind and the knack of extracting the essence of a memo at a glance, he was considered unyielding when opposed and—sometimes to his detriment—given to trigger-quick decisions. It also was rumored that at the Supreme Headquarters of the Allied Expeditionary Force (SHAEF), Eisenhower had been surprised at the sudden appointment and that his chief of staff, Bedell Smith, had had his eyes on the job for himself.

The Deputy Military Governor opened the meeting with a brief statement.[1] The planning phase of the U.S. Group Control Council had come to an end, he said. All the officers should therefore try to assist the people at the American side of SHAEF who were presently responsible for military government operations in the field. That was where the action would be. By pitching in, the staff of the Control Council would acquire some much-needed practical experience. Once hostilities had ended and SHAEF was dissolved, they would return to their present positions. They then would be joined by some of the experts who now were working at SHAEF.

Turning the floor over to the staff, Clay listened to the reports of his division directors, some of whom seemed intimidated by his probing questions or merely by a look from his piercing dark eyes. Clay ended the gathering by announcing that there would be regular division directors meetings on Saturdays at the same hour. He wanted full attendance, he said. In particular he desired the attendance of members of the group who acted in dual capacity by virtue of their positions in SHAEF. In this manner close coordination would be achieved.

Visitors from the War Department in Washington had commented on previous occasions that the work of the U.S. Group Control Council was more or less aimless and ineffective and that accordingly there was a feeling of frustration among the staff. If such sentiments actually prevailed, Clay's appearance had tended to dispel them. Speaking firmly in his usual quiet manner without ever raising his voice for emphasis, he evoked an impression of total control, total personal control, one of the staff later remarked. It seemed that he had thought through the problems facing the group, reached some conclusions, and thereafter would be adamant in remaining with these conclusions. When the meeting ended a brief hour after it had begun, nobody among those present was in doubt that American military government for Germany had found its leader.

Clay had arrived in Paris on April 7, several weeks before the meeting at the Trianon Hotel. Unknown to him, the search for a deputy to Eisenhower had actually been in progress for many months. It had been debated at some length in Washington's top government circles and mentioned in dispatches to and from Eisenhower's headquarters in Europe. Before selecting the right candidate, a question of policy had to be answered—should it or should it not be a military man? President Roosevelt, always with an eye on the electorate, wanted a civilian, but as the American armies entered Germany and the chaotic conditions of the country became apparent, the arguments for a military man gained in force. The military governor would wear "two hats." He would be commander of all American troops in Europe and would carry, nominally at least, the essential civilian responsibilities of military government in Germany.

Henry Morgenthau had objected to anybody with close connections to the business world such as John J. McCloy, who as Henry Stimson's Assistant Secretary of War seemed to many a logical choice.[2] Morgenthau, the influential Secretary of the Treasury, did not elaborate, but with good reason he could expect anybody with a business background to be slow in implementing the drastic deindustrialization of Germany which he had in mind. Judge Robert P. Patterson, the Undersecretary of War, figured prominently among the civilian candidates. Initially he had indicated interest in the job, but after extensive deliberations with Henry Stimson the two agreed that it ought to be a military man. General Omar Bradley, John Lee (Eisenhower's supply chief), Brigadier General Kenneth Royall, and Clay were some of the names mentioned.[3]

On October 25, 1944, McCloy informed Eisenhower that the War Department believed the first phase of the occupation should be a military one. He added that Judge Patterson had turned down the job; if Ike wanted him, however, "he would not refuse."[4] Eisenhower in his reply indicated that he would be "delighted to take Judge Patterson or a senior army officer whom the Secretary and General Marshall consider to possess the necessary qualifications."[5] A few days later, Walter Bedell Smith, Eisenhower's Chief of Staff, followed up by suggesting to John Hilldring, the head of the War Department's civil affairs division, to "either make a major general of Judge Patterson and to send him along or to send the best soldier you can find. The decision should be made as quickly as possible."[6] The reference to a temporary rank of major general was indicative of Smith's plans for his own future. A lieutenant general at the time, he expected to retain complete control over civil affairs, as military government in a liberated country was called. The resulting conflict promptly surfaced when Clay arrived in Paris.

For several months no progress was made. Both the German offensive in the Ardennes and the President's preoccupation with the Yalta Conference were delaying factors. By March, however, the Third Reich was in its death throes and a decision urgently required. On March 3, Smith, possibly aware that Clay was his principal competitor, wrote to Hilldring that he would like to have Clay for the European Theater Civil Affairs (G-5) position, which job he described as "being as important or more important" than the deputy military governor's.[7] About the same time, Stimson and McCloy had concluded that military government in Germany would have to be independent from the army and that its head would report directly to Ike rather than being buried in the general staff. "Smith had indicated that he thinks he could run it in addition to his other duties. This is silly and I won't stand for it," Stimson wrote in his diary.[8]

Since the President still seemed opposed to a military appointment, the War Department had prepared alternative choices although Clay remained the favorite. The issue came to a head in the latter part of March, when John J. McCloy entered the Oval Office and was received by the President with the Hitler salute and the greeting "Heil Reichskommissar for Germany."[9] Taken aback, McCloy pointed out that he would be the wrong choice at this time. Under the prevailing conditions in Germany, he said, an army officer with training for situations like the Mississippi River disaster was needed. (The "disaster" was a scenario during which the Mississippi River flooded during high-water season.) The man chosen would have to reorganize the German communities in the American zone—to put electric plants, water works, and hospitals in running order; and to round up and demobilize German soldiers and weed out Nazis. He was also to repatriate millions of forced laborers and construct camps for those who could not or would not return home. Preferably it should be an engineer, and McCloy named Clay. The President did not know him, but after listening to Jimmie Byrnes' emphatic endorsement—as Byrnes said in *Speaking Frankly* (see Bibliography), "I found no army officer with as clear an understanding of the point of view of the civilian"—he acquiesced.

The period between the two wars had been a time of stagnant advancement. The man who Byrnes had said could run anything—General Motors or General Eisenhower's armies—had served twenty-two years as a company-grade officer mainly building dams and teaching at West Point. Only the coming of the war and the ensuing important responsibilities had brought about a series of rapid promotions to colonel. He had been appointed temporary brigadier general in March 1942 and major general nine months later. Except for his short stay in Cherbourg and an earlier mission to Brazil to establish military airports, Clay had spent most of the war in Washington applying his administrative and engineering skills to the solution of production problems.

He made enemies, but he also made a reputation within the army. In his driving efforts to get munitions produced and delivered to the fronts, he knew only one rule: the army came first, civilians second. "His grim insistence on war priority, his sometimes arbitrary ways of getting it, gave some civilian officials and even some of his army colleagues a feeling that he had forgotten that the United States, even in war, was a democracy."[10] When his appointment to Germany was announced, *The New York Times* referred to him as the Pentagon's "stormy petrel" and the *Washington Post* concluded that "General Clay's exceedingly high abilities are better suited to the German situation than to our own. . . that task calls for authoritarianism."

Drew Middleton's comments in *The New York Times* were similar: "General Clay was a leader in the campaign against the antiquated methods which had clung to the War Department." He wrote:

He was vigorous in executing the theory that production must be controlled only by the necessities of war. He cut through red tape and unnecessary delays, he found materials in 'unexpected places' and filled military schedules. He led the fight against reconversion putting his case this way: 'Our need and demand for military supplies will be at their peak on the date the Germans quit. Those who think that date is predictable and would taper off military production accordingly risk prolonging the war.' Such statements did not make General Clay popular, but they did an enormous amount to keep American industry on an even keel in 1944 and early in 1945. Clay has incurred the wrath of junior and senior officers, prominent and powerful civilian industrialists and politicians. He has in most of his arguments been proved right in time. This, one feels, is all General Clay cares about. He gives the impression of not giving a hoot about public or private opinion of Lucius Clay.[11]

Clay himself had not sought the military-government appointment, which carried a promotion to lieutenant general. "I wasn't interested in the job," he later used to say; "it was the last thing I wanted."[12] To him, the West Pointer, it seemed disgraceful to serve in two world wars without seeing combat, but his requests for transfer to Brehon Somervell, the Commanding General Army Service Forces, all were turned down. Moreover, when trying in January 1944 to change jobs with his good friend and classmate, Hugh Casey, who served on Douglas MacArthur's staff, he was equally unsuccessful. Somervell knew Casey well, and with a suitable replacement on hand Clay thought he would be permitted to leave. He was even willing to go as a colonel, he said, but Casey—who was a brigadier then—was unwilling to swap.[13]

Although the war in Europe was about to end, a landing in Japan was still on the army's agenda and Clay expected to take part in it. He therefore reacted sharply when first confronted with a German assignment. "This is ridiculous," he remarked in an angry manner when Robert Murphy came to congratulate his future boss. "I don't know what you are talking about."[14] He still had his eyes on the Pacific Theater when Murphy's information was confirmed. Clay tried once more to have his orders changed, but again he failed.[15]

The War Department did not give him much notice. "I was kicked out of Fort Myer immediately," Clay commented. "That's the lovely way the army is. When your difficulties start they make it more difficult." Obliged to vacate the attractive house at Fort Myer diagonally across from the officers' club, he did not have the time to seek an apartment for his wife. Washington was overcrowded during the war, but after some search and with the help of friends, Marjorie Clay settled in the Marlyn Apartments at Cathedral Avenue, where she was soon joined by her son Lucius' young bride.

Clay did talk at some length, however, with General William Draper, an investment banker in civilian life who agreed to serve as his economic adviser. With the assistance of Justice Byrnes he also could secure the services of Lewis Douglas, a former Director of the Budget, as financial counselor. And he had two young lawyers, Robert Bowie and Donald S. McLean, assigned to him as personal assistants. The former had worked for him in the Office of War Mobilization and McLean had represented him in the War Department's Civil Affairs Division. Dr. James Boyd, a mining engineer by profession and Clay's executive officer in the Pentagon job, also agreed to follow him to Germany.

By an oversight, so characteristic of Washington's self-centered and competing bureaucracies, nobody had suggested that he should establish some contact at the State Department—and Clay himself, in the rush of departure, had not thought of it.[16] Prior to departing from Washington, he saw John Hilldring, his old friend in the War Department's Civil Affairs Division. The two generals were in agreement that military government was a job for civilians, to be handled by the military only temporarily as a stand-in. It therefore had to be set up as an independent organization that could be severed promptly from the army.

When talking to Hilldring, Clay learned that the President had initially resisted the army's involvement in civil affairs. But later the experiences of the North African campaign demonstrated that the initial instructions to assign supervision over civil matters to the State Department was impractical. The War Department had originally acceded to the President's wishes with the reservation that matters having impact on military operations had to be excepted. The realities of the war, however, had made it clear that as long as hostilities in North Africa continued, everything would directly affect the military situation. Eisenhower actually had to remind General George C. Marshall that his chief civil administrator, Robert D. Murphy, could not be a member of the theater staff and at the same time be independently responsible to the Department of State.[17] Policy consequently changed and a Civil Affairs Division was established in the War Department. In Hilldring's opinion the State Department was not ready to handle the occupation. The army would have to remain in control, not only as long as hostilities continued but also for considerable time thereafter. It was going to be a difficult and thankless job, he thought. Considering the captious American press, it could ruin any man's reputation.

General Eisenhower had not been consulted about the appointment[18] and John McCloy had made a hurried trip to smooth ruffled feathers. Nevertheless, when Clay reported at SHAEF, he not only was cooly received but also found that he had a title without a job. Moreover, he was well aware that he knew little about Germany and nothing about the policies and tripartite agreements, which were to govern the occupation.[19] Experienced in the workings of the military bureaucracy, he believed it self-evident that under these circumstances two things had to be done. He had to get himself on the team. Moreover, he had to use the available time to observe the current status of civil affairs and to become acquainted with the problems of the occupation as they evolved.[20] Despite some professional rivalry between the two, he respected Bedell Smith. A temporary arrangement to serve as his deputy in charge of redeployment served both purposes. It was a part-time job and left Clay sufficient time to scrutinize military government operations in the occupied parts of Germany as well as the policies governing them. As living quarters he was assigned a requisitioned house in Vauxcusson, the villa Monte Cristo which, on his invitation, assistants Draper and Bowie shared. Housekeeping arrangements were in the hands of Clay's adjutant, Captain William Livingston, who hailed from Arkansas.

At SHAEF, Clay found a newly created general staff division, G-5, responsible for civil affairs. In accordance with SHAEF's standard pattern, responsibilities were divided equally between British and American officers. The top G-5 position was occupied by British Lieutenant General Sir A.E. Grassett, whereas his deputy, Major General Frank McSherry, an American, was in charge of operations. Further down the line were the G-5 staffs of the Twelfth and Sixth Army Groups as well as the parallel sections on army, corps and division levels. Because military-government units had to follow command channels, there were no direct communications between G-5 sections operating on different levels. A message from G-5 SHAEF to the next G-5 level, for instance, had to travel through three offices before it reached its destination. The same pattern prevailed at the lower levels. There was considerable dissatisfaction among military government units with this cumbersome procedure, McSherry remarked.[21] He added that it had been carefully thought through, however, and was decided upon by Bedell Smith because earlier experiences in Italy with dual command channels—the so-called Mediterranean pattern—had proven unsatisfactory. A close integration of civil affairs staffs with the normal staffs of combat units during the war made good sense to Clay also. At the same time, however, he could foresee the problems which the pattern was bound to create for his military government. He was resolved to face the issue at an early date.

While fighting was still in progress, it was mainly the lowest civil affairs units at division levels which had an operating role. When reading their reports, Clay recognized that military government functions at the time were closely related to tactical operations of the units which the detachments accompanied. They kept the civilian population as much as possible out of the way of the fighting units, provided labor supply for military purposes and, when needed, searched for local supplies. Whenever the situation was fluid, they stopped only long enough to post the proclamations and ordinances, issue curfew orders and to appoint an acting *Bürgermeister*. If there was more time they might requisition billets for troops, arrange for the dead in the streets to be buried, issue instructions to the police, and put electricity and water works back into operation.[22] As soon as the combat units moved on, they were followed by military government detachments responsible for taking over the administration of the various German government units. McSherry explained that the smallest detachments were earmarked for areas with populations up to 100,000. Larger units went to the individual German *Länder*, provinces, and some of the very large cities. According to their standard instructions, they were responsible for controlling all aspects of public affairs ranging from public health and safety to utilities, and from transportation and legal affairs to the supervision of food supplies.[23]

Clay saw that some of the problems connected with a more permanent military occupation had already emerged in Aachen. The city had been captured in October, and during the Battle of the Bulge it had been occupied by a succession of different combat commands. The city's military government detachment had three commanders before the end of December.[24] The attempt to organize a competent German city administration without a Nazi taint had turned out be a frustrating job, prompting a stream of criticism in the American press. The continual change of supervising American personnel had made the task even more difficult. It seemed clear to Clay that the difficulties encountered in Aachen would reoccur in other places as the army continued to advance and that denazification, as ordained in his instructions, would become one of his major problems.

As he went through the voluminous G-5 files, Clay noticed a number of disquieting personnel reports. Most of the officers were older men because few below the draft age limit of thirty-eight years had been accepted for civil affairs duty. They had been recruited and commissioned directly from civilian life on the basis of their experience in some professional or business field. After having gone through The School of Military Government at Charlottesville, Virginia, or one of the civil-affairs-training schools at a university, they had been shipped to England. There, in a number of military government pools, they had to vegetate for a year or even longer without meaningful training or work until assigned to a combat unit.[25] The enlisted men were generally much younger, about half below thirty. Although they did not have army civil-affairs training, many had experience much superior to that of some civil-affairs officers, frequently a cause for disgruntlement. Reports indicated a spotty morale, which on occasion was reflected in poor performance in the field. G-5 inspection teams had found an almost missionary spirit in some detachments, but they also encountered cases of complete morale breakdown. McSherry thought that once the war ended, there probably would be a stampede for return to civilian life, but Clay considered this a minor problem. He expected the military government staffs would be rapidly reduced and local administrative responsibilities soon returned to German hands. When summing up his impressions of G-5 in a letter to Hilldring, Clay wrote that he was not too happy with its accomplishments. Actually, its emergency job on an expediency basis had been exceedingly well done, he thought, but the long-range approach—of primary concern to him—left much to be desired. He suggested a continuous and intensive recruiting program and added that any organizational setup Hilldring could establish to this end would be of utmost value.[26]

McSherry had indicated that he expected the top G-5 job in the theater once SHAEF had been dissolved, but Clay had a different plan. Years in the military hierarchy had made him keenly aware of the dangers of an internal power struggle, and he wanted an officer of his own choosing in this pivotal position. The final authority thus would remain concentrated in his own hands. Approaching the issue with consummate skill, he wrote Hilldring: "I think we will take McSherry out of G-5 and place him in charge of Manpower Division in the Control Council. He is particularly qualified for this latter job, although he would much prefer to do the G-5 job. . . . I know of no one in the army who has had a comparable experience in manpower problems."[27]

Before Clay's arrival in Paris, Brigadier General Cornelius W. Wickersham had been in charge of the U.S. Group Control Council on an acting basis. A reserve officer and lawyer by profession, he continued briefly as Clay's deputy, returning to his New York law practice by the end of May. In 1942, Wickersham had set up the School of Military Government at the University of Virginia at Charlottesville, whose commandant and director he became. He subsequently was brought to London where he was assigned to the U.S. embassy and also as a War Department observer to the European Advisory Commission. He and several senior officers at the U.S. Group Control Council had been involved in military government planning from the very beginning. They confirmed to Clay that planners at SHAEF had focused for a long time only on the combat and the early post-hostilities functions of its personnel. The long-range aspects of an extended military occupation required fundamental policy decisions which had to be taken on top governmental levels. Nevertheless, some long-range planning had also taken place at SHAEF. As Wickersham pointed out, there had been increasing frustration at Eisenhower's headquarters because of the lack of political guidance from above. By the end of 1943, a sudden German collapse or surrender seemed a distinct possibility, and army routine demanded contingency plans for such eventuality. When repeated requests to Washington failed to elicit the desired response, a German Country Unit was set up in England with the mission to plan for a long-term occupation of Germany. The new unit, which later was to become the U.S. Group Control Council, was also given the task of writing a Handbook for the guidance of military government personnel after the end of hostilities.[28]

Clay was vaguely aware of a controversy which the Handbook had caused on the highest government levels. He learned more about it from his new staff, who explained that for the drafters of the Handbook practical considerations had outweighed ideology. As they saw it, it was of primary importance that the machinery of military government work efficiently. And since the lack of qualified American personnel in sufficient numbers was obvious, they thought that some officials from previous German administrative offices would have to be retained and on occasion their previous Nazi associations disregarded. Moreover, since the principal agricultural regions of Germany would come under Russian control, arrangements for importing the necessary foodstuffs and other commodities would have to be made. Among its conclusions, the manual recommended the conversion of industrial plants from war to consumer goods; financial support of essential economic activities where necessary; and the reconstruction of German foreign trade, with priority given to the needs of the United Nations. Wickersham said that a copy of the manual was probably given on an informal basis to Secretary Morgenthau by Colonel Bernard Bernstein, who represented the Treasury on the German country unit. In any event, the Handbook had found its way to President Roosevelt, who rejected its approach in the strongest possible terms. As a result, only a limited number of copies had been released, with a warning inserted that the manual did not apply to post-hostilities conditions.

It seemed to Clay that the Handbook incident, in conjunction with the War Department instructions for the occupation, which he was still studying, reflected the prevailing Washington climate as well as the political and psychological confines in which military government would have to operate. This atmosphere was given legal force by a Joint Chiefs of Staff Directive,

JCS #1067. For Clay and his financial adviser, Lewis Douglas, the directive had become an object of deep concern.[29] The two men had no misgivings about JCS #1067's punitive provisions, such as the arrest and trial of war criminals, the dissolution of the National Socialist Party, the automatic arrest of all high-ranking government officials and Germany's industrial disarmament. But they were dismayed at the limited authority which JCS #1067 seemed to give to military government. As Clay first read the directive, it prohibited military government from taking any steps to rehabilitate or maintain the German economy except to maximize agricultural production. Until agreements were reached in the quadripartite Control Council, only the production of light consumer goods and the mining of coal were to be encouraged. As Clay later wrote, "We were shocked at the directive's failure to grasp the realities of the financial and economic conditions which confronted us. It seemed obvious to us even then that Germany would starve unless it could produce for export and its industrial production be promptly revived." Read against the background of the Handbook incident, JCS #1067 showed that it had been composed in the vae victis atmosphere which prevailed in Washington at the time, and that it might be futile to ask for a drastic revision. Nevertheless, upon Clay's request, Douglas returned to Washington and tried to convince John J. McCloy that JCS #1067 ought to be modified. Since he was only able to obtain a minor revision, Douglas soon resigned.

Wickersham was also a good source of information on the inner workings of the European Advisory Commission (EAC). This London-based organization had been established in January 1944 following a decision of the Moscow Foreign Ministers Conference. It consisted of representatives of the United States, Great Britain, and the Soviet Union. The limited role of the EAC was often not fully appreciated, Wickersham explained. Essentially it was a negotiating body which could study issues and make recommendations to the participating governments only on questions specifically referred to it. Since every minor step in the policy-negotiating process of the EAC required governmental clearances, progress was exceedingly slow. Instructions to the American representative, Ambassador John Winant, for instance, had to be cleared and approved in Washington by the State Department, the Joint Chiefs of Staff, the War Department's Civil Affairs Division, and the Working Security Committee.[30] Few papers completed the clearance process. The Soviet governmental machinery was possibly even more complex, because Russian reactions were the slowest among the three member governments. To Wickersham's knowledge, the commission had completed during its entire life span only two significant assignments: the drafting of the terms of Germany's surrender and the preparation of a blueprint for the quadripartite control machinery in Germany.

When the Allies landed in Normandy in June 1944, it had seemed that the EAC would not be able to complete its work. Eisenhower therefore had sent Wickersham to Washington with a memorandum for the Joint Chiefs of Staff requesting authority as Supreme Allied Commander to prepare his own plans for the period after the surrender. As Wickersham related with a sense of accomplishment, he had hand-carried the request through twenty-five offices including those of the President and General Marshall.[31] The final result was the permission by the Joint Chiefs of Staff to set up an American planning staff, the U.S. Group Control Council (Germany), with Wickersham as its acting head. Its mission was to plan for post-hostilities control in Germany preferably in accordance with EAC directives or, in the absence of such directives, in accordance with unilateral U.S. views on subjects pending before the EAC.

The American breakthrough at Avranches on August 6 finally had prompted the Soviet representative at the European Advisory Commission to take action. He presented a Soviet proposal for the control machinery of Germany on August 25, the day Paris fell. Accepted with very minor changes by Great Britain and the United States, the Russian draft resulted in an "Agreement on Control Machinery in Germany," which was signed on November 14.[32] It provided for an Allied Control Authority composed of the three commanders in chief and of a permanent coordinating committee of their three deputies who would carry out the decisions of the Control Council. The staff of the council was to be organized in twelve administrative divisions to oversee with the help of a German administration every phase of the occupied country's life. In Berlin an Interallied Governing Authority (*Kommandatura*) would be formed, which would consist of the three Allied commandants who would supervise the administration of Greater Berlin.

It was a good arrangement, Clay thought, especially since it settled the question of military versus civilian rule. While there had been conflicting views within the U.S. Government on this important point, the London Agreement made it clear that Eisenhower would remain as military governor in the United States zone of occupation even after the anticipated disbandment of SHAEF. At the same time, he would represent America on the Control Council in Berlin. From Clay's point of view, however, the question of organization within the American military establishment was still not fully settled. As he later recalled:

> The minute I was told that I had this job I visualized trouble. I knew that the military people would want to keep it under general staff control. I was convinced that it could not be under general staff control. Even as far back as Cuba we learned that. And we had set up a special branch of the War Department to handle the government of Cuba and the Philippines. I also visualized that whoever was chief of staff at SHAEF would try to see that this was a job that came under his bailiwick. I did not believe it could succeed that way.[33]

At SHAEF G-5, on the other hand, there had been concern that the staff of the newly created U.S. Group Control Council might encroach on G-5's authority. Two directives issued by Smith had tried to deal with the problem. The first stipulated that the U.S. Group Control Council would develop policies in cooperation with the theater staff, i.e., SHAEF; the second charged the theater staff with the execution, implementation, and supervision of Control Council policies.[34] Clay's conception was quite different. He had put it on paper shortly after he had arrived in Paris and had discussed a table of organization based upon that paper with Ike and Smith. Assured of the War Department's firm support, he advised the Supreme Commander in a brief seven-paragraph memorandum that he intended "to work directly through the G-5 divisions with the several command echelons,"[35] a fairly clear indication of where orders would originate. Bedell Smith's reply came two weeks later. It took the form of a detailed directive consisting of seventeen paragraphs which ruled that the Deputy Military Governor would secure coordination through the assistant chief of staff G-5. The Deputy Military Governor in his position as U.S. representative at the Allied Control Authority would participate in developing policies for Germany as a whole, but their execution, implementation and supervision within the U.S. zone of occupation would remain the responsibility of the theater staff, in other words, G-5.[36]

The two papers succinctly presented the underlying conflict. According to Bedell Smith, the U.S. Army would administer the American zone through its commanders in the field. General supervision would be in the hands of the army's general staff, which would receive its directives and policy guidance from Washington. As Clay correctly interpreted this kind of arrangement, the U.S. Group Control Council would merely perform the role of an embassy,[37] representing the American army commander in negotiations with commanders of the other occupying forces. Clay had a very different view of his role. His concept was based on a firm conviction that the functions of military government were essentially civilian responsibilities. As deputy military governor, his primary mission was the establishment of a democratic German government at the earliest possible moment. "I believed it was in the best interests of the army to do everything that we could to show that we were not trying to hold the job; that we wanted somebody else to have it."[38]

Accordingly, in Clay's view, military government should be separated quickly from the army and wherever possible it ought to be staffed by competent civilians. In this manner a speedy transfer of authority to a civil branch of government and later to German hands would be prepared. Clay, as deputy military governor, would receive policy guidance from the War Department in Washington and carry out negotiations with the other three occupying powers. His instructions would go directly to American military government offices in the German *Länder*. These offices would be responsible directly to him and not to the U.S. Army commanders. Clay knew that he would have the War Department's and General Eisenhower's backing if he proceeded with implementing this concept. But his long experience in the military bureaucracy suggested that it was wise to bide one's time.

There were numerous good reasons for a gradual approach. Germany's surrender on May 7 ended hostilities, but it also brought to the fore a host of multifaceted problems. Many of them were temporary, such as the re-deployment and demobilization of the American military forces, the settlement of millions of German refugees from the East and the return of equally large numbers of displaced Allied persons to their homelands. It made hardly any sense for Clay to rush in and to accept full responsibility before a minimum of order had been restored. The U.S. Group Control Council was inexperienced and not fully staffed. As Clay saw it, the staff had lived "too cloistered and academic a life to face the realities of the problem." The file of plans was so great "as to be beyond the ability of one man to comprehend."[39] Moreover, the plans had assumed the existence of German ministries which had to be supervised, but there were not going to be any German ministries. Accordingly, Clay said, the plans had been "just a complete waste of time." Under these circumstances there was no point in bringing the conflict with General Smith to a head.

When he heard that because of an administrative error the wrong documents of surrender had been signed at Rheims, Clay used the example to lecture his officers that the Rheims mixup was "an illustration of concrete realities which it is impossible to plan for in advance."[40] In a similar pragmatic vein, he had several hundred of his officers temporarily assigned to the American elements of SHAEF. "This will get the personnel into 'the mud,'" he wrote to Hilldring, "and give them practical experience."[41] Finally, a more gradual acceptance of responsibilities also gave him, as deputy military governor, a chance to learn by observing the mistakes of others. It was a well thought through and appropriate approach, especially since the conditions before Clay's eyes were highly complex and in a state of flux which resisted quick solutions.

On May 16, 1945, one week after the German surrender, Clay held his first press conference as the deputy military governor. Flanked by Robert Murphy and Frank McSherry and facing a crowd of curious war correspondents at the Hotel Scribe in Paris, he outlined the status and the future of American military government in postwar Germany. SHAEF would be dissolved, but it would take at least several weeks to do so. The boundaries of the four occupation zones were not yet firmly determined, and since the destruction of Berlin was so great, there was even some doubt whether the central Allied government could be established in that city. He continued:

> I would like to make it perfectly clear that the government which we propose to set up in Germany is going to be a military government, and that the Germans are going to know that it is a military government. We have enough time later to consider the long-range terms of Germany and the regeneration of the German people. Our first objective is to smash whatever remaining power Germany may have with which to develop a future war potential; drive the Nazis out of power and keep them out of power. War

criminals will pay for their crimes with their lives and their liberties and their sweat and blood. This is the first objective of military government in Germany. When that has been accomplished we will begin to worry about long-range policies and long-range treatment of Germany.

With the help of some charts, he then explained the twelve functional divisions of the contemplated structure of American military government and mentioned the names of several key officials, such as Lewis D. Douglas, Major General Oliver P. Echols, Joseph B. Keenan and others. Five hundred American specialists in various governmental fields had been assembled in Europe, he added, and were now further preparing themselves for participation in the government of Germany.

The question period found Clay in easy control of the meeting. He used it to project a missionary commitment to the Rooseveltian concept of a single postwar world. When questioned on the chances for success in achieving Allied cooperation, he slammed his fist into the other hand: "It's got to work," he replied.

> If the four of us cannot get together now in running Germany, how are we going to get together in an international organization to secure the peace of the world? We are going to have to give and take and do a lot of things which the American public will not believe in, but we cannot go in there with four nations without being prepared to give and take, and if the people at home will recognize that the experiment of four nations means much to the future of the world then we have hope for the future of the job.[42]

For many months after Germany's surrender the most serious defect of the U.S. military administration was its impermanence. The fighting had stopped, but the fighting units were frequently on the move and the military government detachments moved with them. When SHAEF was dissolved in July, it became necessary for Clay to work through SHAEF's successor organization, U.S. Forces in the European Theater (USFET), which assumed command of the American occupation forces. The American zone of occupation was divided into an eastern and a western military district with the Third and Seventh Armies sharing respective occupational responsibilities. Under this arrangement, G-5 of the Third Army became the office through which military government was administered in Bavaria, whereas G-5 of the Seventh Army had a corresponding function in the area around Hesse and Württemberg that comprised the western military district. During the first phases of the occupation, however, military boundaries did not always coincide with those of the occupied *Länder*. Moreover, because of the prevailing uncertainty about the territory of the French zone, there were repeated occupation border changes. Both factors adversely affected administrative efficiency.[43]

In June, Clay gave permission to reinforce the 250 regular military government detachments attached to Third and Seventh Army units by 200 provisional detachments that had some experience in military government.[44] After they had been deployed, however, USFET determined that fewer but larger detachments would be preferable. Consequently, the provisional detachments were broken up and the personnel assigned to the regular units. Accordingly, during the summer of 1945 most detachments doubled in size. The expansion was more often than not a mixed blessing. To the extent that the officers who were added had adequate experience the increase permitted more specialization. But often the new men lacked substantive professional background and could not be given direct specialized responsibilities for specialized work.

There was frequent confusion regarding the proper duties and functions of military government. Clay had repeatedly made clear his view that the purpose of the American military government was not to govern but to supervise German government authorities. U.S. military forces, he felt, could not provide the manpower under any circumstances. Even so, in many cases when it was difficult to find competent men with no Nazi involvement, military government detachments were obliged to shoulder operational responsibilities much longer than desirable. Throughout this period Clay's principal concern continued to center upon the state of relations between the military government units and the staffs of the army commanders in the field. Although hostilities had ended, the detachments remained within the command channels of the tactical army units. The respective responsibilities of tactical units and military government detachments were not clearly defined and the resulting conflicts were often quite severe. When they occurred before German eyes, they tended to become embarrassing. In one case reported to Clay, the German administrators of a town formally requested their military government not to issue any instructions without prior clearance by U.S. division headquarters.[45] As Hilldring had predicted in a letter to Clay, the task of a detachment commander—at best a colonel—was not enviable if he had to operate near higher headquarters under the command of a major general.[46]

As Clay recognized, the time had come to deal with this issue. In May he had moved his headquarters to Höchst, a town three miles from Frankfurt, where the U.S. Group Control Council occupied an unscathed I.G. Farben building, described by Drew Middleton as "something run up by Rube Goldberg for the Marx Brothers."[47] He had a second office at SHAEF in Frankfurt, and he commuted between the two in a small Plymouth sedan. In a meeting at SHAEF on June 21, convened at his request, Clay bluntly told the army commanders that in the War Department's opinion, military government in an occupied country was not a job for soldiers and that their responsibility for it therefore should not continue beyond the minimum time necessary from a strictly military viewpoint. In his words, "Responsibility should be turned over to the political as soon as practicable." In order to accomplish these objectives, Clay said, the present military government organization was being built up by filtering in highly qualified civilians. This applied not only to the U.S. Group Control Council but also to SHAEF (later USFET) G-5 as well. The ultimate goal was to reach a point when the military would be in a position to turn over to the State Department the entire organization and be relieved of further responsibility for government in Germany.[48]

Having thus prepared the army commanders for the eventual demise of army control, the Deputy Military Governor then reassured them that the U.S. Group Control Council would remain in U.S. Army command channels down to the military districts of the Third and Seventh Armies. He firmly requested, however, that the tactical units should cooperate with military government detachments below the district level. "In the past this had not been done," he said. A week after the meeting, when writing to McCloy, Clay repeated that he considered it his basic mission to create a supervising body for Germany composed of civilians.[49]

U.S. military demobilization after World War II was hasty and, as one would expect, many problems resulted from it, not least among them those which affected the military government of Germany. On V-E day the United States had sixty-one divisions in Germany, making a total of three million men in Europe. The War Department had expected to release a million-and-a-half troops from Europe for transfer to the Pacific and to return an additional 600,000 men to the United States for discharge. The remaining 900,000 in Europe were expected to form the army of occupation. Instructions from Washington stipulated that the units to be shipped to the Pacific were to contain only the troops least eligible for discharge and those being sent home were to be the most eligible.[50] A so-called adjusted service rating based primarily on length of service, service overseas and combat decorations was developed as a criterion for discharge eligibility. Redeployment began promptly, and as public pressure "to bring the boys home" mounted, the number of troops shipped home for discharge increased drastically each month. By August 16, the day after Japan surrendered, first redeployment priority went to the men eligible for discharge. From then on there was no way to restrain the vocal public demand for more rapid demobilization. The nation's mood was reflected in Germany where soldiers carrying placards reading "We want to go home" demonstrated before USFET headquarters. As one of the onlooking officers from Clay's staff remarked: "A few months earlier it would have been mutiny—now it was just a bunch of good guys who had gotten together to let off some steam."

The disintegration of the American army continued at a rapid pace. In August a reduced occupational troop basis of 370,000 was established with strong indications that it might have to be reduced even further. No consideration could be given to the quality and efficiency of those remaining. The point score became the only criterion for whether a man remained or was shipped home.[51] Clay had made some efforts to have military government officers classified as critical personnel not subject to the point system, but the majority of those eligible nevertheless soon were on their way home and qualified replacements were scarce. By November, two million men had been demobilized. Plans to organize an occupation force of ten divisions never materialized and all that remained was one-and-a-half divisions. A combat efficiency report which reached Clay's desk in the fall of 1945 stated that "a trained balanced force of infantry, armor and air and supporting troops no longer exists. As a result the forces within the theater are today unable to perform any serious offensive operations." The capability to carry out limited defensive operations was judged to be slightly better.[52]

The American army which had liberated Western Europe was no more. Lucius Clay, "by birth and inclination an old-fashioned Jeffersonian liberal"[53] according to a perceptive commentator, was much too imbued with the democratic values of the Republic which he served to question the authority of a broadly based national demand. The same democratic convictions, on the other hand, fueled his anger when a stream of reports on the misbehavior of some elements among the remaining American troops began to come in. Clay sprang from an old and socially prominent Southern family, and most such families had suffered from the excesses committed by Northern occupation forces after the end of the Civil War. The reports which Clay read of looting, pillage, wanton brutality and rape were all too reminiscent of a traumatic phase in his family's history.[54] The discipline of the American forces of occupation was not the responsibility of the military government but of the U.S. Army. So when, in addition to his military government function, Clay assumed command of the troops in March 1947, he considered it a priority challenge to restore former standards of conduct as quickly as possible.

As the drafters of the Handbook had foreseen, the food situation which the occupying armies found was critical if not calamitous. This pertained particularly to the Western zones, which always had depended on supplies from Eastern Germany, now in Russian and Polish hands. All of the four occupying powers encouraged agricultural production from the outset, but it was clear that a tough winter lay ahead. All Europe was short of food, but SHAEF nevertheless began shipping wheat to Germany in June. There could be no doubt in Clay's mind that the organization of food imports for Germany and the necessary financial support by the American Congress was going to be one of the key issues affecting the success of his mission.

The only positive aspect of the food situation was its impact on the discharge of German prisoners of war. At the end of the war, close to five million prisoners of war and disarmed enemy troops were in SHAEF custody. For a while captured Wehrmacht stocks were used to feed them. However, when these stocks were exhausted and military government supplies had to be used, it was decided to expedite discharges.[55] Following Clay's recommendations, top priority was given to agricultural workers, coal miners, transportation workers, and others in key occupations. By the end of June, SHAEF authorized what the armies were already doing, a general discharge of PWs except for those who were in the automatic arrest categories.

The problems created by the presence of five million Allied and neutral displaced persons, however, resisted quick solutions and eventually became a matter of great concern for the Deputy Military Governor. Allied wartime propaganda had played up the plight of slave laborers, making their liberation a major war aim. The widespread public interest thereby created helped to shape the policies of the American army of occupation, which were governed by a provision of JCS #1067, "to ensure that . . . displaced persons of the United Nations be cared for and repatriated." While the German ration fell to 1,000 calories a day, Clay saw to it that DP rations in the American zone remained at 2,000 calories even when this meant reaching for U.S. Army stocks. Restrictions on the free movement of DPs held in temporary camps were frowned upon by higher headquarters, with the result that serious problems at the grass-roots level arose. It was relatively easy to return West Europeans to their homelands. Most of them left as fast as transportation could be provided. The shipment of millions of Russians (many against their will) in conjunction with a simultaneous return of captured American and British soldiers, however, required a number of protracted and not always amicable meetings with a Soviet negotiating team. By the end of September all but about 600,000 DPs had been sent home, but those who stayed became a special problem. Many were nonrepatriable Jews. Living idly in dilapidated, cramped barracks, memories of cruel oppression, uncertainty about their future and practical immunity from the German police tended to foster criminality among them. Clay found himself here in a quandary. Back in America the displaced persons had become an object of public sympathy and any restrictions placed on them elicited critical comments by the media.

Clay himself felt that most of them had suffered horribly, and that it would be a greater evil than the disorder and criminality in the camps to place them under German jurisdiction. The Jewish DPs were really quite a disciplinary problem, he later recalled:

> They were not responding to German law. They hated soldiers. Soldiers were a sign of oppression to them and we were the only people, our MPs, that could control them when they got into trouble. We had quite a problem. Anyway with my advisor [for Jewish affairs]—I got him to go up, bring up a group of leaders from the camps and I said, 'I'm going to give you people self-government to the fullest extent that I can. I designate you as a committee and you set up the responsibility in the camps, you set up your police in the camps. If you people go to town, you send your police in, if they are misbehaving and arrest them and bring them back.' It worked. I won't say it worked perfectly, nothing ever works perfectly, but it worked. It gave us the type and kind of control we

never had before. If we sent in MPs to arrest them, why it would be in every headline in the U.S. 'U.S. SOLDIERS INVADING JEWISH CAMP' and so forth just as if the Nazis were back at work and so on. So this was the best thing for us.[56]

At the time the Wehrmacht surrendered, British and American troops had deeply penetrated the territory alloted to the Soviet Union. Churchill had anticipated this situation. Looking at foreign affairs in the pragmatic tradition of Downing Street, it seemed almost inconceivable to him to give up strategic advantages gained in combat without making certain that the commitments made by a likely opponent would be duly honored. He had cautioned Truman already in April against any withdrawal before all the questions concerning the occupation had been settled. The sharing of food supplies from the East was one of the items he had mentioned. In a follow-up, a British aide-mèmoire listed the treatment of Germany as an economic unit and the terms of the occupation of Austria as some of the outstanding issues.[57]

Churchill's approach, however, was not in accord with the new-Wilsonian pattern of America's twentieth-century public diplomacy, and the views at the State Department in this regard were divided. In Germany, Eisenhower pleaded for an early setting up of the Control Council and he recommended a quick withdrawal. The customary American inclination to "getting it over with" also played a role. London was advised that the United States was willing to defer the withdrawal for a short period and that the Control Council should be established promptly. But if the Soviets insisted on prior withdrawal, the United States would feel obliged to comply.[58] The American ambassador in London, John Winant, consequently was instructed to get the ball rolling. At the next meeting of the European Advisory Commission on this issue, he recommended to the four governments that their commanders should meet in Berlin on June 1, sign the Declaration Regarding the Defeat of Germany as well as the Assumption of Supreme Authority, and form the Control Council. At the same time they should put the protocol on the zones of occupation and on the control machinery into force.

The staff of the U.S. Group Control Council was well aware that there was no provision covering access to Berlin in the agreement reached by the European Advisory Commission. When the impending meeting of the four commanders was being discussed at SHAEF, Clay—living up to his reputation as a "stormy petrel"—is said to have remarked that he would advise the Supreme Commander not to sign the declaration unless the Russians agreed without equivocation to unrestricted Western use of roads, railroads, and lines of communication.[59] Whether Clay actually made this suggestion to Eisenhower is not recorded. But the impending ceremonial meeting in Berlin would not have been the proper occasion to exert the pressure that Clay had in mind.

The Soviets accepted Winant's recommendations on June 4, and the meeting was scheduled for the next day. The Supreme Commander and his party, which included Clay and Murphy, arrived in Berlin in the morning.[60] Montgomery and Lattre de Tassigny, although still under SHAEF, traveled in separate planes to emphasize their status as national representatives. When arriving at the bombed-out and only partly repaired Tempelhof airdrome, the Americans were welcomed by Zhukov's deputy, General Vassily Sokolovsky. An infantry battalion was lined up, the first Soviet military unit the Americans had encountered. Steel-helmeted, the plashpalatkas strung over the shoulders, with fixed bayonets glinting in the sun, the Russians appeared to be more ready for combat than to act as an honor guard. Uniforms and equipment were war-worn, but the men seemed clean and in splendid physical condition. As the group proceeded by car through the prostrate center of the city, the odor of death was everywhere. The canals were choked with bodies and refuse. The subway had been flooded by a last-minute order of the Nazis, and thousands who had sought refuge in it had died. Clay was impressed by the look on people's faces in the streets. "You did not see this down in the rest of Germany," he later commented. "They really looked beaten down, frightened, whipped. I guess they'd had a pretty tough deal with the troops coming in there. The rubble— the town was of course badly damaged, but so were a lot of other towns. The people of Berlin were really beaten down."[61] In Wendenschloss, one of the eastern suburbs of Berlin, a villa had been put at the disposal of each of the Western commanders. At a private meeting Eisenhower presented Marshall Zhukov with the Chief Commander Grade of the Legion of Merit and then drove back to his billet, where he was soon joined by the British and French commanders.

The four-power meeting had been scheduled for noon, but several hours elapsed without any sign of the Russians. Finally, when Eisenhower and Montgomery indicated that they would depart without signing, they were taken to the Yacht Club, where the ceremony was to take place. There they learned the reason for the delay—a paragraph in the declaration which could have obliged the Soviets to arrest Japanese nationals in Germany even though the Soviet Union was not at war with Japan. Eisenhower's offer to take out the passage still did not settle the matter because Zhukov had to check with Moscow before accepting the deletion. At his diplomatic best, Clay maintained a smiling face throughout the parley, even suggesting that such delays were inevitable. "If any such delay had occurred in his own office," one of his junior officers whimsically remarked, "I would have gone out and shot myself."[62]

It was almost five o'clock when the Soviets were ready to sign. After a brief ceremony, Eisenhower inquired whether the Control Council which hereby had been constituted could now begin its work. Zhukov replied that the staffs of the Control Council would have to wait until all troops had been redeployed. He could not study questions pertaining to the occupation of Germany as long as he did not control his own zone. When Zhukov inquired how long the redeployment would take, Montgomery suggested that it might take three weeks. General Eisenhower then cut short the banquet that followed, insisting that his departure time had to be observed as scheduled. Contrary to their expectations, Clay and the advance party of the U.S. Group Control Council were not permitted to remain in Berlin. They returned to Frankfurt the same evening.

The following day, Clay drafted the report on the meeting for the Joint Chiefs of Staff. He indicated that the Soviets would eventually join "in some form of control machinery" but that "the Control Council may become only a negotiating agency and in no sense an overall government for Germany." Looking far ahead—as was his custom—he added that "our government should consider now the possible alternatives to quadripartite control of Germany as a whole." He listed tripartite control or an independent administration of the American zone as possibilities stressing "the undesirability of either alternative."[63]

With the withdrawal date still undecided, Churchill made one final attempt to postpone this move. However, neither the inexperienced President nor the war-weary American people could be expected to support some tough bargaining with the Soviet Union at the time. Truman's only concession to Churchill, therefore, was a brief comment in the withdrawal notice to the Kremlin which indicated that the President "considered the settlement of the Austrian problem as of equal urgency to the German matter." "This," Churchill later recalled, "struck a knell in my breast but I had no choice but to submit."[64] Stalin, accustomed to quid pro quos, understood and the Austrian issues were promptly resolved. The withdrawal of the British and American troops began on July 1 and ten days later the United States forces did not occupy any territory that was not part of the United States zone.

Three more meetings with Marshall Zhukov were needed to negotiate the remaining issues. In each case, General Clay represented the United States. On June 29, he and Montgomery's deputy, Lieutenant General Sir Ronald Weeks, settled the details of the mutual withdrawals. They involved the yielding of about 16,000 square miles of the Soviet zone occupied by American and British troops in exchange for the 185 square miles of the Western sectors in Berlin.[65] Zhukov, whom Clay described as affable and with a sense of humor, made it very clear that the quicker the Western divisions moved out, the quicker American and British troops could move into Berlin. Accordingly, the first-suggested nine-day schedule was reduced to four.

The movement of Allied troops to Berlin was raised as the next item on the agenda. Marshall Zhukov remarked that he had received requests for three rail lines, two highways and two air routes. He thought that one railway, one highway and one air route should be enough to supply the contemplated small garrison of 50,000 American and British troops. Clay and Weeks were well aware that there was no provision covering access to Berlin in the agreement reached by the European Advisory Commission, and they therefore argued strongly for the original request. When Clay indicated that there should be unlimited access, Zhukov replied that he did not understand. To him, as to any Russian accustomed to the centuries-old tradition of controlling every step of every foreigner on Russian territory, the thought of free access apparently seemed odd. He repeated the offer of one highway, one rail line, and a twenty-mile air corridor. After some arguments, the American and British deputy military governors accepted, with the face-saving proviso that the access question could be reopened by the Control Council. When Zhukov suggested putting the agreement in writing, Clay refused because he thought "that would be a limitation on the overall agreement. The only thing I would have taken," he told Jean Smith, "would have been that thirty days from now or sixty days from now, all roads and railroads would be open. Otherwise, I would have felt that I was limiting the agreement."[66] In his memoirs Clay accepted responsibility in retrospect for the absence of a written agreement, without, however, mentioning Marshall Zhukov's offer.[67]

There was little sign of personal rapport at the discussions. Clay presented Zhukov with a brand-new Beretta pistol, inscribed "From General Clay to General Zhukov"; the Soviet marshall glanced at it briefly and then handed it to his adjutant, who tossed it in a duffle bag. As one of Clay's friends, Jim O'Donnell, commented, "For a Southern gentleman of the old school, it was a humiliating experience."[68]

The next conference with Zhukov dealt with the quadripartite administration of Berlin. It was equally unsatisfactory. Arriving from Frankfurt on July 7, Clay and Murphy drove from the Berlin airport directly to the British headquarters where they joined the British delegation. Also present was General Floyd L. Parks, the recently appointed American commandant of Berlin, and Colonel Frank Howley, a hard-hitting Philadelphia advertising man in charge of the local military government detachment. Before proceeding to the meeting with the Russians at Karlshorst, the generals conferred while Howley waited outside.[69] When he was called in, he saw that the plan for the *Kommandatura*, drafted by him and Parks, was being discussed. According to Howley, Clay told Parks "in fairly blunt terms" that he did not like the plan, which proposed to administer the city on a divided basis. He insisted that all questions arising in Berlin had to be settled unanimously by all powers.

After listening for a while, Howley spoke up and explained that there was no intention of setting up "a little empire in the American sector." However, there would be many questions that could not be solved on a unanimous basis, questions of religion or education, for instance. "The British, French and Americans may agree on a million things," he said, "but there will be many on which the Russians won't agree." Clay's eyes turned "steely," as his aides used to say.[70] "You are entirely wrong," he told the outspoken staff officer in a most peremptory manner. "I have just come from Washington, and it is certainly the intention of our government to administer Berlin on a unanimous basis." What Clay's own views may have been is not recorded. What is clear is his intention to carry out the intention of his government. As Howley describes the scene:

> The Americans sat on the right side of the table and the British on the left. Neither of the two delegations had brought along any experts. Zhukov called the meeting to order immediately. 'Well, gentlemen,' he said, 'shall we start business?' The two delegations seemed a little stunned. If they thought it was going to be a social call, that fantasy went out of the window immediately. It was obvious both were unprepared. We had no plan. Neither had the British, who had taken over their sector much later than we had. And the first business of the day was the creation of a *Kommandatura*.
>
> The British and American representatives were even more stunned when Zhukov, cynically enjoying the silence around the table, whipped out a one-page statement describing how the *Kommandatura* would be set up, naturally providing for the veto: 'The resolutions . . . are to be passed unanimously.' One or two generalizations were put forth hopefully, in a vain effort to cover the fact that we had no concrete proposals to offer, and finally Clay who had received the single-page statement turned to Parks and asked, 'Do these translations check?'
>
> Parks turned to me. 'Frank,' he said, 'take the interpreters and check this, will you?' With the interpreters, I started out to an anteroom, when the Russians suddenly noticed I was a full colonel. Their officer was also a colonel, but rank consciousness took charge. The colonel was pulled back and replaced by a one-star general. It was a typical Russian move: they refused to be outranked. . . . Back in the conference room, I handed my copy to General Clay, who half-turned and asked, 'Is it okay?' 'Well,' I said, 'as a legal document it stinks, but as a rough note on what you've been talking about, it's all right.'
>
> Clay took his pen out and wrote his name across the bottom of the page, thereby indicating that he had no intention of quibbling about commas, periods, or anything else. We were going to get along with the Russians and we were quite willing to start off on their terms. I think it was a good indication of the policy we were to follow in Berlin for many months, doing almost anything to win over the Russians, allay their suspicions, and convince them we were their friends. . . .

A second unexpected development for the Western representatives was Zhukov's insistence that, SHAEF's view to the contrary, they were responsible for supplying their sectors with food and coal. Howley's story continues:

'Now, gentlemen, we will discuss the question of the food and coal you will supply for the maintenance of Berlin,' Zhukov announced.

An icy blast from the steppes swept the room. The American and British commanders glanced at each other in quick consternation, but retained their composure. This was the first intimation by the Russians that we were expected to feed and fuel Berlin. SHAEF had instructed us that the job of feeding Berlin was solely a Russian responsibility. . . .

'As you know, neither the Americans nor the British zone have a surplus of food,' Clay told the Russians, and he added facetiously, in an effort to relieve the tension, 'I can give you mountains, but no coal. That's General Weeks' problem.' Zhukov smiled, but promptly ended the persiflage, 'What I want to know, gentlemen, is when you will start bringing in supplies. I think there should be no ambiguity about this arrangement. . . .'[71]

Neither Clay nor his British counterpart had the authority to accept this demand and another meeting was therefore scheduled for July 10. Howley, despite his frankness, apparently had made a good impression on Clay, because before departing for Frankfurt the general reportedly told an aide responsible for housekeeping arrangements not to treat Howley "like any other colonel."[72]

At the next meeting, after having settled the supply question to Zhukov's satisfaction, Clay presented the papers on the organization of the Allied Control Authority. Although they had been drafted on the basis of quadripartite agreement in London, Zhukov still insisted that they had to be cleared with Moscow.[73] The first meeting of the Control Council took place on July 30, and even then, because of Soviet objections, the council did not become fully operational. As Zhukov indicated on this occasion, the work of the council would have to wait for a satisfactory outcome of the Potsdam Conference. As a result, it was the middle of August before the Allied Control Authority was in place with an active organization. It consisted of the Control Council composed of the four commanders in chief, of the Coordinating Committee made up of the deputy military governors, and of a dozen functional directorates, their committees and subcommittees. As it soon turned out, there was little real negotiation in the Control Council itself. The Coordinating Committee undertook to direct the work of the lower bodies of the ACA and to resolve their differences that could not be settled. When the Control Council and the Coordinating Committee were unable to agree, the issue was either dropped or referred to governments. The seat chosen for the Allied Control Authority was the Kammergericht, a partly bombed-out Baroque building which had housed the High Court of Prussia. It was here that many of the Germans involved in the July 1944 attempt on Hitler's life had been tried by a "People's Court" under the notorious Nazi judge Roland Freisler. It was located in the American sector of Berlin, and the flags of the four victorious nations now flew in front of the building.

As Clay followed the proceedings of the Potsdam Conference, he began to wonder about the impact of the British elections on British foreign policy and on his own mission in Germany. With his slight background in European affairs, he was greatly impressed with the ease of transition. "It was there," he later said, "that I developed my high admiration for the stability of the British and for the continuity of their government. When word of the election results came, all the Americans in Berlin began pacing the floor." He continued:

> Then a plane arrived with Attlee and staff and departed with Churchill and staff. Another came in with Bevin and staff and carried away Eden and his party. And, by golly, the show went right on as if nothing had happened. The only difference was in accent and that applied only to Eden and Bevin! Remarkable people![74]

With the end of the conference in sight, the Deputy Military Governor began to express some concern about the results. JCS #1067, a unilateral United States document, had become effective on July 15, the day SHAEF was dissolved. It was an interim paper, and Clay therefore had reason to hope that its most onerous restriction might be soon modified. When briefed by Freeman Matthews and James Riddleberger on the just completed (and overriding) Potsdam Agreement, he learned that—at least in part—this was the case. The "hands off" policy of JCS #1067 was replaced by the responsibility of developing a balanced economy, which would put a unified Germany on a self-sustaining basis. The two foreign service officers' warning that the Soviets might not honor the unification provision Clay disbelieved. "It was a policy change of major impact," he concluded,[75] although he remained cognizant that other undesirable aspects of JCS #1067—its radical reformist provisions as well as a basically negative approach—had not been changed. "Bad orders," Clay used to say, "but we have to make them work." Neither he nor his staff was yet aware that there were two other factors—both beyond the Deputy Military Governor's control—which actually would be more significant in impeding progress: the lagging production of coal in the Ruhr, which was a British responsibility, and a currency overhang of 500 billion Reichsmarks whose inflationary impact on the German people led to economic paralysis.

With the Allied Control Authority in place and final policy directives in his hands, Clay could focus again on the administrative setup in the American zone. As he now understood the fundamental aspects of his mission, it was his task to make the American zone of occupation within the framework of a unified Germany self-supporting, to organize a clearly transitional supervisory body with the assistance of as many competent civilians as he could find, and to turn over local administrative responsibility to Germans as quickly as it was technically and politically feasible. Since the concept's fundamental aim was an early transfer of authority and the separation of military government from the occupying army, the concentration of administrative responsibilities in one hand seemed a sine qua non.

By the fall of 1945, the American wartime army had been disbanded and most of the troops had gone home. Millions of German prisoners of war had been discharged; millions of refugees from the East had been temporarily settled; and millions of displaced persons had returned to their homelands. The German communication and transportation systems had been partly restored. At least some signs of normalcy seemed to be visible on the horizon. Having worked patiently within the existing framework throughout the summer, Clay felt that the time had come to move ahead with his organizational plans. With one eye always on his ultimate goals in the military bureaucracy, he had prearranged the assignment of General Clarence L. Adcock, a lifelong friend and former classmate, to the pivotal G-5 position at USFET. Although Adcock reported to Bedell Smith, he saw to it that Clay was always kept fully informed.[76] "General Smith was too damned intelligent not to know what was going on," Clay later said, "and it was not what he wanted. General Eisenhower backed me and Smith knew this damned well and did not want a showdown on this issue."[77] It was indeed an unusual arrangement, but satisfactory to Clay, who wanted to have some input—even indirectly—on military government operations in the field.

In September, Adcock and Clay agreed that their staffs should eventually be combined. This was accomplished in several steps during the following months. The U.S. Group Control Council was renamed the Office of Military Government (U.S.) and USFET G-5 became the Office of Military Government (U.S. Zone). For all practical purposes General Adcock from then on was Clay's deputy.[78] The *Land* detachments became offices of military government for the *Länder* and reported directly to Berlin. Subsequent directives ordered the armies to cease all military government activity and the Office of Military Government (U.S. Zone) became OMGUS REAR. Appropriate transfers of personnel completed the reorganization.

The reins of military government from then on were firmly in Clay's hands. Although he made frequent efforts during the coming years to relinquish them to others, he was entirely unsuccessful in this regard. His repeated requests for retirement were not approved. And not before the summer of 1949 was the Department of State willing to take on the War Department's responsibilities in the occupied parts of Germany.

FOOTNOTES

1. Minutes, U.S. Group Control Council staff meeting, April 28, 1945. OMGUS 60–12/1.
2. *Morgenthau Diary: Germany*, Vol. 1, p. 529.
3. Memorandum for the Secretary of War, October 17, 1944. Stimson Diary, Yale University.
4. McCloy to Eisenhower, October 25, 1944, USFET SGS 334/2.
5. Eisenhower to McCloy, November 1, 1944, USFET SGS 334/2.
6. Smith to Hilldring, November, 1944, Eisenhower Papers, Exchange Library, Abilene, Kan.
7. Smith to Hilldring, March 3, 1945, CAD 014, 7–10–42, sec. 1.
8. Stimson Diary, March 14, 1945, Yale University.
9. John H. Backer, *The Decision to Divide Germany: American Foreign Policy in Transition*, p. 105.
10. *Time*, June 25, 1945.
11. "Uncommon Clay: Our Ruler in the Reich," by Drew Middleton in *The New York Times Magazine*, July 15, 1945, p. 10.
12. Jean Smith interview with General Clay, February 5, 1971, Oral History Project, Columbia University.
13. Author's interview with General Hugh Casey, Bradford, Vt., October 9, 1980.
14. Ibid.
15. Lucius D. Clay, *Decision in Germany*, p. 4.
16. Ibid., p. 6.
17. Harry Coles and Albert Weinberg, *Soldiers Become Governors*, p. 93.
18. Jean Smith interview with General Clay, February 5, 1971.
19. Clay, *Decision*, p. 7.
20. Clay to McCloy, April 26, 1945, in Jean Smith, editor, *The Papers of General Lucius D. Clay*, p. 7.
21. Harold Zink, *American Military Government in Germany*, p. 48.
22. Earl F. Ziemke, *The U.S. Army in the Occupation of Germany 1944–1946*, p. 186.
23. Hq. First U.S. Army, Office of CA officer, Check List for Guidance of Civil Affairs Officers, May 18, 1944, SHAEF, G–5, 17.16.
24. Ziemke, *The U.S. Army*, p. 185.
25. Ibid., p. 66.
26. Clay to Hilldring, May 7, 1945, in Smith, *The Papers*, pp. 10–14.
27. Ibid.
28. John H. Backer, *Priming the German Economy: American Occupational Policies 1945–1948*, p. 9.
29. Clay, *Decision*, pp. 16–19.
30. Ziemke, *The U.S. Army*, p. 130.
31. Memo, Wickersham for Smith, Report of Visit to Washington, July 17, 1944, USFET SGS 319.1/4.
32. Department of State, *Foreign Relations of the United States 1944*, Vol. 1, pp. 185–187; 299–301; 404–406.
33. Jean Smith interview with General Clay, December 16, 1970.
34. Ziemke, *The U.S. Army*, p. 223.
35. Memo, Clay to Eisenhower, April 11, 1945, in Smith, *The Papers*, p. 4.
36. Memo, Hqs. ETOUSA Co. S. Relationship of Dep. Mil. Gov. and U.S. Group CC to Theater Staff, April 29, 1945, OMGUS 416–2/3.
37. Clay, *Decision*, p. 53.
38. Jean Smith interview with General Clay, December 16, 1970.
39. Clay to Hilldring, May 7, 1945, in Smith, *The Papers*, p. 10.
40. Minutes, staff meeting, U.S. Group CC, May 12, 1945, OMGUS 60–12/1. What the Germans signed at Rheims was the Act of Military Surrender, written three days previous in the SHAEF G–3, not the painstakingly negotiated EAC surrender instrument. One slip-up was that, although SHAEF had received copies of the EAC surrender instrument, none had been sent through its channel of command. SHAEF had sent drafts of the Act

of Military Surrender to the four capitals, but no answer from Washington or Moscow had been received. (See Ziemke, *The U.S. Army*, pp. 257–258.)

41. Clay to Hilldring, May 7, 1945, in Smith, *The Papers*, p. 10.
42. *Time*, June 25, 1945, and consolidated daily journal, office staff secretary, May 16, 1945, OMGUS 435–2/3.
43. Ziemke, *The U.S. Army*, p. 306.
44. Ibid., pp. 308–309.
45. Ibid., pp. 313–314.
46. Hilldring to Clay, May 21, 1945, OMGUS 177–1/3.
47. Middleton, "Uncommon Clay," p. 10.
48. Minutes of special meeting with Army Commanders, June 22, 1945, OMGUS 60–12/1.
49. Clay for McCloy, June 29, 1945, in Smith, *The Papers*, p. 40.
50. Ziemke, *The U.S. Army*, pp. 328–334.
51. Ibid., p. 335.
52. Cable, Smith to Hull, November 17, 1945. EUCOM, staff message control July-Dec. 1945. "I don't think we would have had a cold war if we had kept a strong army there," Clay commented in 1972.
53. Delbert Clark, *Again the Goose Step*, p. 36.
54. Interview with Dr. Don D. Humphrey, September 9, 1978. Ziemke, *The U.S. Army*, pp. 220–221.
55. Ziemke, ibid.
56. Ibid., p. 355. Author's interview with Richard Hallock, April 5, 1981; and Jean Smith interview with General Clay, February 9, 1971.
57. U.S. Department of State, *Foreign Relations of the United States 1945. III European Advisory Commission*, pp. 304–305.
58. Ibid., p. 308.
59. General Ranson's Diary. C/S. U.S. Hq. BD. T–570–2/1 in consolidated daily journal, office of staff secr. June 2, 1945. OMGUS 435–2/3.
60. Clay, *Decision*, p. 21.
61. Robert Murphy, *Diplomat Among Warriors*, p. 257.
62. Middleton, "Uncommon Clay," p. 10.
63. From Clay (S. Eisenhower) for JCS. June 6, 1945, FWD 23724. R.G. 200. N.A. *Foreign Relations 1945*. III., pp. 327–332; Clay, *Decision*, pp. 20–23.
64. Winston Churchill, *Triumph and Tragedy*, p. 605.
65. Clay, *Decision*, p. 24.
66. Jean Smith interview with General Clay, February 11, 1971.
67. Clay, *Decision*, p. 26. *Foreign Relations 1945*. III., pp. 353–361. *Foreign Relations . . . The Conference of Berlin*, Vol. I, p. 135.
68. Author's interview with Jim O'Donnell, Washington, D.C., March 8, 1980.
69. Frank Howley, *Berlin Command*, pp. 53–57.
70. Author's interview with Mrs. Sylvia O'Connor (Captain Tint) Hershey, Pa., June 14, 1980.
71. Howley, *Berlin*, ibid.
72. Author's interview with General Frank Howley, New York, N.Y., August 5, 1980.
73. Ziemke, *The U.S. Army*, p. 342.
74. Clark, *Again*, pp. 44–45.
75. Clay, *Decision*, p. 41. Author's interview with Ambassador Riddleberger, Washington, D.C., August 6, 1981.
76. Ibid., p. 53.
77. Jean Smith interview with General Clay, February 5, 1971.
78. Ziemke, *The U.S. Army*, p. 402.

CHAPTER TWO

The Setting

"AT THE BEGINNING OF OUR WORK AT OMGUS," WROTE ROBERT MURPHY, CLAY'S political advisor,

> neither Clay nor I had any precedent to guide us in our assorted German, French, and Russian problems. We had to improvise as we went along. . . . I was rather dismayed to learn that he knew virtually nothing about Germany. But I discovered in Berlin that Clay had much more valuable knowledge than that. In addition to his technical skills, Clay had political know-how. Information about Germany's history, its former financial and industrial ramifications, its prewar personalities, and so forth might merely have cluttered the mind of a deputy military governor.[1]

Murphy's comment could have been made with equal justification with regard to Clay's knowledge about Europe in general and the conclusion that "more information merely would have cluttered the mind of a deputy military governor" should be challenged. There were a number of premises—givens, as it were—determining the setting under which Clay had to operate. Early awareness of them would not only have eased the General's task but in the struggle ahead it would also have aided and sharpened his perceptions. The history of American-Soviet relations, always permeated by mutual suspicions and often only vaguely remembered, is a case in point. It is worthy of a summary here.

The Russian Revolution of March 1917 had been warmly greeted by the American public because it seemed to promise the end of Czarist oppression. The Soviet uprising seven months later, on the other hand, was observed with suspicion. When Lenin's new government decided to leave the war against the common enemy, Germany, suspicion gave way to hostility. Great Britain and France promptly opposed the Bolsheviks and participated in the campaigns of the White Russian armies. President Wilson, by contrast, hesitated for several months but eventually yielded to the pressures of his allies. In 1918 the United States Army landed in Murmansk, Archangels, and Vladivostok. American textbook writers justified the presence of the expeditionary force in northern Russia as a successful move to protect valuable war supplies against a threatened German attack. The same sources stressed that the landings in Vladivostok primarily served the purpose of keeping a check on Japanese territorial ambitions.[2] Whatever the guiding motives of the American government were, from the Bolsheviks' point of view the intervention was a hostile act aimed at throttling the new regime in cooperation with counterrevolutionaries and other capitalist powers. It is recorded as such in Soviet collective memories.

Once it had become clear that the counterrevolution in Russia had failed, the European capitalist countries hastened to grant the new regime in Moscow de facto and de jure recognition. The United States, however, refused to follow suit. The Wilson Administration thought it was not possible to recognize the new rulers of Russia because, as it declared, "the regime is based upon the negation of every principle of honor and good faith and every usage and convention underlying the whole structure of international law. . . ."[3] In the eyes of the following three administrations and of the American public at large, the nonpayment of Russia's debts and the impact of Communist propaganda continued to militate successfully against recognition.

The arrival of the Roosevelt Administration in 1933 changed the prospects for diplomatic acceptance. By then the Soviet regime had been firmly in control for fifteen years and, as Roosevelt told Morgenthau, the use of nonrecognition against an established regime was a futile gesture.[4] In his judgment, the question of recognition had to be examined against the background of world affairs.[5] Accordingly, Roosevelt took matters into his own hands and an invitation went out to Moscow to send a representative. When the Soviet emissary, Maxim Litvinov, arrived, he stressed that the details of a debt settlement could only be worked out after recognition had been granted and normal relations established. It was not a promising beginning because, as anybody familiar with Soviet tactics might have predicted, the Soviet attitude was likely to stiffen once the Russian government had been recognized. The pattern of the bilateral discussions which followed has since become standard for American-Soviet negotiations. The Americans were in a hurry to reach an agreement whereas the Russians firmly held their ground. Litvinov explained that any positive Soviet action with regard to the settlement of debts was bound to revive the claims of Great Britain and France. Also, he said, there was no way the Soviet government could curtail the activities of the Comintern.

Recognition was supposed to be granted, however, and the difficult question therefore was how to appease American public opinion. A formal note from Litvinov addressed to the American President served this purpose. It offered some high-sounding "assurances" with respect to Communist propaganda, which gave the impression that the issue had been settled. Similar assurances were given regarding the legal protection of Americans in Russia and the right of Americans to have religious freedom on Russian soil.[6] A "gentlemen's agreement" signed by the American President and Litvinov that tied the debt settlement to the granting of an American loan was not published.[7] Nor did the American public learn of Litvinov's oral but explicit warning to Roosevelt that Russia could assume no responsibility for the Third (Communist) International.[8]

William C. Bullitt, who as a United States emissary had negotiated with Lenin in 1919 and who had worked for an American-Soviet rapprochement since that time, became the first American ambassador to the Soviet Union. Once exposed to the realities of intercourse with the Kremlin, however, his sympathies for Lenin's heirs quickly evaporated. The tentative debt agreement was never completed and the assurances about the curtailment of Communist propaganda turned out to be worthless. When the seventh congress of the Comintern, the Soviet international political action apparatus, met in Moscow in 1935 and the American government protested, the Soviets declared that it was a private organization for which the Soviet government bore no responsibility. The Kremlin on its part had tried to enlist American assistance in Russian efforts to resist Japanese aggression. Since such support was not forthcoming, the Russians also lost interest in continued cordial relations. As a result, an atmosphere of thinly veiled antagonism prevailed, and many Americans regarded Communist Russia as even worse than Nazi Germany.[9] Subsequently, when Soviet Russia attacked little Finland outright hostility emerged, and there were vocal demands throughout the United States for a break in diplomatic relations.[10]

Hitler's invasion of Russia only slowly changed the climate. President Roosevelt promptly promised substantial war supplies, but at the same time Senator Harry S. Truman publicly proposed that the United States should exhaust the two dictators by alternatingly giving aid to the losing side.[11] It also seemed that many Americans were not displeased to see Hitler and Stalin at war, and conservative papers expressed the hope that "the two alien ideologies would now destroy each other."[12]

Pearl Harbor and the German declaration of war on the United States accelerated a change in sentiment. As Russia and America found themselves in a strange alliance which neither had sought, the fundamental hostility between the strongest capitalist and the leading Communist power was consciously and subconsciously suppressed. Roosevelt, the political realist, correctly appraised the situation. He knew that the United States was ill prepared for the impending combat and that even a fully rearmed America, supported only by Great Britain, would probably be unable to bring the war with Hitlerite Germany to a victorious end. As he saw it, not only a collapse of the Russian armies but also a separate peace between the two dictators had to be prevented by all possible means.[13] Lend-lease seemed the logical answer. Moreover, the traditional distrust between the two nations had to be dispelled. The well-remembered scenario of the Molotov-Ribbentrop pact offered a good example of developments which might but should not be permitted to recur. At that time, a clumsy attempt to entangle Russia through a proposed alliance in a war with Germany while France and England watched from behind the Maginot Line was thwarted by

Stalin turning the tables on the Western powers. The lesson not to try to outsmart the man in the Kremlin was not lost on the American President. Stalin's trust in the American ally had to be strengthened. Accordingly, Russia's requests for war supplies had to be honored to the limits of feasibility and Soviet hopes for an early second front had to be kept alive.

A categorical declaration demanding Germany's unconditional surrender was meant to assure the Russian ally that no separate deals would be made.[14] And a systematic public relations campaign extolling the heroism of the Russian armies served the purpose of creating an atmosphere of amenity and trust—indispensable for an all-out war effort. Consequently, "criticizing Russia in in the fall of 1942 was like criticizing one's son when he is struggling to recover from a crippling paralysis, and nobody except the ultraconservative Hearst-McCormick-Patterson newspaper axis was doing it."[15] As General John R. Deane, the head of the American military mission in Moscow, later wrote, it was clear that "our most compelling motive in sending supplies to Russia was to save our skin." And since the Soviets had no illusions on this point, "there was never gratitude among their leaders and there never will be."[16] Although many Americans and Soviets tried to focus on the virtues of their partners in the common struggle against Nazism, mutual suspicions continued to surface. (Stalin's insulting message to F.D.R., alleging betrayal in the surrender negotiations for the German forces in Italy in 1945, was one such incident.)

At the time of the Teheran Conference in November 1943, a considerable degree of harmony among the Big Three had prevailed. The division of a defeated Germany seemed at that time a common policy aim. While within the State Department considerable opposition to this policy had emerged, the President, Churchill, and Stalin spent some time discussing various concepts of partition.[17] Moreover, Roosevelt recognized the need to give postwar aid to devastated Russia. The topic did not come up when he talked to Stalin, but it was mentioned in the President's conversations with Hopkins and Ambassador Harriman. Accordingly, as instructed by Roosevelt, Harriman raised the issue when he met with the Molotov in Moscow. He explained that in conformity with the provisions of congressional authorizations, lend-lease would have to be terminated at the end of hostilities. It might nevertheless be possible, he stated, to negotiate an agreement whereby the Soviets during a period of transition would continue to receive supplies if terms of repayment and interest could be agreed upon.[18] The proposal was promptly taken up by the Soviet government.

A one-billion dollar shopping list was presented and intensive negotiations followed. The Russians, however, haggled endlessly for the best possible terms and thereby overplayed their hand. By March 1945, no agreement had been reached and the State Department with Roosevelt's concurrence withdrew the American offer.[19] A few months later, when Truman with undiplomatic abruptness complied with legislative restrictions and ordered the end of lend-lease, the Kremlin expressed dismay and resentment.[20] The period of war romanticism (to use Dulles' phrase) was nearing its end. At the State Department, many were aware of the tenuousness of American-Soviet relations. General Dwight Eisenhower and some of his military associates, on the other hand, thought more positively about continued cooperation with the Kremlin. But at Yalta as well as at Potsdam there had been few genuine settlements. It therefore was only a matter of time until mutual suspicions would regain the upper hand.

The complex background of the United States position regarding German reparations, unknown to Clay when he arrived in Germany, was another key factor in the setting under which he was about to operate. The Roosevelt Administration had been slow in focusing on the policies for the occupation of Germany. Not before fall of 1944, with American troops approaching the German borders and a collapse of the Hitler regime a distinct possibility, did the President form a Cabinet Committee to draft guidelines for the occupation. Composed of Harry Hopkins and the secretaries of State, War, and Treasury, it met for the first time early in September and several times thereafter.[21] There was general agreement within the committee that Germany would be treated as a defeated country, that war crimes should be punished and that all vestiges of the Third Reich should be eradicated. Germany was to be disarmed and demilitarized. A federal system of government should be imposed as a safeguard for democracy and as a likely obstacle to plans for future aggression.

There was no consensus on appropriate long-term economic policies, however, as Henry Morgenthau took an extreme anti-German position. During his father's incumbency as American Ambassador in Turkey from 1913 to 1916, Henry Morgenthau was often disturbed by the outspoken intention of visiting German officials to resort to brutality to win the war. Like his father, he sympathized with France and England. He also always remembered one Christmas Eve at the Dardanelles. "There was a German officer sitting there who didn't know that I understood German," Morgenthau recorded in his diary. "I heard him damning Americans in foul language. This made a great impression on me." Later, the persecution of the Jews in the Third Reich reinforced his anti-German feelings.

Eventually, because of the Secretary's closeness to the President, his emotionally colored judgment was to have farreaching impact. Morgenthau's initial proposal in the Cabinet Committee to deindustrialize Germany and to create an agrarian economy in the heart of Europe was opposed by the Secretaries of State and War.[22] In apparent disregard of their advice, however, the President invited Morgenthau to join him and Churchill at Quebec so that he could present his views to the two leaders. The upshot was a memorandum, occasionally referred to as "the pastoral letter," which dealt with the future disposition of the Ruhr and Saar. Their industries would be "put out of action and closed down." Moreover, there would be some international body which would make sure that the dismantled industries were not started again by some subterfuge. The memorandum concluded that "this program . . . is looking forward to converting Germany into a country primarily agricultural and pastoral in its character." Both the President and the Prime Minister "were in agreement upon this program."

Morgenthau's triumph did not last very long, however. Opponents of the plan resorted to the time-honored device of a leak to the press in order to scuttle it. In this they were entirely successful, because under the onslaught of an aroused public opinion the President promptly disavowed his own signature.[23]

For the Secretary of the Treasury this development was only a temporary setback. During the following six months his representatives actively participated with State and War Department lawyers in the drafting of an occupational directive which, as he hoped, would implement his program. Moreover, operating on several levels, Morgenthau at the same time maintained his pressure on the President. Historians have focused primarily on his plan for Germany's deindustrialization, and since it was soon abandoned, the Secretary's influence is treated in many texts as a temporary phenomenon. The fateful link between his reparations policy that precluded reparations from production and the eventual emergence of two Germanys has escaped wider recognition.

The reparations controversy after the First World War had left American public opinion disenchanted. Leading economists at home and abroad agreed that the problem had been caused by Allied insistence on monetary transfers when reparations in the form of deliveries from current production were entirely feasible. In the United States, however, the nonpayment of war debts by America's allies, the freeze on the payments of maturing German bonds, the reparations issue, and the simultaneous economic crisis were all lumped together in the public mind. This led to the conclusion that a collection of reparations after the Second World War would not be possible. Oversimplification like this facilitated the promotion of the Morgenthau concept, which largely influenced American occupational policies in Germany. As the Secretary envisaged it, Germany's reparations payments were to be made almost entirely in the form of dismantled factories and equipment. Reparations from production would require the maintenance or possibly even an expansion of the existing industrial base and therefore were taboo.

When the reparations issue came up at Yalta, mythology emanating from the old reparations controversy promptly came into play. Roosevelt chose to interpret the speculative purchases of German bonds by American investors in the 1920s as a huge foreign aid program financing German reparations at the expense of the American taxpayer. This was not going to be repeated, he said.[24] Churchill, who was admittedly concerned about the competition of a revitalized German industry, echoed the President's reservations. Both leaders nevertheless still felt that the Soviet Union was entitled to some reparations, but their approaches differed. While Churchill refused to be committed even on a tentative basis to any definite amount,

Roosevelt agreed to include the Soviet claim of $10 billion "as a basis for discussion." Subsequent American interpretations of this language diverged. In the eyes of many there was no commitment, whereas others opined that the Soviet request had been accepted as a "ball park figure" and as such it should have been honored by the United States. After prolonged debates, the three leaders agreed that reparations in kind were to be exacted from Germany in the form of dismantled equipment, deliveries from current production, and German labor. Additional details were to be worked out by a tripartite Reparations Commission soon to convene in Moscow.

In Washington, in the meantime, the planners for the occupation were putting the finishing touches on the occupational directive JCS #1067. It was the joint product of the War, State, and Treasury departments and therefore entailed many compromises between drastically disparate schools of thought. Morgenthau's handwriting, however, was clearly visible in the provision that no steps were to be taken "leading toward the economic rehabilitation of Germany or designed to maintain or strengthen the German economy." The additional instruction that there would be no action "which would tend to support basic living conditions on a higher level than that existing in any of the neighboring countries" also had the Treasury's mark. The War Department, on the other hand, represented by John J. McCloy, had fought a stubborn and pragmatic rear-guard action. The ingenious formula permitting positive efforts on behalf of the German economy "in order to prevent disease and unrest" was an important escape clause. The directive placed the authority for the administration of the American zone in the hands of the Commander in Chief of the United States Forces of Occupation. He was to "act jointly" with the British and Soviet commanders and the three would constitute a Control Council which would be "the supreme organ of control over Germany." "The agreed policies of the Control Council shall be determinative throughout the zones," the directive said. "Subject to such policies the administration of military government . . . shall be the sole responsibility of the Commander in Chief." In other words, should the Control Council be unable to reach an agreement, the individual zone commanders were to be at liberty to chart their own course. The inherent and farreaching risks of this policy were self-evident.

Upon returning from Yalta, Roosevelt expedited the planning process by setting up an Informal Policy Committee on Germany composed of department representatives.[25] The committee also assumed responsibility for the drafting of instructions to the American representative at the Moscow Reparations Commission. Its final product reflected a conciliation of two opposing factions. On one side there were those who wanted a strong bulwark against Communist expansionism. This group was opposed to any large-scale reparations because they would weaken Germany's economy. On the other side were Morgenthau and his associates who, desiring a weak Germany, pleaded for deindustrialization, which if promptly and drastically implemented would have preempted the issue of reparations from production.

When Lord Keynes met with Dean Acheson, Averell Harriman, and others in September 1943, he had mentioned the widely held "false conclusion" that any attempt to exact payments from Germany after the war would be fruitless, and he had referred to Germany's "immensely efficient industrial organization capable of vast and substantial output." If the skill and industry and determination which Germany had devoted to evil purposes could be diverted to works of peace, he said, its capacity over a period of years should be very great.[26] In a similar vein, the Federal Reserve as well as the Office of Strategic Services had completed scholarly studies demonstrating the feasibility of substantial reparations from production. As the record shows, however, nobody in authority in Washington at that time was concerned with satisfying the Russian reparations demand.

Moreover, as indicated, public opinion in general was opposed to the principle of reparations itself. According to widely held but vague recollections, it was seen as a crisis-producing economic device with American taxpayers eventually holding the bag. The instructions for the United States representative on the Allied Commission consequently reflected this fundamentally negative approach. They acknowledged that "the primary aim of the reparations commission should be the exaction of substantial reparations and that therefore industrial capacity in Germany . . . dangerous to the security of the United Nations should be eliminated." However, the reparations plan should not be based "on the assumption that the United States or any other country will finance directly or indirectly any reconstruction in Germany or reparations by Germany." The plan should not promote the building up of Germany's economic capacity. And if "for political reasons" it should become necessary to collect reparations from current production, they should be as small as possible "and primarily in the form of raw materials and natural resources and to the smallest extent possible in the form of manufactured products." As a further precaution the drafters of the instructions added that deliveries should not be in such amounts as to require "the continued dependence of other countries on Germany after reparations cease." The United States should not be put in a position "where it will have to assume responsibility for sustained relief of the German people." Accordingly the so-called first charge principle was incorporated into the instructions. It provided for the priority of commercial exports over reparations and it stipulated that "recipient countries should be required to pay for German exports."[27]

While it seems that the head of the American delegation to the Moscow Reparations Commission, Ambassador Edwin Pauley, did not have the necessary qualifications for the job, it also is clear that regardless of who was in charge, the highly restrictive instructions for the delegation insured that no agreement at Moscow would be reached. The deliberations of the reparations commission therefore had to be continued at a governmental level.

By the time the Big Three convened at Potsdam, there was no common enemy any longer to fuse the divergent interests of the three allies. The Soviets were now firmly in control of almost all the geographic areas which they considered necessary for the establishment of a political and military glacis—essentially defensive as they saw it. On the other hand, as far as the United States was concerned, the hour of danger had passed and as usual in the life of individuals and nations a more contentious attitude had surfaced. The eventual outcome of the conference was predictable. The most controversial issues, the Western borders of Poland and German reparations, were tied together by Secretary Byrnes in the form of a "package deal."[28] The result was a de facto recognition of Poland's borders and a deferment of a definitive reparations settlement. A provision that the occupying powers would take reparations in the form of dismantled equipment from their respective zones rather than collecting them uniformly throughout Germany for a common pool actually caused postponement. Since the Western powers had refused to be tied to any specific amounts, within six months the Control Council was to come up with a detailed proposal for the future level of Germany's industry not to exceed the European average. Ten percent of "industrial equipment unnecessary for the German peace economy" would then be transferred from the Western zones to the Soviet Union, it said, and additional equipment would be supplied in exchange for food, coal, and other commodities. In addition to the reparations agreement some "economic principles" established at the conference also affected the reparations issue. Germany was to be treated as a single economic unit and common policies were to be established with regard to production, reparations, and foreign trade.

The Potsdam Agreement itself did not mention the crucial issue of reparations from production. The United States had insisted and the Soviet Union had refused to concur that reparations should be a residual item after consumption, occupation costs, and exports—in payment for necessary imports—had been provided for. President Truman had set a definite departure date and it seemed that if no agreement on this issue could be reached the conference would end in failure.

Eventually, as so often in diplomatic intercourse, refuge was taken in a text that meant different things to different people. The first-charge principle, as it was written into the Potsdam accord, therefore said that

> In working out the economic balance of Germany the necessary means must be provided to pay for imports approved by the Control Council in Germany. The proceeds of exports from production and stocks shall be available in the first place for such imports.

This was in apparent accord with the American position. However, since there were no proceeds from reparations, it could be argued that the formula was not even relevant to the issue.[29] The Soviets signed only after the second interpretation had been made clear to them. As one would expect, within a year the underlying conflict was again in the open.

Once Germany had surrendered, it was inevitable that each of the four occupying powers would approach the social and economic problems of the conquered country in its own particular way. The respective historical past and collective memories of the victors could not fail to play a decisive role. Moreover, since the resulting policies differed, a number of inter-Allied conflicts were likely to arise. The United States considered it its task to break the power of the Third Reich and to remove all vestiges of the Nazi regime. Once this was done, Americans expected that new and democratic leaders in a reborn Germany would "naturally" emerge.[30] In accord with this concept, the deputy military governor was not supposed to involve himself in the political and social life of the occupied country. The structuring of the new society was to remain entirely in the hands of Germans.

These specific instructions separating the United States from its allies were another key premise in the operational framework of Clay's mission. Neither Great Britian nor France—both direct victims of German aggression—was willing to face the risks of such an idealistic concept. Although the deliberations for an appropriate postwar policy had begun much earlier in England than in the United States, no British policy for Germany had been firmed up at the time hostilities in Europe came to an end. There was considerable uncertainty about Washington's and Moscow's likely courses of action. Moreover, it was not clear whether a united or a divided Germany should be preferred. England's economic and financial interests suggested the former, but if military and political aspects were taken into consideration, the division of Germany had considerable attraction.[31] Financially ruined by two wars, Britain had hoped to obtain at Dumbarton Oaks a large not-repayable dollar credit, but Lord Keynes' efforts in this regard had been to no avail. As a consequence, once the huge hard-currency costs of the occupation became apparent, policy-makers in London had to conclude that England's precarious finances would make the conduct of an independent policy toward Germany increasingly difficult. Nevertheless, a modicum of independence was maintained. Especially prior to the fusion of the two zones, British official utterances were consistently more anti-German and pro-Soviet than those coming from across the ocean. Several weeks after Secretary Byrnes' renowned Stuttgart speech promising the vanquished "an honorable place among the members of the United Nations," Ernest Bevin told the House of Commons not to forget "that crimes were committed and millions of Germans were implicated in those crimes, and Nuremberg by no means wipes the slate clean. It is extremely distasteful to see victorious nations courting a defeated enemy for ideological reasons."[32]

England's problems were in part being caused by the need to stay in line with America's occupational policies, but undisturbed relations with France were of equal importance. Even before the war had come to an end, it had been one of Great Britain's postwar aims to develop a strong West European alliance in accord with France and the Benelux countries. The French continued insistence on the separation of the Ruhr and the Rhineland therefore could only be opposed by a creative diplomacy. A British plan to nationalize the Ruhr's coal, steel and chemical industries and to put them subsequently under international control was meant to provide security against future German aggression, while at the same time offering a compromise to the Quai d'Orsay. It made good sense when it was presented in the Parliament, where everybody remembered the role of the German industrialists in financing Hitler's wars of aggression. The prospect of a Labor Party's alliance with the German Social Democrats for purposes of socialization did little to pacify the French, but it caused a bitter and protracted American-British conflict.[33] In the face of Washington's opposition—even more pronounced after the Republican victory at the polls—British plans for the socialization of Germany's heavy industries eventually had to be abandoned.

Not unlike the Americans, the French were to show little interest in any involvement in the political or social life of the conquered country. As they saw it, however, aggressive expansionism was part of Germany's national character and this would not be altered by a change of regime. Security therefore depended on a long occupation and the separation of economically important provinces from a future German state. Even during the interwar period, France had had difficulty maintaining—what it considered to be its historical mission—a dominant position in Europe as well as in its African and Asian empire. The consequences of the military defeat and the chaotic economic conditions after its liberation seemed to preclude a recapture of the traditional power. Undaunted, however, De Gaulle and his successors were to be firm in opposing the reemergence of a strong Germany. Although militarily, politically, and economically weak, France's leaders were to use the tools of diplomacy with traditional Gallic skill. Since all policies were stringently controlled from Paris, the French generals at the Allied Control Council, very much like their Soviet opposite numbers, had little leeway for meaningful negotiations. Neither the incorporation of the Saar nor the separation of the Ruhr and the Rhineland from a future German state were topics to be negotiated in Berlin.

Finally, as far as the Soviets were concerned, the answer to the security problem was the restructuring of the German society under the active participation of the victorious power. From the first days of the occupation, the Russians consequently began to play a leading role in transforming their part of Germany into a Communist state.[34] While initially all "antifascist" parties were admitted in the Soviet zone, the gradual ascendance of and eventual domination by the Communist-controlled/Socialist Unity Party (SED) was to be systematically engineered.

The German people for their part looked at the occupying powers with understandable mistrust and fear. Cut off many years from all foreign sources of information, they invariably had absorbed the dire predictions of Goebbels' propaganda: Germany was to be eliminated as a nation and its people condemned to permanent misery. Constant bombing had added to the demoralization. When Americans in 1945 were greeted with *"Alles kaput"* it not only expressed the sincere belief of the vanquished, but also intimated that any succor and reconstruction now would be the victors' responsibility.

In the first days of the occupation, in the wake of the retreating German armies, loosely organized committees appeared throughout Germany. As the Allied troops entered the larger German cities, they were met by delegations of left-wing antifascists offering programs, nominees for office in the local administration, and assistance in the process of denazification. Among the first of such groups was a National Committee For Free Germany, a Soviet-sponsored propaganda organization and "political movement" recruited from German Communists and officers who had become prisoners of war.[35] Other groups, known as "Antifa" or working committees, were under the influence of spontaneously reconstructed work councils in the major industrial enterprises. Composed mainly of former members of the Social Democratic Party and Communists, Antifa had political and social welfare objectives. Its aim was to fight against all forms of Nazism, to educate the people for peace and democracy, and to provide food for the starving and shelter for the homeless.

Initially some American military government detachments had made good use of these offers of assistance. But this was ended soon by an Eisenhower directive which prohibited all political activity, banned political organizations and in general discouraged anything that suggested a political resurgence on the part of the Germans. The ban had been opposed by Robert Murphy, Clay's political advisor, and others who considered the policy suppressive and "discouraging to the more democratic elements who had begun to express themselves." The prohibition lasted only three months[36] but, as it turned out, the revolutionary zeal of these anti-Nazi elements was difficult to rekindle. By the time the directive was rescinded and political parties permitted, concern for food, shelter, and fuel had won the upper hand, and this preoccupation was usually accompanied by political apathy and lethargy.[37]

As far as the more conservative elements of the German society were concerned, they remained as much as possible in the background. Those who had refrained from closer connections with the party were equally careful not to be stigmatized as collaborators. And those who had given National Socialism their full support had their own reasons not to attract any attention. The enduring tradition-bound bourgeoisie, hierarchical in structure and favorable to the existing social order, had been able to maintain most of its influence since the days of the Kaiser. Guided by the principle of "going along to get along," it had seen the Weimar Republic and the Third Reich come and go. It also was resolved to retain its weight after the victors had gone home.

FOOTNOTES

1. Robert Murphy, *Diplomat Among Warriors*, p. 289.
2. George Kennan, *Russia Leaves the War*, pp. 312–319.
3. *Foreign Relations of the United States 1920*, Vol. III, pp. 466–468.
4. *Morgenthau Diaries*, p. 20.
5. Beatrice Farnsworth, *William Bullitt and the Soviet Union*, pp. 90–92.
6. Adam Ulam, *Expansion and Coexistence*, pp. 212–214.
7. Farnsworth, *William Bullitt*, pp. 99–107.
8. Ibid.
9. Gallup Poll, #90, July 5, 1937.
10. *The New York Times*, December 1, 1939, p. 11.
11. Ibid., June 24, 1941, p. 7.
12. Ralph S. Levering, *American Opinion and the Russian Alliance 1939–1945*, p. 46.
13. John H. Backer, *The Decision to Divide Germany*, pp. 72–76.
14. Ibid.
15. Levering, *American Opinion*, p. 99.
16. John R. Deane, *The Strange Alliance*, p. 143.
17. *Foreign Relations . . . The Conferences of Cairo and Teheran 1943*, pp. 600–602.
18. Ibid., *Europe 1944*, Vol. 4, p. 1033.
19. Ibid., *1945*, Vol. 5, p. 991.
20. Ibid., pp. 1018–1021.
21. Henry Stimson, *On Active Service in Peace and War*, pp. 570–582.
22. Ibid.; *Morgenthau Diaries*, p. 7.
23. Ibid.
24. *Foreign Relations . . . The Conference of Malta and Yalta*, pp. 611–623.
25. Backer, *The Decision*, p. 41.
26. SDF. R.G. 59, Notter Files, N.A.
27. Backer, *The Decision*, Appendix 2.
28. *Foreign Relations . . . The Conference of Berlin (Potsdam)*, Vol. 2, pp. 472–473.
29. Backer, *The Decision*, Appendix 2.
30. John Gimbel, "American Military Government and the Education of a New Leadership," in *Political Science Quarterly*, Vol. LXXXIII, No. 2, June 1968.
31. Donald C. Watt, "Hauptprobleme der Britischen Besatzungspolitik 1945–1949," in *Die Deutschlandspolitik Grossbritanniens und die Britische Zone 1945–1949*. Ed. by Claus Scharf and Hans Jürgen Schröder.
32. House of Commons, October 22, 1946.
33. Horst Lademacher, "Die Britische Sozialisierungspolitik im Rhein-Ruhr Raum 1945–1948," in Scharf and Schröder, *Die Deutschlandspolitik*.
34. Leonoard Krieger, "The Interregnum in Germany March-August 1945," in *Political Science Quarterly*, Vol. LXIV, No. 4, December 1949.
35. Moses Moskowitz, "The Political Reeducation of the Germans, The Emergence of Parties and Politics in Württemberg-Baden," in *Political Science Quarterly*, Vol. LXI, No. 4; Lutz Niethammer, *Entnazifizierung in Bayern*, pp. 132–137.
36. *Foreign Relations . . . The Conference of Berlin (Potsdam)*, Vol. 1, p. 472.
37. Moses Moskowitz, "The Political Reeducation of the Germans," pp. 132–137.

CHAPTER THREE

Bad Orders

AT FORT BELVOIR'S U.S. ARMY CORPS OF ENGINEERS SCHOOL, IN VIRGINIA, Lucius Clay's graduate school, military engineers assigned a project are taught to apply the Critical Path Method, or CPM. It outlines the nature of a mission, identifies its individual elements, sets up an organization with sections generally corresponding to the elements of the mission, and fixes a deadline for completion, with interim dates for each element. Robert Bowie, who was one of Clay's principal advisers during the first year in Berlin, referred to this method in somewhat different terms. Bowie said of Clay himself, "He was basically a man who had to have a picture in his mind of where he was going, what he was trying to accomplish, what the guidelines were, and what the relations of things were to each other"[1]—in other words, he needed a grand design. Once this was fixed in his mind the individual parts would fall into place. After Belvoir, Clay invariably sought to impose this overview on each job, and so far it had stood him in good stead through all his military and civilian assignments. It was as effective in directing the construction of the Denison dam in Texas as it was in dealing with the Pentagon's complex and multifaceted problems of war production and reconversion. It was useful when he opened the port of Cherbourg, and it facilitated his task when he began to analyze his directive for the occupation of Germany. But it was of no avail in a more elementary sense. The plans which Clay laid out for his own life became increasingly hostage to events. In two world wars, fate denied him the combat assignment for which he would have given his eyeteeth. And when he succeeded at last in retiring from the Army he soon realized to his dismay that had he stayed on a little longer, he could have had in Korea the frontline challenges he had sought.

The descendant of a politically prominent Southern family, Clay was born on April 27, 1897, in Marietta, Georgia, a small town just outside Atlanta. Marietta was in the path of General Sherman's march to the sea, and when Lucius Clay grew up, family memories of the cruel devastations of the Civil War were still very much alive. Lucius' father, Alexander Stevens Clay, a lawyer and three-time United States senator, had been so named for Alexander Stevens, the vice president of the Confederacy. Henry Clay, "the great compromiser" and twice a presidential candidate, was a

44

distant relative. Lucius' maternal grandfather, who fought on the side of the Confederacy, had died in the war and left his widow, Sarah G. White, destitute on a looted farm. Alexander Clay's family had also been impoverished by the war so that the future senator had to work his way through college. Afterward he taught school while preparing himself for admission to the bar. One of the pupils he tutored for college entrance examination, Frances White, Sarah's daughter, later became his wife.

Alexander Clay's rise at the bar was rapid—so much so that within a few years his success in the profession had brought him not only prominence but also material reward. The same qualities which had distinguished him here made him a natural leader in his community. As his son Lucius related with some pride, Alexander Clay never lost an election. He served for six consecutive years in the state legislature and subsequently from 1897 until his death in 1910 in the United States Senate. Although a Democrat, he was a close friend of Theodore Roosevelt, with whom he saw eye to eye on the need to curtail the monopolistic power of large corporations. He led the fight in the Senate against the sugar trust and effectively opposed a ship-subsidy bill. These liberal policies notwithstanding, his determined opposition to a big national government marked him, by today's standards at least, as a conservative.

The comfortable Clay home in Marietta where the senator's six children grew up was a gregarious political household. As Lucius described it:

> . . . at home there were discussions of politics all the time. One of my brothers was very actively interested in politics and began to run for office even before my father died. You never knew how many people were going to be sitting down at the table, because every one of us was entitled to bring anybody he wanted. Friends of my father and friends of the children. Part of the life was the entertainment of visiting preachers, clergymen, or officials when they came on their rounds. But life was simple in a lot of ways. We had thirty-five acres right behind our house and we raised most of our own food.[2]

At the turn of the century, Congress alternated between a long session one year and a short one the next. Lucius accompanied his father to Washington for the long sessions and served as a page boy on the floor of the Senate—his first exposure to some of the mechanics of politics. Already he was an avid and exceedingly fast reader. When asked about his boyhood impressions, he said, "I think the thing that impressed me more than anything else was my access to the Library of Congress. I could go down and get all the books I wanted to read and take them out, which I used to do once a week."[3] One of his favorite subjects was military affairs; by the time he left high school Lucius had pretty much made up his mind he was going to be a soldier and, like some of his Confederate heroes, he was going to excel in combat. Even before he entered West Point he had studied all the phases of the War Between the States, as he had been brought up to call it. From popular folklore and the writings of the time, he knew the military leaders on both sides, the terrain on which they fought, the logistic problems they had to contend with, and the course of each of the battles. As General Hugh Casey, Clay's West Point roommate and lifelong friend, was to recall:

> the memories of the Civil War were still fresh in the minds of those boys who came from the South. So that there was a feeling about the North and South, the Union and the Confederacy. And Lucius knew what the confederates had come up against, lack of equipment and other handicaps—so he convincingly argued that they actually had performed better than the armies of the North.[4]

Despite Clay's later comment that West Point "had been pretty easy sledding,"[5] his academic standing was not the highest. He excelled in history and English but had difficulty with mathematics, particularly trigonometry, even with some help of Casey.[6] His main problem, however, turned out to be discipline, which used to count as much as mathematics and much more than history or English. In his last year the demerits accumulated particularly fast because, as Clay explained, "I thought we ought to be let out and go into the war and staying at West Point seemed a rather useless waste of time really."[7] As a result he lost some points and wound up twenty-seventh in his class. A combative nonconformist even then, he was a member of the "Dirty Dozen," a group of cadets organized against the high and mighty cadet staff. That made him very popular with his classmates even though he did not participate in athletics. He tried wrestling, but since Casey outwrestled him repeatedly, he soon gave it up.[8] A born fighter, he had to win whether it was in sport, a game, an argument, or any other form of contest. "He was strong-willed and he was very strongly opinionated," General Casey commented, "and if you got into a discussion with him his view was the correct one. He would persist and it was pretty hard to try to change his mind."[9] It was his habit to listen courteously to any exposition of views, but once his mind was made up he would not give an inch. "He had a mind that was splendid in his capacity for logical and clear thought," Robert Bowie recalled.

> But when he got into an argument he was really quite outrageous. You would make a statement, perhaps a peripheral overstatement that was not quite accurate, he would not hit you on the subject that was central, but he would grab hold of the misstatement, error, or weak statement and essentially seek to best you in that like a debater rather than coping with the subject.[10]

Sidney J. Weinberg, the financier and Clay's occasional golf partner, considered him "an annoying competitor on the last three holes when the chips are really down."[11] And his grandson, Lucius III, with whom he played checkers, remarked, "Grandfather always played to win. You would think that maybe he would let the littlest ones win, but he would always be captured by the game and then it would be over and he would win it."[12]

Clay graduated from West Point in June 1918, early enough for a frontline assignment, but it never came. He wanted the field artillery, one of the principal combat arms, but was brevetted to the engineers instead. Thinking a mistake had been made, he contacted the War Department, only to be told, "Obey orders."

Fate was kinder, however, in another aspect of his life. As a last-minute substitute for a sick cadet, he had gone to the bus station to greet a young lady invited to a West Point prom. When Marjorie McKeown, the attractive daughter of a New Jersey industrialist, stepped off the bus, she slipped and literally fell into the arms of Lucius Clay. This abrupt encounter induced a case of love at first sight. They became engaged, and married shortly after his graduation, with Hugh Casey acting as best man.[13]

The next ten years brought extensive training at Fort Belvoir's Army Corps of Engineers School and teaching assignments at West Point and at the Alabama Polytechnic Institute. As Clay moved from post to post, there always was a steady flow of books from the post libraries to his quarters and back. "He had a definite idea what education should be," his grandson Lucius commented.

> His feeling was that if you were not a scientist or engineer, you probably wasted your time at college. He was dogmatic on that. He completely educated himself in just about every field imaginable from business to art to literature—he had read everything, modern European literature, all aspects of art and his feeling was that if you are going to college you should educate yourself in hard science.[14]

As a consequence, his feats with facts and figures—aided by total recall—were phenomenal. At Fort Belvoir one of his fellow officers, James Stratton, gave him a voluminous novel that had taken him four long nights to finish. As Stratton tells it, Clay returned the book the following morning. Assuming his friend had hardly glanced at the book, Stratton proceeded to question him about the characters and the plots, but Clay knew all the answers.[15] At a wartime conference sometime later, an officer remarked, "We shipped 500,000 tons of those rations in May or June." Clay shook his head: "It was 824,000 on April 14." A check of the record proved him correct.[16] Drew Middleton of *The New York Times*, who saw Clay in Berlin every week, marveled at his knowledge and ability to discuss such diverse subjects as the development of recoilless artillery, the making of the American Consititution, American policy in China, and the personality of Charles de Gaulle.[17] His mind was such, his grandson said, that he would bombard you with an argument and you would have no change to respond because of his command of facts and things at his fingertips. He could easily overwhelm you on just about any topic. I remember, for instance, one night after dinner for some reason we started talking about U.S. history. He sort of gave us an impromptu lecture on all the Presidents starting with Washington. He knew the dates and he gave us a kind of brief impression of what he thought of the man and his political views. He also talked about the elections and he would mention the main opponents they ran against. With each President and each election he would mention the platform and the things eventually accomplished. For this or that reason he was a great man, he said, and for this or that reason he was inadequate for the job. And he went through each President—one through thirty-seven.[18]

Inevitably, of course, there were some weak spots in Clay's intellectual armor. He had had little training in economics, and his knowledge of Europe was rudimentary. He knew little about Germany, but, as Murphy discovered in Berlin, "Clay had much more valuable knowledge than that."[19]

When asked in his late years how his formal education had prepared him for his varied responsibilities, Clay thought "he owed everything in his life to the Corps of Engineers."[20] As far as West Point was concerned, "the basic program which probably stood me in great stead more than anything else was that whatever your job was to do, you said yes and went out and did it or went out and tried to do it anyway."[21]

It was this sense of duty over personal opinions—however strongly held—that was so evident in his later German days and that had indeed attracted the attention of superiors and colleagues early in his career. General Arthur Trudeau, a West Point friend, likes to tell one story about Clay's service in Panama in the late twenties.

I've forgotten for certain who the commanding general was, but Clay, anyhow, Lucius was a first lieutenant. This general, and I think it was General Preston Brown, was very much of a martinet. Brown would always be out riding and looking over the zone and whatnot and getting into the hinterland there, very lush tropical growth. The country was almost overrun by people; small groups of people just literally built a shack, stayed there and tried to make a living with a little fruit in the jungle. So when General Brown went out there one day he observed a small village that had grown up within the American zone, the Panama Canal Zone, and was very much disturbed by it. He made representations to the Panamanian government to get these people out but they were very slow about this, so he set a deadline and said if you don't do this by such and such a date I'm going to absolutely clean the place out because it's polluting everything around it and it's a disgrace to have it here. So he sent word down to the 11th Engineers. General

Clay, then a lieutenant and company commander, was given the job. The regimental commander said, 'Lieutenant Clay, go out there and absolutely wipe out this village, the people have been told the Panamanian government should have their police moving them out, but you are to eliminate the last vestiges of it because it is an eyesore and it causes pestilence.' So Clay went out with some of his company and cleaned the place out. That day Preston Brown, the general, came out on his horse (remember, very much the martinet) and Lieutenant Clay rushed over to report to him. The general looked over this place where there wasn't anything standing and said, 'Mr. Clay,' (he always referred to lieutenants as Mr.), 'Mr. Clay, you certainly seem to have cleaned this place out.' Clay said, 'Thank you, sir,' and Brown said, 'Mr. Clay, who destroyed Carthage?' Clay thought a minute and said 'Scipio Africanus sir.' General Brown takes his time and again very pompously said to Clay, 'And what did he do?' Clay replied, 'He razed it to the ground.' The general nodded, and pointed his horse whip to the completely cleared old village site, then said, 'Mr. Clay, this, sir, is Carthage.'[22]

Clay's years in the Canal Zone were the only time he actually served with troops. An entry in his efficiency rating at that time—"a company commander who genuinely likes his men, is constant in his care of them and gets the most out of them"—reflects his potential as a combat commander. Other rating officers commented on his "mercurial temperament," the "sensitivity to criticism," or "the tenacity in pursuit of his own ideas," but all of them were apparently in agreement that lack of tact, defined as "the faculty of being considerate and sensible in dealing with others," was Clay's principal weakness. A gradual improvement in the ratings on this score nevertheless suggests that he eventually managed to establish a certain amount of self-control. In later years, as Casey confirmed, he still had a low boiling point, but he tended to cut acrimonious debates short. "Damn it, Pat," he would say, "I am not going to talk to you anymore. You have your views and I have mine. We are good friends and I don't want to disturb that friendship; so we just are going to cut it off right now and we are not going to argue about that anymore."[23]

Between the two wars there were few engineer troops to command, and Clay spent most of his time after Panama building dams and fighting floods—essentially nonmilitary tasks. Together with Casey, Clay also spent one year on a water-power survey in the Philippines, an assignment that brought him close to Eisenhower, who at the time was General MacArthur's chief of staff. And for four years, from 1933 to 1937, he worked in the Rivers and Harbors Section of the Washington office of the Chief of Engineers, where as the principal liaison officer to Congress he acquired a thorough understanding of the budgetary and legislative processes. His office in the Old Munitions Building soon became a center of information.

Here a Congressman could get data on the projects in his district and learn what their status was, what had to be done, how he oculd get them through Congress, and everything necessary to get a project studied and examined. "In that way," as Clay later explained, "we developed, I think, a great deal of goodwill. We did have the information and we did make it available to others very quickly." Testifying before House and Senate Committees was invaluable experience for Clay.

> It was in this process that I found many friends in the Senate and Congress, but above all I learned how the government operates. I didn't know when I went there that you had to have an authorization before you could get an appropriation, and there were many ways in which a knowledge of how government works in that period of relative expansion gave me a great advantage.[24]

All through those years he, like his classmates, had remained a company grade officer with low pay and no chance for promotion. A well-trained and widely respected engineer, he had many remunerative offers from private industry. Some of them were tempting, but after consulting with Marjorie he always declined them. After all, he had planned to be a soldier and eventually there might be a war. When the war did approach, he was repeatedly promoted, and ordered to design a defense airport system in South America. When the bombs fell on Pearl Harbor, General Brehon Somervell got his hands on him—first to serve as deputy chief of staff for requirements and resources and four months later as the Pentagon's Director of Matériel with the temporary rank of brigadier general. Clay protested and repeatedly asked to transfer to a combat unit, even if reduced to the rank of colonel.[25] But his requests were turned down, and the war went on.

When the American army landed in Africa, Clay could read about Patton and others he knew leading their troops and finishing off the "Desert Fox." Then came Sicily and Anzio and Normandie and New Guinea and Guadalcanal, and Clay's former classmates were all over the map, battling their way to Berlin and Tokyo. Meanwhile, at the Pentagon, keeping two shifts of stenographers busy and more than once putting in three consecutive 24-hour days, he effectively handled the biggest procurement job the world had even seen. In the army and outside of it, he made a name for himself. But inwardly he was a frustrated, unhappy man. "Day after day," Marjorie Clay recalled, "he came home complaining about the misfortune to be denied a combat command."[26] He was envious of his two sons, both of whom were in combat, one commanding armored units, the other leading a B-26 squadron.

Finally something seemed to break. Eisenhower, a good friend since they had served together in the Philippines, asked for his help in October 1944 to break the Cherbourg bottleneck that had slowed down the American advance. He was given three weeks to deal with the problem, but only shortly after his arrival supplies began to move freely. By the time he left, the flow had quintupled. As Clay tells it with great modesty, it was a routine achievement. The bottleneck had been caused primarily by too much supervision given to an efficient port director, he wrote. But James Stratton, also a general by then, had a different story.

> What Clay did immediately was to take all German prisoners and to organize them into work groups. He practically dismissed all the guards. 'You don't need those,' Clay said. 'These fellows are not going to run away, the only place to go would be the enemy French.' So what he did was to put the Germans under challenge and they organized themselves into work groups and I tell you, the marvelous job that they did. When I visited Clay, Lucius was sitting in a chair reading a book. I said, 'For Christ's sake, Lucius, don't you have anything to do?' He said, 'Well, look around, what the hell could I do, go out there and be a foreman, something of that sort?' And I said, 'Well I don't know but let's tour the port anyway.' And I tell you I was impressed. You talk about organization—this was the kind where he excelled.[27]

When Cherbourg and Clay were mentioned at SHAEF, another story made the rounds. A general stationed in Paris had phoned and asked Clay to expedite the shipment of half a dozen cases of Scotch arriving on the next transport. "For old times' sake, Lucius," he said, "I'll let you keep out two bottles for yourself." Clay speeded the shipment along, but by way of letting it be known that the busy commander of a bustling port could not be expected to concern himself with such frivolous matters for such petty compensation, he kept three cases for himself.[28]

Clay had been promised a combat assignment once the Cherbourg job was done, but fate intervened again. A shortage of heavy ammunition had developed and Clay was asked to return home to convince the War Department of the urgency of the problem. "They will not let me come back," he unhappily predicted, but Eisenhower thought he knew better; a personal letter to General George C. Marshall, the Chief of Staff, would assure Clay's return. Clay's apprehension proved to be justified. Once Justice Byrnes learned that Clay was in town, he requested his services as his deputy for war production. For all practical purposes this was the end. "I never saw a sicker man," one of Clay's associates remarked,[29] and Marjorie Clay later said, "It ruined his life."[30] There remained only the faint hope for an assignment in the Pacific Theater, and this too was soon dashed. "Even you have seen more combat," Clay later used to say to James Riddleberger, his political adviser, who had been bombed in Berlin by the Royal Air Force and in London by the Luftwaffe. "It was a wound that never healed," the diplomat remarked; "it bit into his soul."[31]

In one of his last interviews, Lucius Clay mentioned "doing it anyway" as the principal legacy of West Point's "long gray line."[32] It was this motto that tended to guide him through his German years and kept him in the job despite innumerable conflicts with Washington's hierarchy.

Clay had not sought the Berlin assignment nor did he know much about Germany. Nevertheless, he was eminently qualified. A Southern liberal of the turn-of-the-century variety, with an autocratic temperament and democratic convictions, he knew what a military occupation could be and should not be. Moreover, Clay had political know-how. "The ability to avoid paper roadblocks and to persuade obstinate officials, these universally useful political talents were bred in Clay's bones and nurtured in his childhood."[33] President Roosevelt agreed to the appointment after being told that Clay had a clearer understanding of the civilian viewpoint than most military men. Because he had spent almost all of the prewar years in civilian clothes on essentially civilian projects, he had learned—as one astute observer put it—"to look at the army from the outside in as well as from the inside out."[34] It was this rare combination that had made him a natural choice for the job. With an independent mind that excelled in penetrating and farsighted thought, he combined military decisiveness with an impressive command of the art of public presentation. All these elements of a rich politicomilitary background came into play as he charted his course in occupied Germany.

His initial shock about JCS #1067 soon gave way to a more analytical approach. Accustomed as he was to receiving and meticulously executing clear-cut military orders, ambivalent instructions were a new experience for him. He recognized that some modifications had been made in the spring of 1945. The section listing oil, synthetic rubber, and other commodities as forbidden industries had been deleted. Secretary of the Treasury Morgenthau had protested, but the Pentagon successfully argued that such prohibition would necessitate additional imports, probably at American expense. Later Lewis Douglas' forceful intervention with John J. McCloy, the Assistant Secretary of War, had produced authorization to establish financial controls to fight inflation. But these were only marginal improvements. Clay, however, soon realized that the directive had a major escape clause in the form of the "disease and unrest" formula: in order to cope with a perceived danger of disease and unrest, some of the principal economic restrictions could be waived. Still uncertain about the full ramifications of the clause, Clay wrote to McCloy by the middle of June and pointedly suggested that "like all general instructions, JCS #1067 can be interpreted in different ways."[35]

His denazification orders in JCS #1067 were equally calamitous, but by contrast they were clear and specific:

> All members of the Nazi Party who have been more than nominal participants in its activities, all active supporters of Nazism or

militarism and all other persons hostile to Allied purposes will be removed and excluded from public office and from positions of importance in quasi-public and private enterprise such as (1) civic, economic and labor organizations, (2) corporations and other organizations in which the German government or subdivisions have a major financial interest, (3) industry, commerce, agriculture and finance, (4) education and (5) the press, publishing houses and other agencies disseminating news and propaganda. . . . No such person shall be retained in any of the categories listed above because of administrative necessity, convenience or expediency.

Not only were there no escape clauses, but the continuous press attacks on the military government also indicated that American public opinion was clamoring for enforcement.

The National Socialist German Workers Party by the end of the war had twelve million card-carrying members, about one-fourth of whom resided in the American zone. As Clay had to interpret his orders, all of them were guilty unless proven innocent, whereas others whose applications for various reasons had been rejected by the Party or who had preferred to support the system without formally joining it were innocent unless proven otherwise. Some of the lawyers on his staff seemed uncertain about the validity of the concept of collective German guilt. They pointed out that the Hitler government after all had been legally elected. To make support of one's legal government a punishable offense by retroactive laws seemed contrary to the most fundamental concepts of democracy.

When Clay, still undecided, discussed denazification with the representatives of Great Britain and France, he realized that their views also differed from those of his own government. For the British, denazification entailed a systematic and thorough search for the principal culprits without paying much attention to the smaller fry. On the other hand, for the French, who had suffered three German invasions, each justified in different terms, the concept of denazification was of little consequence; unwilling to differentiate between "good" and "bad" Germans they considered all Germans *boches*. It developed too that the Russians had a highly unprincipled approach to the problem. They would solve it by proclaiming that all Nazis except top party leaders could redeem their past by joining the Russian-backed and Communist-dominated Socialist Unity Party. Robert Bowie recommended the British policy. As he saw it, only by really focusing on the upper 200,000 could an effective job be done. Clay, keeping the verbatim text of his instructions in his mind, nonetheless remained uncertain.

As he followed the critical reactions of America's media to the denazification practices of SHAEF, it seemed to him that a comprehensive enforcement of the prescribed policies could hardly be avoided. "The British and French did not have the same feelings toward the Nazis we did," Clay explained when discussing the issue in later years. "Neither one had a huge Jewish population," he said, "that had developed a hatred you can well understand. . . . I am not critical of it at all. . . . Nevertheless this was a pressure that did not exist in England and France."[36]

It was a rational but highly simplistic interpretation of a complex American phenomenon that foes or friends of Jews on occasion offered. Certainly to Clay's mind, the sensitivity of the American Jewish community toward military government policies in Germany was an element of great significance. But there was much more to it. Of even greater importance was the traditional crusading fervor of Americans, the world's "almost chosen people" in Abraham Lincoln's words, that had a pervasive influence on the German policy of the United States. As a prominent American put it, "Americans want to know who the fellows are in the white hats and who the fellows are in the black hats. A cowboy movie is still the archetypical American morality play."[37] Often in American history the realities encountered had prevented the implementation of moralistic policy aims,[38] but in 1945 it was going to be different. As America's policymakers had decided, denazification was going to be used for purposes of an artificial revolution. An entire nation was to be remade by a series of bureaucratic decrees.[39]

The antifraternization policies of the American directive had similar roots and were equally unrealistic. Operating under the rigid instructions issued by SHAEF, the army commanders did their best to insure compliance. The provost marshall of the American 82nd Airborne Division, who was imprudent enough to invite a German nurse to a social gathering of his unit, was promplty relieved of his command and heavily fined.[40] There were numerous other instances. When in a relaxed mood, Clay liked to quote the colonel who, trying to explain the controversial issue of fraternization to one of his men, had said, "I guess it means when you stay for breakfast."[41] Nonetheless, with one eye always on Congress, he advised Eisenhower to exercise caution on the subject. "While it is recognized that discipline in the army should not be governed by public opinion," he wrote,[42] "we cannot forget the effects of public opinion. . . ." He indicated that relaxation of the nonfraternization policy, except possibly with respect to small children, would be "misunderstood by the press and the public." A few days later he informed McCloy: "Our nonfraternization policy is extremely unpopular with our soldiers and in many ways you cannot blame them. . . . Frankly I do not know the answer to this problem as yet, and I think we must feel our way a little longer before making any changes."[43]

All these issues were on Clay's mind when, during the Potsdam Conference, Eisenhower invited him to a luncheon with Secretary of War Henry Stimson, who was visiting Germany at the time. "You might tell him about some of your concerns," Ike remarked. As the three men sat in the warm sunlight of a summer day on the terrace of General Eisenhower's Bad Homburg villa, Clay seized the opportunity to unburden himself.[44] It was self-evident, he said, that the United States in its area of responsibility could not let starvation and mass death take place. The cost to the United

States was going to be terrific unless the military government could get in there and get things moving again. But if he followed instructions literally, the military government was prevented from doing anything to help the Germans financially or economically. This was his principal concern, but other parts of JCS #1067, he said, would also be difficult to implement.

The 78-year-old Stimson was perhaps the leading American public servant of this century—he had been Secretary of War under Taft, Governor of the Philippines under Coolidge, and Secretary of State in the Hoover Administration; he listened sympathetically and then gave his views. As Clay later recalled, the Secretary recognized the need for controls and adequate security measures. Only a few months earlier he had announced that the military government in Germany would be "ruthless" in carrying out the "important task of denazification."[45] He still considered the arrest and trial of Nazi leaders and war criminals of utmost importance to future peace. But he would have no part of a policy of vindictiveness and he could see no purpose in the deliberate destruction of the German economy. "No matter how vindictive the American public may feel now," Stimson said, "no matter how stringent your operations may be, just remember this, that in the long run, unless you restore an economic life to these people under which they have some hope of living you will be repudiated by the very people who gave you these instructions. Sure, you have got to live with 1067," Clay quoted Stimson, "but don't live with it to the extent that you let this country starve to death or break down with a lack of opportunity for economic life. In the long run, the American people will never tolerate an area under American control in which there is chaos and hunger."[46]

Here at long last was the guidance Clay had been looking for. Rigid denazification clearly remained a must. On the other hand, he could allow himself some leeway as far as his economic policies were concerned. "I was helped far more than I then realized by the Secretary's visit," Clay later wrote. "Both General Eisenhower and I were impressed by his talk and it had a lasting effect on my conduct of responsibilities."[47]

A few days after the Bad Homburg luncheon the Potsdam Agreement was in Clay's hands. Stimson had offered general guidelines, but the tripartite protocol contained new provisions that superseded JCS #1067 whenever the two were in conflict. In contrast to the former entirely negative policy, the military government was now instructed to promptly restore transportation, communications and utilities in the occupied country. Agriculture as well as coal production was to be stepped up. Whereas 1067 forbade basic living standards in Germany to reach "a higher level than that in any of the neighboring United Nations," the Potsdam Agreement ruled that "living standards were not to exceed the average level of European countries excluding the United Kingdom and the Soviet Union." These were significant modifications, Clay thought, and—as he promptly recognized—Potsdam's emphasis on the economic unity of occupied Germany was the most important one.

By the time Clay and his headquarters moved to Berlin, the division directors and other senior members of his staff had become used to the general's modus operandi. Clay made it clear at the outset that he did not like oral briefings but preferred concise memoranda. Reading and digesting pages as fast as he could turn them, he then often conducted an adversary debate meant to test the weak points in the position presented. "He would almost invariably be able to ask you questions about the one part of the memorandum that really was worth talking about," Robert Bowie recalled.

> He would be able to zero in on the essential issue that might be doubtful or uncertain or worth talking about for some reason. He had a very fast, sharp mind and a very succinct command of the language. He was able to express things very clearly and sharply. At times it seemed to me he made decisions almost too quickly. He had such a capacity to take things in, that it sometimes seemed to me he would make decisions, take a position before he really had thought through all of the implications or all of the aspects of the problem. In terms of personality, it was almost like a shaft of light; when he turned his attention to you it almost felt like a physical blow if he was testing something. I can illustrate this. A man who was in Berlin was a very distnguished lawyer from Chicago, a senior partner of one of the principal law firms in town, with a fine reputation and a high standing—a man of sixty or sixty-five. I can still remember, and this is what he said himself, that he would go into a discussion with Clay and he was almost frightened by him; and here was a man who dealt with all sorts of large legal matters. But the focus of Clay's personality and his intensity when he contested or argued something—it was almost like a physical blow.[48]

"He would pick their brains and tear their papers apart," another close associate remembered. "He had the know-how of bringing out of his people things just so that he would be sure to make the right decisions. He would work them over, up and down, down and up. Continuously fighting was part of his character and technique." "He liked to fight to Mickey Finn," John J. McCloy commented. But Riddleberger thought that "Clay was very reasonable below an adversary shell."[49]

He was not immune to second thoughts, but there was no recorded instance of him ever conceding his position during an argument. After a debate he might quietly adopt the other position and proceed accordingly, but he would not acknowledge it. If events proved him wrong—a rare occurrence—his only comment was, "I did not do too well then."

On the other hand, when he realized he had spoken too sharply and no disagreement over substance was involved, his innate Southern courtesy would make him readily apologize. In one minor altercation with General Sir Brian Robertson, his British counterpart, he made an unwitting remark that cut Robertson. As Delbert Clark of *The New York Times* tells it:

> Clay didn't notice, but when he had returned to his office one who had been present said to him, 'Sir, I think you ought to know that you hurt General Robertson's feelings this afternoon.' 'The hell you say!' exclaimed Clay. Leaping to his feet, he seized his cap, told his secretary over his shoulder to call British headquarters and say he was on his way, and dashed downstairs to his car, two steps at a time. Reaching Robertson's domain fifteen minutes later, he strode past military police and flunkeys right into Robertson's private office. He thrust out his hand, smiled with the full voltage of his charm, and apologized. Word of this incident got around among the British and for months afterwards was a source of amazement. Nothing Clay could have done could have so enhanced their respect for him, for they knew how difficult it would be for a Britisher, however well-intentioned, thus abruptly to shed official dignity and be just a human being.[50]

On the basis of JCS #1067, the Potsdam Agreement, and his meeting with the Secretary of War, Clay thought he had the overview he had been seeking for his German assignment. It now was quite clear in his mind that the unification of Germany was the crucial element of his mission. Since the area under his responsibility could not support itself, harmonious cooperation with the Russians seemed a sine qua non. "We have to make it work," he told a somewhat skeptical staff reiterating what he had said to the press a few months earlier: "If the four nations cannot work together in Berlin, how can we get together in the United Nations to secure the peace of the world? Obviously, there had to be some give and take and at the Allied Control Council this was going to be the American policy."

There were four elements of his mission, he told the staff, that required immediate attention and continued coordination—demilitarization, democratization, denazification, and decartelization. The four Ds—as Clay's advisers promptly called the programs—consequently became the subject of a number of high-level meetings in Berlin as well as of a three-day conference in Frankfurt.[51]

"One of the most frequent reports from the field has been that the military government detachments have lacked an understanding of the basic purposes and direction of the occupation," Clay informed McCloy.

> In view of the agreements of Potsdam we decided to hold a three-day conference at Frankfurt on 27, 28, and 29 August for the staff of the District Commanders and the regional detachments in order to discuss the objectives of the occupation and problems in the field. Over 150 attended the sessions.

The commanders of the two American armies in Germany, General George S. Patton and General Wade H. Haislip, were also present. Eisenhower began the opening session with the statement that "the primary task of the Army in Europe was now military government and all elements of the Army must give their complete cooperation and support to that activity." The Commander in Chief also stressed the need for a thoroughgoing denazification program.[52]

His comments did not remain unchallenged. Patton declared in strong language that complete denazification would lead to an administrative breakdown. His opposition was so blatant in fact that Ike after consulting with Clay followed up with a letter to the army commanders advising them "that the discussion stage of the denazification program was past and that any expressed opposition to the faithful execution of the order cannot be regarded tolerantly by me."[53]

By contrast, when it came to the demilitarization program, Clay foresaw little trouble. By the fall of 1945 it had become clear that the German people, at least for the time being, had had enough of war and military life (so much so that ten years later, when a new political constellation arose, great pressure was needed to reintroduce conscription). In fact, the occupying armies had been able to implement most of demilitarization in the American zone before responsibility shifted to the military government. The German armed forces as well as all other military and paramilitary organizations and establishments had been disbanded. Arms, ammunition and implements of war had been seized. All industries with a military potential had been identified for prompt destruction in the framework of the still pending deindustrialization program.

In a collateral effort to remove all vestiges of Germany's military past, Clay ordered not only Nazi names of streets, parks, and public buildings obliviated, but also those of Bismarck, Moltke, Gneisenau, and other historical figures antedating the present century. Even a world-renowned research organization like the Kaiser Wilhelm Gesellschaft was permitted to resume its work only after the name had been changed to Max Planck Institute. In accordance with American public sentiment, the same directive called for the removal of monuments, statues, emblems, and symbols associated with the German militarism. Other measures were under preparation, Clay reported to Washington, "as part of our unrelenting policy of uprooting Nazi influence from Germany."[54]

As far as the second program—democratization—was concerned, Clay thought he knew how to deal with it. "Anyone who seriously believes in democracy," he said, "knows that it is not a commodity that can be neatly packaged, distributed with food rations, and digested with magical effects. Nor is there, to put it negatively, any wondrous political serum whose injection can immunize the patient against the disease of militarism."[55] Accordingly, he considered it his task to foster democratic leanings where they were found without backing any individual or party. As he told Delbert Clark, some sort of democratic regime could be developed in Germany if the country could be united and means found to correct the desperate situation regarding food, heat, housing, clothing, and so on. "But you cannot build real democracy in an atmosphere of distress and hunger," he said.[56] The fall of 1945 was still too early to start with the job, but as Clay saw it, the institution of democratic machinery similar to the American pattern would be the quickest and most promising approach. "You have to give them the experience of going to the polls and voting and making a choice and living with it,"[57] he used to tell his associates. In the meantime, as a first step, he ordered the withdrawal of textbooks issued to schools by the Third Reich and the destruction of all Nazi literature, and he initiated the printing and distribution of several million schoolbooks whose text had been prepared in advance of the occupation.[58]

As was his custom he expected prompt action. At one of his staff meetings he mentioned Nazi literature found in his own requisitioned home. "I suppose this is the condition in most houses throughout Germany. What do you intend to do about it?" he asked Colonel William S. Paley, who represented the Information Division. The reply, that all the books would be turned over to special committees of German citizens with instructions to have them repulped, was unsatisfactory to the Deputy Military Governor. "I don't think that's enough," he said. "I think it's dangerous for that material to be here and I want it destroyed promptly." Paley, a reserve officer about to be demobilized, dared to object; such action would emulate Nazi practices, he suggested, and therefore be counterproductive as far as world opinion was concerned. Clay's eyes turned steely. "I don't agree," he said. "And since you seem in opposition, I'll ask my chief of staff to prepare orders immediately that call for the destruction of all Nazi literature throughout Germany. That will be all, Colonel." It was a characteristic performance by the Pentagon's "stormy petrel," but there was an atypical ending: using all his powers of persuasion and working through Clay's chief of staff, Bryan Milburn, Paley eventually won his point and his proposal prevailed.[59]

As the Patton-Eisenhower disagreement at the Frankfurt conference had indicated, of the four Ds denazification was proving the most troublesome. During the early summer of 1945 many of Clay's officers had still been on temporary duty with SHAEF. Since they reported to him at his Saturday staff meetings, he had been able to keep abreast of current developments in the zone.

Initially the task of denazification had been entrusted to the occupying armies operating under the guidance of miscellaneous directives in SHAEF's Handbook for Military Government in Germany. They prescribed the apprehension of war criminals, automatic arrest categories, the dissolution of the Nazi Party, and the dismissal of all active Nazis or ardent sympathizers from public office. As a basic instrument for the cleansing process, millions of *Fragebogen* (questionnaires), each with 131 questions, were distributed in the American zone.

Clay was aware that under "wake-of-battle" conditions the detachments in the field had been mainly concerned with the security of the advancing troops and conversely with the necessity of keeping the German administrative machinery in operation. Later a SHAEF directive, based on Joint Chief of Staff instructions, established 1933 as a cutoff date for mandatory removal: those who had joined the Party after the Nazi takeover in January 1933 would not be dismissed if they could show that they had been active only to save their jobs. By the time Clay arrived in the theater, however, the SHAEF directive was amended under critical pressure by the American press and now stipulated that all Party members appointed to an office of political importance had to be dismissed regardless.[60]

In conformity with established army channels, the directive went from Supreme Headquarters to the army groups, where it was redrafted before being relayed to the individual armies. There a similar rewriting process produced the final orders. The result was that during the summer of 1945 the American military government detachments in the field were operating under four different denazification directives. Since still another set of orders mandated the early reestablishment of German administrative machinery, the implementation of the denazification program varied from place to place.[61] As reported at Clay's Saturday meetings, in some areas it was vigorously implemented, in others it got mere lip service.

Automatic-arrest orders were executed swiftly, and in the first months of the occupation more than 100,000 individuals had been apprehended and their property impounded. But where denazification of public service was involved, the main problem was to find appropriate replacements. All the prominent Nazis had for the most part fled before the Americans arrived. The more substantial local citizens tried to stay in the background to avoid association with the occupation. The Germans who approached the military government detachments were often opportunists or schemers. Because the rejection of Nazi ideology by the Catholic clergy was a matter of public record, military government personnel frequently sought the advice of local priests. But they discovered that the priests' resistance had usually taken the form of passive political neutrality rather than active opposition. Although the selected local administrators might satisfy the paper requirements of the directives, the concepts of American democracy were just as alien to them as to their Nazi predecessors. As Walter Dorn, James Pollock, and other experts on Germany at American headquarters liked to point out, the First World War ended the reign of the Kaiser but left the fundamental structure of an essentially autocratic and feudalist society intact. The fifteen years under the Weimar Republic had only confirmed the deep distrust of democracy. The new men chosen by the detachments, therefore, often were middle-class Germans with authoritarian, nationalistic, pan-German, and militaristic convictions. It had not been the authoritarianism but the anticlericalism or some of the socialist programs or the lower-class leadership of the Nazi Party, that had turned them off.

Clay, who knew little about Germany's social structure, listened intently to these comments of his scholarly experts on Germany. They complemented the critical editorials back home and gave credence to a report of the Psychological Warfare Division that had been circulated in the European Theater of Operations. Based on an inspection of Aachen, the first captured German city, the report had charged the military government with having allowed the emergence of a new elite—one made up of technicians, lawyers, engineers, businessmen, manufacturers, and churchmen, and one that was perhaps not Nazi but certainly did not fit the American concept of democracy.[62] The *Oberbürgermeister* in control of the city government was a corporation lawyer for the diocese of Aachen as well as for the Vertrup armament firm that had made parts for Nazi tanks and the V-1 and V-2 rockets. He was anti-Nazi all right, but he was clearly an authoritarian who had no sympathy for some of the fundamental principles of American democracy. His fourteen assistant mayors and department chiefs, all appointed by him, held similar views. These men were reactionaries in the eyes of the visiting PWD officers, although only one of them had been a member of the party. All had prospered during the war with good management jobs in the armaments industry. They were quite willing to hire party members who had changed their minds or who had become party members for business or professional reasons.[63]

Subsequent, dramatic headlines in American newspapers ("How the army blundered in dealing with Nazis"—"We're still giving jobs to Nazis in Reich"[64]) prompted some drastic changes in the Aachen administration but failed to affect military government operations in other areas.[65] As Clay learned to his dismay, the Aachen experience had not even been communicated to other detachments in the field, and military government directives about denazification remained as vague and confused as ever.

Mindful of Hilldring's warning that he would need the support of his government as well as "the best public relations counsel in Christendom," Clay had made it a habit to drop in occasionally at the army's makeshift press club in Berlin. With his courteous manners and easy Southern charm, he had no difficulty maintaining good relations with newsmen. The advantages of informal exchanges were mutual, with Clay benefiting from unfiltered reports on developments in the zone. Reporters roaming the Bavarian countryside thought that many military government detachments had chosen the easy way out, putting primary emphasis on the establishment of an efficient local administration. Encouraged by an equivocal attitude at General Patton's Third Army headquarters, the political past of the new appointees was often overlooked. Moreover—so it seemed—wily Bavarians, having taken the measure of their occupiers, had concluded that their bark was worse than their bite. Exposed for more than a decade to the brutalities of Gestapo rule, they did not consider the open or tacit flouting of military government decrees a particularly risky undertaking. Party members dismissed on military government orders remained in their jobs, so the stories went, and *Fragebogen* were not filled out or mysteriously disappeared.[66]

Literary and professional journals with articles on the occupation—frequently on hand in the club but not readily available through military channels—were an additional attraction for Clay. Often these pieces contained sensational charges such as those in a *Christian Century* editorial, "Playing the Vatican's Game in Germany,"[67] or in an article by Philipp Loewenfeld in the *New Republic*, "On the Bavarian Scandal."[68] The latter asserted that "democracy in Germany had experienced its first setback with the appointment of Dr. Friedrich Schäffer, one of the Weimar Republic's most diligent gravediggers, as minister-president of Bavaria." Later, in the 1950s, when the dust of denazification had settled, Schäffer would serve effectively as minister of finance in the Adenauer cabinet, but in the turbulent first months of the occupation he was branded as "representing reactionary clerical forces" and therefore unacceptable to American public opinion. Commentaries like these and the journalists' tales from the field only confirmed what Clay had known all along: this was not a job for soldiers!

The principal shortcoming of the American approach to denazification was the attempt to put everyone into categories. It was easy for leaders of American opinion to say "get rid of Nazis," but as an American journalist who knew Germany from before the war wrote,

> There were all degrees of Nazis. There were those who joined under pressure, there were the opportunists, there were the 'idealists'—Nazis who later became disillusioned and fell away—there were people who had supported the Nazis under the Nazi regime but had never signed a membership card.[69]

The difference between the Communist concept of the Party as a small activist elite and Hitler's practice of organizing a mass following had never been explained to the American people.

During July and August of 1945, Eisenhower and his staff made valiant efforts to cope with the problem of an aroused public opinion, which they knew would eventually affect the attitude of congressional appropriations committees. The first result was a denazification directive of July 7, 1945, prepared over a period of months by the Public Safety Section of the U.S. Group Control Council and G-5 SHAEF. With a policy statement taken verbatim from JCS #1067, it replaced the previous patchwork of regulations and established May 1, 1937, as the earliest "nonremovable" date for Nazi Party membership.[70] Its aim was to establish a uniform denazification program throughout the American zone, and subordinate headquarters were accordingly forbidden to modify it in any way. The directive's mandatory removal categories pertained to all officials and employees in public administration but only to policymaking and personnel officers in the private sector. Moreover, all persons in public and in prominent private positions were to be "vetted" on the basis of a six-page personnel questionnaire. It was estimated that in the American zone more than 1.5 million Germans would have to go through this procedure.

Only one month after this new order had been published, Clay ordered it applied to private business and industry as well.[71] This extension was often referred to as the "Butcher of Augsburg" directive. According to William Griffith, Clay's order was inspired by a discussion about what should be done with a butcher in Augsburg who favored Nazis in the distribution of meat.

Despite Eisenhower's and Clay's efforts to develop a rational denazification program, the press attacks on military government continued, and Patton's action's and public statements added fuel to the fire. On September 16 Clay alerted McCloy that "things are not entirely smooth in Bavaria" and that Dr. Schäffer, "who had performed a useful service," probably would have to be replaced by an "official of more liberal leanings."[72] But a headline in *The New York Times* a few days later ("Nazis still hold key jobs in the Reich") made it quite clear that the dismissals of a few officials would not suffice. Castigating "a tendency to evade or circumvent Eisenhower's explicit orders," the paper reported "conflict between the policy laid down at high level and its execution by the operating branch of the army and military government. It had become fairly common for military government officers to remove an important executive of industry for Nazi activities," the article said, "only to be ordered by army officers to reinstate him." The paper finally quoted a Patton remark that "it was silly to try to get rid of the most intelligent people in Germany."[73]

If there was still any doubt at U.S. headquarters in Frankfurt and Berlin, Patton's provocative statement on September 22 that "this Nazi thing is just like a Democrat and Republican election fight,"[74] convinced Eisenhower and Clay that prompt and drastic action was required. Judge Charles Fahy, Clay's legal advisor, was told to quickly prepare a radical denazification law, and the assembled division directors in Berlin were informed that "a decision has been reached to denazify all phases of German life." When Fahy, dissatisfied with his first draft of the law, tried to retrieve it, it was too late. Clay was in a hurry and had already departed for Frankfurt with the decree in his pocket.[75]

On September 26, four days before all military government operations in the field came under Clay's direct control, Military Government Law #8 was published. In the meantime, Ministerpräsident Schäffer had resigned and Eisenhower had decided to relieve General Patton of his command. The main focus of denazification had so far been on public service. Concentrating by contrast on the private sector, the new law prohibited the employment of Party members in any supervisory or managerial capacity.

It applied to industry, commerce, finance, education, civic and labor organizations, the press, and publishing. Local German labor offices were made responsible for enforcing compliance. A business enterprise that wanted to stay open had to certify that it had no Nazis in supervisory positions; noncompliance resulted in closing of the enterprise. Where owners were involved, the military government detachments would take the businesses under property control and appoint non-Nazi trustees.[76] The law applied the legal presumption that every Party member was to be considered an active Nazi until he could prove otherwise. In short, the burden of proof was on the individual. Party members who claimed nominal membership could appeal their discharges to German review boards, but the final decision rested with the military government. The review boards were to be composed of reputable non-Nazis appointed by the local mayor and approved by the military government.

From Clay's point of view, Law #8 represented a vigorous implementation of the denazification orders as encompassed in JCS #1067. It was in full accord with public opinion at home, which would not countenance any obstruction—not even on the part of a national hero like George Patton. It was also the first move toward turning over responsibility to the Germans—one of Clay's priority aims. Moreover, with everybody back home focusing on the Patton incident, the General saw an opportunity to demonstrate that the military government was operating "in a goldfish bowl," as he had often reminded the staff, and thereby to get public opinion on his side. At a hastily called press conference, he cited General Eisenhower's policy of "uprooting the whole Nazi organization regardless of the fact that we may sometimes suffer from local and administrative inefficiency," and then announced the principal provisions of the law. "Our policy is complete denazification of Germany as quickly as it can be done and as ruthlessly as necessary," he said. Answering the assembled journalists' questions with his customary skill, he ended the conference by setting the tone for future cordial relations with the press. "I would like to ask you a few questions now. Are meetings of this kind helpful for you? Would you come up here when I put out my part of it and would you put out your part of it? Is that a fair proposition? I would like to make it informal and get your views and reactions. Thank you very much."[77] It was one of his first moves toward an honest and open relationship with the press corps, free of self-serving propaganda, and it paid dividends. His press conferences soon became known as electric affairs. "They crackle and sparkle and the boys love it," one observer commented. Moreover, with the General's door open to the press at all times he won the support of most American correspondents. As far as the denazification issue was concerned, the American media were temporarily pacified and turned their attention to another war aim of the United States—Germany's deindustrialization.

Clay recognized from the beginning that the reparations issue was crucial to the success of his mission. Accordingly he conferred at some length with Ambassador Pauley, the head of the American delegation to the Allied Reparations Commission, both before and after the aborted Moscow Conference in June 1945, and he sought to reconcile the reparations provisions of the Potsdam Agreement with those of the Yalta protocol signed six months earlier. Whereas at Yalta an amount of $20 billion had been accepted by the Big Three as a basis for discussion, no definite sum was agreed upon at Potsdam. Instead, the understanding was that 10 percent of the dismantled industrial equipment in the West would go to Soviet Russia and that an additional 15 percent would be exchanged for industrial raw materials from the East. A quadripartite Level of Industry Committee was to be formed to determine a floor for the dismantlement process (i.e., the industrial equipment necessary for Germany's peacetime economy). The Yalta protocol, moreover, had listed dismantled equipment and current production and labor as the sources of reparations, but there was no reference to current production in the Potsdam text. Clay discussed this discrepancy in a number of meetings with the staff.

As William Draper, Clay's economic adviser, interpreted it, there had been agreement at Potsdam that current production was excluded. He cited in support of his thesis a provision stipulating that "the proceeds from exports from current production shall be available in the first place for payment of imports." Others on the staff argued that "in the first place" suggested merely a priority and that the so-called first-charge clause which Draper had cited could be read another way: since there were no proceeds from reparations, they said, the clause might not even be relevant.[78]

Having ruled that in the initial planning process there should be no provision for reparations from production, Clay was greatly surprised by a press statement Ambassador Pauley released on his return to the States. "With respect to the amount of and the time limit on annual recurring reparations," it said, "reparations extracted in the form of current production from year to year, no decision can be made until the character and amount of removals of industrial capital equipment have been determined by the Allied Control Council and the future of Germany is more clearly defined."[79] Troubled by this apparent contradiction, Clay sought clarification. "A number of points remain unsettled," he wrote to McCloy. "In deciding what production facilities are to be removed or destroyed as excess, should provision be made on payment of reparations out of current production?"[80] As so often happened in the first two years of the occupation his query went unanswered, leaving it up to him to find his way through a thicket of ambiguous instructions and to chart his own course.

From the Potsdam text before him he could only conclude that Morgenthau's concept of Germany's deindustrialization was still very much alive and that the overriding purpose of reparations was the elimination of German industry. Its only limitation was the provision that sufficient resources had to be left for Germany to support itself without outside financial assistance at a standard of living not higher than the rest of Europe. As Draper remarked, the volume of reparations would be simply a byproduct consisting of the plant and equipment surplus to a level-of-industry plan. Obviously this surplus would have to be determined before dismantlement could begin.[81]

This appraisal was to be handled by a four-power committee, but Clay—impatient as usual—was unwilling to wait until it was formed. "We might as well go ahead right now and firm up an American position," he instructed the staff. The result was a study group in the form of a German Standard of Living Board under the chairmanship of Calvin Hoover, the dean of Duke University's economic department. As Benjamin Ratchford, one of Hoover's principal assistants, wrote,[82] the economic provisions of Potsdam concerning reparations were in a number of respects unclear and even contradictory. German living standards were not to exceed the European average, but were consumer goods and services alone to be considered or did the standard of living encompass all elements of a country's economy? Should it be expressed in physical or in monetary terms? Was Germany itself to be included in the computation of economic data? Did the average pertain to each industry? Was there to be compensation for industries where because of extraneous circumstances there was little or no German production?[83] Finally and most important, what time period was to be used as a basis? After some research, Hoover concluded that a 26 percent reduction of the German standard of living would have to be made in order to implement the Potsdam formula. Since by coincidence the contemplated future level corresponded to the actual German standard of 1932, the production and consumption of that year—with some exceptions—was taken as a guide. The resulting calculations of the board—performed on a factual and professional basis that "reflected neither a hard peace or soft peace bias"—provided among other things for an annual steel output of 7.8 million ingot tons, an installed electric generating power capacity of 11 million kilowatts, an annual production of 100,000 passenger cars, and an output of 408 million Reichsmarks worth of machinery. Exports and imports were estimated to be in the vicinity of 4 billion RM as compared with an actual total of 4,619,000.000 RM in 1936.[84]

Clay had given Hoover specific questions which he wanted answered by Sepember 10. The board accordingly was to determine

> The measure of the standard of living visualized at Potsdam; the items—by category and quantity— needed to support that economy; how much of that was available in Germany; what had to be brought into Germany to maintain it; and finally what source of exports within Germany could be found which would provide the money to bring in these imports.[85]

When Calvin Hoover and board member Don Humphrey brought their report to Clay's office on September 10, they felt the board had accomplished its mission. Clay's questions had been answered, although there were some serious reservations in Hoover's mind. The report said in its final conclusions:

> It was difficult if not impossible to carry out a severe program of industrial disarmament spread over a number of key industries while still providing for a minimum standard of living as well as for the costs of the occupying forces. One of the principal reasons for the difficulty was the loss of Germany's eastern food land, and the fact that the displaced population would have to be supported in truncated Germany largely by industrial exports.[86]

Clay quickly went over the paper and raised no objections.[87] Some of Hoover's conclusions were obviously debatable; nevertheless, the report would be an appropriate contribution to the impending deliberations of the four powers. It would be promptly referred to the Control Council, he merely said.

When Clay learned a few days later that Hoover had stopped in Washington on his way from the Berlin assignment to discuss reparations with some government officials, Clay sensed trouble. The Patton affair was at its height and Clay was more sensitive than ever to the reactions of the American press. "While I have no objections to these discussions," he wrote to Hilldring,

> I would like to point out that it [Hoover's study] is being used only as a basis for discussion both internally and in quadripartite discussions. Hoover abhors destruction and his personal views are towards leniency. I want you to understand so that you may advise others, if it becomes neecessary, that his views reflect his personal studies but do not necessarily represent our official views over here.[88]

It was an appropriate and timely message because the "flanking fire from U.S. sources" Clay had been cautioned about followed soon.

Clay's letter had barely reached the Pentagon when *The New York Times* reported in a sensational front-page story from Berlin that the American experts at OMGUS, misinterpreting the Potsdam Agreement, had suggested that the German standard of living should be guaranteed.[89] About half of the exports cited by Hoover would come from machinery, chemical products, and precision and optical industries, "all of which are on the borderline of war industries." The article further mentioned "increased Russian suspicions" that the British and Americans were adhering "nominally" to the Potsdam Agreement while hoping to maintain a stronger Germany than the Russians believed was envisaged in Potsdam. In contrast to the Russians, who wanted German steel production limited to three million tons annually, the United States was ready to concede that Germany needed ten million tons a year. The article finally suggested that the Hoover report reflected the influence of big business because men like William Draper, formerly with Dillon Read; Rufus Wysor, formerly with Republic Steel; and Peter Hougland, formerly with General Motors Opel works, occupied key economic positions in the military government.

The story, which an OMGUS staffer later described as "an astute composition of misstatement and innuendo interlarded with substantial fact,"[90] set off such a storm of criticism in the press and on the radio that objective public discussion of the issue became virtually impossible. It was not the first or the last time that facts became unimportant and the emotional defense of opposing ideologies governed public debate. In the United States Morgenthau promptly demanded that the Secretary of War, Robert Patterson, repudiate the report, whereas the anti-New Dealers like Senator Burton K. Wheeler decried the contemplated "harsh peace."[91] In a long cable to the pentagon, Clay defended the integrity of the report: the instructions to Dr. Hoover had asked for "his considered and unbiased views based on an analysis of all available data under the terms of Potsdam." And no guarantee of any standard of living was even implied in the study. The Soviet "suspicions" reported by *The New York Times* "are news to me," Clay cabled, and he wondered where the paper had obtained its inaccurate data on steel. "I know of no way to proceed in determining a reparations program," he angrily concluded, "other than by calling for studies of the type of the Hoover report. Its entire purpose was to apply the Potsdam formula . . . any prophesies with respect of this report on reparations are entirely premature at this time.[92] Two days later, facing a curious crowd of reporters in the "goldfish bowl" at Berlin headquarters, Clay stressed that Hoover had merely given his own conclusions. "I am not prepared," he announced, "to comment at this time on whether or not I agree with them. . . . I have a very high regard for Dr. Hoover, and certainly shall give careful consideration to his report."[93]

During the remaining months of 1945 little progress was made with the reparations questions, and the determination of Germany's future level of industry remained in the hands of the quadripartite committee formed by the Allied Control Council. The few decisions OMGUS was able to make in this regard pertained chiefly to the restitution of identifiable articles taken without payment by Germany. Some war plants were also earmarked for advance deliveries. Early in the fall the Soviets had submitted a detailed list of forty industrial plants they wanted from West Germany, nine of them located in the U.S. zone. While his industry division was making a survey to determine whether they should be dismantled, Clay advised McCloy that he "was anxious to make available those which will clearly not be needed for the German peace economy." He was firmly resolved to make four-power control work.[94]

Decartelization, the last of the four Ds, attracted the least public attention in the first years of the occupation. When Clay took up the issue with his economic and financial advisers, he encountered a number of objections. Draper said it was one thing to proceed with denazification which could be handled within the American zone of occupation and quite another to try breaking up industrial combines. The network of cartels and private business arrangements for the control of marketing conditions extended over the four zones and frequently even beyond national boundaries. For technical and other reasons it would have to be handled on a four-power basis. Moreover, since the principal German cartels embracing the coal, iron, and steel industries had their headquarters in the Ruhr, it seemed appropriate to let the British military government take the lead. Others on the staff pointed out that the European attitude toward industrial concentrations differed from that of the Justice Department in Washington. The Weimar Republic, for instance, had exercised no control of trusts whatsoever, the only regulation of cartels being a requirement for registration. Contrary to wartime propaganda, they said, the dominating influence of Germany's big combines in Europe's heavy industry was not Nazi-generated; the German Ministry of Economics under Dr. Hjalmar Schacht had simply continued an already existing trend when it harnessed private enterprise to the objectives of a totalitarian government.[95] More to the point, Draper said it made little sense to proceed with decartelization as long as the future of German industry was still undetermined. At Potsdam it had been decided that many of the German industries would soon be dismantled, so any efforts toward decentralization seemed premature.

Clay, ever impatient, would not brook delay. JCS #1067 as well as the Potsdam Agreement had made it quite clear, he said, that excessive concentration of economic power and monopolistic arrangements had to be broken up. So far the press had focused mainly on denazification but this could change any day, he warned. Although only 15 percent of the gigantic I.G. Farben combine, seized by the army in July, was located in the American zone, forty-eight manufacturing plants were in the hands of trustees appointed by the army, and it was necessary to move ahead, he insisted.[96] Like most military men, Clay was only vaguely familiar with the intricate economic and legal ramifications of American antitrust legislation and unaware, it seems, that business interests represented in his economic division would eventually fight the decartelization of German industry. But this opposition had not surfaced in 1945 and Clay was able to act promptly.

At the second meeting of the Control Council's Coordinating Committee, the decision was made following a motion of the U.S. delegate to draft a law to govern the decentralization of Germany's industries. A few days later, at the third meeting of the Control Council, General Clay introduced an American draft providing for a quadripartite commission empowered to dissolve big combines and to terminate all contracts with monopolistic or restrictive aims. According to the proposed law, arrangements on restraint of trade would be illegal, and excessive concentrations of economic power prohibited. The precise meaning of "excessive" remained undefined.[97] The American draft was routinely referred to the Economic

Directorate, where the Soviets soon came up with a counterproposal. Rather than leaving it up to a commission to determine in each case what constituted an excessive concentration of economic power, they suggested a clear definition. The upper limit they proposed was a sales figure of 25 million Reichsmarks and a total of 3,000 employees. Companies exceeding this limitation would be broken up "unless there was a showing of economic necessity" or "unless the size or practices of a particular combine was harmless."[98]

The Soviet proposal seemed reasonable, but the British, who had no substantive tradition of business regulation, regarded all antitrust legislation simply as an American hobby.[99] Sir Henry Percy Mills, the British representative, accordingly made it clear that any "mandatory" disapproval was unacceptable to his government. Instead, an administrative tribunal should be set up, he said, with the power to investigate and to make its own rulings. Now it was the American turn to object. Acting under Clay's instructions, General Draper pointed out that the British proposal required unanimous four-power agreement in each particular case whereas mandatory standards would require agreement only on exemptions. There also was the question of constitutionality—the Germans should know in advance what kind of marketing arrangements would be illegal. Draper then proposed a compromise: all cartel agreements would be prohibited; the market share as well as size would raise a presumption of excessive concentration, but dissolution would not be mandatory. When Sir Henry Mills again objected, Clay turned to Washington for advice. The State Department felt it was up to the Control Council to clarify the concept of illegal power concentration, and accordingly instructed Clay to insist on a mandatory definition.

This made the impasse complete. By the end of November the American, French, and Soviet representatives at the Control Council had reached agreement on mandatory provisions of a law, but the British dissented. Stymied on his level, Clay then asked for support through diplomatic channels. "We hope that strong State Department representation might result in a change of British viewpoint," he cabled to the Pentagon. "We have little hope that a law without mandatory provisions would be really effective as each separate case would require quadripartite agreement."[100] The State Department complied by instructing Ambassador John Winant in London "to discuss this refusal with appropriate members of the British Government to determine the Government's reasons for this position and to suggest modification."[101] With the British reply outstanding, the negotiations in Berlin came to a standstill.

In the meantime, denazification efforts in the American zone had continued. Military Government Law #8—the one Charles Fahy had so hurriedly drafted in September 1945—represented a rigid enforcement of United States denazification policies, and the immediate consequences of its promulgation should have surprised no one. USFET reported "bitterness and despair,[102] and there were rumors among the Germans that this was just the beginning of a plan to destroy their economy. The law affected potentially every Party member employed in work requiring skill or responsibility as well as the operations of every Nazi-owned business establishment. Some military government detachments closed down all the businesses in their areas and would not let them reopen until the Nazis had been identified and removed. Hundreds of Germans appeared at the various headquarters to assert their nominal Party membership or, in numerous cases, simply to present the keys to their offices.[103] American Public Safety officers were often in tacit agreement with the Germans that the eventual result of the law would be chaos. Colonel William W. Dawson, commanding the Württemberg-Baden *Land* Detachment, reported:

> Never before have military government measures been received with such open hostility and their wisdom questioned as today. The belief in the avowed purpose of encouraging the growth of democracy in Germany has been shaken and aspersions are being cast against the personnel of Military Government, the CIC, and other U.S. Army units.[104]

From Clay's point of view he was merely following orders. He accordingly reported to Washington that "so far 42,000 Nazis have been removed," and he added that "the change from Dr. Schäffer to a more liberal Bavarian President-Minister [Ministerpräsident Wilhelm Högner] was all to the good and I am sure will pay dividends.[105] Denazification was clearly slowing the return to normal conditions, but Clay had made sure that some key sectors of the economy were protected. There were a number of official exemptions as well as unofficial loopholes in the law. Agriculture was exempted from the beginning; for the medical profession, with a better than 80 percent Party membership, a special system of revocable temporary work permits was introduced and the permits never revoked. Reichsbahn employees working for the European Theater Service Forces were initially able to secure an exemption; and when it was later revoked they were authorized to continue on the job until their appeals had been heard. Moreover, mounting public pressure forced an amendment that exempted business with fewer than ten employees from the law's application.

One of the most detrimental effects of Law #8 was the reduced respect among Germans for military government policies and regulations. As the Germans soon discerned, the law did not stipulate outright dismissal but permitted continued employment of Nazis as common laborers.[106] Consequently, job titles were simply changed and deals were made with friends or relatives who served as trustees. Since the burden of proof that he had not been an active Nazi rested with the individual, there was a veritable flood of certificates and declarations—the so-called *Persilscheine* (Persil is a popular German detergent). It threatened to make a farce out of the entire process of denazification; fraud and corruption were commonplace.[107] Nonetheless an initial military government report on denazification suggested that "industrial production was at such a low level that no serious effect was caused by the denazification of management. While it was true that inconveniences and handicaps had been caused by the denazification program," it said, "such considerations are not regarded as of primary importance in the long-range program for a denazified and rehabilitated Germany."[108] It was the language of the bureaucracy defending a controversial policy of the American government. Carl Friedrich, the distinguished Harvard scholar, offered a more convincing comment when he wrote, "Seen in perspective of essential democratization and pacification of Germany, this removal of all Nazis should be considered part of the war.[109]

Actually, it was Lucius Clay himself who in an unguarded moment gave a clinching explanation for his actions. Don Humphrey, a deputy to Draper, believed, like many of his colleagues at OMGUS, that the Deputy Military Governor was too rough on the Germans, and he made no bones about saying so. But Clay was playing this one close to the chest. For many months, he sipped coffee, chain-smoked, and listened quietly from behind the big walnut desk in his office to the critical remarks of his staff. Finally one day when Humphrey had been particularly outspoken on the subject, Clay fixed him with piercing eyes and said, "Haven't you learned, Humphrey, the quickest way to get a bad order changed is to carry it out vigorously?"[110]

FOOTNOTES

1. Author's interview with Robert Bowie, Langley, Va., February 28, 1979.
2. Jean Smith interview with General Clay, February 9, 1971. Oral History Project, Columbia University.
3. Ibid.
4. Author's interview with General Hugh Casey, Bradford, Vt., October 9, 1980.
5. Jean Smith interview with General Clay, September 23, 1970.
6. Author's interview with General Hugh Casey, October 9, 1980.
7. Jean Smith interview with General Clay, September 23, 1970.
8. Author's interview with General Hugh Casey, October 9, 1980.
9. Ibid.
10. Author's interview with Robert Bowie, Langley, Va., February 28, 1979.
11. E.J. Kahn, Jr., "Soldier in Mufti," *The New Yorker*, January 13, 1951.
12. Author's interview with Dr. Lucius Clay III, New York, N.Y., June 4, 1980.
13. Demaree Bess, "American Viceroy in Germany," *Saturday Evening Post*, May 10, 1947.
14. Author's interview with Dr. Lucius Clay III, June 4, 1980.
15. Author's interview with General James Stratton, Washington, D.C., November 12, 1979.
16. Kahn, "Soldier," p. 36.
17. Drew Middleton, *The Struggle for Germany*, p. 128.
18. Author's interview with Dr. Lucius Clay III, New York, N.Y., June 4, 1980.
19. Robert Murphy, *Diplomat Among Warriors*, p. 289.
20. Harold Kanarek interview with General Clay, August 16, 1977, in files of Historical Division, U.S. Corps of Engineers.
21. Ibid.
22. Author's interview with General Arthur Trudeau, Washington, D.C., August 14, 1978.
23. Author's interview with General Hugh Casey, October 9, 1980.
24. Jean Smith interview with General Clay, October 8, 1970.
25. Ibid.
26. Author's interview with Mrs. Lucius D. Clay, McLean, Va., February 2, 1980.
27. Author's interview with General James Stratton, November 12, 1979.
28. Kahn, "Soldier."
29. Bess, "American Viceroy," p. 16.
30. Author's interview with Mrs. Lucius Clay.
31. Author's interview with Ambassador James Riddleberger, Washington, D.C., February 21, 1980.
32. Harold Kanarek interview with General Clay, August 16, 1977.
33. Murphy, *Diplomat Among Warriors*, p. 289.
34. Bess, "American Viceroy," p. 146.
35. Clay to McCloy, June 16, 1945, in Smith, *The Papers*, pp. 23 and 24.
36. Jean Smith interview with General Clay, February 9, 1971.
37. Jacqueline Simon interview with Secretary James Schlesinger, *Washington Post*, February 3, 1980, p. C5.
38. Ernest Lefever, *Moralism and U.S. Foreign Policy*.
39. John D. Montgomery, *Forced to be Free: The Artificial Revolution in Germany and Japan.* Harold Zink, "The American Denazification Program in Germany," in *Journal of Central European Affairs*, Vol. 6, October 1946, No. 3, p. 239.
40. Personal information.
41. Author's interview with James O'Donnell, Washington, D.C., March 8, 1980.
42. Memo, U.S. Group Control Council. Office of the Deputy Military Governor for General Eisenhower, May 23, 1945, in USFET SGS 250.
43. Clay to McCloy, June 29, 1945, in Smith, *The Papers*, pp. 35–45.
44. Clay, *Decision in Germany*, pp. 53–54.
45. *The New York Times*, May 12, 1945, p. 1.
46. Clay, *Decisions*, pp. 18 and 54. Jean Smith interview with General Clay, February 5, 1971.

47. Ibid.
48. Author's interview with Robert Bowie, February 28, 1979.
49. Author's interviews with Edloe Donnan, Manchester, Mo., October 27, 1980; Ambassador Riddleberger, Wash., D.C., August 6, 1981; and John J. McCloy, New York, N.Y., April 23, 1980.
50. Delbert Clark, *Again the Goosestep*, pp. 41–42.
51. Author's interview with Robert Bowie, February 28, 1979.
52. Clay to McCloy, September 3, 1945, in Smith, *The Papers*, p. 66.
53. *The New York Times*, September 28, 1945, pp. 1 and 10.
54. Clay to Stimson, August 18, 1945, in Smith, *The Papers*, pp. 59–61.
55. *Life*, February 2, 1950, p. 48.
56. *The New York Times Magazine*, November 17, 1946, p. 2.
57. Clay to McCloy, September 3, 1945, in Smith, *The Papers*, pp. 62–69.
58. Karl-Ernst Bungenstab, *Umerziehung zur Demokratie? Re-education-Politik im Bildungswesen der U.S. Zone 1945–1949*, pp. 101–102.
59. William S. Paley, *As it Happened*, pp. 169–170.
60. Earl F. Ziemke, *The U.S. Army in the Occupation of Germany, 1944–1946*, pp. 381–382.
61. Harold Zink, "The American Denazification Program in Germany," *Journal of Central European Affairs*, Vol. VI, No. 3, October 1946.
62. S. R. Padover, *Experiment in Germany*, passim. Zink, "The American Denazification," p. 231.
63. Ibid.
64. Max Lerner in *PM*, February 19, 1945, and March 6, 1945.
65. Ibid.
66. Memo for Record. USFET, G–5 Advisor (Dr. Walter Dorn) sub. Min. Pres. Friedrich Schäffer and the Tardy Denazification of the Bavarian Government. October 2, 1945, in USFET SGS 000.1.
67. June 29, 1945.
68. June 18, 1945, pp. 841–842.
69. Russell Hill, *Struggle for Germany*, p. 74.
70. Elmer Plischke, "Denazifying the Reich," in *Review of Politics*, April 1947, and "Denazification Law and Procedure," in *American Journal of International Law*, October 1947. After May 1, 1937, civil servants were compelled to join the Party. They consequently were to be exempted from automatic removal.
71. William E. Griffith, "The Denazification Program in the United States Zone of Germany," Doctoral Dissertation, Harvard University, pp. 82–83.
72. Clay for McCloy, September 16, 1945, in Smith, *The Papers*, pp. 81 and 82.
73. *The New York Times*, September 20, 1945, p. 11.
74. *The New York Times*, September 23, 1945, p. 26.
75. U.S. Group Control Council, Staff Meeting, September 24, 1945, in N.A. OMGUS 12–1/5. Charles Fahy, "Memoirs." Oral History Project, Columbia University.
76. Griffith, "The Denazification," Ch. VI. Ziemke, *The U.S. Army*, p. 388. "By December 45 property control had become the largest single military government activity everywhere in the U.S. Zone."
77. Press conference, September 26, 1945. Headquarters, U.S. Group Control Council, Public Relations Service. Albert C. Carr, *Truman, Stalin, and Peace*, pp. 187–188.
78. Probably nobody at OMGUS was aware that the Soviets had signed the Potsdam Agreement only after this second interpretation had been made clear to them. See John H. Backer, *The Decision to Divide Germany*, Appendix 5.
79. Ibid., Appendix 4.
80. Clay to McCloy, September 3, 1945, in Smith, *The Papers*, pp. 62–67.
81. Don Humphrey, private papers.
82. Ratchford, B. U. and Ross, W. D., *Berlin Reparations Assignment*.
83. Ibid., pp. 47 and 48.
84. Ibid., p. 81.
85. Clay for War Department, October 10, 1945, in Smith, *The Papers*, pp. 99–100.
86. Ratchford, B. U. and Ross, W. D., *Berlin Reparations*, pp. 79–82.
87. Author's interview with Don Humphrey, Winchester, Mass., September 1978.
88. Clay personal for Hilldring, September 1945, in Smith, *The Papers*, p. 86.
89. *The New York Times*, October 1945, p. 1.

90. Don Humphrey, private papers.
91. *Congressional Record*, 79th Congress, 1st Sess. Senate, November 27, 1945, pp. 11015, 11033.
92. Clay for War Department, October 10, 1945, in Smith, *The Papers*, pp. 99–100.
93. Press Conference, October 12, 1945, in OMGUS 17–2/5 v 102–6/1.
94. Clay to McCloy, September 3, 1945, in Smith, *The Papers*, pp. 62–67.
95. Graham D. Taylor, "The Rise and Fall of Antitrust in Occupied Germany, 1945–1948," in *Prologue* Spring 1979, pp. 23–39.
96. Clay, *Decision*, p. 327.
97. James Stewart Martin, *All Honorable Men*, pp. 166–174.
98. Ibid.
99. Taylor, "The Rise and Fall."
100. Clay for War Department, November 28, 1945, in Smith, *The Papers*, pp. 125–126.
101. *Foreign Relations of the United States* 1945, v. 3, p. 1573.
102. Ziemke, *The U.S. Army*, p. 386.
103. Ibid., pp. 387–389.
104. History of Military Government, *Land* Württemberg-Baden in OMGUS 410–1/3, Vol. 1, p. 1440.
105. Clay to McCloy, October 3, 1945, in Smith, *The Papers*, pp. 89–90.
106. Ziemke, *The U.S. Army* . . . , *p.* 389.
107. Richard Schmid, "Denazification: A German Critique," in *American Perspective*, Vol. II, No. 5, October 1948, p. 235.
108. Monthly Report of Mil. Govt. "Denazification and Public Safety," November 1945 in OMGUS 146–1/11.
109. Carl J. Friedrich, *American Experiences in Military Government in World War II*, Ch. XII, Denazification 1944–1946, p. 258.
110. Don Humphrey, private papers.

CHAPTER FOUR

The Power
of the Purse Strings

LIEUTENANT CLAY, WITH HIS EXPERT KNOWLEDGE OF THE ARTICLES OF THE
Constitution, was puzzled when he read the *Washington Post*'s headlines one
day in January 1923. The U.S. Senate had by an almost unanimous vote
just decided to bring the American occupation of the Rhineland to an end.
Clearly this should have been the Commander in Chief's initiative, yet the
Post assured its readers that the vote was no encroachment on the White
House's prerogative. The President would ultimately decide. As Clay well
knew, however, appropriations would soon be running out and the Senate's
request to President Harding to "order the immediate return to the United
States of all troops of the United States now stationed in Germany" was
consequently tantamount to a mandate. Within a few months the last
American troops would be departing from the Rhine.

The recollection of this experience was permanently fixed in Clay's
mind. Even many years later, he was to be alert to the critical comments
on the military government by Congress and the press. Whenever budget
questions were discussed in Berlin, he reminded his associates of the 1923
precedent when a congressional resolution rather than an executive policy
decision had brought to an end the last occupation of Germany. "When I
served in Washington in the thirties," he said, "I was in almost daily contact
with congressional committees and I learned how quickly sentiments can
change on the Hill. What happened after the First World War could happen
again. They can always cut off your appropriations." As he proceeded with
his plans for the occupation, it was his constant worry that the American
army would be pulled out by Congress before the job was completed.[1]
From the outset it had been clear to him that only the economic unification
of Germany could eliminate the financial burden on the American taxpayer.
However, this would require time. The Level of Industry Committee, set
up at Potsdam to determine the limits for Germany's deindustrialization,
had six months to complete its task, with little progress toward unification
expected in the meantime. A sharing of all of Germany's resources and a
common import program for the entire country would be a first critical
step. But as Vassily Sokolovsky, Clay's Russian counterpart, had remarked,
there was no point in raising the issue at the Control Council until the

future level of Germany's industry was determined first. There was considerable merit in this argument and Clay reluctantly had acquiesced. As he saw it, however, there were certain activities such as transportation and communications where unification could and should be sought. He was resolved to press at the Control Council for early quadripartite action in these functional areas.

In the meantime it was necessary to keep the costs of the occupation under tight control. A three-pronged approach would serve this purpose. The American staff would have to be drastically reduced and departing personnel replaced by Germans. The costs of essential imports would have to be determined and incorporated in the next War Department budget. And finally an export program would have to be developed promptly to reduce the unavoidable foreign trade deficit expected for the first years of the occupation.

As the General in later years explained,

> We—at least I—didn't know how long the United States was going to be willing to support an occupation, and therefore if I was going to establish law and order, I felt that the best way to do it was by utilizing Germans. Secondly, I felt that the more we could reduce American personnel and military government, the more apt we were to be able to obtain the proper support at home by doing the job. And thirdly, I thought they could do it better than we could.[2]

Some parts of this concept were also spelled out in his letter to McCloy:

> I doubt if the government of a defeated country has ever had to be undertaken under existing conditions. The American public is accustomed to rapidity in organization and in execution of policies, which will make it difficult for it to understand the apparent delay in getting underway in Germany. I know of no answer to this except to continue in every possible way in our own zone to strengthen and improve our own machinery by trying to create from the anti-Nazi forces in Germany a new, even though inexperienced, administrative machine and to patiently and with faith meet in quadripartite council to work out the problems which can only be solved by treating Germany as a unit or by completely recasting of the economies of the several parts.[3]

Among the resulting organizational problems, the question of his staff's size and quality took priority. From past experiences Clay knew only too well that any critical scrutiny by Congress would focus quickly on his administrative overhead. Accordingly he told the personnel section that the original military government staff of 13,000 would have to be cut in half by spring of 1946 and reduced further to about 5,000 by the end of the year. Moreover the military would have to be gradually replaced by civilians. Clay thought that routine attrition would take care of the reduction in force and that it could be expedited by an early transfer of responsibilities to Germans. This worked all right at the lower ranks, but with the high brass there were some difficulties. At the end of hostilities many generals and full colonels with excellent combat records, but without the now-needed civilian qualifications, found their work finished. After having served in company grades for many years, they understandably were reluctant to revert to their lower permanent ranks. Since early retirement often was equally unattractive, an assignment to the occupation forces became a preferred solution. To some of these officers, the running of a military government unit in Germany was essentially the same as operating a military post or an airfield back in the United States. With little understanding for the job to be done or respect for the military government phase of the war effort, they constituted a fairly heavy liability.[4] As John Hilldring, who had anticipated this development, commented on occasion, military government would not be able to succeed "until the heroes had been brought home."[5]

At some of the Deputy Military Governor's meetings with personnel officers the danger of Germany becoming a retirement center for surplus brass was mentioned, but this statement of the issue did not necessarily entail a solution. An unsatisfactory efficiency rating was usually tantamount to destroying an officer's career in the American army, and Clay was unwilling to use this device. He had been trained to wring the maximum out of resources at hand with minimum loss and waste. He therefore shifted incompetent men around until he found a place for them where they could not get in the way of better people.[6] He knew that administrative changes in the field would be coming so fast that in the end most of the military government offices would be abolished. In his own headquarters, as one observer put it, "he telescoped functions, dealt with useful parts, periodically shook up the formal parts with reorganization to keep dead wood off balance and out of action."[7] Moreover, rather than fire incompetents he took on additional responsibilities, making OMGUS more and more a one-man show.

Not only was it difficult to get rid of surplus colonels and generals, it was also equally cumbersome to obtain the services of qualified civilians. It was a new experience for Clay and others who, during the Pentagon war years, always had an ample supply of qualified personnel. On occasion the search for administrative talent caused some friction even in Clay's Berlin headquarters. When a frustrated Draper tried to "borrow" the services of Bowie and Mclean, Clay, a strong believer in "do your own," turned him down abruptly. "Look, Bill," he reportedly said, "I took care of my personnel requirements before I came to Germany and if you did not, I am not going to bail you out."[8]

With an annual salary of ten thousand dollars for top positions and a one-year contract the only incentives, recruiters for occupation personnel stationed in the Pentagon had a difficult task. Many of the new arrivals had ulterior motives for accepting employment in Germany. Some sought revenge, others easy profits, and still others simply wanted to run away from something. Moreover, as Clay later discovered, there were a good many fellow-travelers and even some card-carrying Communists who joined military government headquarters in the early days. With some notable exceptions, Clay consequently was obliged to work with a temporary, frequently changing emergency staff that had to deal with emergency situations and which consequently led to an occasional sarcastic comment about the "feet of Clay."

Early elections on the local level and the setting up of German governmental machinery not only would relieve the military of a job for which they were ill-equipped, but in Clay's judgment would also expedite the process of democratization. "If the Germans are to learn democratic methods, I think the best way is to start them off quickly on the local levels," he wrote to McCloy.[9] He remarked to Dr. James Pollock, his senior civil affairs advisor, who was skeptical about early elections like most of his colleagues at OMGUS, "In order to swim you have to get into the water." "I enjoyed teasing him," Clay was later to recall of Pollock, "about liberal professors of political science trying to restrain a hard-bitten soldier from restoring the ballot to a people who had been deprived of their right to vote."[10] Village elections were thus set for January 1946 in order to give the *Land* governments time to draft election laws which would preclude Nazis from becoming candidates.

In an important respect it was a timely move, since it brought an end to the official army policy prohibiting political activity, banning political organizations, and discouraging anything that suggested a German political resurgence.[11] As a result of those prohibitions, the military government had been obliged for several months to operate without any means whatsoever of assessing public opinion and/or of evaluating the political attitude of the population. One of the other results was to exacerbate the apathy and lethargy into which the Germans had been thrust by defeat. They were in the dark as to what was in store for them, and this uncertainty about the future produced a deepening state of demoralization.

As far as the setting up of a German governmental machinery was concerned, Clay moved even more rapidly. In part he was influenced by the developments in the Soviet zone, where five *Länder* had been established by the beginning of September and eleven German central administrations had begun to operate. By the middle of the month the American military government followed suit by proclaiming the establishment of three German states: Greater Hesse, Württemberg-Baden and Bavaria.[12] In each case a military government-appointed minister-president headed the German state administration. In Hesse it was Dr. Karl Geiler, a well-known lawyer and member of the democratic party; in Württemberg, Dr. Reinhold Maier, who had been a deputy in the Reichstag of the Weimar Republic; and in Bavaria the social democrat Dr. Wilhelm Högner, who had fled from Nazi persecution to Switzerland and who had replaced Dr. Friedrich Schäffer when the latter had been obliged to resign in connection with the Patton affair.[13] "We cannot expect the Germans to take responsibility without giving it to them," Clay wrote to Adcock a few weeks later. "We don't want the low level jobs; we want the Germans to do it. We are going to move a little fast."[14] In a similar vein, he advised McCloy:

> As you know, the Russians have set up a complete German ad-
> ministrative for their zone. I have been reluctant to create any
> such agency for our zone for fear it might impede the treatment
> of Germany as an economic entity. In view of the delay in establishing
> the central agencies, however, we have concluded that some German
> machinery is essential for coordinating the activities of the three
> *Länder* in our zone. We plan to create a council composed of these
> three *Länder* to meet monthly for this purpose . . . this should enable
> the Germans to work out jointly more of the problems which affect
> several *Länder* and relieve our staff of the direct coordination to that
> extent. I do not think this method will impede the creation of the
> central agencies in the field, agreed on at Potsdam.[15]

On October 5, Clay ordered the military government detachments in the field to divest themselves of the direct supervision of the German civilian administration by the end of the year. They were to be replaced by two-officer liaison and security detachments whose task would be to observe and to act as link to the occupation forces. As the Deputy Military governor envisaged it, the office of military government in Berlin, the *Land* offices of the military government, and the *Länderrat* consisting of the three minister-presidents and lord mayor of Bremen were to comprise the executive machinery in the American zone.[16] Proceeding with his program, Clay summoned the German heads of state to Stuttgart, where in a formal address on October 17 he outlined for them not only the official policies of the American government but also his own plans for their implementation. Citing sections of the Potsdam text, he stressed that the aim of the United States was to destroy the war potential of Germany but not to destroy its people. Accordingly, denazification and demilitarization would be rigidly enforced, heavy industry dismantled, and concentrations of industrial power in the form of cartels and trusts broken up. Since Germany's future standard of living was to correspond to a European average, agricultural production would have to be raised and light industries further developed. Admittedly this would take time because the transportation system and coal production would first have to be restored.

Clay then turned to his own plans, the "positive side," as he called it. Responsibility for self-administration would be quickly returned to German hands, he announced. Governmental authority would be decentralized and entrusted to the individual *Länder*. The American personnel would be largely withdrawn, with the residual staff answerable only for controls and security. Although it was the intention of the military government to strengthen the authority of the individual *Länder*, Clay said, the economic unification of the country and the establishment of a federal administration remained the ultimate goal. For the time being, however, there was neither, and a coordination of governmental affairs within the American zone was therefore indispensable. This pertained particularly to the transportation and postal services which in Germany had traditionally been centralized. "This coordination will be your job, not ours," he said.

> As an interim solution we consequently intend to establish here in Stuttgart a council of Ministerpraesidents for the American zone. You will meet periodically to discuss common problems. Moreover a German secretariat ought to be set up and liaison officers from the individual *Länder* appointed. There also will be a small American staff to oversee the work of the council and to ascertain that it follows United States policies.

Clay ended by asking for prompt action. "I would like to emphasize," he said in his closing comments, "that within the framework of the policies of the United States the responsibility will be yours. We shall not dictate as long as you abide by these policies.[17] Having thus set the course for a rapid reduction of American staffs and of a return of responsibility to German administrators, Clay turned to another pressing problem, the feeding of the occupied land.

The briefing material prepared by the agricultural section of the U.S. Group Control Council had already pinpointed the critical conditions facing the American military government. The topography, soil, and climate of the occupied country did not provide for great productivity. Furthermore, so the reports said, Germany's conservative farming population had always resisted modernization. Even the powerful German Reich under the Kaiser had been deficient in food production and required substantial food imports. This weakness in Germany's economic armor had hastened the defeat of the Central Powers in the First World War. Hence when Hitler came to power his government went to great pains to achieve agricultural self-sufficiency. Farmers were extensively subsidized, heath and moor land was reclaimed, and low land was drained. However, despite these rigorous efforts to increase domestic production, prior to World War II self-sufficiency came only to 83 percent, and even this level was achieved only by the importation of some fodder and fertilizers. To obtain high levels of agricultural production it had been necessary to apply huge quantities of fertilizers. During the war these imports were cut off and most of the domestic production was diverted into ammunition. The resulting sharp drop in agricultural yields led to estimates that three to four years of large fertilizer application would be needed to make up for the cumulative deficiencies.[18]

Anxious not to repeat the mistakes of their imperial predecessors, the German leaders on the eve of World War II had promptly organized an extensive food rationing system built around a "normal consumer" ration of about 2,000 calories. As long as the German armies were able to live off the land in occupied countries and in addition send requisitioned food home, rations for the German population were fully maintained. By January 1945, however, Germany's military and economic situation had worsened so much that the "normal consumer" ration had to be reduced to 1,600 calories and in May, when the war ended, it had dropped to 1,000 calories.

As Colonel Hughes Hester, Clay's agricultural advisor, pointed out, to feed the German population from domestic supplies would have been difficult even under optimal conditions, but the division of the country presented the Western powers with an almost impossible task. Although the Eastern provinces contained only 14 percent of the population, they had produced one-fourth of the country's food output and a considerable part of its fertilizer needs. Moreover, the influx of seven million refugees from the East was creating a food crisis of disastrous proportions. While still operating under SHAEF, the various military government detachments had done their best to cope with the emergency. When they arrived on the scene, most of the indigenous regional food and agricultural offices had already ceased to exist. On the national scene none of the larger Nazi food organizations remained intact. Many officials had gone into hiding, their offices had been closed and records removed or destroyed. Frequently warehouses, grain elevators and food storage places had been heavily damaged. The communications system had broken down completely, and it was next to impossible to transport even essential supplies by either vehicle or rail. Under the direction of Colonel Hester, in July the military government began to organize food distribution. In addition to the basic ration scale for the normal consumer, temporarily set at 1,550 calories and covering about one-third of the population in the American zone, special categories for children, pregnant women, and heavy workers were established. As Clay's advisors pointed out, it was highly uncertain even at this low level how long rations could be maintained. The grain supply that SHAEF had brought along would provide some help. But the principal positive aspect was the large food reserve of the German army which, in the turmoil of defeat, had been distributed among the German population by legal or illegal means. It therefore seemed, the advisors said, that many German homes had a fairly substantial hidden food store which might help them over the coming winter.[19]

It was clear to Clay that until unification could be achieved, and probably thereafter, substantial food imports from the United States would continue to be needed. The question was how to secure congressional appropriations. When he had left Washington in April a vae victis attitude had been very much in evidence, and press reports from back home seemed to indicate that the Wehrmacht's unconditional surrender had intensified this public reaction. The four years with Rivers and Harbors had taught Clay to prepare different game plans for authorization and appropriation committees, an experience he realized would be useful now. Also, since it had been one of his responsibilities during the war to keep a watchful eye on lend-lease shipments, he knew how unpopular this program had been on the Hill. He had no doubt that expenditures to sustain a recent enemy would run into even greater opposition. Accordingly, there had to be an unshakable basis and solid evidence for any fund request.

"We have to make a case to Congress and the Bureau of the Budget," Clay told his economic advisors. "You have any suggestions?" There was none. Some mentioned the "disease and unrest" provisions but also pointed out that there was no unrest. The German people seemed completely subdued; even the threatened guerrilla warfare by the *Werwolf*—an underground organization of fanatic Nazi youth—had not materialized. Clay then called in Morrison Stayer, the Chief Surgeon, to inquire about the general state of health. There were no serious problems, few contagious diseases and no epidemics. How about undernourishment, Clay inquired. The doctor shrugged; obviously there were some cases. How could we find out, was the next question. Stayer hesitated. "Well," he said, "we could take random samples and start a weighing program according to age groups and sex." "Let's do it," Clay decided. "JCS #1067 mandates that we must not permit disease and unrest," he went on, "but we don't have to wait until there is serious trouble. We can make a case for Congress if we demonstrate the probability of both." Thus, barely six months after American and British airmen had ceased to bomb Germany's cities, the orders went out, and shortly thereafter the Deputy Military Governor received the needed data.

"There was a loss of weight and reserve tissue," Morrison Stayer reported, and "any further loss would seriously endanger health and physical fitness." The contemplated ration levels for the fall consequently were bound "to result in widespread nutritional deficiency, inability to work, predisposition to epidemics, increased mortality, and grave unrest." Stayer concluded, "It is my belief that such disease and unrest will occur as will endanger the occupation . . . and that a consumption level of 2,000 calories for normal consumers must be provided . . . if epidemic disease and unrest are to be prevented."[20]

For Clay this was sufficient justification for requesting imports of wheat with a corresponding outlay of $250 to $300 million in the next War Department budget. Always careful, however, to protect his flanks, he also made it clear that his recommendation was made "without information as to ration standards in the surrounding countries and in the firm belief that the input of food into Germany should be restricted to a lower level if in fact the liberated countries have a lower ration allowance." The costs of food imports should constitute a first charge against German exports, but—pointing to the key premise of his mission—he concluded that "unless and until quadripartite authority installs the economic unity of Germany, this is not truly realistic."[21]

To expect in the fall of 1945 a substantial flow of exports from the American zone would have indeed been unrealistic. Leaving aside the critical shortage of coal and the absence of essential raw materials, the realities of the military occupation prevented an early revival of export trade. The borders of Germany were closed hermetically and only members of the occupying armies could enter or leave. Even had German businessmen been permitted to travel abroad, there were no foreign currencies to finance their trips. At the same time, the lack of housing and feeding facilities in Germany militated against the admission of foreign buyers.[22] The Trading with the Enemy Act, prohibiting contacts between German and foreign business firms, added another impediment. Moreover, for technical as well as security reasons mail and telephone service with foreign countries was suspended. It therefore would not have been unreasonable to wait until the traditional channels of business communications were restored. But this was not Clay's way of doing things. Within the framework of Draper's economic division a small export-import section under Roy Bullock from the Johns Hopkins School of Business was set up, and Clay let it be known he expected prompt action.

The Potsdam Agreement stipulated that there should be common policies with regard to Germany's foreign trade. Accordingly, the Allied Control council as one of its early actions approved the general provisions of an interim agreement which in essence authorized the individual zone commanders to proceed independently when regulating exports and imports. Sales would have to be in U.S. dollars or any other currency acceptable to the Control Council, and imports were to be restricted to allow minimum standards of consumption and production. Having thus acknowledged the theoretical aim of a unified economy, the four powers agreed to submit to the Allied Control Authority proposals regarding the setting up of a unified foreign trade machinery.

Accordingly, the foreign trade staff in Berlin began to work on an early draft. At the same time, a concentrated effort was being made to promote exports from the American zone. Here the absence of a viable currency proved to be a major obstacle. From 1935 to 1945 Reichsmarks in circulation had increased tenfold and bank deposits grown fivefold. At the same time, the government debt had climbed from 15 billion to RM 400 billion. In view of this unprecedented RM overhang and the uncertainty created by the four-power occupation of the country, the Reichsmark was no longer quoted on international currency markets. The question then was in what currency should German products be offered abroad.[23]

The European countries depended economically on each other, and the support of their populations required a complex system of trade among themselves which in turn had to be balanced with the rest of the world. During the interwar period their economies had been maintained in a highly unstable balance, with Germany as the principal supplier of manufactured goods. The mechanics of this trade had developed after the Depression of the early Thirties. In a reciprocal effort to protect each other from the damaging consequences of beggar-thy-neighbor policies, most European countries had resorted to a thinly disguised system of barter. Dollars and other freely convertible currencies were in short supply. Accordingly, in the course of bilateral trade negotiations, clearing accounts were set up in order to shield the monetary reserves of the individual nations. Both products and quantities to be exchanged were determined in government offices and, since all payments had to go through the clearing accounts, the individual currencies remained protected. By the end of World War II, Europe's foreign exchange reserves were nearly exhausted and it could not acquire new balances by increasing exports. The prewar pattern of international payments had vanished. Under the prevailing emergency conditions, Clay and his financial and economic advisors were in agreement that it was necessary to concentrate on Germany and the immediate problems facing the military government. Since the principal import item would be wheat that had to be paid for in U.S. dollars, it was only logical, they jointly concluded, to insist on dollar payments for German exports.[24]

Don Humphrey, "a lone and ineffective voice opposing the dollar requirements," argued in vain for a return to the traditional forms of intra-European trade. As he relates, "Clay thought in terms of importing the barest minimum of wheat that could prevent starvation, of selling exports for dollars, and of asking Congress to appropriate funds for the residual deficit. His views were so determined on this issue that he probably could not have been shaken whatever the rest of the staff advised."[25] Clay's approach in this regard was undoubtedly parochial. However, he also knew that the alternatives to his dollar policy—barter deals or sales in nonconvertible currencies—not only were beyond the competence of his staff but also an invitation to adverse congressional criticism. Consequently, when State Department pressure for a change of policy after the first year of the occupation increased, he cut off the bitter debates which resulted by retreating to a convenient alibi: "I am just a simple country boy in these affairs. I want my money in the bank and I want it in dollars so that I can spend it when I have to."[26] As he singlemindedly focused on his German mission, he could not and did not foresee the eventual consequences of his policy, namely a dramatic demonstration that the German economy could not be reconstructed in isolation.

As far as the foreign trade officials at OMGUS were concerned, Clay's dollar policy was accepted as one of the ground rules of the occupation. Since no exchange rate existed whereby controlled prices within Germany could be translated into dollar prices obtainable on the international markets, it became clear that their office would have to assume the role of a Soviet-type ministry of foreign trade.[27] It would have complete operational responsibility for all aspects of exports and imports including the arbitrary determination of export prices by government fiat. To accomplish the promotion of foreign trade, export-import sections were also set up in the military government offices of each of the three *Länder*, namely in Munich, Stuttgart, and Wiesbaden. Berlin headquarters, however, remained responsible all through 1946 for the negotiation of imports and the determination and approval of exports.

In other words, during the initial phase of the occupation the entire decision-making machinery in this sphere was entrusted to a small group of American officials in Berlin, which for many months in addition to other problems was faced with inadequate means of communication with the field.[28] The highly centralized procedure provided for obligatory operational channels which necessitated the transmittal of all correspondence from exporters to the German ministry, to U.S. Export-Import Section at *Land* level, to Export-Import Section Berlin, to U.S. embassies in the importing country and finally to the eventual buyer. Communications going in the opposite direction had to observe the same route. There was a complete lack of incentive for the German exporter. The local bureaucracy was disorganized and ineffective. Also, as Clay was aware, the military government was not a good instrument to administer a planned economy. Under these circumstances it was no surprise to him that a few million dollars worth of hops were the only immediate export from the American zone; moreover, the administrative machinery was so cumbersome that months were required to sell those.

The Control Council's Level of Industry Committee had taken Calvin Hoover's report as a basis for its deliberations and expected to come up with its final conclusions by February of the following year. Since there was little Clay could do to expedite the committee's initial research, he turned to areas where administrative expediency and mutual benefits might help in overcoming politically motivated opposition. The prompt establishment of all-German agencies for communications and transportation as well as of a central German statistical agency fell into this category.

In his initial meetings at the Allied Control Authority, Dwight Eisenhower had found some personal rapport with Marshall Grigori Zhukov, the Soviet military governor. The presence of military men in high places has often been seen as an impediment to the pursuit of peace. But the two Allied commanders, having had first-hand knowledge of the horrors of war, found agreement on the great political, economic and military benefits of continued American-Soviet cooperation. In the summer of 1945, the same positive attitude still prevailed in Washington as well, and in many of Ike's exchanges with Clay the Supreme Commander stressed the need to get along with the Russians.[29]

Only a year earlier, Clay had dealt with the Kremlin long distance and by proxy. He had represented the interests of the U.S. Army at the War Department's so-called protocol section, which was chaired by Harry Hopkins. It was responsible for clearing lend-lease shipments to Russia and Great Britain, and Clay's hard-nosed approach to these authorizations had been notorious. Columbia University's John Hazard, at that time the secretary of the protocol section, relates that every Soviet request was challenged by Clay unless it clearly and unambiguously contributed to winning the war.[30] The General, for instance, had no problems with the allocation of huge quantities of copper telephone wire, Hazard recalled. As Clay explained, "In a fluid combat situation they would be needed. In case of a retreat telephone lines would have to be abandoned and advancing troops would have no time to roll up wire and take it along." But according to Hazard, Clay was very suspicious of the Russians, and when a request for landing barges came in, he promptly turned it down. "I can't see where they are going to use landing barges except on the Caspian Sea," Clay said. "And if they want to use them on the Caspian Sea they must be to invade Iran. They want to extend their influence on the southern frontier of the Caspian Sea. I am not going to give them the barges and help in doing that."[31] Similarly, he blocked the shipping of chemical factories or petroleum refineries that might aid the expansion of Soviet power after the war.

The astute politician in this son of a United States Senator made it easy for him to adjust promptly to a new and very different relationship with the Russian ally. Clay's Soviet counterpart at the Control Council was Lieutenant General Vassily Danilovich Sokolovsky, the victor of Smolensk, who had been in command when this strategic keystone of the German defenses was taken. A former schoolteacher of poor peasant stock,[32] Sokolovsky had joined the Red Army during the civil war and risen rapidly through the ranks. Later, while serving as a general staff officer prior to and during the Second World War, he had been close to Zhukov in a number of assignments.[33] Despite different background and opposing ideologies, he and Clay were intellectually compatible. During the first years of the occupation their personal relations were pleasant enough. "I liked Sokolovsky," said Clay in later years. "He could quote the Bible more frequently and accurately than anybody I had known. He was very intelligent, very interesting."[34] As Delbert Clark confirmed,

> There was a great deal of mutual respect and each appeared to recognize that the insults and denunciations that were a standing feature at their meetings had nothing personal in them. . . . Sokolovsky, because he had been trained in a school of diplomacy where the calculated insult was a standard weapon, and Clay, be-

cause he was alert and adaptable, never stood on their dignity once the fishwives' session was over. Out they would go to the bar, arm in arm, and have a drink.[35]

In this favorable atmosphere, Clay managed on occasion to score some points by applying quiet diplomacy in the course of off-the-record conversations. One day at the Control Council, when the Soviet deputy military governor had read a particularly offensive statement obviously drafted by one of Moscow's party hacks, Clay took Sokolovsky aside and politely pointed out that such speeches were hardly helpful toward continued cooperation of their two countries. The Russian listened quietly and did not reply. But for a long time no such provocative speeches were forthcoming.[36] In a similar fashion, Clay was able to end the kidnapping of German prisoners, probably in an effort to gain intelligence, from trains from Berlin to Helmstedt under American control. After a number of such incidents, he again had a private conversation with his Soviet counterpart. He would be constrained, Clay said, to put guards of fifty soldiers with machine guns on each of the American trains with instructions to shoot anyone who boarded the train or interfered with its operation. He added that such an incident would be unwelcome in America as well as in Russia. Throughout the meeting, he was consistently polite and thoroughly businesslike. Shortly after this conversation, Sokolovsky issued an order forbidding any train jumping or kidnapping.[37]

By contrast, Clay could not anticipate the difficulties that the weakest of the four occupying powers—France—would cause. Charles de Gaulle had not been permitted to participate at the wartime conferences of Teheran and Yalta nor at the Potsdam meeting of the Big Three, but upon America's insistence France had nevertheless been handed a seat at the Allied Control Authority as well as the veto right. In his parental home and later in the military service, Clay had been sufficiently exposed to the workings of the American governmental machinery to be aware of the disjointed fashion in which critical decisions were often arrived at. So while the incongruity of the French status came not as a surprise, he had reason to assume that France, considering its military and economic weakness, would have to follow the American lead in Berlin. Often not privy to communications on top governmental levels, it took some time for Clay to discover his error— a disappointing and increasingly exasperating learning process.

In fact the French government had put its cards on the table from the start. The Potsdam Conference had hardly ended when the Quai d'Orsay dispatched a number of letters to the ambassadors of the United States, Great Britain, and the Soviet Union rejecting some key provisions of the tripartite agreement. German economic unity, a centralized German administration, and the readmission of political parties throughout Germany were not acceptable terms to France.[38]

De Gaulle was even more specific when he met with President Harry S Truman at the White House at the end of August. Echoing Clemenceau, who twenty-six years earlier had expressed identical thoughts, he could not have stated the French position more clearly. "The Rhine is French security and I think the security of the whole world. But France is the principal interested party. It wishes to be established from one end to the other of its natural frontier." De Gaulle went on to say that all invasions of French territory from the east had always come through the Rhineland and that therefore France should have a guarantee that this would not occur in the future. "Separation of the Rhineland from Germany was a necessary geographic guarantee and it was also a psychological necessity for the French people." He added that despite the loss of Silesia a unified Germany would still have an enormous industrial potential if it retained the Ruhr, and that the Ruhr should therefore be placed under an Allied administration. In conclusion, De Gaulle warned that the unified Germany might be under the influence of a strong and powerful Slav bloc which was now being consitituted in Eastern Europe.[39]

The United States government had been forewarned. France was the weakest of the four members of the Allied Control Authority but it was resolved to use the veto power. Because of France's almost panicky fear of a reemerging German power, its representative at the Control Council, General Louis Marie Koeltz, was instructed to block all moves toward unification. On September 22, at the Control Council's ninth meeting, Clay encountered the French opposition for the first time. A British proposal to set up a central German statistical agency to serve the control authority prompted the French delegate to warn his colleagues about "the danger of such an organization as a means of mobilizing." Koeltz was even more vocal in rejecting a British-American-Soviet plan for a central transportation department. He remarked that France was opposed in general to a central administration of Germany and he rejected in particular a central administration of railways as having a crucial war potential. A tripartite plan for a central organization of communications and mail also elicited French objections. As General Koeltz indicated, "The French government has made its reservations known through diplomatic channels," and he added that General Koenig, the Commander in Chief of the French Forces of Occupation, might have new instructions by the time of the next Council meeting on October 1.[40]

Clay's response was very much to the point: "I feel the problem right now is the fundamental principle of how we are going to govern Germany . . . . If the Control Council isn't going to establish German administrative machinery it might as well fold up as a governing agency and become a negotiating agency." In a similar vein, he cabled the War Department:

The establishment of sufficient central administrative machinery to govern Germany as an economic unity at earliest possible date is essential to execution of our policy in Germany and of the policy agreed to at Potsdam. Russians and British are in full agreement with us as to the desirability of establishing this machinery. However the French are in opposition . . . we have our *Länder* units established now and with central administrative machinery as agreed upon at Potsdam would be able to operate effectively. However if such administrative machinery is not established promptly we will have to establish overall German administrative machinery for the United States. . . . We are apprehensive that it would lead to practical if not actual dismemberment.[41]

In case the Deputy Military Governor was still uncertain about the rationale for French obstructionism, General Koenig's statement at the next Control Council on October 1 gave him the necessary background. "France is unable to concur with the establishment of centralized German agencies," this out-and-out de Gaullist declared, "as long as the future of the Rhineland and Westphalia has not been settled."[42]

Under these circumstances there were only two approaches that could be taken with any promise of success. Clay could request authorization to proceed on a tripartite basis, or he could exhort his government to apply diplomatic pressure in Paris. True to his customary modus operandi, he tried both, but having received authorization to proceed on a tripartite basis, he unexpectedly was first rebuked by the British and later by the Russians.[43] In both cases the argument was that no separate agreement could be negotiated because the Potsdam decisions called for central organs for all four zones.

In the meantime French obstructionism continued. On October 9, when the creation of a central finance agency was under discussion, France sent only an observer. A few weeks later, when an American-British proposal to open all zonal boundaries to the passage of Germans was on the agenda, France again objected. Even a proposal to permit the federation of trade unions in all of Germany was opposed by General Koeltz because "trade unions are political structures."[44]

Clay had taken up his German assignment as directed and without any enthusiasm. Even before he arrived in Paris, he knew that the Army would try to keep the military government job under the general staff, an approach he considered disastrous. Thanks to the support of Eisenhower, he had been able to avert this development. By fall of 1945 he also had become confident that another impediment to the fulfillment of his mission, the restrictive economic provisions of JCS #1067, could be effectively neutralized. As Secretary Stimson had suggested and John McCloy recognized, he would apply them selectively.

A third area of concern was the Allied Control Authority. Clay was increasingly worried that his work there was being endangered by the attitude of his own government. First there was the French opposition encouraged, as he thought, by the State Department's ostensible unwillingness to intervene through diplomatic channels. Second, there was an ominously negative tone to the dispatches from the American Embassy in Moscow and in the State Department's replies. Since Clay on his level had established good working relations with the Russians, he feared that in the long run the mutual suspicions of the two governments would jeopardize the success of his assignment.

The unexpected appearance in Berlin of George Kennan, eminent expert on the Soviet Union, gave Clay an opportunity to air his grievances. He also became exposed to a new trend in American political thought. At a dinner in Bob Murphy's house, Clay mentioned his own friendly experiences with Sokolovsky, even suggesting that he might trust the Russians more than the British. He also expressed concern about the role of the Moscow embassy. As George Kennan recalled,

> I was being upbraided by the general over what he considered to be our anti-Soviet prejudices. I remember him somewhat suspicious of the Moscow embassy because he lived in the atmosphere that radiated at that time, not only from General Eisenhower but from other high military figures including ones for whom I have great respect. I think it included General Marshall, too. These men were strongly influenced toward the end of the war by the feeling that they could get along with their Soviet military opposite members much better than any of us had been able to get along with the Soviet government in general. I'm sure that Zhukov's personality played a considerable part in this. I think it is quite true that a number of the Soviet military, senior military figures, like their American counterparts, were influenced by the fact that they had a certain comradeship of arms with their American opposite numbers during the war, and would have liked to continue to have close and good relations with them. I'm sure this was as true of Zhukov as it was with Eisenhower. However, I think this atmosphere and these mutual feelings were somewhat misleading, because the military did not play so great a part in the Soviet Union as our people thought. In fact, Stalin kept things under very close control and rather eliminated them from influence as soon as the war was over.[45]

It probably was an unexpected experience for Kennan to express such views in front of a public servant accustomed to complying implicitly with the policies of his government and who, moreover, was aggressively vocal in their defense. "Clay took seriously the line of policy," Kennan conceded, "that had been developed in the wartime conferences and in the Potsdam Conference, whereas I was skeptical about all this. This is important. . . . I had the impression of a very strong man," he went on, "who looked in one direction and persisted in that direction with great physical and nervous intensity. I don't believe he thought much of me."[46] It was a perceptive conclusion. "Kennan is all theory," Clay commented to his wife,[47] apparently still unaware that at the State Department and in the White House similar views were in the ascendance.

In the fall of 1945, President Truman had dispatched Byron Price, a wartime director of censorship, to Europe to survey relations between the

American forces of occupation and the German people. Among other recommendations, Price had suggested changes in JCS #1067 and an American
intervention at the Quai d'Orsay in support of Clay's mission at the Control
Council.[48] In spite of this dual pressure, however, no responses from the
State Department were forthcoming, and since other issues also called for
direct consultations. Clay, accompanied by Robert Murphy, spent the first
days of November in Washington.

The political climate had changed since he had departed for Germany.
When Clay had left in the early spring, Franklin Roosevelt was President;
Soviet Russia was still the coveted ally, with war romanticism in full swing;
at the same time, new evidence of concentration-camp atrocities had added
fuel to the hatred of the Nazi enemy. Half a year later a more rational
attitude toward the problems of the occupation had begun to emerge, with
Germans the indirect beneficiaries. Moreover, since the tactical support by
the Russian army was not any longer needed, some of America's opinion
leaders did not feel compelled to suppress their anti-Soviet biases. The new
President's principal foreign affairs advisor was now Admiral William
Leahy, who considered agreements with the Soviet government "without
value."[49] Truman himself, keenly aware of his limited capabilities, felt an
exaggerated need to flex his muscle. He had signed without reading an order
to cancel lend-lease to the Soviet Union. He bragged that in his April
conversation with Molotov he had given the Soviet foreign minister "the
one-two, right to the jaw." And as Churchill commented to Lord Moran
at Potsdam, the new President took no notice of delicate ground. "He just
plants his foot firmly down on it." The American people were still unaware
that their President was becoming "tired of babying the Russians" and that
after the failure of the recent meeting of the Council of Foreign Ministers
in London a policy of "no appeasement"[50] had been born which in its
ultimate consequences was to preclude all compromises. The record of
Clay's meeting with the State Department's European hands reveals this
gradually changing political scene. His factual evaluation of the proceedings
at the Control Council did not fit in with the newly emerging thought
patterns and consequently could only be rejected.

"The past performances of the Allied Control Council have demonstrated that the Soviet Union is willing to work with the other powers in
operating Germany as a single political and economic unit," Clay declared
at the meeting. "The U.S.S.R. has blocked no more than one or two papers
in the Control Council, whereas the French have vetoed all legislative moves
toward creating a central administrative machinery." He added that in his
judgment the American relations with the Soviet Union in governing Germany were of decisive importance for the foreign policy of the United
States. "Unless the two countries succeed in working effectively in that
laboratory the entire foreign policy of the United States with regard to
Russia will be in jeopardy."[51]

The State Department's old European hands (so critically described
by John Kenneth Galbraith[52]) listened politely. It quickly became clear to

them that this General was out of step with the Administration's new policies. Jim Riddleberger, the Chief of the Division of Central European Affairs, picked up the cudgels for the department by asking rhetorically whether the Soviet Union actually was willing to carry out the political and economic principles of the Berlin protocol. He did not mention the Anglo-American support of the cruel expulsion of the Sudeten Germans from their homelands as he began to castigate the Russian "inhumane transfer of population" from the East. Barriers to interzonal movement, the failure to develop interzonal trade, the control of the press in the Russian zone, Soviet support of the favored political parties and unilateral action on land reform were other items on the department's bill of particulars in support of the new "getting tough" policy.[53] As he did quite often when defending his views, Clay reacted sharply to the suggestion that it was the U.S.S.R. which was failing to carry out the Berlin protocol. The Russians favored the creation of central administrative machinery, he reiterated, but they also failed to understand the American attitude in the face of French obstructions. Some of his Soviet colleagues actually had expressed the thought that the French obstinacy was receiving tacit support from the United States and Great Britain.[54] He added heatedly that in his opinion the Soviet Union had gone further than the French in the introduction of democratic procedures. The French had even refused to permit trade unions within their zone to establish connections with unions in other zones. Nazis removed from positions in the American zone had been employed by the French. As far as the land reform in the Eastern zone was concerned, in the absence of a quadripartite agreement, the Soviet military government had of course acted unilaterally. But the same could be said about certain measures taken by the Commanding General of the United States Forces in Europe. The Deputy Military Governor finally asked for a definition of the U.S. government's views concerning the French proposal to internationalize the Ruhr and the Rhineland.[55] Since the Berlin protocol required that the level of German peacetime economy be determined by February, it was essential to know whether these areas would be separated from Germany, he said. It was a highly pertinent question, but it was not a surprise to Clay when the answer was dilatory. Freeman Matthews, the Director of the Office of European Affairs, spoke up and said that the Secretary of State had invited the French to discuss the matter in Washington and that it was "unlikely that the Secretary would desire to prejudge the United States position in advance of hearing the French arguments." The department's response to Clay's question as to whether any pressure had been put on France to cooperate with other members of the Control Council in setting up a central German administrative machinery was equally unsatisfactory. There had been no pressure.

The meeting also gave Clay an opportunity to air his grievances about some of the confusion prevailing with regard to restitution and reparations. In the early fall of 1945 an Interallied Reparations Agency (IARA) had been set up in Paris to distribute reparations among the Western Allies, but its responsibilities and those of the American representative, Walter Angell, had been poorly defined. Clay asked for clarification of the United States representative's role on the Reparations Commission vis-à-vis the Office of Military Government for Germany.[56] The instructions to Angell, he said, involved an apportionment in which he could not concur. There had to be a clearcut decision as to who should determine the amount and character of reparations removals. Recommendations as to the removal from Germany of capital equipment was a very heavy responsibility, Clay went on. He was willing to undertake such responsibility if his government so wished, but he did not feel that the United States member of the Reparations Commission should be in a position "to fill the record with dissents, second-guesses, and criticisms." Having thus stressed the army's traditional predilection for proper channels, he turned to the problem of restitution requests by some of the Allies. He suggested that reparations should be given a higher priority than restitution, and—ever protective of the congressional budget—he added that restitution should not necessitate additional imports.[57]

As he flew back to Berlin, Clay had an opportunity to collect his thoughts on the Washington meetings. It was quite obvious that the *Zeitgeist* was changing. A suggestion to reconstruct Germany's economy no longer exposed one to "the risk of getting hung on the obelisk in Washington," as he liked to say. On the other hand, there were now strong anti-Soviet feelings in evidence. He still was hopeful that his good relations with Sokolovsky would continue, but unification seemed far away. Murphy had mentioned the State Department's preoccupation with the domestic situation in France. Communist influence there was in ascendance and Secretary James F. Byrnes apparently was reluctant to apply pressure. It might topple the weak French government and bring Maurice Thorez to power, Murphy said. But it was not Clay's way to take such outside factors into consideration. "Looking and persisting with great intensity in one direction," as George Kennan had recognized, he considered it his primary task to work toward unification at the Control Council. Any opposition, regardless of source, had to be overcome. There was no choice but to continue the same policies as before and to demand diplomatic assistance whenever appropriate. This was his twenty-seventh year in the service, and he could always retire if the powers that be wanted him replaced. By February, when the Level of Industry Committee had to come up with its plan for Germany's future economy, the crucial policy decisions would have to be made. In the meantime, he was going to take a hand in the committee's work, making sure that there would be no delays.

It is in keeping with Clay's uncompromising views on the responsibilities of the public servant that the dispute at the State Department is not mentioned in his memoirs, which were published one year after his 1949 retirement from the army. As his code of professional ethics prescribed, discretion was a life-long obligation. Moreover, by the time his book came out, there was no point in dwelling on his earlier appraisal of Soviet good intentions. The fundamental direction of his mission in Germany had been changed, and General Clay had fallen in line with the new policies of his government.

Upon his return to Berlin, Clay asked for an up-to-date report on the work of the quadripartite Level of Industry Committee. It had met for the first time on September 18, but in the following two months little meaningful progress had been made. In part this was due to Soviet and French staffing problems. During September and October the Soviet representatives had made almost no positive contribution to the work of the committee. In November a new Soviet delegation joined the staff. They were more competent than the first group, but still appeared unfamiliar with the issues. It was not until the first of December that a team of fully qualified Soviet experts, consisting of economists, government officials and engineers, arrived. The French delegation however remained poorly staffed and contributed very little constructive work.[58]

In addition to these personnel problems, divergent views on some fundamental issues continued to impede progress. Because the standard of living was to be computed on a per capita basis, the projected size of the German population was of basic significance. However, there had been no census since 1939 and both the number of refugees from the East and of Germans killed in the war could only be estimated. The three Western powers held that 68 million was a minimum estimate for future Germany, whereas the Soviets first said 62 and then 65. The result was a mathematical compromise at 66.5 million, but the Soviets nevertheless proceeded unilaterally with their calculations on a 62-million basis.[59]

The question of interpreting "industrial disarmament" was even more troublesome. Plants suitable only for the production of armaments, of course, would be destroyed. Beyond that the concept of industrial disarmament was unclear. As the United States and Great Britain saw it, heavy industry was to be reduced sufficiently so that Germany would have no surplus capacity above the minimum civilian requirements. But the Soviets and French also wanted to reduce extensively some branches of peaceful industries. The Soviets, moreover, did not regard it as mandatory that facilities should be left to provide a German standard of living equal to the average European standard. Any standard below the average would be in accordance with Potsdam, they argued. Since Germany was less self-sufficient in food and raw materials than the rest of Europe, it needed more industry to maintain a comparable standard of living. The Soviets rejected this interpretation.[60]

By the time Clay returned from Washington, the Level of Industry Committee had examined a wide range of issues and debated about a score of industries, but agreement had been reached only on agricultural equipment, motorcycles, paper, and rolling stock. Among the score of issues, one outstanding difference in principle had emerged.[61] The Soviets were determined to apply the prewar per capita average of European steel production to an extremely low estimate of German population. The result was a suggested production limit of 4.6 million tons of ingot steel, compared to 9.0, 7.8, and 7 million tons, respectively, proposed by Great Britain, the United States, and France. Since no agreement could be reached in the Level of Industry Committee or the Economic Directorate, it was clear that the underlying question of principle would have to be settled by the Coordinating Committee.

December was the American month in the chair and, using this advantage, Clay called a special session for the last day of the year. If he could settle the actual level of the steel industry he believed the decisions on other branches of industry would follow. The Coordinating Committee had been asked to resolve the issue of principle with steel mentioned as an illustration, but Clay, in a characteristic manner, chose a different tactic.[62] His primary concern continued to be the establishment of unified administrative machinery which, among other tasks, was to implement a quadripartite export-import plan. Viewed against this fundamental goal, the details of any level-of-industry plan seemed of secondary significance. Moreover, in light of a current steel production of less than 2 million tons it made little sense to fight too long to reconcile the British and Soviet proposals. A recently received Department of State policy paper on reparations finally also seemed to invite a pragmatic approach to reparations.

Clay recognized that the department in this latest statement walked a tight rope in an attempt to perform a delicate balancing act with "strict adherence to Potsdam" on one shoulder and a unilateral "conception of the meaning of Potsdam" on the other. The essence of the new interpretation was that deindustrialization, level-of-industry control, and standard of living formulated in the Potsdam Agreement after all were not for the purposes of limiting the German level of industry and standard of living permanently, but had only the narrower objective of eliminating existing war potential and the providing of reparations. "In the view of the Department of State," the statement said, "the Berlin Declaration is not intended to force a reduction in German living standards except as such reduction is required to enable Germany to meet her reparations payments."[63] As Clay concluded, according to the new policy there would be a drastic once-and-for-all cut in German industry for the purpose of determining reparations. Thereafter, however, Germany would be free to rebuild its industry and raise its standard of living. Having questioned the performance of any level of industry plan all along, Clay thus had his early skepticism confirmed. From now on reparations were going to be the primary purpose with deindustrialization only a temporary restriction. Under these circumstances, rather than fight for any theoretical principle he was resolved to reach an agreement—almost any agreement—on the limitations of Germany's steel industry.

As he sat down with his three colleagues in the austere courtroom, where only a year earlier the 20th July conspirators against Hitler had been tried by the infamous People's Court, Clay had his game plan ready.[64] Ignoring the question that the Coordinating Committee had been asked to resolve, he opened the meeting with the blunt announcement that the level for steel would now be settled. There were few in the room who believed this possible since a spread of almost 100 percent between the high and low positions seemed too great for compromise. Moreover, as steel went, so would go the entire German industry. Sir Brian Robertson—he not merely represented the British Empire, he was the British Empire, some Americans quipped—promptly objected. A brilliant officer, who could look back at a successful army and international business career, he recognized what his American colleague was up to. He disapproved of Clay's turning the issue, he said. He argued that the principle should be settled first and specific figures be determined later. But Clay, who knew how to take advantage of his position in the chair, proposed two questions: What level of steel industry should be permitted, and how much industrial capacity should be left? At first this was taken to represent merely two aspects of a single question, and each side lined up where it had stood earlier in the Level of Industry Committee.

Clay now repeated his double-barreled question, for which his colleagues were unprepared. The idea that they faced two questions instead of one threw everyone just enough off balance to enable Clay as chairman to hold the initiative. He drove hard, not so much to sell the American figure of 7.8 million tons as to get an agreement. When the Soviets, hell-bent on the low figure, argued their case, Clay talked level of production. When the British, equally determined on their figure twice as great, justified their position, Clay talked level of capacity. Then he tried the simplest possible compromise: add the four positions and divide by four.

Sokolovsky, standing on principle, would not buy it. German consumption should be limited, he said, to the per capita of the rest of Europe (excluding the Soviet Union), which would be 4.6 million tons; but he might concede something additional for export material.[65]

General Kloetz then pointed out that the Soviet figure had to be based on the German population of 62 million, whereas that committee had just recently accepted the population estimate of 65,285,000; in addition, the plan for the transfer into Germany of 6,650,000 Germans from outside territories had been approved. The Soviet member then agreed to base his position on the population of 65 million, which raised his figure about 5 percent. Clay opposed the Soviet method, but offered to come down to 5.5 million tons for production.

Robertson, in turn, proposed two conditions: first, the figure set for production should be reviewed annually, and second, capacity for nine million tons ought to be left in Germany. The Soviets did not accept either the 5.5 million for production or the nine million for capacity. But it was now clear that Clay's two concepts were not technically related. As Don

Humphrey, who was present, suggested, "The minutes do not convey an adequate impression of the sublety with which Clay employed a dual conception, or the agressiveness with which he drove for a decision."[66]

Clay then taunted his colleagues with loss of prestige if the issue had to be referred to diplomatic channels. He then tried another compromise, this time using both barrels: annual production of six million and retained capacity of 7.5 million tons. The French agreed. The British were favorable but wanted eight million capacity. Sokolovsky had turned down cold the 7.5 million for capacity but eyed the six million for production an instant too long. Seeing this, Clay declared stoutly that the United States government would never agree to less than six million tons production, nor to as much as eight million capacity. The impasse had been broken, since the divergent positions had obviously been brought within range of compromise. It was New Year's Eve and Clay adjourned the meeting.

At the next session the Soviets were prepared to accept an annual production of 5.8 million tons and a capacity of 6.5 million tons. Clay agreed to accept 5.8 for production provided the Soviets would accept seven million for capacity. The French agreed. The Soviets agreed. But the British held out for 7.5 million tons of productive capacity. Sokolovsky came up to 7.2 but held out for three days until the next meeting of the Control Council before swallowing the last 300,000 tons.

There was an agreed decision on steel, which many observers had thought to be impossible. As Don Humphrey wrote, "The 5.8 production figure was due to Soviet insistence, the 7.5 capacity figure was due to British insistance, the decision was due to Clay's insistence." Clay had kicked overboard the issue of principle and fought for the naming of specific figures in the belief that agreement on the basic industry would open the gate.

The real significance of the steel decision was, of course, the light that it threw on Clay's strategy at the Control Council. "In the steel negotiation he told Sokolovsky, in effect, that he was not standing on principle or technicalities but was out to get an agreement and would drive the British along. Not only was he still courting the Russians at the time, but he also was resolved not to tolerate any delay."[67] Once the level of industry plan had been accepted, he was going to bring the issue of reunification promptly to the fore.

The Deputy Military Governor was about to prepare a year-end report on the state of his mission when he received a War Department message requesting his comments on a review of JCS #1067 as suggested to the President by Byron Price. By that time, it had already become clear to Clay that the directive was not at the root of his problems. Its most restrictive economic provisions had been superseded by the Potsdam Agreement, which called for a balanced and self-supporting German economy. Both the disease and unrest concept as well as the need to produce for export left him sufficient elbow room, especially at a time when production levels were far below any reasonable limitations. Moreover, according to Washington's new interpretation of Potsdam, there would be no permanent restrictions on the economy nor on Germany's standard of living. "I am getting along all right. I have no suggestions to make," Clay remarked complacently to Don McLean,[68] as he drafted his interim reply: "On the whole JCS #1067 as modified by Potsdam has proved workable. I don't know how we could have set up our military government without JCS #1067." He nevertheless instructed his chief of staff to query the division chiefs and to send their suggestions—they turned out to be of little consequence—to the Pentagon.[69]

The General did not request any relaxation in his denazification orders because he knew that public opinion was not ready for this. Also, he was resolved to turn the program over to the German authorities, and he expected that this would take care of its many problems.

Ever since Military Government Law #8 had been enacted, there had been complaints from American and German sources in the field. Apparently there were numerous violations because—hastily drafted and promulgated—the law had failed to provide for any effective enforcement machinery.[70] Moreover, the existing procedure dealt only with party members employed in public or private offices; the owners of businesses, active Nazis living on wealth acquired during the Third Reich, and nonparty members who had been active supporters were not affected by the law. Of equal importance was the loophole whereby anyone dismissed from a supervisory or managerial position could be employed in a minor position by the same company. As Dr. Walter Dorn, one of Clay's advisors, remarked, Law #8 had merely meant a change of official signatures as well as a large number of highly competent clerks. As a result, the actions of the military government seemed arbitrary and capricious to the Germans and tended to alienate even those who favored denazification. "There was general agreement by all German officials and military government officers interviewed," an inspection report from Bavaria read, "that Law #8 has not and cannot in its present form and method of application carry out its stated purpose."[71]

Obviously changes had to be made. Some detachments in the field had suggested forbidding dismissed personnel from holding any position not only in the same firm but also in the same type of business or industry.[72] On the other hand, there were proposals from the German side to abandon the mandatory criterion of party membership in favor of a thorough and realistic evaluation of an individual's role under the Third Reich.[73] Having earlier acted hastily under the pressure of public opinion, the General now decided on a more deliberate course of action. The ministers of justice of the three *Länder* in the American zone were asked to submit proposals for a new denazification law. Similar instructions went out to a newly formed Denazification Policy Board composed of several division chiefs and chaired by Judge Fahy. January 1946 was the deadline for the requested draft of a new law that would put responsibility into German hands.

As Clay recognized, modifications of JCS #1067 would not affect his principal predicament—the opposition at the Allied Control Authority.

"Changes in our directives are not so important now as the establishment of a central administrative machinery," he wrote to Hilldring. "This is the real stumbling block for further progress."[74] He was firmly resolved to force an early showdown. If the four zones could not be reunited, a different solution would have to be sought. The economic unification of the American and British zones seemed to be a most logical move, especially since economic experts had indicated that within three or four years a self-supporting region would thereby be created. Until then $250–300 million of appropriations would be needed annually. However, if a final end of these expenditures could be shown, Congress might actually be willing to go along.

FOOTNOTES

1. Author's interview with Don Humphrey, Winchester, Mass., September 9, 1978. Richard D. McKinzie interview with General Clay, New York City, July 16, 1974.
2. Jean Smith interview with General Clay, February 19, 1971.
3. Clay to McCloy, June 29, 1945, in Jean Smith, ed., *The Papers of General Lucius D. Clay*, pp. 35–45.
4. Harold Zink, *American Military Government in Germany*, p. 29.
5. Author's interview with Don McLean, Andover, Mass., August 16, 1979.
6. Author's interview with Edloe Donnan, Manchester, Mo., October 27, 1980. Demaree Bess, "An American Viceroy in Germany," in *Saturday Evening Post*, May 3 and 5, 1947.
7. Author's interview with Richard Hallock, Washington, D.C., April 5, 1981.
8. Author's interview with Don McLean, Andover, Mass., August 16, 1979.
9. Clay to McCloy, September 16, 1945, in Smith, *The Papers*, pp. 74–82.
10. Lucius D. Clay, *Decision in Germany*, p. 88.
11. Moses Moskowitz, "The Political Reeducation of the Germans: The Emergence of Parties and Politics in Württemberg-Baden." May 1945–June 1946 in *The Political Science Quarterly*, Vol. LXI, p. 534 ff. Also: Lutz Niethammer, *Entnazifizierung in Bayern*.
12. Clay, *Decision*, p. 55.
13. Earl Ziemke, *The U.S. Army in the Occupation of Germany 1944–1945*, p. 312.
14. Memo, USFET Civil Admin. Br. for C. of S. sub: Proposed Directives in USFET SGS, 0.14.1.
15. Clay to McCloy, October 5, 1945, in Smith, *The Papers*, pp. 91–97.
16. Earl Ziemke, *The U.S. Army*, p. 404.
17. Heinz Guradze, "The Laenderrat, Landmark of German Reconstruction," in *The Western Political Quarterly*, June 1950, p. 191.
18. John H. Backer, *Priming the German Economy: American Occupational Policies 1945–1948*, pp. 35–55.
19. Ibid.
20. Don D. Humphrey, private papers.
21. Ibid.
22. Backer, *Priming*, pp. 107–118.
23. Ibid.
24. Author's interview with Jack Bennett, Chapel Hill, N.C., May 9, 1981; E. A. Tennenbaum, "Why do we trade for dollars?" OMGUS. Office of the Finance Advisor, February 15, 1948, 82–2/1.
25. Don Humphrey, private papers.
26. Ibid.
27. Backer, *Priming*, pp. 110–121.
28. Ibid.
29. Heath to Riddleberger, November 26, 1945, 861.5048/11–2645, State Department Papers.
30. Author's interview with Dr. John Hazard, New York, N.Y., October 8, 1979.
31. Ibid.
32. Author's interview with Colonel John Bates, Maplewood, N.J., April 23, 1980.
33. Grigori Zhukov, *Memoirs* passim.
34. Jean Smith interview with Clay, February 11, 1971.
35. Delbert Clark, *Again the Goosestep*, p. 41.
36. Author's interview with Colonel John Bates, Maplewood, N.J., April 23, 1980.
37. Walter Millis, *The Forestall Diaries*, p. 182.
38. Ministère des Affaires Etrangères, *Documents français relatifs l'Allemagne*, pp. 7–11.
39. *Foreign Relations of the United States, 1945*, Vol. 4, p. 661 ff.
40. Clay, *Decision*, p. 110.
41. Clay for War Department, September 24, 1945, in Smith, *The Papers*, pp. 84–85.
42. *Documents français*, p. 16. Koenig had a very gallant record with the free French forces, from desert areas in Africa to Montgomery at el Alamein. Murphy and Clay always suspected that he took his orders from De Gaulle rather than from his government.

43. *Foreign Relations . . . European Advisory Commission . . .* 1945, Vol. 3, p. 911.
44. Clay, *Decision*, p. 110.
45. Letter, George Kennan to author, November 20, 1979. Author's interview with Kennan, Princeton, N.J., March 19, 1980. Author's interview with Ambassador Jacob Beam, Washington, D.C., June 3, 1981.
46. Ibid.
47. Author's interview with Mrs. Lucius D. Clay, McLean, Va., February 2, 1980.
48. Memorandum, Byron Price to the President, OMGUS records 177–2/3, November 9, 1945.
49. Admiral William Leahy, Diary. U.S. Library of Congress, April 17, 1946.
50. John Foster Dulles, *War or Peace*, p. 30.
51. Hilldring, Memorandum for Assistant Secretary of War, "Résumé of meeting at State Dept., November 3, 1945." W.W. II records, ASW 370.8, Germany. N.A.
52. John Kenneth Galbraith, *A Life in Our Time*, p. 242.
53. Hilldring, Memorandum for Assistant Secretary of War, "Résumé of Meeting at State Department, November 3, 1945."
54. Ibid.
55. Ibid.
56. Ibid.
57. Ibid.
58. B. O. Ratchford and W. D. Ross, *Berlin Reparations Assignment*. Don Humphrey, private papers.
59. Ibid.
60. Ibid.
61. Ibid.
62. The author has drawn on the description of this Control Council meeting in an unpublished manuscript, "Clay Settles Steel," by Don Humphrey.
63. U.S. Department of State Bulletin 13, No. 338, December 16, 1945, p. 960.
64. Don Humphrey, private papers.
65. Ibid.
66. Ibid.
67. Ibid.
68. Interview with Don McLean, Andover, Mass., August 16, 1979.
69. Memorandum, Bryan Milburn to all divisions, December 2, 1945, OMGUS 367–2/5, N.A.
70. Office Memorandum, "Failure of Law #8." December 29, 1945. OMGUS 124–3/15. File 13. N.A.
71. Ibid.
72. Ibid.
73. German Draft of Denazification Law. OMGUS. Dec. file 014.3 Box 15, File 5.
74. Clay for Hilldring, December 10, 1945. CC 20130. N.A.

CHAPTER FIVE

A General Sets Policy

THE IVY-COVERED HOUSE IN LARGELY UNDAMAGED DAHLEM THAT CLAY HAD chosen for his Berlin residence was comfortable and, in comparison with the elaborate mansions requisitioned for the other military governors, unpretentious. Built before the First World War as an English-style country home for a British woman who lived in the city, it was located on spacious grounds and surrounded by poplar and beech trees. By 1939, when the house changed hands, Dahlem had become one of Berlin's fashionable suburbs. The new owner, prominent in the German business elite, had like many of his peers given the party tacit support without formally joining it. When Clay took over the house there were stacks of Nazi literature on the shelves and photographs of parties given there, with everybody except the host in Nazi regalia.[1] The dining room and the two drawing rooms on the main floor lent themselves to a modest amount of entertaining. There were also two guest rooms on the third floor. The general decided he could host the larger functions at the nearby Harnack House or at the Wannsee Guest House, both of which had lodgings for visiting dignitaries.

Since the beginning of the war Clay had set for himself a seven-day week with an eleven- to twelve-hour workday. He liked to come home for dinner and have a drink while relaxing in casual conversation. In Vauxcusson and in Höchst he had shared his house with Draper and Bowie, but Draper's habit of bringing up business matters during and after dinner bothered Clay. When his headquarters moved to Berlin in August he decided to live alone until Mrs. Clay could join him.[2] His personal aides thought he was alone in the evenings too often and were looking forward to her arrival as much as he was. After the long office hours, Clay usually ate a solitary meal with his beloved Scottie, George, as his only company. His office staff was also concerned because the General paid so little attention to his health, refusing to consult a doctor when he obviously needed medical attention.[3]

The question of permitting dependents to come to Germany had been debated in army headquarters in Frankfurt and back in the Pentagon for many months. Clay had urged approval because he believed their arrival would bring a more normal life to the American communities and would be reassuring evidence that the United States was in Germany for a long stay.[4] Moreover, he argued, it would be difficult to recruit qualified personnel willing to spend years in Germany if it meant separation from their families. Concern for the security of women and children, however, caused postponement of a favorable decision until the spring of 1946. There were no exceptions until that date. When Mrs. Clay and Mrs. Hugh Casey asked for passports to attend the Frankfurt wedding of their children, Frank and Patricia, they were turned down.[5] They missed the ceremony and also one of the last social events that reflected a warm feeling of American-Soviet friendship. After the wedding reception, General Casey and Marshall Sokolovsky and a group of Allied officers stayed until the early morning hours, toasting each other and singing American and Russian army songs.[6]

Finally, on an April evening in 1946, the first train from Bremerhaven with dependents pulled into Wannsee station. As a U.S. Army band struck up a popular tune, the Deputy Military Governor was among those waiting to greet their wives. Many of the military personnel on the platform had not seen their loved ones for several years and there were scenes of happy reunion often mixed with tears. But Marjorie Clay's joy was dampened by concern for her husband's health. A year of continued tensions and frustrations without relief had taken its toll. He looked haggard and worn, she thought.[7] The following day a tour of the bombed-out city and the sight of pale, sullen-looking men and women and emaciated children in the streets added to her distress. If she had to stay in Germany, she decided, a charity program for German children in the American communities throughout the U.S. zone would be her first challenge.[8]

Clay had not wanted the military government job in the first place but as long as the war was on he had had no choice. This changed with Japan's surrender and with it his last chance for a combat assignment—or so he thought. (Only in 1950, after the attack on South Korea that followed his long-sought retirement from the army, did he realize with regret that he had misjudged the course of history.) He had mistakenly assumed the job would be a short tour with civilian agencies taking over after a few months.[9] Not many were aware that it was the General's singular devotion to duty that alone kept him in Germany after V-J Day. But the Washington meetings in November and Eisenhower's departure prompted him to reappraise the future of his job. Under Ike he had enjoyed virtually a free hand. "He gave me almost complete delegation of responsibility as long as I would keep him informed," Clay said. "We were seeing eye to eye on policy."[10] Under the new man, General Joseph McNarney, it would probably be different; at least, there were some early indications to that effect according to observers close to the scene. The new military governor showed little interest in German affairs but nonetheless insisted on his command prerogatives.[11]

There was also another consideration: Clay's position was financially demanding. His expenses were high, never fully reimbursed, and probably would eat up a good part of his $12,000 annual salary. He would do better to retire from the army and take a lucrative position in the business world.

Marjorie had grown up in greater comfort than he had been able to provide and it was about time, he thought, to give her some of the luxuries she had once been accustomed to. But the State Department was bound to take over from the military soon, so he decided to wait and see how things worked out. Uncertain about his own future, however, he chose for the time being to do without an aide-de-camp. Bill Livingston, who had been with him in this capacity since Versailles, had returned to civilian life. Before departing for Washington in November, Clay had promised the job to Major Charles O'Connor who was with the Field Intelligence Agency, Technical (FIAT), in Frankfurt but upon his return Clay told him that the future of the Berlin assignment was uncertain, and he was not going to make any personnel changes now.[12]

A perceptive American correspondent assessed the General's attitude toward his assignment:

> Even as a youthful lieutenant he was also a fully qualified civil engineer equipped to work outside as well as inside the army. As the years have passed, his qualifications have steadily increased for a wide range of jobs in the civilian world. Moreover, his two sons now are army officers themselves, his wife has inherited a modest independent income, and his own retirement pay is on tap. Consciously or subconsciously his sense of personal independence must be partly responsible for the extraordinary initiative he is taking on the job.[13]

Personal circumstances were indeed part of it, but the continued lack of adequate policy guidance and diplomatic support from his government also forced Clay into independent action.

The last months of 1945 had been marked by a series of disappointments, and the new year brought more of the same. The lack of a qualified staff and frequent administrative conflicts with Washington were particularly exasperating. Some of Clay's principal advisors—William Draper, Don Humphrey, Joseph Dodge, and Edward Litchfield among others—were excellent by any standards; some were reasonably effective; but many others had little to recommend them.[14] "The caliber of the professional personnel that we are getting recently is going downhill," Clay told Hilldring. "It is a difficult problem, but of course your recruiting officer measures his success by getting people. But I would rather operate here at half strength with good people than to fill up with people that are no good."[15] To hold some key people, Clay tried personally to guarantee them work for two years, but much longer contracts would have been needed to attract really first-rate administrators. Many competent men therefore went home and Washington seemed unable to find the right replacements.

Clay himself was part of the problem. His "one-man-show" had already been noticed when the Denison Dam in Texas was being built. Jim Stratton, who had joined Clay as his deputy in charge of all engineering, found himself "as a dangling member on the staff . . . without any duties or assignments. I had no position or any responsibility," Stratton recalled, "but the civilian engineers loved Clay, because he did all the hard thinking. They were technicians in a way and they could perform the technical duties. . . . He had a picture in his mind and he'd tell them to work on it." Similarly many of Clay's associates at OMGUS felt that the General did not make full use of his experts and often took matters into his own hands without even consulting them.[16] "Clay fell short in his capacity to use the perception and wisdom of others. The army teaches that a great leader must be a good follower," Don Humphrey commented, and he explained that "the General did not make optimum use of the available talent." On occasion, as Robert Bowie pointed out, the intimidating impact of Clay's personality played a role. "He makes up his mind by himself with the almost mystical belief in his rightness as America Thinking," another staff member thought. Some officers at OMGUS accordingly remarked that "Clay does not need a staff but only aides," but others were impressed with the General's command of particulars. "I have yet to find a division chief who knows more about the details of the division than Clay does," was the kind of comment frequently heard at the American press club in Sven Hedin Allee.[17]

The political division under Robert Murphy with a crew of professional foreign service officers did not have this kind of personnel problem. Serious friction developed, however, because of the political division's reporting directly to the State Department using a separate code. For Clay the very thought of several government agencies working independently in the American zone was anathema, and a unified communication channel from and to his area of responsibility was an administrative must. His firm insistence on this management principle caused repeated conflicts with Washington's entrenched bureaucracy. The General was accustomed to having his way in these matters, even when facing one day as formidable an opponent as Averell Harriman. However, when Murphy threatened to close down his Berlin office rather than give up the use of a separate code, Clay's political savvy told him to accept a compromise.[18] Under its terms only information exchanges were to go via the State Department channel, whereas all instructions from State and reactions thereto had to travel the established War Department-OMGUS route.[19]

But Clay did reject a December 1945 Commerce Department request to send special teams into Germany to conduct an independent technical investigation of German industry. He reminded the War Department, his only official channel of communication, that this task was in the hands of the Field Intelligence Agency, Technical, an organization he had set up a few months earlier under Colonel Ralph Osborne, one of his Pentagon associates. He did not want any outside agency reporting directly to Washington and dealing with matters for which he would be ultimately responsible, Clay advised Hilldring. If Commerce wanted its representatives to work with and through FIAT there would be no objection, he said.[20] The solution was a joint operation with headquarters in Höchst and later in Karlsruhe, which for two years systematically collected technical, industrial, and scientific information.

Clay had set up FIAT with mixed feelings. The ever-present possibility of carpetbagging was very much on his mind, triggered no doubt by memories of his early childhood in his grandmother's home and the tales of her life on a looted farm after the Civil War. It was not always easy, however, to draw the line between the legitimate prerogatives of the victor and private profiteering. In an effort to stay on top of the job, the General at first wanted FIAT to operate out of Berlin. Only when Osborne listed the administrative complications involved did he yield on this point. "All right," he said, "have it your way, but I want you to report to me in person every week."[21] The Deputy Military Governor also imposed some restrictions on FIAT. Documents and any materials that belonged to German industrial enterprises were not to be removed, but had to be microfilmed in place for eventual public use. Moreover, in order to demonstrate America's good faith to its Soviet ally, copies of the reels taken from Berlin's patent office had to be given to Marshall Sokolovsky. During the first year of the occupation Clay even managed to arrange for a limited exchange of American and Russian investigation teams. In the fall of 1945, FIAT had sent a number of requests to the Soviet authorities in Karlshorst, asking permission for its investigators to visit specified industrial plants in the Russian zone. They all were rejected. Later, following Clay's advice, FIAT invited a team of Soviet technical experts to visit an I.G. Farben plant near Frankfurt. Months went by without an answer. Then one day around Christmas a Soviet general with a large entourage of technicians unexpectedly appeared at FIAT. On instructions, Osborne's deputy, Jack Boyle, refused them access to the plant. "I am sorry," he said, "but there is nothing I can do. We have sent you a number of requests for admission of our teams; they all have been turned down." The Russian officer persisted for a while, then recognized that the Americans would not give him a free ride, reached into his boot, and pulled out FIAT's original requests—all stamped approved.[22]

As time went on and the reconstruction of the West German economy became a priority task of the American military government, Clay began to have second thoughts about the operations of FIAT. The agency was taking from Germany all the information it could about trade processes and advanced scientific know-how. Even though most of this information was made available to the public, Clay knew that because of America's industrial advancement it was of greater value to the United States than to others. He was aware too that the Joint Chiefs of Staff had set up a screening process to select the information it did not want released to American industry or to other nations.[23] In sum then, as his penetrating and incorruptible mind recognized, FIAT's job was essentially the collecting of hidden reparations for the United States.[24] "The taking of this information without accounting," he wrote in October 1946 to General Oliver P. Echols, Hilldring's successor, "to my mind is parallel to Soviet action in taking current production."[25] French action in removing capital equipment apart from reparations belonged in the same category, he said. Accordingly, he suggested there ought to be an evaluation "not for payment but to include in final reparations accounting." The War Department merely replied that it was impractical to put a value on the FIAT materials because there was no way of knowing how they would eventually be utilized. Since no action was taken by Washington, Clay repeated his proposal in January 1947 to General Daniel Noce, who had taken Echols' place as head of the War Department's Civil Affairs Division.[26] When once again nothing was done, Clay's concern for the German economy gained the upper hand and he proposed to terminate FIAT's investigative work by March 31, 1947.[27] The Department of Commerce protested, but by now the General knew how to make his viewpoint prevail. He advised the War Department that he would proceed with his plan unless ordered otherwise; since decisions overruling field commanders were rarely made on the Potomac, Clay got his way and by midsummer 1947 FIAT closed up shop.

Clay remained sensitive to the dangers of carpetbagging all through his German years. Unaffected by sustained pressures on the part of the State and War departments, he made certain that no foreign buyers would be admitted to Germany until the economic and financial interests of its people could be duly protected. In his judgment, even the appearance of exploitation by the military government had to be avoided. When the transfer of captured German art objects for safekeeping to the United States was under discussion, the General insisted there had to be a simultaneous official commitment that this was a temporary move and that once normal conditions had been restored all objects would be brought back to Germany. Two years later he again was objecting to any delays and demanding the prompt return of German art.[28]

Clay had expected that his office would take an active hand in the collection of Germany's external assets and that these funds might eventually be used to compensate for the rising costs of the occupation. He possibly underestimated the complexity of the issue, but during the spring of 1946 the developing controversy with the State Department became increasingly irritating. Under a compromise reached at the Potsdam Conference, German assets in Eastern Europe had been assigned as reparations to the Soviet Union and those in the West to Great Britain and the United States. Clay had followed up on President Truman's suggestion that there ought to be a Control Council law vesting title to all German assets abroad in a quadripartite commission.[29] A bill was quickly drafted and pushed through at the lower levels of the Allied Control Authority. When it reached the top, however, General Brian Robertson, the British deputy military governor, objected. In the opinion of his government, he said, the proposed law was legally unsound and tactically unwise. It would probably not be recognized in neutral countries and a diplomatic approach suggesting the voluntary surrender might be more appropriate.

After several weeks of extensive lobbying by Clay, the bill creating a German External Property Commission was nevertheless passed, but new complications promptly arose. The British proposed that the commission should be broken up into two branches, one dealing with assets in the East and the other with those located in the Western countries. Clay saw this as another breach in four-power unity, but learned to his dismay that his own government approved of the British proposal. The State Department, moreover, came up with the suggestion that German assets in the Western hemisphere should not come under the authority of the new commission.[30] Since negotiations with neutral countries had started at the State Department and Clay had not been informed, the consequence was an exchange of acrimonious cables. "This office finds itself completely at sea with respect to responsibilities of the German External Property Commission,"[31] Clay complained, and recognizing the "impractibility" of the commission's work, he proposed its abolition. "The results of actions and correspondence to date leaves us more confused than ever," he cabled, "and we are unable to proceed intelligently in any quadripartite discussions of the problems involved as we do not know what American views are being expressed elsewhere, by whom, and where."[32] As a result, negotiations with the neutrals continued through diplomatic channels, and OMGUS merely maintained an investigating and bookkeeping staff.

At the Allied Control Authority, meanwhile, there had been lots of activity but little significant progress. Agreements had been reached on a number of essentially negative measures, such as a law for the control of scientific research and a directive prohibiting the supervision of political parties by the police. General Clay, when talking to the press, tried to maintain a good front. He stressed the few constructive four-power agreements reached, although he knew that the directives from the Control Council were implemented by each zone commander as he saw fit.[33]

On the main issue of Germany's unification, however, no progress at all was being made, and French obstructionism continued. On January 21, France vetoed a British proposal for a central German finance department.[34] As General Koenig explained it, the proposal was "incongruous with French policy" because the authority of this department would extend over all of Germany, the western boundaries of which had not been fixed. When Clay and Murphy subsequently flew to London to discuss the matter with Byrnes, the Secretary agreed that the French position was slowing recovery and doing grave injury to Europe's economy, but he could not suggest any way out of the impasse. "It has become evident," an increasingly bitter Deputy

Military Governor wrote in his February report, "that only the solution at government level [of the western boundary issue] will permit further progress in the establishment of central German administrative agencies."[35] Against the background of a deteriorating German economy the French opposition was particularly exasperating.

The food situation in the American zone had always been bad, but in February it became critical. The debilitating effects of suppressed inflation were more and more noticeable and industrial production hovered at around 28 percent of the prewar level. In the fall of 1945, half of SHAEF's grain reserve had to be sent to the British and French zones, where food supplies were even lower than in the mainly agricultural regions occupied by the American army. The remaining 320,000 tons had been distributed among the German population in the American zone.[36] Only because of these supplementary supplies had it been possible to distribute a "normal consumer" ration of 1,500 calories during the winter of 1945—clearly less than the 2,000 calories recommended by medical authorities. But in January, Clay received urgent requests from the French for an advance of 110,000 tons of wheat from American stocks to avoid an immediate cut in German rations to 1,150 calories. "I am convinced the situation in the French zone from a food viewpoint is quite serious," Clay cabled to Hilldring. "However, it results in substantial part from failure of the French to look ahead and particularly from their initial policy of supplying their forces in the occupied territory from indigenous sources." He suggested an American intervention at the Combined Food Board[37] in Washington, and stressed the consequences of the French problem for the other Western zones. "In view of the French failure to adhere to central administrative machinery," Clay concluded, "any cooperation in the existing food shortage in the French zone might well be conditioned on a change of attitude by France to quadripartite government."[38]

The French appeal for assistance was soon followed by a drastic curtailment of food rations in the British zone, and Clay made desperate efforts to avoid a similar course of action in his zone. The barrage of cables to Washington pleading for supplies reflected his frustration. "The reduction of this ration will be damaging to the United States prestige and particularly to my own personal relationship with the three *Länder* minister-presidents," he cabled on March 16. "It is our belief that the Russian zone is feeding approximately 1,500 calories and will continue to do so until the next harvest season," he said in another message. "We have insisted on democratic processes in the United States zone and have maintained a strict neutrality between political parties. As a result the Communist party has made little progress. However, there is no choice between becoming a Communist on 1,500 calories and a believer in democracy on 1,000 calories."[39] His wrath was directed mainly against the French. "We have not used German indigenous resources to meet our own needs," Clay wrote in a personal message to Hilldring.

However, while we were conserving our resources, the French in particular used large quantities of indigenous resources to support their own needs. It would seem unjust to the Germans in the United States zone who have met our requirements to make them pay the penalty for such actions in other zones. . . . Perhaps I am off-base, but I find it difficult to understand when we see the exploitation which has taken place and is taking place in at least two other zones, why the United States should divide its resources without requiring as a condition thereto an agreement for the future treatment of Germany as an economic unit.[40]

The real reason for the foot-dragging on this issue in Washington was implicit in the exchange of cables between the State Department and the American Embassy in Paris—beyond Clay's channels of communication. De Gaulle had resigned in January and the American ambassador, reporting on the resignation, indicated the likelihood of a coalition government with the head of the French Communist Party, Maurice Thorez, as President. When a tripartite cabinet under the moderate Socialist Felix Gouin eventually emerged, Washington was anxious to avoid shaking its weak foundations. Secretary Byrnes suggested that when talking to Foreign Minister Georges Bidault on the subject of establishing central German agencies, Ambassador Jefferson Caffery "might discreetly inject the thought that any steps which the French government may publicly take at this time in the way of cooperating with American aims should help to create a more favorable atmosphere for the impending economic and financial talks in Washington." When Caffery commented four weeks later on his fruitless conversations with Bidault, he assured the department he would continue his efforts to bring about an evolution in French thinking but cautioned that Bidault's resignation might cause a governmental crisis "on which the Communists would certainly capitalize." As he saw it, "It would be definitely unwise at this juncture to press this matter further." To this the State Department replied that "the French should not be pressed to a point where there is real danger of Bidault's resignation and of a split in the coalition government which would have wide political ramifications in France."[41]

Even if Clay had been privy to these exchanges, it probably would not have made much difference. As one of his critics commented, the General never understood "and even less respected the French visceral fear and distrust of Germany."[42] He might have added that in Clay's modus operandi there was simply no room for "understanding or respect" of an opponent's motivation; his mission called for Germany's unification and, as far as he was concerned, nothing else mattered. His reaction was, therefore, one of utter exasperation when he recognized that his appeals for help had been ineffective and that the average consumer ration in the American zone for the summer would have to be lowered to 1,200 calories.[43]

Rations were even lower in the British zone, and there was no area in the West where the impact of wartime destruction and inflation was more debilitating than in the Ruhr. Contrary to cursory observations, however, plants, mines and factories largely had escaped bombing during the war or had been quickly repaired. As the U.S. Strategic Bombing Survey had determined, at the end of hostilities most of the industries were in fair shape. It was the center of the towns that had sustained the greatest damage, and the inhabitants of the Ruhr rather than their capital equipment had suffered most.[44] When Clay complained about the lagging production of coal, his British colleagues invariably referred to the food and housing situation. There was one "dwelling unit" to every three or four families, they said, which meant that each person enjoyed about four-and-a-half square yards of space—much less than in most German jails. A great many of the coal miners lived in cellar rooms threatened by the wreckage piled up above them. It was true that at the current starvation level their basic food ration cost only about two marks a week. But a man making even fifty marks a week—a good wage anywhere in Germany—could not afford the escalating black-market prices for butter and meat unless he worked in the black market himself. As a consequence there was little incentive to work more than absolutely necessary to buy the basic ration, a development reflected in a production rate at 45 percent of the prewar level, compared to 90 percent or better in the Soviet zone. The Ruhr steel industry depended entirely on Ruhr coke, and its production was equally unsatisfactory.[45]

The British military government was slow to act. With a staff of 20,000, more than twice as large as OMGUS, its only move had been the expropriation of the owners of the coal mines. "It was ironic," *Fortune* magazine commented, "that the British with all their domestic coal difficulties were running the Ruhr. They had set up shop in their zone as if they were somewhere in darkest Africa. . . . As usual," the journal concluded, "they will doubtless get around to doing something about it all—sooner or later."[46] In the meantime all of Germany's industry was forced to stagnate. Even the London *Economist* had to acknowledge that "clearly something was wrong. It was a quite inexcusable state of affairs which cannot be blamed— as it often is—on the Potsdam decisions."[47] As far as Clay was concerned, there was hardly anything he could do about the inadequate supply of coal and the lack of industrial raw materials. Like everybody on his economic staff he was aware that the failure of the British to speed the production of coal was one of the major scandals of the occupation period.[48] Without any say in the administration of the Ruhr, he could do no more than scold his British allies at the meetings of the Control Council and make sure his critical comments reached the British press. As for raw materials for Germany's industry, he had to turn down General Draper's repeated requests for "a billion dollars to finance essential imports other than food." "No such money is available," Clay said, "and we could and must build up our capital until it is sufficient to start a real flow of exports."[49] During the first two years of the occupation, however, proceeds from exports were insignificant, and as Clay admitted it was an effort to pull the German economy up by its own bootstraps.[50]

By the end of the first winter, victors and vanquished in Germany had sized each other up. It was clear by then that the fear of guerrilla warfare in the occupied country had been unwarranted. The defeated Germans, docile and apathetic, were unlikely to resort to violence. Americans had come to recognize that the Hitler regime had engaged the active or passive support of the people, and that Germans fully in accord with Western concepts of democracy were hard to find. The still-vivid memories of runaway inflation after the First World War had a pervasive impact on the entire population, but only after the 1948 currency reform and the resulting dramatic recovery did Americans fully grasp the paralyzing effects of a suppressed inflation.

To the Germans in the American zone, however, it had become obvious that their occupiers were quite human. Having been bludgeoned into submission for twelve years by the Gestapo, they quickly became aware of the differences in administrative practices and how easily they could circumvent the rules and regulations in a liberal system—even when administered by military men. Food rations were inadequate, but though they might go hungry, they would not starve; the widely discussed weighing program was evidence of that. But the unsettling doubts about the country's political and economic future remained. Goebbels' propaganda about the Morgenthau Plan was still alive and no one knew how far the collection of reparations would go. In this situation, consciously or subconsciously, two general goals emerged: to protect one's property and to stay alive. Because printed money was abundant and obviously would soon lose all its value, the rule of thumb was to sell as little as possible using payment in the threatened currency and to seek protection in the acquisition of *Sachwerte*, i.e., real property. For the farmers, it meant delivering as little as possible at the official prices while bartering the remainder for needed industrial supplies. For laborers and employees, it meant working only enough to pay for rationed food, rent and utilities at controlled prices. People devoted their spare time to foraging on the black market, carefully conserving the little physical energy their meager rations provided. Dealers and manufacturers resorted to barter whenever possible and hoarded all commodities against the day a new currency would be introduced. This was the pattern in the Western zones.[51]

It was different in the East, where the Russians seemed to demonstrate how a totalitarian regime can have certain advantages in dealing with an emergency situation. In contrast to the West, where only the bank balances of leading National Socialists and Nazi institutions had been frozen, Marshall Zhukov had promptly ordered all banks closed and all deposits blocked. Subsequently municipal savings banks and agricultural credit cooperatives were reopened, but payments of RM 300 were permitted only to depositors whose total account did not exceed RM 3,000; depositors with more than that amount were considered undeserving capitalists and received no funds at all.[52] All financial claims and liabilities of financial institutions were voided, along with the Reich's debt, which served as their main backing. As a result of these ruthless measures, the economy in the Soviet zone was drained of nearly four-fifths of its monetary assets. While this action was compensated in part by the issuance of Moscow-printed occupation currency, the purchasing power of the German people was drastically reduced, inflationary pressures eased, and work incentives reestablished. Communist sanctions and methods of exhortation also stimulated production. Party managers who did not fulfill their production quotas had to expect the accusation of sabotage,[53] and fear of secret arrests or deportations was widespread. In contrast to the Western zones, there was full employment and a much smaller black market. The people simply had less time and money for it and the penalties for being caught were harsh.[54]

It is not recorded whether Clay and his financial advisors ever tried to evaluate the economic consequences of the Soviet approach to inflation. But even if they did, being the servants of a democratic laissez-faire system, they could not emulate the Russians. Although Clay interpreted the restrictions of JCS #1067 very liberally, he knew they precluded the drastic reform the German economy required.

By spring of 1946, inflationary pressures had become most ominous, however, and Washington's attitude toward the defeated country had changed. The initiative for a currency reform, it seems, came from Joseph Dodge, Clay's financial advisor, who was in Washington in January 1946 conferring on economic policy. Clay's initial reaction to the proposed dispatch of some monetary experts to Germany reflected his predilection for a quadripartite solution. "I am not enthusiastic over a special mission," he cabled to Hilldring.

> Anti-inflationary measures will be so varied in type as to require many months in execution. They can be carried out successfully only by a permanent organization within military government. . . . At present anti-inflationary measures must be confined to those measures which can obtain quadripartite approval. If and when central German machinery is established, the problem will be simplified as the responsibility for avoiding inflation can be placed squarely on German shoulders. . . . However, if, after receiving this radiogram, Dodge and you still believe mission desirable, I will accept your judgment.[55]

In March, then, a group of economic experts arrived in Germany to study the problem and arrive at appropriate recommendations. The resulting "Plan for the Liquidation of War Finance and the Financial Rehabilitation of Germany" was the work of Gerhard Colm, Joseph M. Dodge, Raymond

W. Goldsmith, and a small staff. It was on Clay's desk by the end of May. In the eight intervening weeks, the American economists had talked to British, Soviet, and French members of the quadripartite Finance Directorate; made trips through all four zones; met with German tax officials, bankers, industrialists, and academic experts; and presented an outline of their recommendations to a special meeting of the *Länderrat* in Stuttgart.

Their recommendations proceeded from the premise that Germany was threatened with the repudiation of the Reichsmark by its own people and the consequent disintegration into a number of localized barter economies. The principal cause, of course, was a 1,000 percent increase in currency in circulation since 1935 and a 27-fold growth of the Reich's debt. Although a prompt currency reform would not remove all the obstacles to a rapid increase in industrial and agricultural production, it would at least "draw away a confusing veil of money" and reintroduce a firm accounting basis for the recovery of the German economy.

As the report correctly predicted, the real danger was not a sudden collapse of the economy but a creeping paralysis. The reform was needed not only to support price controls, which were so far quite effective, but also to protect production and prevent economic chaos. If a substantial amount of production continued to be diverted from regular channels of supply, the whole body economic would be endangered. Inflation controls become illusory, the report said, when services are no longer rendered and goods no longer sold at official prices. An increasing portion of total output was going into the black market, where prices were often fifty to several hundred times greater than official prices. Black market purchases could hardly be made out of current earned income, only out of money hoarded or from the sale of property or from black-market profits. The general knowledge that a worker could collect a day's wage by selling just one cigarette in the black market was bound to affect his willingness to work. The result was a labor scarcity in spite of the fact that productive employment was at a low level. In a similar way businessmen's incentive to sell was greatly affected by abundant funds and the lack of confidence in the currency: "To sell as little as possible has become today's art of business." The German people believed the situation simply could not continue as it was, and this attitude alone was bound to prevent an economic recovery.

Clay summed up the committee's recommendations in a message to the War Department. "In general, the conclusion calls for a program in three steps," his message read. "The first step would create a new currency and reduce claims and obligations in the ratio of ten Reichmarks to one Deutschmark. It calls for cancellation of the Reich's debt but sufficient amounts of a new debt issue would be assumed by Germany as a whole and allocated to banks, insurance organizations, credit cooperatives, etc., to enable them to meet their reduced obligations." The second step, he went on, was to make the devaluation of the currency more equitable to Germany as a whole by imposing mortages on real estate, equipment, and inventories; the third step is a progressive capital levy.[56]

Clay was in full agreement with the plan and its desirability as a whole, but he felt that "the imposition of these measures by military dictate is not entirely consistent with our desire to have responsibility for such measures taken by the German people or their officials." At the same time, he wondered how long a newly established, democratically elected German government could survive if it had to initiate such measures itself. The General then asked for Washington's earliest reaction so the formal proposals could be introduced into the quadripartite machinery.

Clay did not anticipate that the very thoroughness of the plan would prevent its early enactment. The proposed capital levy and new currency caused controversies and delays. Even though the psychological advantages of issuing new notes were self-evident, the ensuing American-Soviet dispute about the location of the printing plant delayed matters long enough to prevent its adoption as a quadripartite solution.

Stymied in the field of economics, unable to further expedite the work of the Level of Industry Committee, Clay now focused on the areas where he had more elbow room. The denazification Law #8 had been drafted in a hurry against the background of the Patton affair and under the influence of an aroused public opinion back home. It was an interim solution and Judge Fahy, the drafter, conceded that he "should have avoided the poor draftsmanship" and claimed he "expected to have another shot at the draft."[57] While the promulgation of the law seemed to have pacified the American press at least temporarily, it also caused a critical reaction from Germans and Americans in the zone.

Fahy, as well as Bowie, had already recognized in October the need for integrating denazification into a more coherent and definite program. "We do need to clarify our own approach to the whole denazification policy," Fahy suggested to Clay, "and make the policy more understandable to the people of Germany as a whole with clearer legal proceedings for its effectuation."[58]

The experiences of the first year of occupation had shown that individuals who had played an important role in the Third Reich could escape the purge because, for one reason or another, they did not fall into any of the categories listed by the military government. Important sections of the German social elite that supported the Nazi system were thus shielded from prosecution. On the other hand, there were large numbers of minor or merely nominal Nazis who, because they happened to occupy a certain rank or position, could be deprived of jobs and livelihood.[59] Like most Americans, Clay was unable to visualize the everyday social realities of the Third Reich, especially the permeation of all relationships by political pressure and terror.[60] Unacquainted as he was with Germany's societal patterns, it took some time for him to recognize that many middle-class Germans with nationalistic and pan-German convictions had been less exposed to

Nazi pressure than others and therefore not compelled to join the party. He listened when his denazification advisors pointed out that if the *Fragebogen* gave no evidence of party membership or active party support, it was practically impossible to bring a Nazi to justice.[61] But even the often-cited example of the judge who could not be fired* only made him reach for the JCS #1067 file, "the most frequently called-for document in his office," according to Captain Allen.[62]

Obviously, the General replied, it would not always be easy to determine who was a Nazi, but nevertheless the pertinent provisions of JCS #1067 and Potsdam had to be scrupulously observed. His instructions to Fahy, who was to chair the new Denazification Policy Board, reflected the same concept. The board was to work closely with the minister-presidents of the *Länder*, who were submitting their own proposals.[63] Clay stressed that a new comprehensive denazification law would have to satisfy three principles: it would have to be in accord with the denazification policies enunciated at Potsdam, it should conform to the quadripartite provisions he expected to be codified soon, and it should promptly put the responsibility for implementation into German hands.

The subsequent negotiations between the board's working group headed by Robert Bowie and the *Länderrat* in Stuttgart brought into the open some fundamentally divergent points of view. The Germans, basing their contention on personal observations during the thirteen years of the Third Reich, insisted that membership was of secondary significance at best. "Formal membership in an organization shall not be decisive," they insisted, and their first draft recommended that "Any person who is an activist, militarist, profiteeer, political defender or a follower should be judged exclusively by his actual conduct taken as a whole."[64] In other words, the Germans concluded that Nazism was a personal characteristic that could not be deduced from military ranks or jobs held. If they had committed crimes, they should be prosecuted and punished—but not excluded from the political process on the basis of party membership or position alone.

From Clay's point of view, on the other hand, punishment was important but secondary. As he saw it, the principal aim of denazification was to remove all former Nazis from positions of influence so that individuals untainted by the past could gain control and forge a democratic Germany. Accordingly, as it was enunciated by the Denazification Policy Board, "the first basic objective of denazification was to change the governing elements. Political and economic authority must be shifted from those who dominated German society and the Nazis to others who will establish a free and

---

* During the last days of the war, the judge in question had sentenced a man to death for having removed antitank road blocks, but there was no time to execute the sentence. The condemned man had been a party member and under military government law had to be discharged from his position. The judge, not having been a party member, remained the highest-ranking judge in town. (C. J. Friedrich. *American Experiences in Military Government in World War II*, p. 263. See Bibliography.)

peaceful society." As expressed by the board, Clay considered "denazification as a means for assisting in this transfer of authority from those who usurped and abused it."[65]

As negotiations between the Americans and Germans in Stuttgart continued, to his great satisfaction, Clay scored some points in the form of a quadripartite directive which, while substantially similar to the basic American directive of July 7, 1945, implemented the Potsdam Protocol and JCS #1067. Under the heading "Removal from Office and from Positions of Responsibility of Nazis and of Persons Hostile to Allied Purposes," the new directive covered all positions of importance in the public, quasipublic, and private sectors, and listed ninety-nine categories of persons to be classified as "major offenders" or "offenders."[66] As Clay later wrote, quadripartite conformity in this matter was particularly desirable because Germans removed from offices in the American zone had often found good posts in another zone. In practice, however, the Control Council Directive was of questionable value since America's allies continued to pursue their own denazification procedures which, especially in the Russian case, differed drastically from the American approach.

Clay liked most of the elements of the first German draft[67] but felt more than ever committed to a quadripartite policy.[68] And he was up against continued criticism of his military government by the American press, which presumably would disapprove of the transfer of denazification proceedings to German hands—a sine qua non in Clay's eyes. To go even beyond this transfer of proceedings, which was part and parcel of the General's grand design, in the aftermath of the Patton affair seemed foolhardy indeed. Accordingly, Robert Bowie was told to work toward reconciliation of the two approaches and to insist that the presumption of guilt through party membership alone be incorporated in the new law. The Germans were "thunderstruck" and fought back vigorously. On several occasions the Stuttgart negotiations threatened to break down. From the German point of view, membership in the party or in a Nazi organization, the date of joining, and the duration of membership were irrelevant. It was up to the public prosecutor, they said, to prove the accused guilty. But General Clay remained adamant. While accepting other essentials of the German draft, he demanded that the law be supplemented by an appendix in which party organizations were listed and membership remained prima facie evidence of guilt, thus "indicting the German ruling class in all its branches."[69] It was this provision as well as Clay's insistence that the legislation had to be a German law representing the first step of the new democracy that brought about a dramatic confrontation.[70]

Faced now with a virtual ultimatum, German delegates at the *Länderrat* conferred frantically among themselves then rushed home to seek instructions from the *Land* governments. Two of them gave in immediately, but the third, Württemberg, decided not to yield. Thereupon a full joint meeting of the American and German representatives was called and Reinhold Maier, the minister-president of Württemberg, had his cabinet's refusal read. However, it was only one year after Germany's unconditional surrender and the time for sustained resistance to the occupying power had not yet come. When the American delegates predicted the Deputy Military Governor's "unfavorable reactions," Dr. Maier quickly gave in. He would not insist on refusal, he said; the statement was meant only for home consumption.

Shortly afterward the bill was promulgated as a German law in the form designed by the American military government. It provided for a special ministry of liberation in each state, the head of which would be a member of the cabinet. The real responsibility for the enforcement of the law was given to local, quasijudicial bodies called *Spruch Kammern*, which resembled local draft boards in the United States in that they were drawn from local citizens. These tribunals were given the job of vetting more than thirteen million Germans in the American zone and classifying them into one of the five categories—major offenders, who might be subject to as many as ten years of imprisonment, permanent exclusion from holding public office, and property confiscation; offenders, who could be imprisoned, fined and/or excluded from public office but eligible for probation; lesser offenders, who might be fined; followers, who regained their civil rights after paying a small fine; and, finally, nonoffenders. The Germans did win judicial independence for the tribunals and appelate tribunals and they won the right to classify respondents, irrespective of presumptive categories, at their discretion.[71] In order to implement the law, 545 German tribunals with a staff of 22,000 had to be set up.[72]

As it turned out, 3.5 million individuals had to be tried, a development that caused the Deputy Military Governor to assert that three-fourths of the Germans in the American zone were called on to judge the other fourth.[73] The implied proposition that the great majority of the Germans had kept themselves free from Nazi taint and therefore were in a position to judge their fellow citizens who had succumbed to Nazism did not remain unchallenged. As Harold Zink, the distinguished historian, wrote with considerable justification,

> It was very difficult to accept this argument. With more than 80 percent of the teachers and approximately proportionate numbers of other professions in National Socialist organizations of one kind or another, with virtually the entire German economy under Nazi control, and with German life almost completely geared to Nazi operations, even the most ardent defender of the German people cannot with straight face maintain that the majority were anti-Hitler and opponents of the Nazi regime.[74]

While the General managed to make some progress with denazification, the decartelization program was blocked by the British refusal to consider any mandatory provisions. American-British negotiations had shifted to the diplomatic level, but in spite of considerable pressure by the Department of State no progress was made.[75] In the meantime, most of the personnel assigned to the decartelization division in Berlin had returned to the States and Clay was trying to find competent replacements. James Stewart Martin, an antitrust lawyer who had been temporarily with the finance branch of SHAEF, seemed to fill the bill and Clay was able to have him assigned to Berlin.[76] At the same time, possibly unaware of General Draper's strong opposition to the decartelization program, the Deputy Military Governor agreed to the abolishment of the Decartelization Division and to the transfer of most of its responsibilities to a newly created Decartelization Branch of Draper's Economic Division.[77] The stage was thus set for an eventual clash of ideologies.

On his arrival in January 1946, Martin, the newly appointed head of the Decartelization Branch, promptly resumed negotiations with Sir Cecil Weir, Draper's opposite number. In accordance with instructions from Washington, the American proposals were now amended to overcome London's objections. The mandatory approach remained, but "excessive concentration" would be gauged by the value of gross assets as well as by size, sales and market shares. A firm exceeding these criteria still could avoid deconcentration if it demonstrated that "technological efficiency would be seriously impaired by such action." Unwilling to give ultimate authority to a joint commission instead of to their zone commander, however, the British continued to object.[78] Negotiations continued, and Clay eventually indicated that if no agreement was reached he would proceed unilaterally in the American zone.

He was more successful in his democratization efforts, at least in a formal sense. The village elections—scheduled in January against the advice of his staff—went off well, with 86 percent of those eligible voting. The next step, elections for county and city councils, was equally successful. Encouraged by these developments, the General then asked the minister-presidents to draw up preliminary constitutions and to arrange for the election of constitutional assemblies to consider the drafts.[79]

The newly formed *Länderrat* (Council of States) in Stuttgart also made good progress. Composed of the three minister-presidents and the Mayor of Bremen and supported by a large German staff, it had played a significant role in the negotiations for a zonal denazification law. In conjunction with Clay's continuous efforts to reduce American personnel, the *Länderrat* was given increasingly more responsibilities. Although effective in such areas as resettlement of refugees, transportation, and postal services, the handling of the critical food collection remained a major bone of contention. Its most important work was done in 1946 and early in 1947, when its powers were assumed by the new bizonal agencies. A Regional Coordinating Office in Stuttgart under Dr. James Pollock, who reported directly to the Deputy Military Governor, was the principal channel between Clay and the German state governments. When setting up the *Länderrat*, Clay had hoped it might set an example for the other occupying powers and thereby serve as a forerunner for a central German administration. Grass-roots efforts toward unification were therefore actively encouraged by the General but produced no real results.

His monthly meetings with the minister-presidents in Stuttgart were nonetheless a source of considerable satisfaction for Clay.[80] After the official part of the sessions, he appreciated informal conversations over a cup of coffee, and obviously enjoyed talking to the German press. "You know," he reminisced many years later, "the German reporters first could not believe they were permitted to question the Deputy Military Governor. They watched the give and take with the Allied press for several meetings before they gained enough confidence. They never had this experience. It's a funny thing," he said with some pride, "press conferences are held in Germany to this day."[81]

It would seem that Clay's satisfaction with the Stuttgart meetings was apparently shared by his audience. As one observer described it,

> The General's speeches, concerned with subjects frequently un-
> pleasant but always vital, were master species of statements. De-
> livered for the most part without notes in an unobtrusive but sol-
> dierly and distinct voice, concise and to the point, occasionally
> spiced with a sprinkling of humor, he minced no words without
> being offensive. Never repeating or correcting himself, the General
> spoke in brief sentences which were individually translated. He
> never failed to impress the audience with his sincerity and deter-
> mination. It was through Clay's appearances before the *Länderrat*
> that the American government presented itself at its best to the
> representatives of the German people.[82]

Whether trying to cope with the dismal food and coal situation, French obstructionism, denazification or any other problem, the General kept an eye on the work of the Level of Industry Committee. Its final report, he thought, would be the logical device to force a decision on his German assignment. He had already told Byrnes in London that without unification the major elements of the Potsdam Agreement would have to be scrapped and—since the American zone by itself was not economically viable—Clay's mission reconsidered. Sokolovsky and his deputy, General Mikhail Dratvin, had told him repeatedly that a joint foreign-trade program and a pooling of resources could be developed only after a level of industry agreement had been reached. As time went on, Clay had become increasingly suspicious of the Soviet position as simply a stalling tactic. He was only waiting for the completion of the plan to bring the underlying confict to a head.

Thanks to his negotiating skills, a four-power compromise on the fundamental steel question had been reached, but the controversy over other production levels continued. As the Deputy Military Governor saw it, the protracted haggling about individual figures was time-consuming and the ultimate results probably irrelevant. The plan itself would be an estimate only. The actual German production levels in 1946 were far below the expected limitations and it would take at least three or four years to catch up. In the meantime, all kinds of political changes would take place and almost certainly render the plan's data obsolete.

The Level of Industry Committee, under sustained American pressures, finally produced a plan at the end of March 1946. For all practical purposes it constituted a compromise among four independent drafts, with the levels proposed by the Soviet Union usually the lowest and those by the United Kingdom the highest. As Don Humphrey explained it, in the last phases of the negotiations political considerations were as a rule decisive. "Often differences were settled after everyone had made a speech or two by the simplest of all methods—namely adding and dividing by four."[83] Unaware that Clay was resolved not to permit a break with the Russians over the level of industry issue, some of the American industry specialists were critical of the compromises made. But they also felt that if the decision went to Clay he would settle for even lower levels if necessary.[84]

Once the committee's final plan was on Clay's desk, he quickly moved ahead. "The groundwork for the collection of reparations has now been laid," he announced at the Control Council. "A joint export-import plan is logically the next step." The Soviet reply immediately dispelled any hope for genuine progress. "We will adhere to the principle of zonal foreign trade and individual responsibilities of the countries for the results of the occupation of their zone," the Soviet representative declared.[85] "We will substitute this for the collective responsibility of all the powers. In accordance with this, the Soviet Delegation cannot accept any other position than that of a zonal principle."[86]

It was the long-sought clarification which Clay had been waiting for. "The Potsdam Agreement provides for a common export-import plan," he replied the next day. "The level of industry plan is based on a balanced export-import plan and if such a plan was not to be established, then the reparations plan has no validity. Reparations deliveries are still in an early stage," he stressed, "and thus it is time to consider this problem. . . . And," he added with quiet emphasis, "if a common import-export plan cannot be agreed upon then at a suitable time in the not too distant future the United States Delegation would request revision of the reparations plan."[87] The Russians had been put on notice and, knowing Clay, they were aware that he was not bluffing.

During subsequent meetings of the Control Council Clay made several unsuccessful attempts to reach an agreement on the common utilization of resources. When Mikhail Dratvin, who had replaced Sokolovsky on the Coordinating Committee, denied any connection between reparations and a joint export-import plan, Clay blew up. "I submit that reparations are only one of the bricks that built the house," he said sharply.

> If you pull out any of the bricks the house collapses and it seems to me we have pulled out so many already we're on the verge of collapse. I don't believe we can ever reach a solution on any one

of them without reaching a solution on all of them. Certainly the
question of the ability to meet the export-import program is tied
up definitely with the question of reparations.[88]

He gave them a few more weeks before he carried out his threat.
Finally, on May 2, the ax fell. At a meeting of the Coordinating Committee,
with French and British support, he introduced a paper providing for the
pooling of resources. As expected, Dratvin again objected and, turning to
General Koeltz, he inquired whether the French were now ready to establish
a central administrative machinery. The answer was the usual one. France
favored treatment of Germany as a single economic entity but it opposed
central administrative machinery. Then Clay spoke up.

> I think I understand the position of the Soviet Delegation putting
> the cart before the horse instead of behind it. I can only say that
> with the exception of advance reparation plans, all further repar-
> ations have been stopped in the American zone. We will be very
> glad to continue preparations, but we have no intention of imple-
> menting them until the entire question has been resolved. We do
> not want to be put in the position where we are without plants
> and without an agreement.[89]

The threatening storm had broken. But while the Eastern press thundered
against the "illegal General Clay" and American pundits debated whether
the reparations halt was directed against Russia or France, the Deputy
Military Governor felt that he had accomplished something more important.
By making it clear that he would not permit any outgo from his area of
financial responsibility until the income from Allied sources had been assured, he had moved the policies of the four powers off dead center. ("If
economic unity is not achieved," he told a reporter, "the four governments
would have to decide what to do next."[90])

To make certain that his message was understood on the policymaking
level, Clay submitted a comprehensive review of the German problem to
the heads of the departments in Washington. The general pointed out that
if a common economic policy could not be fully implemented in all the
zones of Germany and if the present boundaries were going to be changed,
the concept of Potsdam would be meaningless. Economic unity could be
obtained only through free trade within the country and through a common
foreign trade policy to serve the nation as a whole. A unified financial policy
and drastic fiscal reforms were equally essential. The territorial questions
involving the Rhineland, the Ruhr, and the Saar should be promptly decided.
The loss of the Saar would not require a serious revision of the level of
industry plan, but the loss of the Rhineland and the Ruhr would necessitate
complete revision. The principal problem for the military administration,
the General suggested, was that economic chaos would "particularly affect

the U.S. zone, which had no raw materials and would create a continuing financial liability for the United States for many years." On the other hand, Clay saw no reasons why the reparations plan should not be implemented promptly if economic unity could be achieved. But he was apprehensive of developing pressures to revise the reparations plan in favor of production of reparations, and he actually repeated the Morgenthau thesis that "reparations from current production ignores the real danger which Germany would still present if restored to full industrial strength." He proposed the early establishment of a provisional German government with the *Länderrat* serving as an initial model, and the creation of a Ruhr control authority for the coal and steel industry in that area. Clay predicted strong French resistance (unavoidable since all the French parties wanted Germany dismembered), but he suggested that his proposals might be acceptable to the Russians (who were interested in a unified Germany although preferably under their tutelage). If the four powers failed to reach agreement, then Clay proposed an economic merger of the British and American zones, which could become self-sufficient within a few years and provide relief in accordance with congressional wishes.[91]

To Clay's disappointment, the United States government was not quite ready yet to endorse his "either-or" posture. An Acheson-Hilldring proposal, sent to Paris for Secretary Byrnes' consideration, suggested a compromise instead. Under its terms there would be a "resumed implementation of the reparations program during a period of 60–90 days on condition that Soviets agree to join with other occupying powers in instructions to the Allied Control Authority to proceed during this period with negotiations on a phased plan for the adoption and implementation of common economic policies focusing on adoption of an export-import program. . . ."[92]

For Clay, that was the end—or so he thought. Marjorie was not happy in Berlin in the midst of German misery, and the General himself was now more than ever convinced the time had come to leave. His relations with General McNarney had become increasingly unsatisfactory. A number of directives out of USFET headquarters in Frankfurt had angered him.[93] And there were underlying animosities between army and military government staffs[94] and between a much-decorated aviator who had seen combat in two wars and an officer who had spent the whole war in Washington. The new Military Governor showed little understanding for the problems of the occupation;[95] even outsiders could not help noticing what little interest he took in his work. As one witness described it, during deliberations of the Control Council "McNarney had to bend his ear toward Clay, making it embarrassingly plain that he had not done his homework."[96] He was frequently away from Germany but insisted on his prerogatives and on final approval of all important decisions.[97]

On June 15, in a cable to McNarney, General Clay applied for retirement.[98]

FOOTNOTES

1. Author's interview with Mrs. Lucius D. Clay, McLean, Va., February 2, 1980.
2. Author's interview with Mr. Robert Bowie, Langley, Va., February 28, 1979.
3. Author's interview with Captain Margaret Allen, Washington, D. C., October 2, 1980. Clay had a painful eye infection and refused to see a doctor. He was furious when the staff sent the garrison's eye specialist to his residence.
4. Lucius D. Clay, *Decision in Germany*, pp. 70–71.
5. Author's interview with Mrs. Clay, McLean, Va., April 1, 1981.
6. Author's interview with General Hugh Casey, Bradford, Vt., October 8, 1980.
7. Author's interview with Mrs. Lucius D. Clay, McLean, Va., April 1, 1981.
8. Ibid.
9. Demaree Bess, "American Viceroy in Germany," in *Saturday Evening Post*, May 3, 1947. p. 146. Robert Murphy, *Diplomat Among Warriors*, p. 289.
10. Jean Smith interview with General Clay, February 17, 1971.
11. Author's interview with Ambassador Jacob Beam, Washington, D.C., June 3, 1981.
12. Author's interview with Mrs. Charles O'Connor, Hershey, Pa., June 14, 1980.
13. Bess, "American Viceroy in Germany," p. 146.
14. Harold Zink, *The United States in Germany, 1944–1955*, pp. 71–75.
15. Teleconference, Clay-Hilldring, March 1, 1946. TC-5756.R.G.200.N.A.
16. Author's interviews with General Frank Howley, New York, N.Y., April 23, 1980; James Sundquist, Wash., D.C., May 5, 1980; and General James Stratton, Wash., D.C., November 12, 1979.
17. Don Humphrey, private papers, and author's inverview, Winchester, Mass., October 10, 1980. William Harlan Hale, "General Clay—On His Own" in *Harpers*, December 1948.
18. Murphy, *Diplomat*, p. 292. Clay for Hilldring, November 17, 1945. CC 19086 R.G.200.N.A.
19. Ibid.
20. Clay for Hildring, December 8, 1945. CC 20113. R.G.200.N.A.
21. Major General Ralph Osborne to author, May 26, 1980.
22. Author's interview with Lieutenant General A. J. Boyle, Allaway Farms, Mitchells, Va., April 12, 1980.
23. USFET from McNarney to OMGUS, October 10, 1946. R.G. 165 file WDSCA 014 Germany.N.A.
24. War Dept. to USFET, October 8, 1946, R.G.165 WDSCA 014 Germany. N.A.
25. Clay to Echols, October 4, 1946. R.G.165 file WDSCA 387.6.N.A.
26. Clay to Noce, January 22, 1947, CC 7783.R.G.200. N.A.
27. Clay to AGWAR for Petersen. January 30, 1947. R.G.165 file WDSCA 014 Germany. N.A.
28. Clay for War Dept., August 7, 1945. CC 14167; Clay for War Dept., September 4, 1945; Clay for McCloy, September 21, 1945; Clay for War Dept., September 27, 1945; Clay for Hilldring, August 14, 1945, CC 18900; Clay for Echols, October 4, 1946, CC 4908; Clay for Draper, January 31, 1948, CC 3050; Clay for Draper, February 6, 19468, CC 3111; Clay for Draper, April 13, 1948, CC 3853; Clay for Draper, April 20, 1948, CC 73134. Teleconference, Clay-Draper, April 23, 1948. TT 9402.R.G.200.N.A.
29. Clay for War Dept., October 1, 1945; Clay for Hilldring, December 5, 1945; Clay for Hilldring, January 25, 1946, CC 22138; February 8, 1946, CC 22830; February 9, 1946, CC 22881; February 17, 1946, CC 23226; February 18, 1946, CC 23277; Clay for Echols, April 5, 1946, CC 2599; R.G.200.N.A. Also *Foreign Relations of the United States 1945*, Vol. 2, pp. 904–906; Vol. 3, pp. 836–845.
30. Ibid.
31. Ibid.
32. Ibid.
33. Clay, *Decision*, p. 116.
34. Murphy to Secretary of State, January 23, 1946. R.G. 59. File 740.00119 Control (Germany) Box 3730.N.A.

35. OMGUS, *Monthly Report of Military Governor*, No. 7, February 20, 1946, p. 1, N.A.
36. Clay, *Decision*, pp. 263–264.
37. The Combined Food Board had been set up during the war by the United States, Canada and Great Britain to ensure equitable distribution of food to the Allied nations. The board was succeeded by an International Emergency Food Council in Washington, which eventually became the International Emergency Food Committee of the UN's Food and Agricultural Organization. Membership in the IEFC included all important food exporting and importing countries with the exception of the U.S.S.R. and Argentina. The IRFC was a voluntary organization regulating the distribution of exportable surpluses of the world's scarce commodities. Although it had no legal authority, there was general compliance with the council's recommendations.
38. Clay for Hilldring, January 23, 1946. CC 22247 R.G. 200.N.A.
39. Clay for Hilldring, February 27, 1946, CC 23681; Clay for Berry, March 6, 1946, CC 1530; Clay for McNarney, March 18, 1946; Clay for Petersen, March 22, 1946, CC 1854; Clay for Petersen and Echols, March 27, 1946; Clay for War Dept., April 11, 1946, CC 2903; Clay for Echols, May 18, 1946, CC 5315; and May 24, 1946, CC 5693, all in R.G.200.N.A.
40. Clay for Hilldring, March 6, 1946, CC 1033.R.G. 200.N.A.
41. *Foreign Relations . . ., Commonwealth, West and Central Europe 1946*, Vol. 5, pp. 403–404; 498; 509–511.
42. Wallace R. Devel, "The Army in Power," in *Survey*, February 1950.
43. John H. Backer, *Priming the German Economy*, p. 57.
44. "Second Battle of Germany," in *Fortune*, December 1946, p. 132.
45. Ibid., p. 133.
46. Ibid., p. 137.
47. "The German Crisis," in *The Economist*, April 6, 1946, pp. 527–532.
48. David Ginsburg, *The Future of German Reparations*, The National Planning Association, February 18, 1947.
49. Clay, *Decision*, p. 196.
50. Ibid.
51. Gustav Stolper, *German Realities*, pp. 95–108.
52. Hans Adler, "The Postwar Reorganization," in *Quarterly Journal of Economics* 63, No. 3, (August 1946), p. 333; Manuel Gottlieb, *The German Peace Settlement and the Berlin Crisis*, p. 58.
53. Wolfgang Friedman. *The Allied Military Government of Germany*, pp. 192–194, 202. J. P. Nettl, *The Eastern Zone and Soviet Policy in Germany, 1945–1950*, pp. 162–165.
54. Ibid.
55. Clay for Hilldring, January 27, 1946, in Jean Smith, editor, *The Papers of General Lucius D. Clay*, p. 151.
56. Clay for Echols, May 23, 1946, CC 5635.R.G.200.N.A.
57. Charles Fahy, Memoirs, Oral History Project, Columbia University, New York City.
58. Charles Fahy, Memorandum for Clay, October 8, 1945, Dec. File 1945–1946, Box 15. N.A.
59. John H. Herz, "The Fiasco of Denazification," in *Political Science Quarterly*, Vol. LXIII, No. 4, p. 571.
60. Richard Schmid, "Denazification—A German Critique," October 1948 in *American Perspective*, Vol. 2, No. 5, p. 239.
61. Ibid., p. 234.
62. Author's interview with Margaret Allen, October 2, 1980.
63. Extract Special Orders #228, November 30, 1945, Sec. 17, Dec. file 1945–1946, Box 15, N.A.
64. German Draft of Proposed Denazification Law prepared by *Land* Ministries of Justice, December 22, 1945. Sec. 1, Dec. file 014.3, Box 15, N.A.
65. Report of Denazification Policy Board to Deputy Military Governor, January 15, 1946, p. 1, Dec. file 014.3, Box 15, N.A.
66. Earl Ziemke, *The U.S. Army in the Occupation of Germany*, p. 430.
67. William Griffith, "The Denazification Program in the U.S. Zone of Germany," p. 174. Doctoral Dissertation, Harvard University.
68. Clay for Hilldring, January 14, 1946. CC 21576. R.G.200.N.A.

69. Alvin Johnson, "Denazification," in *Social Research*, 1947, p. 71. Carl Friedrich, *Military Government in World War II*, pp. 266–267.
70. Schmid, ibid., pp. 236–237; Friedrich, ibid., pp. 266–267; Griffith, ibid., Chapter VIII.
71. Schmid, ibid., pp. 239–240; Lutz Niethammer, *Entnazifizierung in Bayern*, pp. 310–325.
72. William Griffith, "Denazification in the U.S. Zone of Germany," in the *Annals*, January 1950, p. 70. Elmer Plischke, "Denazification Law and Procedure" in *American Journal of International Law*, October 1947, p. 824.
73. Clay, *Decision*, p. 259.
74. Zink, *The United States*, p. 162.
75. James Stewart Martin, *All Honorable Men*, p. 165.
76. Ibid. pp. 153–154.
77. Ibid., p. 163.
78. Graham D. Taylor, "The Rise and Fall of Antitrust," in *Prologue*, Spring 1979, pp. 32–33.
79. Clay, *Decision*, p. 97. Ziemke, *The U.S. Army*, pp. 427–428. "Some observers believed the Germans had voted mainly to convince themselves and their neighbors that the stigma of Nazism had been eradicated. . . ."
80. Clay, *Decision*, p. 97.
81. Jean Smith interview with General Clay, February 19, 1971.
82. Heinz Guradze, "The Laenderrat: Landmark of German Reconstruction," in *Western Political Quarterly*, June 1950, p. 196.
83. Don Humphrey, private papers.
84. Ibid.
85. Statement by K. I. Koval at ACA, April 5, 1946. OMGUS records, 5–1/1, N.A.
86. Ibid.
87. Clay, *Decision*, p. 121.
88. Ibid.
89. Ibid., p. 122; Clay for Echols, May 2, 1946, CC 4227, R.G. 200.N.A.; Clay, *Decision*, pp. 73–78.
90. OMGUS. PRO. Transcript of Clay Press Conference, May 27, 1946. OMGUS records 1–1/4 N.A.
91. Clay for Eisenhower, May 26, 1946, CC 5797, R.G. 200.N.A.
92. *Foreign Relations . . . , The British Commonwealth, West and Central Europe 1946*, Vol. 5, pp. 550–555.
93. Teleconference, Clay-Hilldring, March 1, 1946. TC-5756; R.G.N.A.
94. Jean Smith interview with General Clay, February 19, 1971.
95. Author's interview with Jim O'Donnell, Washington, D.C., March 8, 1980; Author's interview with Ambassador Jacob Beam, Washington, D.C., June 3, 1981.
96. Author's interview with Colonel John Bates, Maplewood, N.J., April 23, 1980.
97. Author's interview with Jim O'Donnell, Washington, D.C., March 8, 1980.
98. Clay for McNarney, June 15, 1946, CC 7029; Clay for Echols, June 17, 1946, CC 7038, R.G.200.N.A.

CHAPTER SIX

A Temporary Expedient

CLAY'S FRUSTRATION WITH THE JOB WAS THE PRINCIPAL REASON FOR HIS WISH to retire, but the friction with the Military Governor was probably the last straw. McNarney, replying to his deputy's cable, indicated little regret at the prospect of losing him, but by that time Robert Murphy had become convinced that Clay was indispensable.[1] He secretly sent word of the crisis to the Secretary of State. Byrnes' personal and urgent appeal to his friend brought forth the desired reaction. Clay promised he would stay on at least for the time being.

One month after the General's dramatic reparations stop, there was a ready response to the challenge from the Kremlin. Soviet seizure of "war booty" actually had begun as soon as Russian troops entered Germany.[2] A detailed plan encompassing the collection of foodstuffs, animals, farm machinery, transportation equipment and miscellaneous household goods had been prepared and special "trophy brigades" made responsible for its fulfillment. Simultaneously, the principal targets for reparations, i.e. coal-mining installations, railway-repair shops, power stations, electrical works, and locomotive factories, were quickly dismantled. However, the work fell to unskilled crews who received no overall direction or essential technical instructions and caused extensive damage. In addition, due to the shortage of railway transportation facilities the dismantled equipment was often left to rain and weather. Now, after Clay's reparations stop, the Soviets extended their grasp. Two hundred of the largest industrial works in the Russian zone—properties of monopoly capitalists and Nazis, as they announced—would be expropriated. They would be transformed into Soviet cooperatives producing exclusively for the Soviet state or for exports on the Soviet account.[3] A number of the seized firms had originally been earmarked for dismantlement. As Draper therefore suggested, the Soviets probably also had recognized that reparations could be taken more promptly and cheaply if factories were left in their places.

Outwardly, the cordial relationship between the American and Soviet deputy military governors was not affected by the reparations dispute. However, the East German press, disregarding a Control Council ruling against criticism of Allied personalities, reacted with slanderous comments about the "illegal" General. Apparently thinking amends were in order, Sokolovsky drew his American colleague aside at the next meeting of the Coordinating Committee: "We have always been good friends and I hope we will remain so despite the political differences between our governments." Clay smiled and in an astute display of Southern charm stuck out his hand. "Yes, you are still my friend and I like you," he replied, "but I don't like the low-down, scoundrelly newspapers that take orders from you."[4]

Contrary to Clay's expectations, his initiative at the Control Council had not generated any active support from his own government. At the May meeting in Paris with Secretary Byrnes and Senators Arthur H. Vandenberg and Tom Connally, he again had brought up the option of a bizonal merger. Congress' negative reactions to open-ended deficits were predictable, he said. On the other hand, a self-supporting bizonal economy might well stave off a curtailment of funds. Three or four years would be needed to achieve economic stability, but the Soviet Union might, in the meantime, come around.[5] Bizonia—the economic amalgamation of the American and British zones—would be a temporary expedient providing more time to work toward an all-German settlement at the Control Council. He presented his concept most convincingly, but even as he spoke it became clear to him that his government was not yet willing to act.

On July 9, at the Foreign Ministers conference in Paris, the General listened to the Soviet Union's official response to his challenge. Facing an unperturbed Clay and an increasingly annoyed Byrnes, Molotov castigated "the illegal reparations stop." The 25-year treaty guaranteeing the demilitarization of Germany which the United States had proposed could not be considered, he said, until the reparations issue which Potsdam had left open had been settled.[6] The statement about the unresolved reparations question was true enough. But instead of pursuing this point, for which ample evidence was on hand, Molotov rather clumsily brought up the reparations claim of $10 billion. His allegation that President Roosevelt at Yalta had accepted this figure infuriated the Secretary of State, causing a sharp and unproductive debate.[7]

The next day Clay had the confrontation provoked by the reparations stop. Using the Morgenthau concept as a propaganda device, Molotov played on the Germans' raw fears about their future by declaring that it would be a mistake to contemplate Germany's annihilation as a state or to plan its agrarianization and the destruction of its principal industries. The aim of the Soviet government was not to destroy Germany, he said, "but to transform it into a democratic and peace-loving state which besides its agriculture will have its own industry and foreign trade."[8] A policy directed toward the creation of a pastoral state and the elimination of its principal industries would only result in making Germany an incubator for dangerous sentiments of revenge. With regard to the detaching of the Ruhr, Molotov remarked that since it was self-evident that Germany could not exist as an independent and viable state without this area, such concepts simply complemented the plans for the country's agrarianization. The Allies, he went on, should put no obstacles in the way of increasing the German output of steel, coal, and manufactured products of a peaceful nature. Molotov failed to mention that at recent meetings about the future level of German industry it was always the Soviets who had voted for the lowest figures.

The Secretary's response was still conciliatory. Byrnes merely expressed the hope for the early establishment of central German administrative agencies, which were necessary to secure the economic unity of Germany. However, if no agreement in this regard could be reached, "the United States as a last resort would make another suggestion." No zone of Germany was fully self-sufficient, Byrnes declared, thus the treatment of any two zones as an economic unit would improve conditions in both zones. "Pending agreement among the four powers to implement the Potsdam Agreement requiring the administration of Germany as an economic unit," he then announced,

> the United States will join with any other occupying government in Germany for the treatment of our respective zones as an economic unit. The continuation of the present situation will result in inflation and economic paralysis. It will result in increased costs to the occupying powers and unnecessary suffering to the German people. The United States is unwilling to share the responsibility for the continuance of such conditions.[9]

Although this was the diplomatic move Clay had been waiting for, he was not satisfied. As he saw it, a more direct response to the Soviet propaganda blast was urgently needed.

From his almost daily conversations with reporters, the General was only too well aware that not even the American press, much less the German people, were informed about U.S. plans for the postwar treatment of Germany. Actually, there existed only a few guideposts: the Morgenthau Plan whose validity as an instrument of U.S. policy had neither been officially acknowledged nor denied; the Potsdam Agreement of August 1945; the Joint Chiefs of Staff Directive #1067 of May 1945, which was released for publication only five months later, leaving unclear the fact that some of its stringent provisions had been annulled by Potsdam; and finally the quadripartite Level of Industry Plan of March 1946. While all these documents stressed the resistive aspects of American policies, none of them extended to Germans any hope about their future as a nation.

Clay had known for some time that an official policy statement on the part of the United States was required. Molotov's inflammatory speech had merely accentuated this necessity. Besides, all the General's fighting spirit revolted against leaving the Soviet foreign minister's provocative remarks unanswered. Upon his return to Berlin he therefore recorded for the Pentagon his own understanding of United States policy and objectives. This, he thought, should be released throughout the military government, and possibly be made available to the German people. "I hesitate to publish it without the full concurrence of the War and State departments," he told General Echols. "While occupied Germany is busily discussing the Moltov statement," he went on, "our own military government people have no ready up-to-date summarized version of our policy or objectives which they could use in discussion with our German people."[10] The extensive and complex summary of United States objectives which followed covered the broad spectrum of U.S. policies in Germany.

Starting with Potsdam, Clay's paper confirmed that the United States adhered to the Tripartite agreement but it insisted:

> on the treatment of Germany as an economic unit with indigenous resources to be used first to meet the essential requirements in Germany and second to provide exports to finance essential imports into Germany. Plants in excess of the agreed level of industry should be promptly removed but there should be no other reparations that would represent a further tax on the German economy.

The Level of Industry Plan was a minimum essential to a reasonable German standard of living which, however, also required the removal of the present zonal boundary restrictions. If German exports in the immediate future should be insufficient to pay for essential imports, the occupying powers should have to consider financing them. A drastic and early monetary reform placing Germany on a sound financial basis was therefore of paramount importance. Moreover, the five central administrative agencies provided for by Potsdam should not only be created promptly but a central agency for agriculture added as well. It was also "desirable to establish concurrently a provisional government to which these agencies would report."[11] It would "consist of a council of the minister-presidents or other chief officers which have been established in each of the four zones. . . ." The Council of Minister-Presidents would also be charged with the preliminary drafting of a constitution, the essentials of which Clay then outlined.

As far as Germany's future boundaries were concerned, Clay's interpretation accepted the eastern de facto border. It conceded the economic unification of the Saar with France but it ruled out the severance of the Rhineland and the Ruhr. Instead, it proposed the internationalization of the coal and steel industries. As to the future, Clay opposed any permanent industrial limitations which would deny Germany a hope of raising its standard of living. The trial and punishment of war criminals and adherents of the National Socialist Party should be brought to an early conclusion. As soon as Allied objectives in Germany had been achieved, the size of the occupation forces should be drastically reduced. Allied military government would be exercised by the Control Council and "sufficient field inspection teams to insure the accomplishment of its directives." A federal Germany consisting of a number of smaller states would eventually be accepted among the United Nations of the world on terms of equality.[12]

As so often happened, Clay's concept of what United States policy ought to be was more advanced than what emerged from the policy-making process at the State Department. Then Undersecretary of State Dean Acheson promptly created a special study committee "to consider and report on long-range U.S. policy for Germany and to prepare a policy summary to be used by military government."[13] At the same time the War Department advised Berlin of Acheson's view that the paper had broad implications and therefore a public policy statement of such magnitude should be made by the Secretary of State.

When Clay learned of the proposed study, he was furious. "I did not send the paper back to obtain a revised policy but a statement of policy under which we are operating now," his cable to the War Department said. "We are really in a mess if we are unable without days of delay to give a summarized statement of policy to our own people. Unless instructed otherwise, I propose to issue it to military government personnel in one week."[14] Within five days, he had his instructions. The summary was not to be published. "We are fearful that issuance now," the War Department said, "might commit the Government in a manner more binding than is desirable." A State Department committee headed by James W. Riddleberger would be proceeding shortly to Berlin to discuss framing a policy statement in conjunction with Clay. In particular, the State Department objected to Clay's comments about the early establishment of a provisional government, an eventual admission of Germany to the United Nations and United States acceptance of Germany's eastern frontiers.[15]

It took a week for Clay to calm down. On August 15, in a personal letter to Hilldring, he complained

> that we are operating only under what we thought to be government policy but have found out is not government policy. . . . You tell us now that you are sending a committee here to develop a revised policy. With all due respect to the committee and the chairman, Mr. Riddleberger, it cannot expect me or my staff to enter into some discussions.

"Believe me, John, retirement and a tour of catfishing look awfully good to me," the closing sentence read.[16] Apparently the General had second thoughts about the letter because it was filed unsent. Instead, he advised the War Department the next day, "Your message will of course be followed, but I must say that it leaves military government at sea since it is obvious that we have no firm policy."[17] And in a personal letter to Secretary of War Robert P. Patterson, he wrote that he had thrown his own memorandum "in the wastebasket." "I believe the memorandum has been misunderstood," he added. "It was not my intent to submit it as a recommended policy for Germany. I realize that it is not our task to originate or even recommend policy but it is distressing to find after more than a year that our interpretation of policy must be variant with facts."[18]

Apparently there was real concern in top government circles that the irate General actually would walk out on them, and the Clays were invited to spend an evening with Justice Byrnes in Paris. When Marjorie Clay commented years later that the Secretary always had been "like a father" to them, she must have had this and similar occasions in mind.[19] As it seems, Byrnes quickly managed to placate his enraged former associate. The Secretary's promise to make a comprehensive statement on German policy early in September settled Clay's controversy with Washington and— alas only temporarily—raised the General's morale. "Marjorie and I enjoyed our trip to Paris more than I can express," he wrote to Byrnes the following day. "Particularly because it demonstrated again to me the true value of your friendship and confidence. How you could take time to raise my spirits in the midst of your worries is almost unbelievable. I want you to know," the handwritten note concluded, "that until you say the word I shall continue to do my best to carry out my part of the task in Germany. I would be ashamed otherwise."[20]

Yet, "mercurial in temperament," as one of his rating officers had noted, only two days later Clay again asked McNarney for an early replacement. He confirmed this oral request in a letter indicating that "when the date is established I would like to return to the United States on leave of absence, as I have accumulated the maximum accrued leave. During the leave I would submit my request for retirement. . . . In the meantime," he concluded, "I assure you that I shall continue to give my best efforts to military government and to the accomplishment of our objectives in Germany."[21] Walter Bedell Smith was visiting Germany at the time, and a couple of days later Clay showed him the draft of a letter to Eisenhower asking for relief and if necessary for retirement. Smith told him to wait until he could talk to Ike personally, and alerted Eisenhower, who at the time was Chief of Staff. "McNarney is doing a good job," Smith wrote, "but it is simply very difficult to like him. . . . It must be hard," he added, "to serve in a very close staff relationship with a commander whom one does not like. However, I think Clay is still indispensable in Germany."[22]

The date finally agreed upon for Byrnes' appearance in Germany was September 6, and the place chosen for the occasion the Stuttgart Opera House. "If it had been in Frankfurt," Clay later commented, "it would have been really a spectacle too much for our own headquarters, for our own people. Obviously Berlin wasn't the place. So the logical place for our Secretary was the seat of the German government under our jurisdiction, and that was Stuttgart."[23] Byrnes, accompanied by Vandenberg and Connally and their wives, arrived in Berlin early in the afternoon of September

5. Met at the Tempelhof airport by Clay and Murphy, the group first went
to the headquarters on Kronprinzenallee and then quickly toured the city.
When going over the speech which Ben Cohen had drafted—it contained
the major portions of the General's controversial policy message—the Deputy Military Governor only suggested he "put in there that as long as
anybody else's troops were in Germany, ours would be there too."[24] Byrnes
agreed, but recognizing the ramifications, he first tried to get the President's
approval. "He did not get Truman on the telephone, although he tried very
hard," Clay later explained,

> but he went ahead and put it in his speech anyway and of course
> it was at least to my way of thinking the major important thing
> in his speech. To the Germans there were other things that were
> very, very important but to the Europeans the fact that the United
> States had committed itself to stay in Germany and in Europe
> probably did more to stop the Communist political games in West-
> ern Europe than any other thing that ever happened.[25]

Later in the day the party boarded the Fuehrer's luxurious train and
departed for Stuttgart. They were met by the minister-presidents of the
three states in the American zone, who then had an opportunity to meet
and talk with Justice Byrnes before he made his speech.

The Secretary's visit was the most colorful event in the American zone
since the occupation began, and the setting was dramatic. The streets leading
to the Opera House were lined with spic-and-span soldiers wearing shiny
helmets circled in blue and yellow and marked with the big *C* of the U.S.
Constabulary, an elite unit recently formed by General Ernest Harmon.
The intersections were blocked off by armored cars and tanks garnished
with the unit's flashy colors. Behind the lined up troops there were thousands
of Germans on the sidewalks. Inside the Opera House a constabulary band
played while officers, soldiers, and civilian officials of the American military
government slowly filled stalls and tiers. Some of the sections in front were
reserved for invited German officials and visiting British and French officers.
On the flower- and flag-bedecked stage stood five chairs.[26] Shortly before
one P.M., General McNarney escorted Secretary Byrnes, the two senators
and Ambassador Robert Murphy to the stage. Clay, who had chosen to sit
in the orchestra with the minister-presidents, later explained that this enabled him to "observe German reactions."[27] Acutally it was a clever gesture
demonstrating publicly that the Deputy Military Governor was there together with his German associates to listen to his government's policy decisions. For informed insiders it was a far cry from the early days of the
occupation when Germans calling on the Deputy Military Governor were
not asked to sit but had to remain standing.[28]

The Secretary's speech[29] was the official United States response to
Molotov's propaganda statement in July. It reconfirmed the terms of the

Potsdam Agreements whereby Germany was to be demilitarized and compelled to pay reparations. Germany's war potential was to be reduced by the elimination of its war industries, and its economic power curtailed by the reduction and the removal of industrial plants not needed for its peacetime economy. The aim was to enable Germany to maintain average European living standards without assistance from other countries. Addressing himself to the Soviet Union, the Secretary remarked that in many important respects the Control Council was neither governing Germany nor allowing Germany to govern itself. The United States regarded a common financial policy as essential for the successful rehabilitation of Germany and considered it quite certain that a runaway inflation accompanied by economic paralysis would develop unless the German house could be put in order through a common financial policy. With regard to territorial issues, Byrnes indicated "the American government would support the French claim to the Saar" and was also prepared to recognize Poland's annexation of some territory in East Germany.

While German listeners could derive little comfort from the above, they were undoubtedly pleased to hear that the United States considered the Ruhr and the Rhineland indisputably German. America therefore would not support any encroachment on this territory nor any division of Germany not genuinely desired by the people concerned. Byrnes summed up his speech by declaring the United States could not relieve Germany from the hardship inflicted upon it by the war which the National Socialist regime had started, but would attempt to give the German people "an opportunity to work their way out of these hardships so long as they respected human freedom and clung to the path of peace." Contrary to a popular interpretation, the speech contained no change in substance when compared with previous American policy statements, but there was a very considerable difference in the tone; furthermore, while the priming of the German economy in the American zone had been underway for more than a year, this was now officially recognized as a major policy aim of the United States.

There also was the short paragraph in the speech which Clay had insisted on: "Security forces will probably have to remain in Germany for a long period," Byrnes declared. "I want no misunderstanding. We will not shirk our duty. We are not withdrawing. We are staying here and will furnish our proportionate share of the security forces." For the first time, the world was thus put on notice of a radical shift in the political views of the United States. Whereas at Yalta, in accordance with prevailing sentiments back home, Roosevelt had suggested that American forces might remain in Europe for two years, and whereas the world—based on the United States' past record—had arrived at similar conclusions, Byrnes' declaration heralded an entirely new foreign policy approach. The barrier of the Atlantic thus seemed removed, with the fate of the United States officially tied to that of Western Europe.

From Clay's vantage point, the Secretary's speech had the great merit of clearing the air and eliminating numerous misapprehensions. Washington's official stance was now in line with the grass-roots activities of the military government; the American position as to territorial changes had been clearly defined; and friend and foe were given notice that the United States would not withdraw. With regard to the Deputy Military Governor's primary concern, the attainment of economic self-sufficiency, Byrnes had also declared that "Germany must be given a chance to export goods in order to import to make [the country] self-sustaining. European recovery will be slow . . . if Germany . . . is turned into a poorhouse." This complemented the envisaged economic merger of the British and American zones.

The event at the Opera House ended with the band playing "The Star Spangled Banner." The audience remained standing as Secretary Byrnes and his party withdrew. "I walked backstage to meet them in the wings," Clay wrote, "and to congratulate him on a speech which I believed would live through the years. Senator Vandenberg, whose eyes were moist, as were mine, remarked: 'And they played "The Star Spangled Banner" with the same authority as if they were on the steps of the Capitol.' "[30]

The Stuttgart speech had lessened some of the strain under which Clay was working. The Russians were given the answer which his personal fighting impulses demanded. The impasse at the Control Council was now on the diplomatic agenda; and his last controversy with the State Department had been settled. But other stresses remained, and contrary to what a cursory first impression of Clay might suggest he was not an iron man with no nerves. When Marjorie Clay had arrived in April in Berlin, she was shocked to see in her husband's face the effects of overwork and continuous tension. Thereafter the pressures of the job had been steadily mounting. "Clay is a fine fellow when he relaxes," one of his associates at OMGUS quipped, "the only problem is that he never relaxes." In the office, his aides, Captain Margaret Allen and Edna Shelley, continued to appreciate the General's easygoing manner and never-failing courtesy,[31] a facade often maintained only by iron self-control. Others, including George Kennan, noticed his "great physical and nervous intensity."[32] Delbert Clark observed an angry Clay whose "eyes contracted until they were opaque black pools of anger";[33] whereas Don Humphrey concluded that the General "was thin skinned and all nerves."[34] James Forrestal, who talked to Clay for an hour after the Deputy Military Governor had returned from Paris in July, felt that the strain was beginning to tell on the General. When he returned to the United States a few days later Forrestal wrote a memorandum to the Secretary of War: "I think you should order General Clay to take a ten-day or two-week holiday—nothing else will make him do it; and if he doesn't get some break, he runs the risk of blowing up entirely."[35]

The General's physical stamina seemed phenomenal, an impression enhanced by his unwillingness to admit to any illness or pain. "He wanted to be twenty-four hours in the saddle," Edloe Donnan said. But nature has its way of reacting to deep-seated repressed tensions. Countless cups of black coffee and three to four packs of cigarettes a day were also detrimental to his health. Like so many overworked executives, Lucius Clay developed stomach ulcers—the "managers' malady." Following the Stuttgart speech the Clays joined the Washington guests for two days in the Bavarian Alps. The General expected a "delightful and memorable" break, but during the first night in Berchtesgaden, nature took its toll. He became violently ill, vomiting all night. "I thought he would die," Mrs. Clay recalled.[36] In the morning he again appeared self-composed and courteous, guiding his distinguished guests to Hitler's former home, now an American club, and up the winding mountain road to the renowned "Eagle's Nest."[37]

When Clay returned to Berlin he found a note from General Eisenhower in response to Bedell Smith's letter. Ike was to be in Germany in the latter part of September, Clay was informed. "I shall of course await your arrival," the Deputy Military Governor replied. "Marjorie and I have been looking forward too long for a visit from Mamie and you to even think of missing it. I hope it will give us a chance to talk. However, I am more convinced than ever that it would be a serious mistake for me to continue here."[38] "It was not a very happy period," Clay recalled, and he conceded that "Military Command had something to do with it." McNarney was the chief, but, in Clay's view, he neither understood the problems of the occupied country nor cared to understand. Nevertheless, the last word was often his. "I really didn't see for myself what future there was to it," Clay explained twenty-five years later. "If I wasn't in a position to make the decisions I couldn't even be helpful to the situation in Germany, and if I was going to do all the work and still not make the decisions I didn't see any point to that."[39] The meeting with Eisenhower settled the matter. Clay was told that McNarney would soon be leaving and Clay was to take over the European Command in addition to his present responsibilities in Berlin.

It was easier getting rid of an ill-chosen commander than to alleviate the two fundamental and interconnected problems of the occupation, shortage of food and a suppressed inflation. With the SHAEF grain reserve running out, rations in the American and British zones for the summer had been cut. Fortunately the 1946 German harvest was good and in the fall the former rations could be restored. However, by then it also had become clear that even full implementation of the 1,550 calories for the "normal consumer" would not suffice to sustain a working population. It would thus prevent an early recovery of the economy. The continued undernourishment had resulted in lowered body weights and a general deterioration of health among the German population. As Clay's nutritional survey teams reported in August 1946, there was on the average a 10 to 14 percent deviation from a minimum satisfactory weight. A combined British, French, and American committee of health experts concluded that "while part of the population of the cities of the three zones of Western Germany is in fairly good nutritional state, a significantly larger proportion is in an unsatisfactory condition, and of these an increasing number show signs of severe under-nutrition. . . . The longer this situation continues, the greater becomes the risk of nutritional disaster."[40]

The inability to deal effectively with the interlocking inflation-food problem was the source of continuous frustration for Clay. On the one hand he was stymied by the slow progress in the Control Council toward a currency reform; on the other, he was impeded by limited appropriations and world food shortages. Moreover, and this was the most galling aspect, he was in no position to enforce a rigid collection of food in his own area. Since most of the American supervisory personnel had departed, he depended on German administrators, whose loyalties were divided.

Since hardly any farm machinery or spare parts were available through legal channels, the farmers, rather than fulfilling even low delivery quotas, used part of their produce for barter. It was estimated at OMGUS that about 20 percent of the harvest was hoarded or reached the black market,[41] but as the currency reform in the summer of 1948 dramatically revealed, 50 percent would have been a more accurate assessment.[42] Conditions in the factories paralleled those on the farms; many of the workers maintained regular jobs only in order to be entitled to ration cards and the social benefits that depended on regular employment.[43]

With Reichsmarks practically worthless, cigarettes assumed the role of printed money since they fulfilled some of its prerequisites—durability, divisibility into small "denominations," transportability, and wide accept-ance. Millions of cartons of cigarettes were mailed to U.S. Army personnel directly from the United States, while additional quantities entered the country via Switzerland.[44] The going black market rate of RM1,000 to 1,500 for a carton of cigarettes with a conversion rate of one dollar for ten marks readily created small fortunes.[45] During the first year of the occupa-tion, administrative rules were inadequate and enforcement lax. When dollar instruments in the form of military scrip finally replaced the Allied marks in the summer of 1946, the U.S. Army—to the Pentagon's embar-rassment—held over $200 million worth of nonconvertible Reichsmarks. (Since a set of plates for the printing of the Allied occupational currency had been given to the Soviet government in 1944, "Communists" in the U.S. Treasury became a convenient scapegoat for the Army Finance Office's neglect.[46]

Under the prevailing conditions of moral decay, advanced by a legal twilight, Clay's uncompromising sense of justice stood him in good stead on many divergent issues. Friendly relations and frequent contacts with the press, moreover, helped in preventing coverups. When *Newsweek*'s Jim O'Donnell mentioned the then only suspected theft of the Hessian crown jewels by an American colonel and his mistress, Clay's first reaction was utter disbelief. "A West Pointer and a full colonel," he exclaimed. "It can't be true." But when the information was confirmed, he threw the full weight of his office behind the prosecution.[47] He maintained the same criteria of fairness when Germans were involved. By the end of 1945, under the automatic arrest provisions about 120,000 functionaries of the Third Reich were still held without trial in American internment camps. As the General saw it, the war was over and normal legal procedures in accord with American standards should be quickly restored. Accordingly, in the absence of specific charges, more than half of them were set free, and those remaining in the camps became as of July 1946 a German responsibility. The War Department objected vigorously, but having set the course for a gradual American withdrawal, Clay remained adamant.

The Deputy Military Governor had no responsibility for the International War Crimes Court in Nuremberg itself except for providing administrative support. The sentences, however, were reviewed at the Control Council in executive session with its four members pledged never to disclose anything that transpired at those meetings.[48] Twenty-five years later Clay would only say that "we tried [unsuccessfully] to reduce or change the punishment in a couple of cases. The Western powers tried at least to get General Jodl's sentence changed from hanging to being shot, which was something that was very important to him and to his wife. But the Russians wouldn't permit any changes."[49] Having studied the records carefully, he thought that on balance the trials had served a useful purpose. A substantial number of German lawyers had occasion to examine the evidence, he said, and he himself had made sure that the record was widely printed in the German press. The General, nevertheless, had difficulties with the sentences of some of the military men. He especially wondered about Admiral Erich Raeder, who was sentenced to life imprisonment because of the illegal use of submarines. "I am not too sure," Clay remarked, "that when we talk about that kind of use of submarines and at the same time we lay down bombs on Nagasaki and Hiroshima, that we aren't making a distinction that won't stand up in the light of history."[50] He also differentiated between Field Marshall Wilhelm Keitel's actions, "which were not those of a soldier carrying out orders," and General Alfred Jodl's, who as chief of staff did "what almost any other military man would have done." "When a soldier is given orders to do something, and then is charged with a crime because he is carrying out orders, it is very difficult for my conscience to tell me when it's wrong and when it's right. I don't know. The point is: don't lose the war," he concluded, "that's all."[51]

When the Control Council authorized the zone commanders in December 1945 to establish appropriate tribunals for war crimes trials, Clay saw to it that an American military court with Brigadier General Telford Taylor heading the prosecution staff soon succeeded the international tribunal. During 1946, 185 military leaders, government ministers, industrialists, and members of the SS were indicted and tried by this court. Simultaneously a Dachau military tribunal ran trials of about 2,000 war criminals charged with specific crimes, such as participation in the murders and atrocities in the concentration camps. These cases came under the authority of the United States Army rather than of military government,[52] but by the time the sentences were rendered, Clay had also become the final reviewing officer as U.S. Commander in Chief, Europe.

It was more difficult to uphold the law when trying to deal with the black market. Compensation trading, as barter was called, had been forbidden in the Third Reich, and the ruling was easily enforced because there were adequate supplies through legal channels. By contrast, the relevant policies of the American military government were contradictory and local German enforcement measures inadequate. Some efforts were made to distinguish between "legal" and "illegal" barter, the latter pertaining to trade in rationed food. But as some officers at OMGUS saw it, there was nothing objectionable in barter deals. If an American soldier acquired a valuable rug, a painting or a collection of fine china for a pack of cigarettes, the cigarettes would eventually reach the more affluent Germans, it was argued, whereas people in need would resell their cigarettes at black market prices to those who could afford to smoke them. Others, mainly Europeans, regarded the acquisition of valuable assets in such a manner as indirect looting and castigated the Americans, who alone among the occupying armies had at their disposal an abundance of consumer goods.[53]

Since the beginning of the occupation, private barter shops had sprung up all over the American zone and Clay himself finally reached the conclusion that he might as well sanction what he was unable to prevent. The American barter shops, which he authorized on an "experimental" basis, and Washington's query as to their "ethical or moral basis," brought forth an official defense which tells much of the General's moral quandary. This office always viewed the barter market with some misgivings," his answer read,

> and accepted it as the lesser of two ills. Admittedly, an operation which takes people's cherished possessions for consumer items is not pleasant. However, these possessions are going to second-hand stores anyway where the return to the Germans is much less. In the [American] barter market he does get a fair value because it is operated on a high plane with expert German appraisals evaluating fair exchange prices.

Asserting that the American shop had "materially reduced uncontrolled trading" and "was making it much easier for black market operations to be prevented," Clay also pointed out that "the German is getting a better exchange in the controlled barter market than on the forced rent of his house for American occupancy." Finally, in a terse reply to Washington's question he declared that "what is moral in an occupied country is difficult to determine"—this from a son of the Confederacy![54]

Twenty-five years later, Clay still thought that his barter market "was a good out."[55] Obviously, prices were somewhat in favor of Americans, he conceded, but nevertheless, "no German had to come in." When asked how he would have felt if Union troops in Marietta had done the same, he had a ready answer.

> I would have felt a lot better about it than if they were doing it around the corner with uncontrolled and unregulated prices. We certainly tried to set up what at least gave some reasonable return to the Germans, far more than they were getting around the corner and [from] off-the-street-business where they were operating [with] three and four and five go-betweens who were operating illegally. I don't think this is quite necessarily a problem of occupation because I had just as much trouble in a way with my people when they would go to France and Italy, buying their money in the black market where they got four and five times as much for their money as they did at the official rate of exchange, and this was the same thing we are talking about now. How do you do that? How do you prevent people from doing it? I don't know. The British and French just didn't pay any attention to it.[56]

The Stuttgart speech had cleared the air regarding United States objectives in Germany. Coming closely as it did after Clay's announcement of the reparations stop, the men in the Kremlin apparently had grasped the message. At least it seemed to the General that they now were ready for a compromise. In the meantime, however, he had his hands full with internal problems in his zone. Neither denazification nor decartelization was going the way he had hoped. Moreover, political developments on the German side caused controversies with Washington and within his own headquarters.

The 25-page Law for Liberation from National Socialism and Militarism and its 20-page appendix had been promulgated early in March 1946. The solemn Munich ceremony in General Clay's presence marking the enactment and the accompanying congratulatory press comments did little to alleviate the dissatisfaction of American and German officials who had participated in drafting the law. On the one hand, there was the American concern that the transfer of the program to Germans came too early, on the other hand, the Germans objected that party membership alone should not be a prima facie evidence of guilt. Before the first trials could take place the Ministries of Liberation in the three *Länder* had to be established to implement the orders drafted, and trial tribunals set up and staffed. The new offices had to operate under the handicaps of an economy paralyzed by the black market, which as the only source involved a continuous battle for space, typewriters, paper, and other supplies.[57] Of course, the question of finding the right personnel was of critical importance. The people chosen, however, were hastily selected and often unfit for their jobs. Many were very old or individuals whose educational level had prevented their employment in the administration of the Third Reich. In numerous cases the chairmen and prosecutors appointed had to be removed because of corruption and favoritism in office.[58] Hastily chosen with little attention to objectivity, fairness, and judicial training, these men came more and more under public criticism. Since one-fourth of the population in the American zone had to be put on trial, an expeditious handling of the program was well nigh impossible. Party members whose involvement in the system had been only nominal consequently pressured for early trials, whereas others, whose consciences told them of their guilt, hoped to remain in the background until the political atmosphere changed. Moreover, during the first months under the new law, there was little supervision because of Clay's specific orders to hold interference by the military government to a minimum.[59]

In a long memorandum, a perceptive member of Clay's legal staff had cautioned that "even the anti-Nazis in Germany are good Germans and they have to live with their people. . . ." He went on to say:

> It should be clearly realized that once denazification is handed over to the Germans themselves it will be handled by them not on the basis of abstract principles of justice but in the climate of misery, operating through extralegal media such as social contacts, political pressure, [and] public opinion hostile to the occupation, and favoring whatever efforts could be made for frustrating its aim and extricating the people from the defeat. . . .[60]

Already the first statistics coming in on the trials demonstrated the wisdom of this warning. They showed that employment restrictions were imposed only rarely and that most of the individuals tried were declared followers or were acquitted. As a consequence there were many complaints by disillusioned Americans and Germans about flagrant cases of "whitewashing."[61] The spreading dissatisfaction with the law was accentuated by the ruling that the maximum penalty for individuals declared to be followers was a fine of RM 2,000. Whereas German officials in accordance with traditional German juridical customs had fought for a schedule of fines related to a person's wealth or income, Clay personally had been adamant in this regard. Having been brought up under American standards of justices he firmly believed that the German proposal had to be rejected as undemocratic even if it meant that the actual fine was merely nominal.[62]

When American criticism of the denazification tribunals mounted, Clay first reacted in a typical army fashion by instructing military government personnel

> to refrain from destructive criticism of the law and to devote their efforts wholeheartedly to constructive action directed toward the successful completion of the denazification program. . . . If Nazism and militarism are to be permanently suppressed only the German people themselves will do it and arbitrary interference by military government would completely negate this principle. . . . It is only to be expected that errors and even corrupt acts will be encountered in its enforcement. The administration of criminal justice is not without its abuses in any democracy.

As he saw it, it was "as challenge to military government officers to detect these errors and abuses and to secure the prosecution of the corrupt."[63]

His denazification plans had been made, and—as always—pursuing any elected policy tenaciously and intensely, the General was not going to allow any changes. He chose to express his disappointment to the *Länderrat* only when the visiting chief counsel of a Senate investigating committee[64] pointed out to him that, according to most military government officers, the Germans were whitewashing Nazis and high officials were escaping with practically no punishment.[65] Out of 575 cases charged by the prosecutors to be ardent Nazis, Clay said, the tribunals had found almost 400 to be followers and only twenty-five to be major offenders.

> Military government cannot in full conscience restore self-respon-
> sibility of government to German people who had shown that they
> are unwilling to denazify their public life. I shall follow the work
> of your tribunals during the next sixty days with special attention
> . . . in the hope that there will become evident the will to do their
> job which is not present today. . . . Regardless of its effect on the
> German economy . . . if this will does not develop, military gov-
> ernment will necessarily have to take measures to see that dena-
> zification is carried out. . . . Let us have no misunderstanding.
> Denazification is a 'must.'[66]

But contrary to some interpretations of his speech, he did not in so many words threaten that if there was no improvement denazification would revert to American hands.[67] He knew only too well that there was no way of turning back the clock.

With the increasing encouragement of Washington, the General had used a liberal interpretation of the economic restrictions in his orders. By contrast, as far as denazification was concerned, he felt that there was no leeway and that the mass roundup of all party members, required by JCS #1067 and American public opinion, was mandatory. The enormity of the task was of course clear to him, and he considered a system of gradual amnesties the best way to comply with the literal text of his directives on the one hand and the realities before his eyes on the other. In July, he had issued an amnesty to those born after January 1, 1919, except for ardent Nazis who had occupied positions of leadership. As a result, nearly 900,000 cases were removed from the pending trial list.[68] He was resolved to follow the same route with additional amnesties.

In the meantime he remained convinced of the correctness of his policy. Clay fought back with his usual combative vigor when General McNarney's intelligence officer criticized corrupt and inadequately trained denazification personnel, illegal attempts to obtain favorable affidavits, and the judges' and the witnesses' fear of reprisals, and concluded that the resulting loss of respect for military government laws represented a very serious threat to the security of any American agency in Germany.[69] His office was continually reviewing the denazification program to improve its operation, Clay said, and recently had put into effect a more rigorous supervisory system. In any analysis of the denazification program it ought to be remembered that 25 percent of the population in the American zone was chargeable under the law "and that this in itself will make for an unbelievably large amount of criticism of the law by Germans." He rejected most of the army's specific charges as "very general and supported only by the most hearsay evidence."

Experienced in bureaucractic infighting, he then counterattacked: "If dangerous Nazis are not interned," he wrote, "it is because our mandatory arrest provisions were inadequate or the arrests were not made. The establishment of the mandatory arrest categories was previously a function of G-2 and the arrest of persons in these categories was likewise a function of G-2." And he concluded that "the Army Chief of Staff G-2 has drawn conclusions from the acceptance of only unfavorable reports without a detailed knowledge of the purpose of the program" and that "his criticism is largely destructive." "I cannot agree," Clay finally said, "that the execution of the law is creating a threat to security, nor can I accept the conclusions of the [G-2] report as other than an expression of opinion."[70]

Clay had anticipated that the reaction of American public opinion to a slow implementation of the decartelization provisions of Potsdam would be not as drastic as in the case of denazification failures. It also seems that General Draper's arguments against the program as highly detrimental for a zonal economic recovery had made some impression. Nevertheless, when James Stewart Martin returned in June from a Washington recruiting trip, Clay told him that in his absence the decartelization program had lost considerable ground. Congress was becoming economy minded, the spotlight was turning to "recovery" and "saving the American taxpayers' money." In Clay's opinion, OMGUS would have to move rapidly because the pressure to do nothing at all might be expected to increase.[71] As Martin soon discovered, the views of a stream of visiting American industrialists seemed to reinforce the opposition to decartelization in Draper's economic division. Early in August, Clay lost patience and instructed Martin to go ahead with drafting a decartelization law. Simultaneously the three Allies were informed that pending a four-power agreement the Americans would proceed unilaterally in their zone.

Martin promptly complied, but there was further delay when Murphy questioned the wisdom of proceeding without the British. Draper also claimed Washington was changing its views regarding the mandatory aspects of the law, and Lawrence Wilkinson, his deputy, suggested at a briefing of American editors that decartelization was responsible for delaying Germany's economic recovery. Apprised of these developments, Clay reacted angrily. "It seems to me that a lukewarm attitude toward decartelization is certain to develop if we begin to preach that decartelization will stifle German economy," he wrote to Draper. And he added,

While I am not attempting to carry a brief for small business against big business in the United States, I am certain that the revival of democracy in Germany is dependent on our ability to develop an economy which is not controlled by a handful of banks and holding companies. I would appreciate it if you would make this policy fully understood as representing the official view of OMGUS.

Subsequently, the Deputy Military Governor made it clear that he personally was in favor of mandatory decartelization based on size, and he reminded Draper of his duty as an officer regardless of his personal views.[72]

Progress remained slow, however, because the impending amalgamation of the British and American zones made it necessary to coordinate decartelization procedures. And since the British firmly opposed mandatory controls, with influential Americans at OMGUS in silent sympathy, the eventual outcome was predictable. During the next round of negotiations the Americans continued to modify their position. On instructions from the State Department, the criteria of size, including gross assets, numbers of employees, and sales volume were all dropped, leaving only the question of market share, the most difficult to determine accurately.[73] This was where the issue rested by the end of 1946.

Despite this personal close involvement in the decartelization and denazification processes, General Clay had kept a careful distance from all political entanglements. In his judgment, a policy of neutrality was the only democratic way to give the Germans freedom of choice. By contrast, Marshall Zhukov and his political aides had made it a practice to invite the leaders of political parties to Karlshorst once a week to dinner and a long talk.[74] At least one Soviet liaison officer was permanently assigned to each party's central headquarters and maintained his office there. At the Karlshorst meetings, party leaders were told what attitude they must take toward every issue of the day.[75] If they did not abide by this advice they were either directly removed by the Soviet military administration or were engineered out of office by pressure and terror.

The *Landtag* elections in the Russian zone coincided with the first elections in Berlin. Consistently, from the early days of the occupation on, the Soviets had urged the Social Democrats to unite with the Communists, a pressure which eventually had results. The new Socialist Unity Party (SED) had a radical Marxist program which threatened revolution in case "reactionary capitalists" resisted socialism. By refusing to register the two non-Communist parties in most of the communities in the Russian zone and by granting about fifty times as much newsprint to the SED as to the two other parties combined, the Soviets set out to assure a Communist victory.[76] Moreover, while the SED could hold public meetings without restrictions, the other parties had to apply for permission for each meeting and submit all details about it in advance. Under one pretext or another, permission was frequently denied.

Concerned about the situation in the East, some of Clay's political officers repeatedly urged the General to speak up at the Control Council in opposition to these developments. He flatly refused.[77] As long as unification was the fundamental part of his mission, to do so seemed counterproductive to him. In a similar vein, he disagreed when Washington suggested material and moral assistance to the democratic parties of the West. "If we did," he cabled the War Department, "military government would have clearly violated its announced principles of complete political neutrality and such action would be misunderstood in Germany and would prove a step backward in teaching democracy. I do not wish to be pushed into premature action by ill-advised tactics of the Socialist Unity Party."[78] He went even further by refusing to license a "political press" as he called it, because there was no need for it. "While newspapers controlled by political parties are not permitted at the present time," he advised Washington, "this results from the need for the establishment of a strong independent press in the American zone. We do not believe that we can establish a free and independent press in Germany if we deviate from our present policy by attempting to establish party-controlled newspapers with the limited newsprint now available."[79]

He remained adamant in his refusal to imitate the Soviet methods of favoring one party over the other. The best way to diminish Communist strength, he said, was to raise the economic levels of Western Germany. In accord with his somewhat theoretical concept of American democracy, he believed that once the mechanics of a democratic system had been established, leaders would naturally emerge to be confirmed by their compatriots. The idea that the military government might actively promote future leadership was repugnant to his basic democratic creed.[80] In other words, in contrast to the Russians who were resolved to be a factor within German social and political life,[81] Clay conceived of military government as a factor outside German political life.[82] He therefore also declined to intervene when the SPD, acting on its own, refused to merge with the SED in Berlin.

The results of the elections, a testimony to German democratic backbone, confirmed the judiciousness of his policy. Even in the Soviet zone the SED got only 47.5 percent of the votes, the balance going to the non-Communist parties. In Berlin the SPD was the big winner with 48.7 percent of the votes. The SED, with 19.8 percent, had fewer votes than the Communist Party alone had gotten in any election from 1928 to 1933. The election marked a turning point in Berlin politics. A new city government was formed in accordance with these results, although until 1948 the Soviets—using their veto in the Allied *Kommandatura*—were able to largely nullify the popular decision.[83]

In the West, as of September 1945 OMGUS had licensed all applicants except former Nazis to form political parties. The result was a multiplicity of parties, but only four—the Social Democrats, the Christian Democratic

Union, the Liberal Democratic Party and the Communists—assumed wider importance. As it turned out, under the "nonpolitical" auspices of the Clay regime the old social groups in Germany managed to consolidate conditions along the lines of the pre-Nazi social order and thereby prevent radical changes. The General neither engineered a social revolution in German political life nor had he orders instructing him to do so. As a result, under to auspices of the American military government, the pre-Nazi political pattern and behavior emerged almost intact.[84]

Clay was equally consistent in the defense of his democratic princples when it came to a debate with some bureaucrats at the State Department. At the department's request, in August he had submitted copies of the draft constitutions of the three *Länder*. In his covering message he indicated that the military government had given the German authorities the basic principles necessary for a democratic constitution. As long as these principles were safeguarded in the constitutions, he did not intend to comment on the details. "These constitutions must go to the German people as a free creation of their elected representatives and with the least possible taint of military government dictation."[85] Clay therefore exploded when two months later he received from the War Department a long list of constitutional changes suggested by the State Department. In an angry reply he pointed out that "the constitutional assemblies of the three *Länder* composed of representatives freely elected by the people had devoted three months of sincere and conscientious effort to the drafting of these constitutions. Our own experts have worked with them through this period but by power of suggestion rather than by instruction. The changes that Washington proposed, he went on, could not be obtained by suggestion but only by military government decree. "Accordingly, with the concurrence of Assistant Secretary of War Peterson, who happened to be in Berlin, he recommended that if the State Department persisted the issues should be brought to the attention of the President.[86] That quickly settled the matter. By December 8 the three constitutions were confirmed by popular referenda. Two days later, when addressing a zonal meeting of military government officers in Stuttgart, Clay announced that the constitutions of the German states "must become the Bible for our action. . . . When the constitutions recently voted in the three *Länder* go into effect," he said, "you must be as zealous in guarding German rights as if you were constitutional lawyers in the United States."[87]

General Clay had followed the progress toward a bizonal merger with mixed feelings. In the Control Council, General McNarney, as instructed, had repeated Secretary Byrnes' invitation to proceed with economic unification, but only Great Britain accepted. "We have cast the die here in economic integration with the British zone," Clay wrote to Dodge. "This is forcing the issue and while we hope it will expedite quadripartite action, it may just have its reverse effect. However, I could not continue longer in economic stagnation and this at last will help. . . ."[88] Although he himself had suggested the merger as a temporary expedient, the Deputy Military

Governor knew that it was no panacea. American and British views on the economic organization of the combined area differed, and the socialization issue in particular was bound to cause conflicts.

At the same time, Clay had not given up on a quadripartite solution. He was concerned about "the old red scare" which, he thought, was gripping the United States.[89] And George Kennan's "Long Telegram" from Moscow, stressing the Soviet danger and recommending a policy of containment, had been distributed to senior military commanders abroad and had aroused Clay's ire. The General was "pretty violent against it," Murphy advised Freeman Matthews at State.[90] But even Matthews' assurance that it represented "the now dominant virtually unchallenged outlook in high policy circles" failed to affect Clay's doggedly held views. "If things go on this way, a scrap with the Russians is inevitable," he told Stuart Symington, the Assistant Secretary of Air, who visited Berlin in July. "However," he insisted, "the situation is far from hopeless."[91] A Soviet offer to compromise received a few weeks later encouraged this optimistic outlook.

Faced with conflicting pressures and a still undetermined policy of his government, the Deputy Military Governor concluded that he had no choice but to move simultaneously in two directions. Both the bizonal solution and the negotiations with the Soviets would have to be actively pursued.

Accordingly, in a meeting on August 9 with Sir Brian Robertson, a bipartite board composed of the two deputy military governors was established to "act as the final seat of authority for the unification . . . subject only to the policies of the two governments." A common standard of living, a sharing of economic resources and a common export-import policy were some of the agreed-upon principles. Proceeds from past exports were to be placed in a common account to be utilized in payment of approved imports. Also, five German executive agencies would work directly with the two military governments "with no German machinery interposed." It also was agreed that these agencies would not be located in only one town, which might give the impression that a joint capital for the two zones was being created. Political unity was not an aim of this arrangement, and the German authorities were informed that there was no intention of interfering with the political structure of either zone or of setting up a unified government.[92]

Because the delegation of administrative and legislative authority to Germans was much more advanced in the American than in the British zone, Clay had some special problems to contend with. Since its creation, the *Länderrat* had been an agent government, subject in its legislative moves to military government concurrence. However, as soon as the constitutions of the three states of the American zone had been voted on by public referenda, there arose the embarrassing problem of reconciling democratically arrived-at legislation with authoritative controls.[93] In a similar vein, the relation of the respective authorities of the new bizonal German executive agencies and the *Länderrat* had to be clarified. The General tried to square the circle by issuing a directive concerning "Relationship between Military and Civil Government (U.S. Zone) subsequent to adoption of *Land* constitutions." He followed this up by instructions which tried to define the relationships of the new bizonal agencies and projected *Länder* governments.[94] While he specified the extensive restrictions to be imposed upon civil government, he was less successful in other respects. The real authority of the *Land* governments in the American zone remained unclear, and conflicting interpretations caused administrative and legislative conflicts as soon as Bizonia became a reality.[95]

Undoubtedly the Soviet government also realized that a period of critical decisions was on hand. The bizonal initiative following closely after the American-British determined stand in Iran demonstrated that Western patience had its limits. The time for Russian concessions was on hand. Accordingly, a diplomatic "feeler" was forthcoming. The opening move came at the economic directorate when one of Don Humphrey's Soviet colleagues (apparently Boris T. Kolpakov) cast off his usual aloofness and asked to be shown an American film. Invited to Humphrey's home and having seen the film, the Russian with ill-assumed casualness began to complain about the reparations stop. It was "needlessly harsh," he declared. He then turned to an emotional description of his country's desperate economic need for consumer goods, and became really impassioned on the topic of bicycles. Fifty years must elapse, he declared, before the Soviet per capita production would equal Sweden's. In the end he said in so many words that the Soviets would go to great lengths in making other concessions in order to get the required reparations deliveries. This Soviet initiative was followed by American-Soviet pourparlers which moved up to the levels of Draper-Koval and eventually Clay-Sokolovsky. The final result was the draft of a compromise that entailed the supply of Russian raw materials to Germany in exchange for a flow of German goods, and a dismantlement halt for at least ten years. As envisaged at Potsdam, there would be an immediate economic unification of the four zones, the establishment of German administrative agencies, a monetary reform, a sharing of resources and a common export-import plan.[96] The recently completed Level of Industry Plan would be discarded with total permitted industrial production about doubled.

It was clear to Clay that the Soviet move could not have been made without an explicit sanction by the Kremlin. Don Humphrey was therefore instructed to prepare a tentative financial plan which would implement the suggested compromise.[97] Accompanied by Murphy's enthusiastic commentary, an outline of the proposals was reported to Washington. "In addition to economic and financial unity," Murphy's cable read, "we should try to obtain equally important political objectives. This may be our last opportunity to use such a potent bargaining position in Germany for this purpose."[98] There was no immediate response. Since Clay had been called to New York by Byrnes in connection with the bizonal talks, he decided to present the Secretary with a comprehensive and up-to-date overview of the German problem.[99] It listed four issues which could not be solved at the

General's level: the disarmament treaty, the peace treaty, the question of German boundaries, and the conditions which had to be fulfilled for the economic unification of Germany. The first two items were intergovernmental problems. "It would be presumptuous for military government," Clay wrote, "to comment or to offer suggestions." As to the question of boundaries, he merely summarized earlier comments on the respective economic consequences of ceding the Ruhr and the Saar. It was the impasse in obtaining political and economic unity in Berlin which occupied the greatest part of this exceptional memorandum. As Clay pointed out, the stalemate resulted on the one hand from French opposition to any unification proposals until boundary claims had been settled, and on the other hand from Soviet resistance to a common utilization of German resources and to a common acceptance of responsibility for deficits.

With regard to France, Clay concluded that only full agreement by the three other powers and a firm presentation of their agreed-upon views would succeed in obtaining French cooperation. In addition, the Saar would probably have to be ceded to France. As to Soviet opposition, Clay acknowledged that "it rested primarily on [the Soviet Union's] need and desire for current production as reparations." Fully aware of the crucial significance of the issue, Clay then summarized some promising reparations studies by his economic experts and, after listing the pros and cons of a compromise, he offered the following appraisal:

> It is impossible to evaluate specifically the advantages and disadvantages until there is an agreed plan for the German economy in which the cost of reparations from current production is determined in dollars and cents. . . .
>
> The question is, therefore, whether or not such a proposal deserves full consideration. . . . If in fact, German unification is impossible unless this question is resolved, a *failure* to investigate it fully means the partition of Germany. . . . Obviously this establishes the frontier of Western democracy along the Elbe. [Clay's emphasis.]
>
> Certainly no consideration should be given to a plan for economic unification in which production for reparations is authorized without complete understanding that political unification would be undertaken simultaneously, and that production for reparations would cease if political unification proved impossible along democratic lines. . . .
>
> We have much at stake in gaining the opportunity to fight for democractic ideals in Eastern Germany and in Eastern Europe. This opportunity would result from the true unification of Germany under quadripartite control.
>
> Therefore, it does appear worthwhile to investigate fully this possible solution to the internal German problem. How much we are willing to pay to achieve our objectives is unknown, but *it is possible that the investigation may indicate that the cost in dollars and cents*

is not too high, particularly when measured in terms of European stability and the possible contributions of such stability to world peace.[100] [Emphasis added.]

It seems doubtful that this remarkable document with its prophetic implications received serious consideration. When questioned on this score in 1975, the General replied that the proposed study was never made and that he was not sure of the reasons.[101] By November 1946 Secretary Byrnes was on his way out. Also, as Ben Cohen recalled, "Byrnes was very sensitive to the forces about. . . . Byrnes would go as far as he could to make a settlement based on the highest common denominator of the forces above him. And so, as the forces began to stiffen, he began to stiffen."[102] In this case, the tracks for a stiff new policy had already been set, under the auspices of Clark Clifford and Admiral William D. Leahy as Truman's foreign-policy advisors, of General Walter Bedell Smith as Ambassador in Moscow and of George Kennan at the State Department. "No appeasement but containment" was to be the United States doctrine. Clay's farsighted recommendations—if considered at all—were set aside and the decision reached to proceed at least on a tentative basis with the fusion of the two zones. Accordingly, unification was formalized in December 1946 by a Byrnes-Bevin agreement which provided for a pooling of all economic resources and imports in order to achieve a common standard of living. It also stipulated that the two zones were to be treated as a single area for economic purposes. The economic unification was to be accomplished by German administrative agencies scheduled to operate under the joint control of the American and British commanders in chief. While working out the details of the merger, the two military governors were initially under instructions to avoid the appearance of a bipartite political action that might tend to reduce the chances for the unification of all of Germany. For tactical purposes as well as for reasons of protocol, the Soviet Union and France not only were repeatedly invited to participate in the bilateral venture but also were kept informed as to American-British plans for the bizonal organization.

FOOTNOTES

1. Robert Murphy, *Diplomat Among Warriors*, pp. 290–291.
2. Vassily Yershov, "Confiscation and Plunder by the Army of Occupation," in *Soviet Economic Policy in Post-war Germany*, ed. by Robert Slusser.
3. Peter Nettl, "German Reparations in the Soviet Empire," p. 304. *Foreign Affairs* 29, No. 2, (January 1951).
4. Demaree Bess, "American Viceroy in Germany," in *Saturday Evening Post*, May 10, 1947, p. 78.
5. Lucius D. Clay, *Decision in Germany*, p. 78.
6. James F. Byrnes, *Speaking Frankly*, pp. 175–176; *Foreign Relations of the United States 1946*, Vol. II, pp. 846–857.
7. Ibid.
8. Clay, *Decision*, pp. 127–129; *Foreign Relations . . . 1946*, Vol. II, pp. 868–873; Byrnes, *Speaking*, pp. 177–182.
9. *Foreign Relations . . . 1946*, Vol. II, pp. 897–989.
10. Clay to Echols, July 19, 1946. OMGUS 177–1/3 N.A.
11. Ibid. Respectively these five agencies were to operate in such fields as finance, transportation, communications, industry and foreign trade.
12. Ibid.
13. AGWAR to OMGUS, August 12, 1946. OMGUS 177–3/3.
14. Clay to Schulgen, August 7, 1946. CC 1378. R.G.200 N.A.
15. W-97164 in Jean Smith, ed., *The Papers of Lucius D. Clay*, p. 254.
16. Clay for Hilldring, August 15, 1946, in Smith, *The Papers*, p. 252.
17. Clay for War Department, August 16, 1946. CC 1731 R.G.200 N.A.
18. Clay to Patterson, August 17, 1946, in Smith, *The Papers*, pp. 254–255.
19. Author's interview with Mrs. Lucius D. Clay, Washington, D.C., August 4, 1979.
20. Clay for Byrnes (handwritten), August 19, 1946, in Smith, *The Papers*, p. 255.
21. Clay for McNarney, August 21, 1946, in Smith, *The Papers*, p. 259.
22. Bedell Smith to Eisenhower, August 23, 1946, in Smith, *The Papers*, Eisenhower Library. As cited in *The Papers*, p. 260.
23. Jean Smith interview with General Clay, February 25, 1971.
24. Ibid.
25. Ibid.
26. *Der Tagesspiegel*, September 7, 1946. Nr. 209 Beiblatt; Clay, *Decision*, pp. 79–80.
27. Clay, *Decision*, pp. 79–80.
28. Don Humphrey, private papers.
29. *Department of State Bulletin*, September 15, 1946, p. 496 ff. Byrnes, *Speaking Frankly*, pp. 188–192.
30. Clay, *Decision*, p. 81.
31. Author's interviews with Margaret Allen, Washington, D.C., October 25, 1980; Edna Shelley, St. Louis, Missouri, October 27, 1980.
32. Author's interview with George Kennan, Princeton, N.J., March 19, 1980.
33. Delbert Clark, *Again the Goosestep*, p. 35.
34. Don Humphrey, private papers.
35. *The Forrestal Diaries*, p. 183.
36. Author's interviews with Mrs. Lucius D. Clay, McLean, Va., April 1, 1981; Edloe Donnan, Manchester, Mo., October 27, 1980.
37. Clay, *Decision*, pp. 81–82.
38. Clay for Eisenhower, September 8, 1946, in Smith, *The Papers*, p. 263.
39. Jean Smith interview with General Clay, February 25, 1971.
40. Hoover Report—Food and Agriculture, US-UK Zone of Germany, February 1947, pp. 56–57. OMGUS records N.A.
41. Gustav Stolper, *German Realities*, p. 96.
42. Hans Schlange-Schöningen, *Im Schatten des Hungers* Anhang 18. After the currency reform, the German collection of domestic wheat and other cereals promptly increased by 50 percent.

43. Stolper, *German Realities*, pp. 95–108.
44. *Foreign Commerce and Navigation of the United States* 1946, Vol. I; Foreign Trade Statistics, Part A.
45. "Import of Cigarettes," OMGUS records 82–3/8. File 14.N.A.
46. John H. Backer, *The Decision to Divide Germany*, pp. 123–131.
47. Author's interview with James O'Donnell, Washington, D.C., March 8, 1980.
48. Jean Smith interview with General Clay, February 9, 1971.
49. Ibid. Colonel R. Joe Rogers interview with General Clay, New York, N.Y., January 24, 1973.
50. Ibid.
51. Ibid.
52. Clay, *Decision*, pp. 250–253.
53. Wolfgang Friedman, *The Allied Military Government of Germany* p. 43.
54. Clay for White, November 2, 1946. CC 6679, R.G.200.N.A.
55. Jean Smith interview with General Clay, February 19, 1971.
56. Ibid.
57. William E. Griffith, "The Denazification Program in the U.S. Zone of Germany," Doctoral Dissertation, Harvard University, April 1950, pp. 302–316.
58. Ibid.
59. Ibid.
60. Memorandum by Dr. Karl Loewenstein as cited in Griffith, "The Denazification," pp. 172–173.
61. Griffith, "The Denazification," pp. 315–316.
62. Lutz Niethammer, *Entnazifizierung in Bayern*, pp. 348–349.
63. OMGUS letter to Director OMGH, September 6, 1946. Subject: Defeatist Attitude toward Denazification on the part of some Military Government personnel. A.G. Records OMGUS papers, N.A.
64. November 5, 1946.
65. Confidential Report to the Special Senate Committee Investigating the National Defense Program, November 22, 1946. George Meader, Special Counsel.
66. Griffith, "The Denazification," pp. 326–330; Niethammer, *Entnazifizierung*, p. 354.
67. Ibid.
68. Clay, *Decision*, p. 260; Niethammer, *Entnazifizierung*, p. 354.
69. USFET (G-2) memorandum to C/S. Subject: "German Denazification Boards." Dec. File 014.3, Box 15, OMGUS records N.A.
70. First endorsement, Clay to Commanding General USFET, December 26, 1946. Dec. File 014.3, Box 15 N.A.
71. James Stewart Martin, *All Honorable Men*, pp. 192–193.
72. Ibid., pp. 194–204.
73. Graham Taylor, "The Rise and Fall of Antitrust in Occupied Germany, 1945–1948," in *The Prologue*, Spring 1979, p. 33.
74. Louis Wiesner, "Organized Labor in Postwar Germany," p. 195.
75. Ibid.
76. Ibid., p. 213.
77. Ibid., p. 214.
78. Clay for War Department, CC 2135, August 20, 1946, R.G.200 N.A.
79. Clay for War Department, CC 7385, December 15, 1946, R.G.200 N.A.
80. Leonard Krieger, "The Interregnum in Germany, March-August 1945," in *Political Science Quarterly*, Vol. LXIV, December 1949, Number 4.
81. Ibid.
82. Ibid.
83. Wiesner, "Organized Labor," p. 194.
84. Seymour R. Bolton, "Military Government and the German Political Parties," in *The Annals*, January 1950.
85. Clay for War Department, August 23, 1946, CC 2417. Clay for Echols, October 15, 1946, CC 5554, RG.200 N.A.
86. Ibid.
87. *The New York Times*, October 10, 1946, p. 8.
88. Clay to Dodge, July 31, 1946, Dodge Papers, Detroit Public Library, Detroit, Mich.
89. Clay to Dodge, July 25, 1946, Dodge Papers, Detroit Public Library, Detroit, Mich.

90. Murphy to Matthews, April 3, 1946. 861.00/4–346. State Dept. Papers, N.A.; Matthews to Murphy, April 18, 1946. Matthews file N.A.

91. W. Stuart Symington, Memorandum to President; Interview with General Clay, July 25, 29, 30, 1946.

92. Joint U.S.-British Meeting on Economic Unity, August 9, 1946, Box 435–2/3. OMGUS records N.A.

93. Clay to Robertson as cited in John Gimbel, "Education of a new German Leadership," in *Political Science Quarterly*, Vol. LXXXIII, No. 2, June 1968.

94. Edward Litchfield et al, *Governing Postwar Germany*, pp. 26–27.

95. Lia Härtel, *Der Länderrat des Amerikanischen Besatzungsgebietes*, Anlage 16; Gimbel, "Education," pp. 262–263.

96. Joseph Alsop, "Russian Need for Reparations May Avert Partition of Germany," *New York Herald Tribune*, November 11, 1946, p. 7. *The Economist*, "Reparations from Germany," November 23, 1946, pp. 833–834. Author's interview with Don Humphrey, Winchester, Mass., October 10, 1980.

97. Don Humphrey to Draper, November 2, 1946. CFM file OMGUS records 177–3/13. N.A.

98. *Foreign Relations . . . 1946*, Vol. V, The British Commonwealth, pp. 621–623 and 624–625.

99. Clay for Byrnes, November 1946, in Smith, *The Papers*, pp. 279–284.

100. Ibid.

101. General Clay's letter to author, August 18, 1975.

102. Daniel Yergin interview with Ben Cohen. As cited in Yergin, *The Shattered Peace*, p. 162.

CHAPTER SEVEN

The President Sets Policy

THE RESULTS OF THE CONGRESSIONAL ELECTIONS IN NOVEMBER 1946 WERE EVEN more startling than had been expected. A Democratic majority of 53 in the House had to give way to a Republican majority of 58, and in the Senate the Democratic majority of 19 was transformed into a Republican one of 6. A congressional assault against the occupation's costs, which had always concerned Lucius Clay, was to be expected. Familiar as he was with the highways and byways of Capitol Hill he feared that the authorization and appropriation committees of the two houses, if left to their own devices, would court disaster for the military government. As the Republican tide grew through the summer and autumn of 1946 it became increasingly clear to him that some countervailing action would have to be taken. There had to be an intensive and systematic lobbying effort on behalf of the army, which only a Republican of some stature could provide. Herbert Hoover was a natural choice.

In the early spring of 1946, the former President and Truman-appointed chairman of the Famine Emergency Commission had traveled 35,000 miles and visited twenty-two countries, alerting Truman upon his return that "hunger was hanging over the houses of 800 million people—over one-third of the world." In the course of this round-the-world trip, Hoover also had stopped in Berlin, where the Deputy Military Governor had seen to it that he was briefed by American agricultural experts and by the minister-presidents of the three *Länder* in the U.S. zone. The parting promise of the former President that "the American people would do whatever possible to help and that in this regard they would look at the future and not at the past" had been a source of considerable encouragement for the German officials who had participated in the briefings.[1] Now it was necessary to call on him again.

The 1946 harvest had been good, with favorable weather counterbalancing the shortage of fertilizers and seeds. However, the winter of 1946–47 was accompanied by numerous setbacks, which affected food distribution in Germany. Because of a number of strikes in the United States, imports from America did not arrive as expected. Furthermore, the indigenous grain collection left much to be desired, and—to make matters worse—Germany was visited by the most severe winter freeze in a generation. Inland waterways were completely blocked for two or three months, electric power failed and railway locomotives broke down in the hundreds. As Clay expected, the cumulative result of these misfortunes would be a new food crisis in the spring of 1947 with less than 1,100 calories per day available for distribution in the bizone. More help was clearly needed.[2]

In the course of his frequent communications with the Pentagon concerning the food situation and the need for additional appropriations, Clay had made it clear that in his opinion Hoover's help was of critical importance.[3] Accordingly—when election returns were barely in—Robert Patterson, the Secretary of War, sent word to the former President that he would appreciate a meeting. "We have some problems on food that I would like very much to discuss with you," the telegram read. When the two men met, and also in subsequent pourparlers, Hoover intimated that he would be willing to make an economic survey of the German and Austrian territory under American occupation, but his mandate would have to go beyond an examination of food problems alone and the invitation ought to come directly from the White House. Moreover, in accord with Clay's thoughts, he indicated that his principal service would be to assist in keeping the Republican Congress in line so that the army's program would have the necessary support.[4]

There was some concern in top government circles that a broad mandate might lead to encroachments on the State Department policy prerogatives,[5] but in Hoover's two meetings with Truman an agreement was nevertheless reached. The former President was going to Germany on an economic mission directed to food and its collateral problems, he personally announced to the press.[6] The purpose was not so much to determine Germany's needs for the next two or three months, he said, as it was to conduct a long-range study with the aim of easing the U.S. taxpayer's burden. Although the trip was termed a fact-finding mission, Hoover apparently had a definite notion of the facts he was going to find: the need for increased exports and foreign exchange, the necessity for an upward adjustment of the level of industry plan, and the exigency for an indefinite deferment of reparations.[7]

Hoover left New York on February 2 in the company of Tracy L. Voorhees, who represented the Secretary of War, and a group of agricultural, medical, and nutritional experts. Frankfurt, Berlin, Hamburg, Stuttgart, Vienna, and Rome were his principal stopping points. In Frankfurt he was joined by Clay, who had put the Commanding General's six-car train—operated by a German crew and originally owned by Herman Göring—at the mission's disposal.[8] The former President and his entourage slept and ate on the train while the dining car served as a conference room for the almost uninterrupted series of meetings with German economic, financial, and nutritional experts.

Among the staff accompanying Hoover were two men intimately acquainted with German affairs. One, Louis Lochner, had for many years headed the Associated Press office in Berlin. The other, Dr. Gustav Stolper, an Austrian-born publicist, had been a member of the pre-Hitler parliament, the Reichstag. He had edited several well-respected economic journals and had also written a book on Germany's prewar economy. He had emigrated to the United States because of his Jewish ancestry and had become an American citizen. Stolper was a conservative; most of his personal contacts were among Germany's upper middle class, generally nationalistic in its outlook. Men like former Secretary of State Bernhard von Bülow, the ambassadors Adolf Köster, Leopold von Hoesch, and Herbert von Dirksen, as well as Graf Albrecht von Bernstorff, were some of his prominent friends.[9] Like Hoover, Stolper had gone to Germany with some definite ideas about what the problems were, and before leaving America he had outlined them to the former President. Next to the food problem of "a truncated Germany after Russian and Polish annexations" were the "stymieing of German entrepeneurial spirits" by the dismantling of industry and "the arrests of thousands of managers in the course of denazification." The "threatening socialization or neutralization" of the Ruhr through the British Labor Government was another issue very much on Stolper's mind.[10] He shared many of Hoover's political and economic views and his influence was therefore considerable. As one Berlin observer put it, "He was always at Hoover's elbow." Thanks to his extensive contacts in German society, Stolper was able to assemble within a few weeks the background material that Hoover needed for his reports.

The bias of Stolper's German background and anti-Soviet leanings, however, made him fail to draw attention to a critical factor in the German economy which might have affected Washington's political outlook. The German in the Western zones, for all practical purposes, was essentially passive, interested only in protecting his caloric and financial substance while observing the rescue efforts of his occupiers. Weighing and food programs, although necessary, actually aggravated this situation. Only a currency reform would have provided the missing work incentives, money that had some value. In its absence, the prevailing economic, moral, and spiritual paralysis was bound to continue, thus rendering any judgment about the actual state of the German economy incomplete at best, delusory at worst.

Clay was on Hoover's train most of the time. As it approached Hamburg the General's relentlessly driving personality left an indelible impression on one of his lowly subordinates. The train commander, Oliver Margolin, was standing in the bay when the door was opened and he was brusquely ordered to "stand aside." "It was General Clay in a voice and manner I never forgot," the former chief warrant officer recalled. "We had arrived in the yards at about 8:00 A.M. but the British, in whose zone Hamburg was, had set our arrival for 9:00 A.M. Ordered a few minutes later "to take the train in," Margolin still can see "the puzzled expression on the engineer's face" when he relayed the order.

It was one of unheard disbelief [sic], but take the train in he did, upsetting I suppose other rail traffic in the station at that time. Needless to say no one—British authorities or other—was there to meet us. So we passed the time at the platform until the reception party arrived. . . . It was the flavor of the man, the impression of him towering over me at close quarters in the bay of that train's open door with the unexpected imperious voice—that impression sticks with me as authentic. [11]

Three reports on the trip were expected to go to the White House— one on Austria and two on Germany. The report on German agriculture and food requirements dealt primarily with short-term problems and was drafted to support the army's current appropriations request. Clay's staff provided the statistical data and wrote most of the text, which vividly described the housing situation ("the worst that civilization had ever seen"); the shortage of coal and its consequences; and the deplorable condition of seven million children and adolescents as well as the increased death toll among the ages. [12] The report suggested that "a great mass of Germans . . . have sunk to the lowest level known in a hundred years of history," and it concluded that "our flag flies over those people. The flag means something besides military power." [13]

Whereas the report on Germany's food requirements was meant to justify the increased burden on the American taxpayer, the third report aimed at demonstrating how in the future the cost could be eliminated entirely. Labeled "The necessary steps for promotion of German exports so as to relieve American taxpayers of the burdens of relief and for economic recovery of Europe," it was drafted in its main parts by Stolper. [14] It was an important document not only because of its political ramifications but also because it reached the White House at a strategic time when winds of history were shifting. War romanticism had been fading and Soviet expansionist policies around the world—in Romania, Poland, Iran, Bulgaria—had convinced America's decision makers that they could not sit down with the Russians and resolve questions. [15] Lucius Clay, stubbornly engrossed with his German mission, was increasingly isolated in his endeavor to find an accommodation with the Kremlin. Eventually there had to be a clash of antipodal perceptions.

Although the Republican ex-President knew better, Hoover used as a starting point for his report a politically motivated attack on the defunct Morgenthau Plan and JCS #1067 which, thanks to Clay's political skill, had by that time also become a dead letter. Hoover's next statement, to the effect that Europe's production could not be restored without the restoration of Germany—a forerunner of the Marshall Plan concept—was already common wisdom in the spring of 1947. He avoided acknowledging that about 85 percent of Germany's prewar industrial capacity was intact by asserting that the extent of the "loss of peaceful industry had not been determined."

In a similar fashion he escaped any entanglements in the still popular de-nazification and decartelization programs by suggesting only "that certain phases of them limited recovery." And he ignored the key issue of economic paralysis by merely stating that "an inflated currency and no adequate banking system hampers all forward movements." This was followed by a broadside against the level of industry concept and "the illusion that Germany's light industry could pay for imports making Germany self-supporting." The State Department's announcement of December 1945 that the level of industry concept was temporary "and not designed to impose permanent limitations on the German economy" was again not mentioned. Nor was there any reference to informal Soviet suggestions that there had to be an upward revision of the level of industry.

Hoover then presented his principal recommendations—namely, the end of dismantlement, the end of level of industry, with no limitations on German heavy industry, the return to their German owners of the industrial enterprises expropriated by the Soviet military government and no separation of the Ruhr and the Rhineland. Negotiations with American allies should continue on these premises and if no agreement could be reached the Bizonia project should be actively implemented. In most respects Hoover's proposals coincided with the current thinking of the Truman Administration. Only the emphasis on the revitalization of Germany's heavy industry was new and considered still somewhat provocative.[16]

On the return flight to America, Hoover had stopped in London to inform the British government of his findings and of the recommendations he was going to make.[17] But even before his departure from Germany, he had urged Clay to release certain stocks of available American food and to start a child-feeding program promptly. About $19 million worth of highly nutritious food had been stockpiled for displaced persons, and on Hoover's instruction it became the first allotment assigned to a program to provide 350-calorie noon meal for more than 3.5 million children in the bizonal area.[18] Widely advertised as it was, the program could leave no doubt in German minds that under the aegis of their conquerors no starvation would be tolerated.

As Clay had calculated, the former President's intervention became decisive for the continuation of the occupation's financial support. An experienced politician, Hoover saw to it that his appearances before congressional committees were preceded or accompanied by radio addresses and covered by influential papers and journals.[19] His appeals to the conscience of the American people aimed at building up a grass-roots movement in support of his presentations to Congress. Moreover, he personally lobbied individual senators before testifying at the various congressional committees.

The obstacles that had to be overcome, however, were formidable; Eisenhower was correct when he had informed McNarney in February that "Congress was determined to cut drastically the amount of civil relief."[20] As customary and as foreseen by Clay, the first attack of the Washington solons was directed against "an unreasonably large staff." But the personnel at OMGUS had been cut to the bone and it was a charge that could be easily refuted, especially since there were vocal and well-founded complaints that the remaining Americans were too few to make effective controls possible. Charges that the Germans were not doing their share and that they were increasingly lax in fulfilling their agricultural quotas, on the other hand, were much more difficult to disprove. Clay himself, when testifying before Congress in November, had indicated that "strong-arm methods" might have to be used to assure compliance.[21] When the food crisis in Germany became most acute in the spring of 1947, press reports on the cut to 1,300 and later to 1,100 calories were often juxtaposed by others describing the uncontrolled black market, and questioning whether Germans were trying to help themselves or were actually sabotaging the food effort.[22] Headlines such as "German buys 620 pounds of food in two hours in starving Bavaria" and the detailed description of how easily this was done could not fail to undermine the army's position before the appropriations committees.[23] Clay was in a quandary. On the one hand he had to exhort German officials to do a better job and sometimes—although he had no illusions in this regard—to threaten the enforcement of delivery quotas by the U.S. Constabulary. On the other hand, when pleading with Washington for additional food supplies, he had to counter vocal charges that the Germans were not doing their share and that the Military Governor's own public statements were testimony to that effect.[24] Actually there was considerable doubt even among the Berlin staff about the effectiveness of food collection. Some officers had calculated that the large food shipments from the United States should have made available a ration of 2,300 calories rather than 1,500 calories or less; some of this information apparently was leaked to the press.[25]

Well-documented reports about black-market operations in American cigarettes also hurt the army's case, although the full deleterious impact of these transactions both on American prestige and on the morale of the occupying army was hardly recognized at the time.[26] When the army, with the Deputy Military Governor's reluctant concurrence, tried to put a stop to it in March 1947, the direct mailing of cigarettes to occupied Germany came to a temporary halt.[27] The problem was not solved, however. Shipments of tobacco products to the PXs continued. Moreover, as Clay had expected, astute exporters simply shipped to Switzerland, whose porous borders with the French zone were beyond American control.[28] The Pentagon's admonition to Clay "to take appropriate action to prevent imports of this nature from perimeter countries" only showed the perceptual gap that separated Washington from the field.

The Appropriations Committees of the House and Senate had become in many instances the arbiter of policy in areas where jurisdiction was unclear or incomplete or mixed. When it came to the occupation, the most important formulation of policy rested in the hands of the Appropriations

Committee of the House.[29] Fortunately, the powerful Chairman of the committee, John Taber, was a great admirer of Hoover and had complete confidence in the former President's judgment.[30] Thanks to Hoover's persuasive testimonies in the committee's open and executive sessions, and with Taber's active support, the formidable legislative hurdles were eventually overcome. A deficiency appropriation of $300 million for fiscal year 1947 to cover the occupied areas' requirements for food, chemical fertilizer, and seed was passed by Congress, as was an appropriation of $600 million for the following year.

While still in Germany, Hoover had shown great interest in the status of German export trade. Clay, with the assistance of Draper and others, had given him some detailed briefings. An early American plan for an Allied export-import bureau as a forerunner to a German foreign trade agency, Clay said, had been rejected in December 1945 as too advanced even by the British.[31] Consequently, in the absence of a four-power accord, OMGUS was attempting to promote exports on its own but, even apart from the shortages of coal and raw materials, the difficulties encountered were tremendous. German manufacturers showed little interest in selling abroad since their prices were frozen, and in any event all they would receive in return were Reichsmarks of little practical value. The European countries, however, traditionally the principal partners in Germany's foreign trade, were unwilling to share their scant dollar reserves. Instead they were eager to balance accounts by shipping commodities such as vegetables from Holland or fruits from Italy. As Clay explained,[32] Germany could ill afford under the prevailing emergency conditions to spend severely restricted funds on foods low in calories; they request high-calorie food, and that requirement had to be the decisive factor in food imports. His export-import policy, the General said, had therefore become the source of frequent frictions with the State Department, which always took the European side. However, as he emphasized, he had handled appropriated funds for many years, and he felt strongly that they had to be zealously used only for the purposes voted by Congress.[33] The budget for Germany was his and not the State Department's responsibility.

The Belgian and Dutch governments had been particularly vocal in their complaints, which therefore often had made headlines. In particular, the General said, their demand to use the Low Country ports for imports into Germany had become a celebrated controversy. But port charges in Rotterdam and Antwerp would have to be paid in dollars, while German port charges for imports were paid in Reichsmarks provided by the German authorities.[34] The State Department naturally wanted to assist the liberated countries and to subsidize Europe indirectly at the expense of his German budget, Clay concluded, but this he was not going to permit.

When questioned by Hoover about the details of the bizonal fusion agreement that had recently been signed in New York, the General pointed out that the initial responsibility for the development of German foreign trade in the bizone had been assigned to a Joint Export-Import Agency. It was expected, however, that its mission would be transferred to a German agency for foreign trade that would operate under joint American-British supervision. Clay himself had taken the position that the respective financial responsibilities should be related to the population figures of the two zones, a proposal which would have favored the United States. The British, on the other hand, hard pressed for the dollars needed for the importation of food, insisted that the United States should carry 60 percent of the burden. He and Robertson had not been able to settle this point, and it therefore had to be referred to the government level. Eventually an even division was agreed upon.[35]

The Deputy Military Governor also remarked that a Joint Foreign Exchange Agency was in addition being created to facilitate the work of JEIA. It would be authorized to open accounts in the names of the two military governments with banks of the countries where the agency would be operating. All proceeds from bizonal exports were to be paid into those accounts. In the course of the Hoover briefings, Clay indicated that OMGUS was trying to restore normal business practices as quickly as possible. Foreign buyers would soon be given free access to the bizone and the restrictions on business communications between Germany and other countries removed. The original export procedure, whereby all transactions were channeled through Berlin, had caused a time-consuming bottle-neck. He therefore had delegated procedural authorities to military government offices in the *Länder* and ordered the transfer of personnel to these offices. The initial results of these moves seemed encouraging, he said.[36] Undoubtedly an early currency reform would also help Germany's foreign trade, and all the occupying powers wanted one. The negotiations at the Control Council had recently made very good progress, he added, until a snag was created by the Soviet insistence that the new currency be printed in Leipzig. Although the Russians later conceded supervision of the printing by a quadripartite committee, Clay was uncertain at that point how to proceed. He had asked the War Department for instructions, he told the former President.[37]

Hoover's report to President Truman claimed that decartelization was retarding Germany's recovery. But Clay, aware that this was a controversial program, had proceeded here slowly and with deliberate caution.[38] Testifying in November before the Senate Special Committee Investigating the National Defense Program, he had discussed the voluminous report that the committee's Chief Counsel, George Meader, had submitted upon his recent return from Germany. On the subject of decartelization Meader drew on his conversations with James Martin and reminded the committee of Hitler's effective use of Germany's industrial combines in his program of aggression. Because German industry had been concentrated in large units, he claimed, it had been comparatively simple for the Nazi state to promote the secret conversion of manufacturing enterprises to the production of armaments. Moreover, Meader contended, Hitler had been able to weaken his potential enemies industrially through the foreign operations of German cartels.[39] The difficulties in the production of synthetic rubber at the beginning of the war were a case in point.

Meader had also brought up what he termed the "effects of assigning key positions in military government to individuals recruited from American business organizations." There were many American officials who could be fitted into this category, but Meader mentioned only one by name: William Draper, "a Vice President of Dillon Read," who "in the 1920s had floated in the United States large amounts of German securities including those of the *Vereinigte Stahlwerke*." Since there were publicly made denouncements that "business representatives of American firms were serving their companies' interest rather than their country's interest in positions of economic power in military government," Meader recommended that "the facts ought to be fully ascertained."[40]

As Clay saw it, there was no validity in these charges. He nevertheless could not fail to recognize that these recommendations carried some weight when, following the November elections, Meader's secret report was released to the press. On the other hand, Clay had also become aware of a growing American opposition to the decartelization program. Within the American business community there was a vocal body of opinion suggesting that OMGUS decartelization policy was the work of extremists from the Department of Justice, and that the policy hampered economic progress.[41] These were of course the views shared by Hoover.

Clay decided to keep to the middle ground. After returning to Berlin, he mildly criticized James Martin for having expressed his frustration before Meader, and he again refused to free him from Draper's control.[42] He also rejected Martin's offer to resign and tried to assure better cooperation between the two offices. The result, as Martin put it, was a "standstill" agreement which was used to justify a continuation of the difficult negotiations with the British on levels of concentration in bizonal industry. The number of German combines considered to enjoy too great a market share was reduced by Anglo-American agreement to twenty-one, and eventually the concept was dropped completely. The new draft accord provided instead for the establishment of a joint commission that would examine firms and determine whether their size and scale of operations were justified on the grounds of technical efficiency. Whenever excessive concentrations of power were found, the commission could recommend appropriate action to the zone commanders. These firms were then to be reorganized and separated into workable but independent economic units. Since the concept of "mandatory" had been dropped, it was not difficult to agree with the British on a common text of a law.[43] Issued in February as Military Government Law #56 for the United States zone and as ordinance #78 for the British zone, it was one of Clay's concessions to the concept of Bizonia. Philip Hawkins, a middle-of-the-roader on the issue who soon was to follow Martin as head of the decartelization branch, put it this way: the new law was "a retreat from the Potsdam Agreement and a complete tactical victory for the traditional British position"[44]; the General had decided to accommodate the British. But, as Martin noted with regret, "Law #56 was still nothing but paper and printer's ink."[45]

Clay's rigid denazification law, on the other hand, was a source of continuous trouble, and the demands for amendments were steadily mounting. They came not only from the Germans but also from the Deputy Military governor's own staff. In spite of the General's threatening November speech and a constant stream of directives, orders and plans from military government offices, little progress was being made.[46] American denazification officials continued to ask that the major offenders be tried first,[47] but the efforts of millions of party followers to obtain speedy action and absolvement were overwhelming the system. Restricted to common labor, they were naturally anxious to be cleared quickly, to pay the nominal fine and to be done with it. There was little the German tribunals were willing to do in order to resist these pressures.

Lucius Clay, always dogged in the pursuit of his established objectives, was as unwilling to give up his denazification policy as he was his design for Germany's unification. But while in the latter instance his persistance was soon to cause a confrontation with the new Secretary of State, in the former the device of the amnesty gave him an out. The reaction of the American press to the earlier youth amnesty had been positive, and the move had cleared the tribunals of about 900,000 pending cases. Accordingly Walter Dorn, who had replaced Fritz Oppenheimer as Clay's denazification advisor, suggested an amnesty for lower-income groups, a proposal supported by the German trade unions and speedily accepted by Clay. Ceremoniously proclaimed by General McNarney on Christmas Day 1946, the new amnesty pertained to individuals who were "not chargeable as major offenders or offenders . . . , whose financial status shows that they have not profited from Nazi greed and ambition . . . or who suffer from more than 50 percent disability."[48] An implementing instruction issued by OMGUS indicated that the amnesty covered persons with an income of less than RM 3,600 and a taxable property of less than RM 20,000 at the end of the war. From Clay's point of view, the Christmas amnesty had the advantage of clearing away about 900,000 cases while leaving the principle of the denazification process intact. And it took some of the steam out of Soviet charges that in the American zone the little Nazis were being tried while the big ones remained scot free. Nevertheless, one million cases remained to be tried, and at least initially the amnesty itself caused further delays. It took the tribunals more than three months to sort out the cases covered by it. It also was quite clear that by using the amnesty device Clay had not solved but merely evaded the basic problem. However, as one of the program's staunchest critics acknowledged, "the amnesties did to some extent relieve the political, economic, and social tensions with which the denazification program had burdened a prostrate society."[49]

The General still maintained that the cornerstone of his denazification policy, i.e., the prima facie guilt of all party members, had not only been ordained by JCS #1067 but also still had the support of American public opinion. Possibly to counteract any impression of weakening in his resolve, he publicly stated in January that he "stood 100 percent" behind the Law of Liberation.[50] Not only members of Nazi organizations but also non-members who were active participants in the Nazi machine had to be completely eliminated from positions of power and influence. "If the Germans do not do this job," he said, "I will not hesitate to take it over." When Delbert Clark reminded him that most Germans regarded this threat as impossible to fulfill because of lack of personnel, Clay responded, "It is not so difficult as some may think. It is not necessary to replace German tribunals but only to place an American officer on each with the deciding vote." He did not elaborate any further on such possible admission of his policy's bankruptcy. With similar toughness he ordered the cancellation of all the temporary work licenses that had been issued earlier in blanket form by the military government. The move principally affected the state railway system (the Reichsbahn), for which an exception had been made so that railroad operations could continue. Faced with a public calamity of first order, the Ministers of Political Liberation, responsible for denazification, issued blanket licenses to find themselves soon rebuked by an OMGUS directive. Eventually a compromise was worked out on lower administrative levels, but Clay had upheld his principle.[51]

A few weeks after the Hoover mission had completed its fact-finding tour, General McNarney left Germany. On March 15, Lucius Clay, as the new Commander in Chief and Military Governor, assumed command of all American forces in Europe. Although the fourth star accompanying this assignment undoubtedly pleased the General, it still was not enough to change his basic unhappiness with the job. When Clay was advised in December *after the fact* that the United States had agreed to France taking over the Saar, his fundamental dissatisfaction again came to the fore. "I know I have talked a lot about leaving Germany, perhaps too much," he told Assistant Secretary of War Howard Petersen in the course of a tele-conference.

> However, if State Department is reported correctly, I feel my usefulness here is at an end and I would like to be recalled immediately. My difficulties with France have been too real over too long a time for me to continue to sit with them in view of State's repudiations of my actions, which were based on specific State Department instructions.[52]

The incident was smoothed over, but during the following two years the same feeling of frustration emerged even more frequently. It was only Eisenhower's and other friends' emphatic appeals to his patriotism and sense of duty which made the General withdraw his repeated requests for retirement.

Having known for some time that he would succeed McNarney in March as U.S. Commander in Chief in Europe, Clay had been able to prepare for the demands of this additional function. The American army of occupation, with the possible exception of the small constabulary, was in very poor shape. Undisciplined, disorganized, engaged in the black market, with high AWOL and VD rates, it was a blemish on the United States.[53] Because Clay's principal responsibility continued to be military government, he knew he would have to spend most of his time in Berlin. He devised a three-pronged approach to cope with his new responsibilities.

He sent for Lieutenant General Clarence Huebner, who had come up through the ranks and who was known as a superb troop trainer. As Clay's deputy, chief of staff and commander of the ground forces, he was delegated broad authority to whip the occupational forces into shape. As Clay envisaged it, he would combine his weekly inspection of troops in the field with a monthly meeting at Huebner's Heidelberg headquarters. There, armed with the appropriate statistics and other data on operations compiled by James Sundquist, his management control officer, he would make the necessary command decisions. (According to Sundquist, "Clay's concept was that the number in the reports would throw up red lights and the lights would tell him act here, act this way. . . .") Also, as advised by the U.S. Bureau of the Budget, Clay established European Command (EUCOM) in Berlin. Consisting of the inspector general, the directors of intelligence, personnel, and management control, in addition to his own economic, financial, political and government affairs advisors, the command was to serve as the military governor's principal instrument of supervision over the Theater.

Finally, with the aim of keeping OMGUS and EUCOM on the same level, he set up an office of the Commander in Chief, Europe (CINCEUR). It was to be free of operational functions and serve as his personal headquarters. The assumption of additional command responsibilities thus was almost routinely accomplished.

The bizonal merger was more complex. As Clay had expected, the initial phases of Bizonia had brought a host of problems to the fore. He recognized that they resulted from three contradictory policies: the creation of German legislative bodies in the U.S. zone, the establishment of bizonal agencies, and his own continued efforts to comply with the policies laid down at Potsdam. Striking a balance among these contradictions remained one of his main preoccupations during the coming months.

He had tried to accelerate the country's unification indirectly by giving Germans in the United States zone increasingly more authority and responsibilities. Moreover, he had insisted on early elections, on the drafting and passage of democractic constitutions, and on creating the nucleus of an all-German administration in Stuttgart. By the beginning of 1947 the *Länderrat* consisted of democratically elected representatives of the German people who expected to be heard and on occasion to cast a meaningful vote.

"A combative nonconformist as a cadet [at West Point, 1915–1918], he was a member of the dirty dozen."—General Hugh Casey
(*U.S. Military Academy photo*)

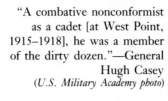

"A company commander who genuinely likes his men, is constant in his care of them, and gets the most out of them."—efficiency-rating entry
(*U.S. Army photo*)

U.S. Deputy Military Governor for Germany. "The last job I would have wanted."—Clay to an interviewer
(*U.S. Army photo*)

A Distinguished Service Cross for wartime service as Director
of Matériel.
"I would have given my eyeteeth for a combat command."—Clay to
an interviewer
From left to right: Mrs. Lucius D. Clay, Jr.; Mrs. Lucius D. Clay;
Major General Lucius D. Clay; General Brehon B. Somervell.
(*U.S. Army photo*)

"Washington must revise its
thinking relative to the destruction
of Germany's war potential as an
immediate problem. The progress
of war has accomplished this."—
Clay to John J. McCloy
(*U.S. Army photo*)

Reconstruction began. German
women are shown chipping bricks
down to size for use in rebuilding
demolished buildings.
(*U.S. Army photo*)

"Quiet, unassuming, and dignified, Sokolovsky was ready in debate, which he flavored with a delightful sense of humor and the frequent use of Russian proverbs. He could cite the Bible better than anybody I knew. I learned to respect his ability."—*Decision in Germany* and interview with Jean Smith
(photo credit OMGUS Public Relations Service, Louis E. Bowlde, photographer; courtesy Mrs. [Captain Tint] Sylvia O'Connor)

The production of coal was all-important. Clay and General Sir Brian Robertson, with German coal miners.
(U.S. Army photo)

"Our nonfraternization policy is extremely unpopular with our soldiers and in many ways you cannot blame them."—Clay to Eisenhower
(U.S. Army photo)

Full day's German ration
combined in one meal.
(*U.S. Army photo*)

The black market could not be controlled.
(*U.S. Army photo*)

A single black-market meal
in a Berlin nightclub.
(*U.S. Army photo*)

Denazification was to be rigorously pursued. General Clay is shown
here outlining a severe denazification law to the American
correspondents, September 26, 1945.
(*U.S. Army photo*)

War Crimes Trials.
"My responsibility as reviewing officer [there was no court of appeals]
and as clemency officer was great and there was no other which
weighed more heavily on me."—*Decision in Germany*
(*U.S. Army photo*)

"I depend upon Clay and trust him without reservation."—Eisenhower to Mamie, December 18, 1944
(*Photo courtesy Mrs. Lucius D. Clay*)

On March 14, 1947, Lieutenant General Lucius D. Clay succeeded General Joseph McNarney as Military Governor.
(*U.S. Army photo*)

"Such was the relationship between Ambassador [Robert] Murphy and me that I know of no decision taken during the four years in which we were in Germany from which he dissented."—*Decision in Germany*
(*Wide World photo*)

"[General William H.] Draper was more than an economic advisor. He and I had worked together for four years and I relied on his ability and judgment in all fields."—*Decision in Germany*
(*U.S. Army photo*)

In the beginning there was still an American-Soviet honeymoon. An informal gathering following presentation of First Order of Kutuzov to Lieutenant General Lucius D. Clay. From left to right: General Eisenhower, Lieutenant General Clay, Marshall Zhukov, General Sokolovsky, Russian interpreter.
(*U.S. Army photo*)

"He never failed to impress the audience with his sincerity and determination. It was through Clay's appearances before the *Länderrat* that the American Government presented itself at its best to the representatives of the German people."—Heinz Guradze, *The Länderrat: Landmark of German Reconstruction*
(*U.S. Army photo*)

German minister-presidents bid farewell to Secretary James F. Byrnes after his Stuttgart speech. From left to right: Dr. Wilhelm Hoegner, Dr. Reinhold Maier, Dr. Karl Geiler, Byrnes.
(*National Archives photo*)

The newly elected minister-presidents of the three *Länder* of the U.S.
zone and the president of the *Senat* of the City of Bremen, who for the
first time participated in a *Länderrat* meeting, were given a reception by
Lieutenant General Lucius D. Clay.
From left to right: Christian Stock, Minister-President of Hesse; Dr.
Hans Ehard, Minister-President of Bavaria; General Clay; Dr. Reinhold
Maier, Minister-President of Württemberg-Baden; and Dr. Wilhelm
Kaisen, President of the *Senat* of the City of Bremen.
(*Wide World photo*)

The Soviet delegation at the Control Council.
From left to right: Major Kudriatzev; Mr. Maximov; Counsellor
Arkadiev; General Dratvin; Marshall Sokolovsky; Minister Semenov;
Counsellor Grivanov; and Lieutenant Colonel Kostenko.
(*U.S. Army photo*)

The decisive Moscow Conference, March-April 1947.
"There was no doubt among the American delegation that a protracted division of Germany had been decided upon. It meant the maintenance of American troops in West Germany for an indefinite period of time."—Edward Mason, "Reflections on the Moscow Conference," *International Organization* 1, no. 2 (May 1947)
(*photo courtesy Sovfoto*)

"The American people want to help the German people to win their way back to an honorable place among the free and peace-loving nations of the world."—Secretary of State James F. Byrnes at Stuttgart, September 6, 1946. Seated behind the Secretary, from left to right: Ambassador Robert Murphy, Senator Arthur Vandenberg, Senator Thomas Connally, and General Joseph T. McNarney.
(*U.S. Army photo*)

Clay and Secretary of State George C. Marshall.

"At the Tempelhof airport, I was instructed to proceed vigorously with the strengthening of the bizonal organization in conjunction with [Sir Brian] Robertson and to expedite the upward revision of the level of bizonal industry to ensure the self-sufficiency of the area. It seemed possible that a wider economic unity in Germany might not take place for years."
— *Decision in Germany*
(National Archives photo)

The Parliamentary Council during a vote on the Basic Law.
From left to right, in the first row: Dr. Walter Menzel, Minister of the Interior, Nordrhein-Westfalen; Professor Dr. Carlo Schmidt, acting State President and Minister of Justice of South Baden; Paul Loebe, President of the Reichstag until 1933; Professor Theodor Heuss; and Dr. Hans Christoph Seebohm.
(*DPA photo*)

Kurt Schumacher addressing a party meeting of the SPD (Social Democratic Party of West Germany).
"Fanatical, strongminded, and of integrity, Kurt Schumacher's opposition was serious."—*Decision in Germany*
(*National Archives photo*)

Konrad Adenauer at the Parliamentary Council.
"When Dr. Adenauer rises above party politics, he has the intelligence and character to act as a statesman. He exhibited this quality of statesmanship at critical periods in the life of the Parliamentary Council."—*Decision in Germany*
(*DPA photo*)

The Berlin airlift.
"When Berlin falls, Western Germany will be next. If we mean . . . to hold Europe against Communism, we must not budge."—Clay to Omar Bradley
(*U.S. Air Force photo*)
(Life *Magazine photo, Walter Sanders, 1947, Time, Inc.*)

The military governors during a meeting
with the Parliamentary Council.
From left to right: Mr. Francois Seydoux (political advisor to General
Pierre Koenig), General Koenig, General Clay, General Sir Brian
Robertson, and Mr. James Riddleberger (political advisor
to General Clay).
(*DPA photo*)

Jewish leaders bid farewell to General Lucius D. Clay, expressing
thanks for his rehabilitation of the Jewish people.
(*U.S. Army photo*)

"The Allied armies will remain in Germany to ensure that the peace and freedom for which the war had been fought might endure."—General Clay in his farewell address to the U.S. Army.
From left to right: General Clay, Lieutenant General Clarence R. Huebner, Rear Admiral John Wilkes, Lieutenant General Geoffrey Keyes, Major General R.W. Douglas.
(*U.S. Army photo*)

Retiring General Lucius D. Clay addresses Congress, May 18, 1949. "A man of the many men I have seen who is able as any man I ever met in the Army or out."—Speaker Sam Rayburn introducing General Clay
(*National Archives photo*)

"A tired man whose face and manner bore the marks of his grueling occupation tasks."—*The New York Times*, May 18, 1949
(*U.S. Army photo*)

A crowd estimated at a quarter of a million welcomed the retired American Military Governor in New York City on May 18, 1949.
(*Wide World photo*)

General Lucius D. Clay addressing the welcoming crowd in Marietta, Georgia, on May 28, 1949, just across from the monument to his father.
(*U.S. Army photo*)

The administrative superstructure of Bizonia, on the other hand, had been created by the two military governors without German participation. In spite of some corrective efforts on Clay's part, the precise nature of the relationship between the new bizonal authorities and the *Land* governments in the U.S. zone had been left unclear. An attempt to find a unifying administrative pattern for the two zones, each of which had its own distinct governmental apparatus by that time, proved exceedingly difficult. In the U.S. zone the emphasis had been on decentralization, unplanned economics and "free enterprise." Anything resembling an economic planning authority had been discouraged.[54] By contrast, the British zone had a highly centralized administration with the military government in direct control, and with no provision made for corresponding German responsibilities.[55] There was a tendency on the part of the British to use their centralized power for purposes of planning and socialization—both taboo in Clay's eyes.[56]

Clay saw that these were all fundamental weakenesses: the differences in authority between the bizonal agencies in each of the two zones, the lack of an executive arm to enforce their decisions, the dependence upon the good will of the *Länder* for the execution of programs, and the lack of coordination between committees located in different geographic areas. Moreover, they were fundamental weaknesses that would soon have to be corrected. In addition, and most embarassing, when the first steps toward a bizonal administration were taken, the effect of the differing denazification procedures in the two zones had become very clear. As a German minister had commented to Clay, the British military government had Germans in highly responsible positions "who in the American zone could not even be employed as letter carriers."[57]

Aside from these factors, a third group of problems arose from the efforts toward a bizonal amalgamation, while the unification of Germany itself remained on Washington's pro forma and Clay's active agenda. The likelihood of unification seemed more and more remote, but the State Department nevertheless insisted that appearances had to be preserved. The Truman Administration's rationale had been spelled out early in September when the Policy Committee on Germany advised the Secretary of State that "if there should be a split of Germany it must be clear to the whole world that it was in spite of U.S. policy and not because of it."[58] The shifting of the onus that accordingly began was reflected in the unduly protracted negotiations for a four-power currency reform, which found the United States pitted against its three allies.[59] The same policy necessitated the geographic dispersion of bizonal agencies, and it militated against the creation of a coordinating authority that might be regarded as the nucleus of a future West German government.[60]

The mounting dissatisfaction of German legislators with the consequences of these contraditions gave rise to a number of open clashes between German officials and military government officers—the first such incidents since the occupation began. Apprised of these controversies, General Clay decided to invite the minister-presidents of the American zone and the *Oberbürgermeister* from Bremen to a Sunday meeting in his headquarters at Kronprinzenallee. When he addressed the group, he assumed the role of a banker who faced supplicant clients.

On his own responsibility, he said, $40 million had been loaned by the Reconstruction Finance Corporation to the military government and a subsidy of additional $300 million was pending. The activation of these funds depended, however, on a successful completion of the bizonal merger and on the necessary German support. He then went over the developments which had led to the present impasse. Starting with the Potsdam Agreement, he acknowledged that it had so far not been possible to unify the four zones and that he had consequently set up the *Länderrat* as a coordinating body. He had approved the democratic constitutions of the three *Länder* while reserving in very general terms the military government's rights of control. The guiding principle had been not to prejudice any provisions of a future all-German constitution. Subsequently, in cooperation with the British, bizonal agencies had been set up. The two military governments had put the executive authority for them into the hands of the *Länder* in order to avoid the establishment of a bureaucratic machinery. It was now up to the *Land* governments to cooperate and overcome the difficulties which the opposition of their respective parliaments might create. In Clay's judgment, there were two methods to safeguard the effectiveness of the bizonal agencies. One was the establishment of local offices which would operate under the full responsibility of the military government. the other would entail the maintenance of the present system. It could succeed if the representatives of the *Länder* at the bizonal agencies were given the necessary powers. Clay admitted that as far as actual legislation was concerned, the American and British views still differed, and accordingly there existed no machinery as yet that would permit the issuance of any binding law for the two zones. Clay then summed up his remarks with the comment that the decision on how to proceed remained with his listeners. The first method would be easier and lead to fast results. However, it would delay the development of democratic institutions.[61]

During the discussion that followed, Clay's experience in dealing with congressional committees stood him in good stead. When pressed hard by the German legislators on the contradictions in the present system, he resorted to the tactics he had successfully used on the Hill. He openly admitted that there were some negative aspects in the present situation, but he considered the problem to be temporary; after the impending Council of foreign Ministers meeting in Moscow, changes would be made. Clearly aware of the power of his office, Clay often evaded precise answers and on occasion found it expedient to equivocate. He stressed that any appearance of creating a bizonal government had to be avoided regardless of the difficult side effects. Accordingly, he "recommended" that the scheduled meeting of his visitors with the minister-presidents of the three other zones should be postponed until after the Moscow Conference. The meeting ultimately took place in Munich on June 6-7, 1947, against the background of a hardening East-West rift. The efforts of German political leaders to prepare the way for their country's unification therefore came to naught.

It seems that the Soviet government had carefully followed these developments in the Western zone. Two days after Clay's meeting at Kronprinzenallee, Vassily Sokolovsky addressed the issue at the Control Council.[62] "The bizonal agreement could have serious consequences for Germany's political future," he warned. If Germany would be dismembered, "this would bring about the creation of a new nest of unrest in Central Europe which could in the future endanger the peace and security of the nations." Sokolovsky took exception to the statements of West German political leaders who had spoken about the creation of a "political directorate" in the West and the necessity of changes in the dismantlement process, and he stressed that the agreement on fusion of the two zones "has failed to expedite either the elimination of war potential or reparations deliveries." He turned to the GARIOA (Government Aid and Relief in Occupied Areas) credits still pending and, using Marxist terminology, he then criticized loans which "are of the nature of bondage" and will "allow the American and British monopolists to dictate the terms of development of the Western German economy." The question arises, he continued, whether the fusion agreement was not aimed at reducing West Germany "to the state of an appendix to foreign monopolies." The stated purpose of Bizonia was to ensure that the industries of the fused zones would be able to meet their own requirements. But "how can one profess a desire for economic unity of Germany," he asked, "while in practice separating her basic industrial wealth from the other parts of Germany?" The Soviet marshall nevertheless ended his statement on a friendly note with the suggestion that the difficulties in the occupation "are perfectly soluble along the path of agreed and farsighted common policies of the Allies in the spirit of the decisions of the Crimea and Berlin conferences."

Sokolovsky had spoken in executive session, and therefore his remarks should not have been published. When nevertheless the text of the statement appeared in the Eastern press, Clay drafted an angry reply, but on second thought released a rather mild response to the press instead.[63] The tentative reparations compromise that he and Sokolovsky had drafted was still on his agenda. With the Moscow Conference only a few weeks away, there was obviously no reason to engage in verbal battles and create more discord at the Control Council.

Clay had no doubt about the critical significance of the impending conference, although, as the new year began, he had become less and less sanguine about its outcome. In the first months of 1947, a great deal of time had to be devoted at his headquarters and those of the Allied Control Authority to preparing for the conference. At the close of its third session in New York, the Council of Foreign Ministers gave the Berlin Control

Council until the end of February to submit a report both on its work and on the problems encountered in administering Germany.[64] There had been difficulties in complying with this assignment, because the Russian and French representatives in Berlin refused to furnish information on capital removals and reparations from current production. These data would be presented in Moscow, they said. Eventually a report weighing six pounds and covering many hundred pages was nevertheless completed. When the Deputy Military Governor was shown a small summary which some diligent staffers had prepared for him, he impatiently pushed it aside.[65] "I don't need that," he said, and those who worked with him closely knew that this was a fact. He had the essentials for each division more clearly in his mind than the individual division chiefs.

The Control Council had spent many hours in a futile effort to develop agreed recommendations. The ACA report merely revealed, as Clay later remarked, the different views about what had occurred and of what remained to be done. It did lay down in black and white the wide divergences which had taken place in an attempt to administer Germany as a unit. Although the report was a monumental accomplishment, Clay thought that it would do little to help the foreign ministers in solving the pressing problems which would be presented in Moscow. "I think," he concluded as the report was finally signed on February 25, "that even Marshall Sokolovsky felt discouraged at the result."[66] For eighteen months, in an effort to continue the wartime alliance, Sokolovsky and Clay had worked toward the common goal of a unified Germany under four-power control. They were too clear-headed not to recognize that the policies of their governments were more and more moving in different directions.

While the Control Council in Berlin had been working on its reports, the State Department had been equally busy preparing a large volume of papers for the Moscow Conference. The Deputy Military Governor had been asked for his comments, and as he reviewed the briefing book he noticed its negative drift. When, in the summer of 1946 on White House instructions, Eisenhower had queried all military commanders "on the manner in which agreements had been carried out by the Soviets," Clay had truthfully replied that "it is difficult to find major instances of Soviet failures to carry out agreements reached in the quadripartite government of Germany." He therefore was struck by the shifting of the onus in the documents, the State Department's apparent reaction to Communist policies in Germany and elsewhere. The all-out skirmish with the Russians in Iran, the Kremlin's brazen attempt to acquire a base in the Dardanelles, and Soviet terrorist tactics in Poland, Bulgaria, Romania, and Hungary, had all made an indelible impact on America's decision-makers. But Clay, captured as always by his own particular fight or game, had failed to enter any of the above into his political calculus.

He had no doubt that unless a compromise on the reparations issue could be reached in Moscow, the conference was doomed to failure. It also was clear in his mind that the ultimate consequences of such a failure would be the partition of Germany, resulting in political and economic competition between a Western and Eastern bloc. As he read the reparations section of the briefing papers, he found no grounds for encouragement.[67] The tentative reparations agreement he had worked out with Sokolovsky followed the example of the peace treaty with Italy, which provided that Russian raw materials be supplied for the manufacture of finished products as reparation goods. The economic data which Don Humphrey had compiled[68] to implement this plan had apparently been examined at the State Department, but in the briefing paper mainly negative conclusions had been reached. Humphrey had arrived at $7.5 billion as a feasible amount for overall German reparations and some of Clay's financial experts at OMGUS had suggested an even larger amount was possible,[69] but the briefing papers doubted the German capacity to pay. There was no reference to the General's pragmatic recommendations that Germany's economic potential be expertly appraised. Instead there only was the misleading statement in which Clay had said "he has no position to recommend to his government."[70]

As he perused the Washington documents, the Deputy Military Governor could not have failed to recognize that his task in implementing the Potsdam Agreement was likely to come to an end. In accord with this sobering conclusion, his comments were restrained. He concurred on subjects tangential to his mission, but he was explicit in opposing suggested restrictions on the authority of a provisional German government and in rejecting the internationalization of the Ruhr, which he considered "unworkable and undesirable."[71]

If anything could have magnified Clay's disenchantment, it was the announcement of Secretary Byrnes' resignation. The news came "as a sudden and almost unbelievable shock." He wrote to the Secretary:

> I had always felt that I was serving you and it gave me both pride and pleasure to do so. . . . That privilege [of working for you] has given me a new faith in America and in democracy. It has proved that an American can spend his life in politics and at the same time keep the faith and maintain the highest ideals of service. The kindness and affection which you have given to those who have worked for you have meant more to them than they can evidence.

And he concluded by summing up his own situation: "Somehow or other my own assignment does not seem the same. . . . I shall continue here in Germany although I shall again urge the War Department to look for an ultimate successor."[72]

In contrast to his close relation with Byrnes, the General had had very little personal association with General George C. Marshall, who succeeded Byrnes as Secretary of State. During the war his official contacts in the Pentagon had been with General Brehon Somervell and Undersecretary

Patterson. On a number of occasions he had attended conferences called by Marshall. When appointed Deputy Military Governor, Clay had called on the Chief of Staff to pay his respects and "had been impressed with his sympathetic understanding of the difficulties I would face."[73] Like everybody in the American army he had great respect for Marshall, but he could not expect the same kind of support from the new Secretary that he had enjoyed from his predecessor, whom he and Marjorie "had come to love."

Clay hoped that he would not have to attend the Moscow Conference unless called for during its progress. Accordingly he cabled Daniel Noce, who headed the Civil Affairs Division, that the conference would be followed with great interest in Germany, and "its proceeding may well become the basis for an intensive propaganda campaign." "Hence a period of unrest may be expected and my place should therefore be in Berlin."[74] It was not a very good argument. The General's later explanation, "I was responsible to the War Department and hesitated to make recommendations on major issues," was more convincing.[75] The bitter controversy with his superiors on the Potomac in the summer of 1946 had evidently left some scars, and he was not about to make the same mistake twice.

It was a disspirited Deputy Military Governor who greeted the Secretary in Berlin on his way to Moscow. John Foster Dulles, Ben Cohen, Charles E. Bohlen, and Freeman H. Matthews were in his company. A Republican victory at the 1948 presidential election was widely expected, which would make Dulles the most likely next Secretary of State. He therefore had been included in Marshall's party. Clay was concerned about Dulles' agreement with the French view on the future of the Ruhr and his influence on the Secretary, and he found his apprehensions quickly confirmed. Marshall had been in office only a few weeks and was still not sufficiently familiar with all the intricate problems before him. According to Clay, his views on Germany "were not very firm."[76] At the State Department he had been briefed daily by Bohlen, James Riddleberger, Cohen, and others, all of whom stressed the Soviet Union's aggressive designs and cautioned that Lenin's slogan "one step back—two steps forward" was still gospel for the men in the Kremlin.[77]

Marshall stayed at the Wannsee Guest House; discussions there were not recorded, but there is sufficient information available to trace the controversy that evolved. Clay summarized his November memorandum to Byrnes, which recommended continued efforts to find an accommodation with the Soviets on the critical reparations issue. By contrast, Dulles had a special paper prepared for the occasion. It proceeded from the premise that there was a worldwide struggle "primarily ideological" between Christian civilization and Communism, "the former led by the United States and the latter led by the Soviet Union." This division, Dulles said, also reflected the classic conflict between the so-called status quo and the dynamic powers. He then raised a number of rhetorical questions: Could a united Germany be relied upon to form a part of the Christian civilization which would resist Soviet Communism; could such a result be obtained without putting France into the Communist bloc; and finally, could the bargaining power of a united Germany be compatible with the stability and peace of Europe?[78]

Answering all these questions in the negative, Dulles concluded that "a united Germany would have an enormous bargaining power which would give Germany the mastery of Europe" and also would put France "almost certainly" into the Soviet bloc. His recommendation therefore was to go slow on unifying Germany "while integrating the Ruhr area economically into Western Europe and not now risking it in an economically and politically united Germany."

Since there could not have been any advice more in conflict with Clay's policy aims, the ensuing debate was necessarily lively. As Marshall listened to the Deputy Military Governor's emphatic plea for Germany's economic unification, he was reminded of similar conflicts on the battlefield. Individual military commanders, without considering the units on their right or left, were concerned only with taking their own assigned targets. "Localitis," Marshall said in conclusion, had also been one of his major problems during the war. The comment indicated on which side the Secretary's sympathies were.[79]

If anything, the meeting enhanced Clay's desire to be left behind in Germany when the group departed for Moscow. When the newly proclaimed Truman Doctrine came over the wire a few days later, he was even more anxious to remain in Berlin. The responsibilities of the Commander in Chief, Europe, which he took over on March 15, gave him additional reasons not to leave. Nevertheless, shortly after the conference of the foreign ministers had begun, he was ordered to come to Moscow. When he asked to be excused, a second telegram told him that these were the Secretary's instructions.

He was met at the airport by Bedell Smith, now the American Ambassador to the Soviet Union, who brought him up to date on the most recent happenings. Demilitarization, denazification, and democratization had made up the conference's first agenda but the critical issues would be coming up the next day, March 17. The Secretary was staying at Spasso House, the ambassador's residence, where the delegation's working space was. Parlors, the billiard room, the ballroom and even the hallways had been converted into offices, Smith said. Clay, like the rest of the delegates, was billeted in the Hotel Moskva. It had been completely refurbished for the occasion and all the doormen and attendants had been put into new uniforms. According to Smith, the Russians were anxious to see the conference succeed and they wanted to make a good impression. The restaurant at the Moskva had been stocked with caviar, smoked salmon and other delicacies all in scarce supply at the time. When the conference began, a fleet of shiny new Zis taxicabs had appeared in front of the hotel. It was incredible, Smith said. The Moscovites were used to trucks with the word "Taxi" painted on the tailgate. Now they might think it was the beginning of the millennium.[80]

As a member of the U.S. delegation, General Clay spent most of the next days at the closely guarded Aviation House, where the conference was held. In the makeshift offices at Spasso House he met some members of his Berlin staff who apprised him of the delegation's internal problems. Among them, so Clay was told, Foster Dulles and his influence on the Secretary figured prominently. Dulles was bitterly opposed to any central powers at all for the German government, and he did not seem to regard as significant what the Potsdam Agreement or the Stuttgart speech said on the topic.[81] A few days before Clay's arrival, Dulles had in effect threatened the entire delegation. He was sick and tired, he said, of being told in response to his points that it was the other way in the Potsdam Agreement or that the Allied Control Council had decreed otherwise. Lots of things had occurred since Potsdam, Dulles reportedly went on to say, including the election of a Republican majority in the Senate. His point of view had to be taken fully into account, he declared, or he would have difficulty when he got back to the United States in defending what went on in Moscow.[82] As Clay learned, Cohen had saved the situation. He had made a bland inconsequential remark, then a joke and finally, laughingly, said that he thought that the United States had a bipartisan foreign policy. That left Dulles without a chance to return to the topic. Everybody had difficulties with Dulles, Clay was told, and were it not for Cohen's cohesive influence and drafting ability, no paper at all worth having would be forthcoming.[83] The conference was not going well on the American side, the Military Governor had to conclude.

At Aviation House, in a number of plenary sessions which started at 4:00 P.M. and lasted late, the Russian custom, he listened to a bitter exchange of charges and countercharges.[84] The Western delegation denounced Soviet unilateral actions in the form of large-scale dismantlement of industries and the creation of Soviet-controlled combines, which the Russians countered by castigating the British government's expropriation of the steel and coal industries, the unilateral incorporation of the Saar into France and the establishment of Bizonia. Molotov spent considerable time demonstrating that Potsdam had implemented rather than superseded the Yalta reparations agreement, and that the question of reparations from production had been left for later decisions. He could have made a stronger point had he been briefed more adequately.[85] Marshall, who did not seem to get a grasp of the subject or the technique of the council very rapidly, was hesitant in debate, which caused British complaints.[86] Because he wanted his remarks written out and edited by him before delivery, his reply that the United States would "not follow the Russians in the retreat from Potsdam to Yalta" and that Molotov was "trying to sell the same horse twice" were good rhetoric but not convincing.[87] When Britain and the United States pointed out that reparations from production were actually and illegally leaving the Russian zone, the Soviet delegate mentioned the unpaid-for or under-priced shipments of coal and timber, which had the same effect on the German economy.[88] It was then that Molotov made a mistake. His complaint about Americans seizing German patents and trade processes for their exclusive use gave Charles Kindleberger, then a State Department hand, occasion to read a letter from the Soviet commercial attaché in Washington, in which he thanked the Secretary of Commerce for the data made available and asking when additional material would be published. It was one of the lighter interludes in an otherwise tense atmosphere.[89] It was less amusing for the Western powers, however, when Molotov compared British coal production figures with those of the Soviet zone and with obvious relish asked why Russians' were about twice as high and nothing was being done about it.[90]

Clay nevertheless noticed that there were a number of important points on which the four delegations agreed at least in principle, namely the prompt establishment of central German administrative agencies, an increase in the contemplated German level of industry, an early monetary reform, and the importation of raw and other materials to assist in increasing German exports.[91] The heads of the delegations, one by one, declared that the views of the four powers had much in common. But the main stumbling block as stated by Molotov—no economic unity without a settlement of reparations—remained.

The General, although visibly uncomfortable to be with the delegation,[92] was doing his best behind the scenes to achieve some results. In a summary of the council's discussions of the ACA report which Clay prepared for the Secretary, he acknowledged that neither the United States nor the United Kingdom could accept a program which required increased appropriations. But he again recommended a careful examination by experts of the economic potential before a final decision for or against reparations from production would be reached.[93] He made the same point in some discussions with other members of the American delegation. As he saw it, it was necessary to indicate to Congress how much German unification was going to cost and then leave it up to them to decide whether to pay the bill. However, Clay's opinion carried less weight than in the days of Byrnes, because everybody at Spasso House was aware that Foster Dulles and Bedell Smith were Marshall's fair-haired boys.[94] Some of the economists at the delegation doubted whether an objective economic analysis could be made in Berlin with any chance of reaching a definite answer, and Ben Cohen, who also was skeptical, tried his hand at a compromise. His plan would provide for some reparations from current German production if the recipient countries supplied foreign exchange or needed raw materials to the value of not less than 75 percent of the value of deliveries. But as Clay saw it, there was no hope of coming to an agreement with the Russians on such terms.[95] The debates among the American delegation were long and the clash of opinions often quite sharp. There were only a few lighter moments for Clay, like the exquisite performance of *Romeo and Juliet* by the Bolshoi Ballet. The General also amused himself at the Soviet's expense. He relished Murphy's astonishment when he bet that he would be able to enter Aviation House without showing his credentials. Accordingly, when the General approached the sentry, he walked rigidly erect, his right hand raised to the seam of his garrison cap; then, as the soldier automatically returned the salute, he quickly entered the building. Having thus tested the vaunted Soviet security, Clay mused,[96] "They are just as human as our GIs."

On March 22, the Council of Foreign Ministers had appointed a special committee to prepare a report listing the principal points of agreement and disagreement reached at the conference. Clay, Hervé Alphand, Sir Brian Robertson, and Andrei Y. Vishinsky were on this committee.[97] This, the General's second week in Mocscow, was pɪ ɔbably the low point of his German assignment. The Military Governor had had several runins with Dulles, who insisted that leaving the Ruhr with Germany would cause a Communist France. Dulles and a small group in the State Department therefore proposed to set up an independent Ruhr area under four-power jurisdiction, leaving the rest of Germany more or less to shift for itself. Clay's invariable answer—that a separation of the Ruhr would result in a Communist Germany while not settling the issue—had left some ill feelings on both sides. Consequently, when Dulles suggested that the American representative on the special committee should not be allowed to make any commitments without prior agreement by the delegation, Clay blew up.[98] He, the Military Governor, Commander in Chief and four-star General, who for two years had spoken for the United States and more often than not had made its policy, was now asked to submit to prior censorship! It seemed outrageous to him. Witnessed by Matthews, Riddleberger, and Murphy, an undignified exchange of bitter words followed. "The blood was all over the floor," a reminiscing Riddleberger quipped. Clay, humiliated at having lost self-control, finally withdrew to a corner of the room. "There he sat sulking and reading his papers," Don Humphrey recalled.[99]

Two days later, at Secretary Marshall's morning briefing, the die was cast. In another attempt to make his views prevail, Clay reiterated his belief that the United States should not be adamant on the question of reparations from production and should investigate Germany's economic potential. He emphasized again that the availability of production for this purpose might be the deciding factor in creating a unified democratic Germany and in fixing United States influence along the Oder-Neisse rather than at the Elbe. It was to no avail. The winds of history had shifted, and a new course had evidently been set in the White House. The decision reached at the meeting was that if it became necessary "to expose a point of view today or shortly it should be one put out in the Stuttgart speech."[100] Despite this resounding defeat, Clay continued to express his anger. "The whole matter is poorly run," he declared. "The Secretary and Cohen don't know what they want. . . . They are disorganized and ultimately are going to throw away Germany." Close to insubordination, he even hinted to the Russians that he had nothing to do with it. "I am not authorized at the time to state the United States position on a study of reparations from current production," he said at the special committee, and in a private conversation with Sokolovsky he commented the two of them should have been allowed to continue their discussions of last December.[101]

Obviously, Clay's German mission as drafted at Potsdam and in his directives had come to an end. He therefore requested and obtained the Secretary's permission to return to Berlin. "There," he remarked many years later, "if I called a press conference, people would listen and my resignation would have some impact. I was worried that Marshall and Dulles were going to submerge our interests to those of France . . . and I was determined to prevent it."[102]

FOOTNOTES

1. "Zusammenkunft mit Präsident Herbert D. Hoover," Rossmann Papers. Bundesarchiv Koblenz.
2. Food and Agriculture in the Bizonal Area, Manuscript 1, October 1947, OMGUS records, N.A.
3. *The New York Times,* January 23, 1947.
4. Tracy S. Vorhees, R.G. 107. File ASW 430, Book I, Box 76, N.A.
5. Peterson to Sec. of War, Subject, Hoover's Trip, December 24, 1946. R.G. 107, File ASW 430, Book I, Box 76, N.A.
6. *The New York Times,* January 22, 1947.
7. *The New York Times,* January 23, 1947.
8. Oliver Margolin to author, February 12, 1980.
9. Toni Stolper, *Ein Leben in Brennpunkten unserer Zeit,* p. 453.
10. Ibid., p. 451.
11. Margolin, ibid.
12. Louis Lochner, *Herbert Hoover and Germany,* p. 183.
13. Ibid., pp. 184–185.
14. Gustav Stolper, *German Realities,* Appendix E.
15. Executive Hearings. Senate Foreign Relations Committee, April 1, 1947; Heath to Riddleberger, November 25, 1946, 861,5048/11–2546, State Dept. papers.
16. Pauley to Truman, April 15, 1947, OF 383 (Edwin W. Pauley), Truman Library, Independence, Mo.
17. Lochner, *Herbert Hoover,* p. 179.
18. Ibid., p. 181.
19. Ibid., p. 188.
20. Eisenhower to McNarney, February 14, 1947. OMGUS papers 148–1/3, N.A.
21. *The New York Times,* November 26, 1946, p. 21.
22. Teleconference, TT-8096, May 13, 1947. R.G. 200, N.A.
23. *The New York Times,* May 19, 1947, p. 7.
24. Teleconference, TT-8096, May 13, 1947, R.G. 200, N.A.; *The New York Times,* May 9, 1947.
25. James Stewart Martin, "German Cartels are at It Again," in *The New Republic,* October 6, 1947, Vol. 117, p. 15.
26. *The New York Times,* May 20, 1947, p. 3.
27. U.S. Dept. of Commerce, *U.S. Export Statistics,* Vol. I, Foreign Commerce and Navigation Exports of Domestic Merchandise. Commodity Group 2. (Actually 1.4 million cartons of cigarettes had entered Germany in 1946 alone, thus fueling inflation at the prevailing black market prices to the tune of RM 2 billion annually.)
28. Ibid.
29. W. Y. Elliott, "The Control of Foreign Policy in the United States," in *The Political Quarterly* XX, No. 4, October-December 1949.
30. Lochner, *Herbert Hoover,* p. 193.
31. Statement of U.S. Proposal for Export-Import Bureau of Germany, submitted to Trade and Commerce Committee of ACA, February 11, 1946. Memorandum, Dr. Roy Bullock to Fred Winant, January 3, 1946, OMGUS records 123–2/3 N.A.
32. Lucius D. Clay, *Decision in Germany,* pp. 59, 196 and 197.
33. Ibid.
34. Ibid.
35. John H. Backer, *Priming the German Economy,* pp. 112–116. (Under the arrangements for the merger, imports in the bizone were divided into Category A and Category B. The former, mostly food, fertilizers and petroleum products, were to be financed by the two governments from appropriated funds, and category B from the proceeds of exports.)
36. Ibid.
37. Clay for Noce, January 17, 1947, CC 7679, R.G. 200, N.A.

38. "Confidential Report to the Senate Special Committee Investigating the National Defense Program on the Preliminary Investigation of Military Government in the Occupied Areas of Europe," November 22, 1946, George Meader, Chief Counsel.

39. Ibid.

40. Ibid.

41. James Stewart Martin, *All Honorable Men*, p. 194.

42. Ibid., p. 226.

43. Ibid., p. 228.

44. Graham Taylor, "The Rise and Fall of Antitrust in Germany 1945–1948," in *Prologue*, Spring 1979, p. 33.

45. Martin, *All Honorable Men*, p. 229.

46. William Griffith, "The Denazification Program in the American Zone of Germany," p. 333.

47. Ibid., p. 333.

48. Ibid., p. 385; Clay, *Decision*, p. 260.

49. Griffith, "The Denazification Program," p. 389.

50. *The New York Times*, January 23, 1947.

51. Griffith, "The Denazification Program," pp. 422–423.

52. Teleconference, TT-1228, Clay-Petersen, December 28, 1946, R.G. 200, N.A. A teleconference is a telex involving several people, with rapid, almost concurrent exchange of information.

53. Author's interview with Richard Hallock, Washington, D.C., April 8, 1981. Oliver J. Frederiksen, *The American Military Occupation of Germany*, pp. 39–41.

54. *The Evolution of Bizonal Organizations*, OMGUS. Civil Affairs Division, March 1948; Edward Litchfield, *Governing Postwar Germany*, pp. 25–30.

55. Wolfgang Friedman, *The Allied Military Government for Germany*, pp. 88–94.

56. Clay for Noce, April 29, 1947, CC 8959, R.G. 200, N.A.

57. Konferenz zwischen Lt. General Lucius D. Clay und Ministerpräsidenten am, 23 February 1947. Rossmann Papers. Bundesarchiv Koblenz.

58. Report of the Secretary's Policy Committee on Germany, September 15, 1946, p. 17. State Dept. Files, R.G. 43, N.A.

59. John H. Backer, *The Decision to Divide Germany*, Chapter 9.

60. James F. Byrnes, *Speaking Frankly*, p. 196.

61. Konferenz zwischen Lt. General Lucius D. Clay und Ministerpräsidenten am, 23 February 1947.

62. Ruth von Oppen, *Documents on Germany Under Occupation*, pp. 211–219.

63. Draft Memorandum, February 26, 1947, in Jean Smith, *The Papers of Lucius D. Clay*, pp. 319–321. *The New York Times*, March 1, 1947, p. 55.

64. Clay for War Dept., CC-7557, January 3, 1947; CC 7590, January 7, 1947; CC 7659, January 9, 1947; and CC 7759, January 21, 1947. R.G. 200, N.A.

65. Interview with Colonel John Bates, Maplewood, N.J., April 23, 1980.

66. Clay, *Decision*, p. 145.

67. *Foreign Relations of the United States 1947*, Vol. II, pp. 214–218.

68. Humphrey to Draper, November 2, 1946, OMGUS 177–3/3 (CFM File) N.A.

69. Manuel Gottlieb, *The German Peace Settlement and the Berlin Crisis*, Chapter VIII.

70. "Principal Economic Issues on Current German Problems for CFM Meeting," Memorandum #2, Reparations. R.G. 43. Records of CFM, N.A.

71. "Memorandum prepared by the Office of Military Government for Germany," in *Foreign Relations . . . 1947*, Vol. II, pp. 223–234.

72. Clay to Byrnes, January 27, 1947, in Smith, *The Papers*, p. 307.

73. Clay, *Decision*, pp. 146–147.

74. Clay to Noce, January 28, 1947. CC 7847, R.G. 200, N.A.

75. Clay, *Decision*, p. 146.

76. *Foreign Relations . . . 1947*, Vol. II, p. 169. Colonel R. Joe Rogers interview with General Clay, New York, N.Y., January 24, 1973.

77. Hickerson to Dunn, February 15, 1947. Relations with the Soviet Union. Memorandum for Secretary Marshall, January 17, 1947. Europ. Affairs File, State Dept. Papers, N.A.

78. Dulles Papers, March 7, 1947, Seeley G. Mudd Library, Princeton University, Princeton, N.J.

79. John Foster Dulles, *War or Peace*, pp. 102–103.
80. Walter Bedell Smith, *My Three Years in Moscow*, pp. 211–215; Georges Catrous, *J'ai vu tomber Le Rideau de Fer*, pp. 221–222.
81. Kindleberger private papers. Kindleberger to John de Wilde, March 17, 1947.
82. Ibid.
83. Ibid.
84. *Foreign Relations . . . 1947*, Vol. II, pp. 234–258.
85. V. M. Molotov, *Speeches and Statements at the Moscow Session of the Council of Foreign Ministers Conference in 1947.*
86. Kindleberger private papers. Kindleberger to John de Wilde, March 17, 1947.
87. Department of State *Bulletin 16.* No. *404* (March 30, 1947): 564.
88. *Foreign Relations . . . 1947*, Vol. II, p. 259.
89. Clay, *Decision*, p. 151.
90. Molotov, *Speeches*, March 19, 1947.
91. Conference of Foreign Ministers, Minutes of 12th Meeting, March 22, 1947.
92. Author's interview with George R. Jacobs, Washington, D.C., September 6, 1980.
93. Clay, Memorandum: Summary of Discussions in CFM on ACA Report, March 21, 1947, in Smith, *The Papers*, pp. 328–331. (March 30 date is an error.)
94. Author's interview with Don Humphrey, Winchester, Mass., September 9, 1978.
95. Kindleberger private papers, Kindleberger to John de Wilde, March 24 and 29, 1947.
96. Clay, *Decision*; p. 148.
97. *Foreign Relations . . . 1947*, Vol. II, p. 276.
98. Clay, *Decision*, p. 149.
99. Author's interviews with Don Humphrey, Winchester, Mass., September 9, 1978; and Ambassador Riddleberger, Wash., D.C., August 6, 1981.
100. Kindleberger private papers, Kindleberger to John de Wilde, March 24 and 29, 1947.
101. Ibid.
102. Jean Smith interview with Clay, February 14, 1970. Cited in Jean Smith, "The Resignation of James F. Byrnes," delivered to the American Historical Association Annual Meeting, December 30, 1977, Dallas, Texas.

CHAPTER EIGHT

Falling in Line

ONCE THE PLANE FROM MOSCOW WAS AIRBORNE, GENERAL CLAY HAD SEVERAL quiet hours to reappraise his German assignment. Although it had been "the last job he wanted" when he reported to Ike's headquarters in April 1945, he had soon been captured by the challenge of a historic mission. Since Clay had entered West Point, Americans had fought in two World Wars to prevent the hegemony of a militaristic Germany. It therefore had been Franklin Roosevelt's design to maintain the wartime alliance with the Soviet Union as a guarantee of peace in the heart of Europe.

Clay's instructions accordingly indicated that the United States aimed not only at the demilitarization of Germany but also at the democratization of the German people and their country's ultimate return to the community of peaceful nations. The reconstruction of the defeated country in the framework of the European economy was to go hand-in-hand with the economic unification of the four zones. Disarmament, denazification, reparations, and a gradual transfer of administrative responsibilities to German hands, along with the creation of strong states as a counterweight to the power of central authorities, were the key elements of this policy. The ultimate goal was the establishment of a democratic nation in the heart of Europe.

As a citizen and as a soldier Clay had fully believed in the enlightened wisdom of Roosevelt's one-world concept. During the first months on the job he had been concerned about the vindictive aspects of his directive until Henry Stimson had pointed the way: flexibility on economic issues but strict adherence to its political provisions. For two years, the General had faithfully followed this advice. Moreover, despite all the difficulties at the Allied Control Council, the lack of support by his government, and the occasional skepticism expressed at his own headquarters, he had always kept in mind the economic interests of the American people and done his utmost to make his mission a success.

But now he confronted a new situation. If there were any doubts that history had taken a new course, Moscow had laid them to rest. Cooperation with the Soviet Union in Germany as a viable policy alternative had evidently been written off at the highest levels of his government. Clay had been too close to the center of inter-Allied controversies to subscribe to all the anti-Soviet charges made at the meetings in Moscow's Aviation House.

He knew that all four Allies shared the blame for the fatal stalemate that had developed. It seemed especially unfortunate to him that the compromise on reparations he had worked out with Marshall Sokolovsky had been rejected by his government.

But he could also recognize the merits of the counterarguments. There was some validity in Bedell Smith's comment, "We are too naive politically to compete with the Russians in the framework envisaged at Potsdam." The State Department's Foreign Service, an elite corps trained only in the stately art of traditional diplomacy, was clearly not ready to take on the wily and unscrupulous Soviets in daily conflicts in Germany. Chip Bohlen, who knew the weaknesses of the American diplomatic service only too well, had expressed a similar thought when he suggested that "the French saved the United States by their early voting action."[1] Probably Secretary Byrnes had harbored identical views when he commented that "the State Department is not adapted to such work." He consistently refused to let the department take over in Germany. The world will never know which course of action would have been the better one.

Clay had seen his mission at the Allied Control Council in the idealistic light of the closing phase of his country's last crusade for democracy. Cooperation with the Russians in the heart of Europe and a disarmed democratic Germany had seemed to promise many years of uninterrupted peace. But now, after the failure at Moscow, he had no doubt that from here on it would be a different ball game. There would be two Germanys rather than one, and American troops would have to remain in Europe indefinitely. Moreover, with Byrnes gone and a new man at the helm, Clay's own modus operandi probably would be affected, too. He thought he had seen early signs of it at Spasso House where some of the State Department people seemed particularly assertive.

On the other hand, as he kept reminding himself, the army was not supposed to make policy anyway. He was still a soldier and he could take orders. Thirty years of army service had taught him how to fall in line and carry on. But as he landed at Tempelhof, he felt his heart was no longer in the job, and a spell of catfishing looked better than ever. He had told Bedell Smith that much before leaving Moscow. The ambassador was eager to take over the military government job and, with George Marshall's backing, there should be no problem. "I was sure," Clay later recalled, "that when Marshall left Moscow one of the first things he was going to do when he got back to the United States was to get General Smith in General Clay's place." "The earlier the better," he accordingly told Marjorie, who was in the hospital with a painful case of sciatica.[2]

The next morning brought the usual routine. Shortly before eight he was at his desk reading the overnight take from the news ticker tape, all forty feet of it. He always read it by pulling out the folds and throwing them over the front of his desk as rapidly as he could pull them. When Captain Allen, who had returned with him from Moscow, brought in the pot of coffee, she noticed he was still angry. During the day, eager for some news about the conference, more correspondents than usual flocked through the always-open doors of his office. They saw no change in his smile or in his frown. The great dark eyes dominated a face that somehow seemed thinner and older.

Clay's apprehension about the future was quickly confirmed by the first messages he got from Draper, who had remained in Moscow. With the failure of the conference in sight, Ernest Bevin had begun to focus on Bizonia. He suggested to Secretary Marshall not only the concentration of the bizonal agencies in one town and a new 10,000-ton production level for the steel industry but also the resumption of reparations shipments and the creation of a bizonal advisory council to include trade union representatives.[3] Clay's response to Draper indicated his barely concealed anger. For two years he had made such decisions at his own level, usually presenting Washington with faits accomplis. He could hardly object to the State Department's direct involvement, but he could and did express his dissatisfaction. One of his cables to Draper read:

> I am not prepared to comment on figures which as far as I am concerned are drawn out of a hat. I do not believe any firm agreement should be made with the British without detailed studies. While I have every confidence in your judgment, we have had no staff discussions relative to possible bizonal agreements being effected in Moscow. Therefore, please make clear that your recommendations are as an individual.[4]

Although Bevin and Marshall decided in Moscow to let the military governors work out the details of the bizonal setup, Clay soon learned of another encroachment on what he considered his bailiwick. Without his knowledge the British government had proposed a conversion factor for the Reichsmark that he himself, in prior discussions with Robertson, had rejected as inflationary. As he saw it, the fate of the German economy had been entrusted to him and, since the management of War Department funds appropriated for the occupation was his direct responsibility, he resented outside interference and felt his decision ought to be final. "I would urge that State Department advise the British Embassy," he cabled to the War Department,

> that the Bipartite Board is a joint agency of our two governments. If the Bipartite Board [i.e., Robertson and Clay] reaches complete disagreement then it should report its disagreements jointly to each of our governments for their decision. The board should be so instructed. If either member of the Bipartite Board [obviously meaning Robertson] is constantly to appeal at government level when agreement has not been reached, then the board might well be abolished and all decisions made at government level. This is an

example of British tendency to make end runs which I witnessed too often in Washington during the war. I believe that we can resolve these problems here but only if we are permitted to do so and individual disagreements are not resolved by ad hoc decisions at government levels. I feel this strongly in view of the financial responsibility which has been assumed by the War Department and for which I expect to be held responsible.[5]

More than anything else it was this problem of British and French "end runs" that was to disturb the Military Governor's relations with Washington during his remaining years in Germany. In the course of the resulting frequent disputes, the authoritarian side of Clay's personality consequently came into focus, causing sarcastic French remarks about the "Clay d'Orsay" as well as the British comment that "he looks like a Roman Emperor and acts like one." As far as the State Department was concerned, its resigned conclusion was that "whenever we go to a conference, we first have to make a treaty with our General."

The Military Governor had no doubt that the work at OMGUS would continue to take up most of his time, but he also resolved not to let this interfere with his new responsibilities as U.S. Commander in Chief, Europe. Neither George Marshall nor Dwight Eisenhower had been able to prevent the disintegration of the U.S. Army once the enemy had surrendered. But facing the demoralized and undisciplined army of occupation, Clay was determined to turn things around. He knew that if any one man could pull the troops back into shape it was Clarence Huebner, who had commanded the Big Red One Division during most of the war, and Clay requested his assignment to Germany. But even if the restoration of military preparedness and discipline had to be left by necessity to the local commander, equally important command functions could be handled in the course of weekly or biweekly field inspections from Berlin. Almost twenty years earlier, in the Canal Zone—the only time Lucius Clay had served with troops—he had been described as an officer who honestly liked his men and got the most he could from them. It was this sincere interest in the welfare of his men that frequently caught the attention of his aides during Clay's two years as CINCEUR.

Dick Hallock recalled Clay's behavior as Commander in Chief:

When he inspected troops, he would not go to army or division headquarters. He would go down to the company and to the platoon. He would go through kind of a half-run with a bevy of generals behind him trying to keep up. He would go through their mess halls and through their latrines to check their condition; and he would look into the squad rooms to see what kind of uniforms, clothing, and laundry service the men had. He would talk directly with the troops and ask questions of the junior officers, the NCOs and the enlisted men. When he found something he thought was wrong, or he could not get the answer to, then he would go back up to division headquarters to run down the solution to the problem. He would have nothing to do with the protocol around higher headquarters. He would go to the end product.[6]

"The high VD rate was of great concern to Clay," Jim Sundquist added.

At the first of his monthly meetings with the unit commanders at army headquarters in Heidelberg, the General backed by my charts and graphs brought up the subject. The rate of venereal diseases was much too high, he said, and he wanted it drastically reduced. Any officer whose unit for three consecutive months would show a rate above the Theater average would henceforth be relieved of his command. He spoke quietly and firmly but I knew there was hell to pay.[7]

The General was really a company commander at heart, Margaret Allen thought.

He was as interested in the morale as in the welfare of his men. Once on a Sunday—a new club for soldiers had been opened the same morning—he came to the office, obviously angry. 'Give me the headquarters commandant,' he said. 'I am closing the Enlisted Men's Club if we can't do things right. The men are standing outside in the rain. I will not tolerate it.' A few minutes earlier, Tommy Ryan, an eighteen-year-old enlisted man assigned to the General's office, had come in—starry-eyed. 'It's beautiful—the new club is beautiful,' he excitedly exclaimed. And now the General wanted to close it down. 'Please General,' he pleaded. 'Please, General Clay, do not close the club, it is so beautiful.' The General never could be persuaded to change his mind, but this was different. 'All right,' he said after Margaret Allen pointed out that at the beginning some deficiencies could be expected. 'I'll give it a couple of weeks. Cancel the call, Captain.'
  Another time, Clay had called in all the chaplains of the army. About ten or twelve of them were assembled in his office. He was concerned about troop morale and asked for the chaplains' advice and help. Various projects were proposed, all involving the outlay of funds. The General became visibly impatient. 'Gentlemen,' he finally said, 'who among you can give me the names of fifty of his men?' Only Father Powers, the Catholic chaplain in Berlin, raised his hand. Clay nodded, 'I know you do, Father,' he said. Since there was nobody else, he closed the meeting. 'Come back,' he said, 'when you know your men.'[8]

Within a year Huebner's and Clay's combined efforts had produced results. It was a spirited combat-ready American army that was standing guard in Germany at the time of the Military Governor's departure in 1949.

Before Moscow, the economic unification of the four zones had been Clay's main task. Now, when George Marshall stopped briefly in Berlin on his way from Moscow, Clay was given new instructions. The unification of Germany was clearly many years away, the Secretary said, and Clay together with his British counterpart, Sir Brian Robertson, was to proceed vigorously with strengthening the bizonal agencies. He also was to expedite the upward revision of the level of bizonal industry to increase the self-sufficiency of the area.[9] Nothing more was said about separating the Ruhr, however, which Clay took as a positive sign. In sum, he concluded after the meeting with Marshall, the temporary expedient of a bizonal merger was to become semipermanent. Moreover, if France eventually did join, a strong West Germany might emerge and become a cornerstone in his government's containment policy.

It was a new concept, a new mission, and a new challenge. For Clay it also was another engineering task involving six key elements. The first of them to be accomplished would be: the creation of an effective German administration; a new level-of-industry plan to settle the reparations issue; the establishment of a coal and steel authority to promote a substantial increase in coal production; and a vigorous promotion of bizonal exports. The final two elements, once the others had been achieved, would be a monetary reform and the setting up of a representative West German government. As engineering school had taught him, a time framework also had to be set up, with interim dates for the completion of each element. The summer of 1948 became his ultimate target date. In the meantime, as Clay anticipated, the work at the Control Council was bound to lose substance and its meetings would go through increasingly empty motions. A four-power currency reform remained the only major active issue on the agenda. Because Washington wanted the appearance of quadripartite cooperation preserved, negotiations for the reform had to be continued, but Clay realized now that more than technicalities stood in the way of a final understanding.

The American and British military governors agreed that the administrative and legislative relations between the bizonal agencies and the *Land* governments had to be put quickly on a new footing, but their views about the most desirable approach differed drastically. The British authorities favored central planning and control. Clay, on the other hand, surely influenced by his Southern upbringing, wanted a considerable degree of regional autonomy. He therefore promptly rejected Robertson's first reorganization plan while advising the War Department that "it would be completely unacceptable to the American public. . . . By astute maneuvering," he added, "the SPD had succeeded in putting Dr. Victor Agarts in the chairman's position in Minden. He had frequently announced that his principal mission was socialization."[10]

In the absence of any guidance from his government, the General had maintained the position that socialization and similar reforms would have to wait until the German people as a whole could vote on such issues.

Accordingly, he had firmly rejected requests from some members of his staff to assist trade unions or to authorize works councils, socialization and co-determination for labor, i.e. its right to participate in management decisions. The military government had to remain neutral in such matters, he had told the staff, and he was not about to yield now to the British. "It looks like a direct effort to introduce socialist controls," he cabled Noce, "which would pave the way to the complete socialization of the Ruhr area. . . . I am sure," he concluded, "that these terms are not consistent with our political objectives in Germany and even more sure that they would not be acceptable to the American businessmen and bankers on whom we must depend in the final analysis for success. . . ."[11]

The second British proposal was less objectionable. The concept of a highly centralized economy had been dropped; instead a powerful bizonal economic council was suggested. Its members were to be elected by the parliaments of the individual *Länder*, thus ensuring socialist majorities and, as Clay advised Noce, "serving British political interests." Given authority to try for a more acceptable setup, the Military Governor brought his negotiating skills into play. The result was a compromise that the British accepted within a few weeks. It converted the existing committees into bizonal functional departments to be headed by executive directors, and it created two new German agencies. One, an Economic Council resembling a parliament, would have 52 members, each selected by the *Landtage* of the eight *Länder* on the basis of one per 750,000 population. The council would have legislative authority only in the field of economics, and it was subject to military government veto. The second new agency was an eight-men executive committee comprised of one representative from each *Land* appointed by the *Land* government. Its function would be to propose ordinances for adoption by the Economic Council, to issue implementing regulations, and to nominate the department directors for appointment by the Economic Council. The Executive Committee was to serve as a full-time executive agency of the bizonal organization, with supervising authority over the directors of the future ministries.[12] To control this new German administration an American-British Bipartite Control Office (BICO), with some nine hundred officers, was created. All these agencies were now brought together in Frankfurt am Main.

In sum, Clay had fashioned the administrative machinery as much as possible in accord with the traditional American principles of checks and balances. Whereas the Economic Council would protect political party interests, the members of the Executive Committee would protect the interests of the *Land* governments that had appointed them. The *Land* governments, finally, were to act as regional administrative agents with the authority to carry out implementing legislation. As exepcted, the newly created Executive Committee was controlled by the Social Democrats, but thanks to Clay's political engineering its power was balanced by the Economic Council, where the conservative parties held a narrow majority. (On July 23 a coalition of the Christian Democratic Union [CDU] and the Christian Social Union [CSU] with the Free Democratic Party [FDP] won control by a vote of twenty-seven to twenty-two.) It was a temporary solution, but the Military Governor anticipated that by the time economic conditions had been stabilized an established pattern would exist with some influence on the political framework of a future German government.

Although the British attempted to limit German capacity in fields competitive with U.K. industries, it was not too difficult to reach an agreement on a new level of industry, the second item on Clay's bizonal reconstruction project. The new plan, completed early in July, raised the much-disputed limitations on steel production from 5.8 million ingot tons to 10.7 million tons and increased other industrial levels accordingly. The effect of the old plan would have been to limit total industrial capacity to only 70 or 75 percent of 1936 German production, but the revised plan was expected to retain sufficient capacity in the bizonal area "to approximate the level of industry prevailing in Germany in 1936, a year that was not characterized by either boom or depressed conditions."[13]

Clay was aware of the largely theoretical aspects of this exercise in economic analysis, because at a time when a steel production of 10.7 million ingot tons was being discussed, the actual steel production in the bizone was about 2 million tons; and when $2 billion of bizonal exports were being planned, actual exports were far below the contemplated modest program of $350 million for 1947. Moreover, only moderate increases for the immediate future were in sight. Of considerable practical significance, however, was the effect of the revised level on the extent of reparations: of the 1,200 nonwar plants originally earmarked for reparations under the four-power program, more than half could now be removed from the reparations list.[14]

The completion of the new level-of-industry agreement happened to coincide with the replacement of JCS #1067 by a new directive, JCS #1779, that did away with all economic restrictions. Furthermore, the tone of the new instructions, compared to the vindictive phrases of the original, was positive and upbeat. Particularly encouraging in the light of Clay's new mission was his government's now proclaimed intention to "create those political and economic and moral conditions in Germany which will contribute most effectively to a stable and prosperous Europe."[15] But the new level-of-industry plan, as well as the new directive, created serious problems on the diplomatic front.

When the Allied Control Council was informed of the bizonal developments, the Soviets confined themselves to the comment that "the latest bizonal arrangements are aimed at further accentuating the split of Germany."[16] But the French government began a diplomatic offensive to block implementation of the new level. For two years General Koenig had successfully worked at the Allied Control Authority against the reemergence of a unified Germany. Because after Moscow this seemed more and more a dead issue, the Quai d'Orsay now focused on containing the growth of West Germany's economic strength. It was this policy that put the American Military Governor and the Quai d'Orsay again on a collision course.

The French representative at the Control Council had under orders based his numerous vetoes on the fact that his government was not a signatory to the Potsdam Agreement. Now he switched to a different tack. General Marshall's speech at Harvard University in early June had launched the European Recovery Program which, in addition to providing American funds, entailed the active cooperation of the European nations and a significant role for France. By using this new influence to the hilt and occasionally playing on Washington's continuous fears of a Communist takeover in Paris, the foreign minister, Georges Bidault, was trying to delay economic progress in the British and American zones.

The new level-of-industry program was still in its final negotiating stage when Clay received some strange instructions from the War Department. On the one hand the new industrial level ought to permit Germany to make a significant contribution to European economic recovery, the message said, and on the other it ought to produce substantial reparations for the countries of Western Europe.[17] Sensing that something was in the wind but still holding his fire, Clay merely pointed out that his calculations "had not been based on delivery of any specific quantities to IARA nations," but only "on the need for a German industry which will provide a self-supporting economy. . . . We cannot negotiate under indefinite instructions," he concluded.[18] Any doubts he might have had about the developments on the Potomac were removed some ten days later, when he and Robertson were about to announce the completed level-of-industry agreement. Although he was told only that the announcement had to be deferred because of "political implications," he had a pretty good idea who was behind it. "It would appear that these political implications result from French opposition," he cabled to Petersen.

> We had no doubt at the time we were instructed to revise the level of industry that it would develop. Moreover the utilization of a method of attack against French government by Communists seems a part of their plan to prevent at all costs an economic revival in Western Germany. It seems to me that in Western Germany we are completely stymied at present. Frankly I am at wit's end to do anything progressive in economic rehabilitation. . . .[19]

Washington did not reply. But when a few days later he was confronted with French newspaper reports of a letter from Marshall to Bidault promising deferment of the level-of-industry decision, Clay decided he had had enough. Since Petersen confirmed the news, he asked to be brought home. The International Coal Conference that Washington had planned would enable him to bow out quietly, he said. And he angrily added that two years had convinced him that the United States could not have a common

German policy with the French. "Still I am held responsible for economic debacle in Germany and I can no longer accept that responsibility. Believe me, I understand full well the State Department's established policy and when we who are responsible for execution cannot accept it we must go."[20]

Because Murphy also advised the State Department of Clay's intention to retire and expressed concern that "Clay may feel obliged to make certain public statements,"[21] Eisenhower was brought into the act. "I thoroughly understand your sense of frustration . . . ," Ike cabled to his friend.

> You and I have served too long in this Army to contemplate se-riously the laying down of a task simply because things sometimes go at sixes and sevens through no fault of our own. Times are too critical for anyone to move out of a post in which he can serve our country's interest. As a final word please remember that now abide Faith, Hope, and Charity, these three, and greater than any is a sense of humor.[22]

Clay's reply indicated how unbearable he considered the conditions under which he had to operate. Reminding Ike that he could not have run the Allied Expeditionary Force if he had been kept in the dark about conditions elsewhere, he suggested that it might be a mistake for him to continue in a job without the support of the policy makers. "Leaving a job under such circumstances might well be in the best interests of the job and not 'running out!' " he cabled Ike. "Nevertheless, I value your friendship and good will too much not to accept your adivce. If you think that my departure would be running out of the job and failing in my obligation to an Army which had been more than good to me, that is enough to keep me here."[23]

There were two additional messages from Washington that probably helped persuade the Military Governor to remain in his job. They confirmed that both the State and War departments would "support vigorously" the level of industry agreement reached by Clay and Robertson. Moreover, no other country would have "any vote, veto or power of decision as to the bizonal level of industry."[24] Temporarily appeased and unaware that the worst was still to come, Clay advised Kenneth Royall, the new Secretary of War, that he fully understood the possible necessity for amending the agreed level of industry to conform to an overall European program.[25] He objected, however, to letting French Communism play a leading role in fixing the Western occupying powers' German policy, "which means that our program for Western Germany is largely influenced by the Soviets."

The General wanted an early announcement of the new level of industry mainly for the beneficial effect he believed it would have on German morale. Lagging coal production, on the other hand, presented a more direct and crucial problem. It had been clear to Clay from the outset that if his commitments to Congress were to be fulfilled on time and a self-sustaining bizonal economy created, a substantial increase in Ruhr coal output was a sine qua non. Daily coal production in the Ruhr before the war had averaged 400,000 tons; when the British took over in 1945, it had dropped to 105,000 tons; by January 1947 it had climbed back to only 215,000 tons and there was little further recovery in sight. Clay had discussed the problem with John Kenneth Galbraith and other advisors even before the bizonal merger enabled him to take an active hand in the solution. Part of the answer was of course to find a way of giving the miners the food they needed for their heavy work.[26] The British, on very low rations themselves and following a policy of equal shares for all, had objected to any solution that would give more calories to German miners than their own people at home enjoyed. Once the merger of the two zones had been decided upon, Clay was able to bring his influence to bear, and in a January meeting with Robertson and German trade union leaders at the Villa Huegel, the Krupp's family former residence, a new policy was announced.[27] The miners got a healthy increase in their rations, and a filling lunch—not counted against the ration—would be served in the mines. Progress, nevertheless, remained slow. The American coal experts at OMGUS—very much aware of the high production figures in the Russian zone—were prodding their British colleagues as hard as they could. But as they frequently complained to Clay, they encountered a typical colonial civil service attitude: slowness, stubbornness, unwillingness to make decisions and just plain inefficiency. And great quantities of coal continued to disappear from coal dealers' stocks on moving or standing coal trains and from the coal yards of the occupying forces.[28] Despite frequent American admonishments, however, nothing was done to correct the situation.

Continued French insistence on increased exports of coal accentuated the problem for Clay. If additional coal was exported, he argued, and the inadequate domestic supplies even further reduced, the only result would be a further debilitation of the German economy that would drag coal output down with it. It was difficult, he wrote, to convince the French of this when they deliberately interpreted his attitude as an unwillingness to help the countries that had suffered most at German hands.[29] While in Moscow, he had been able to work out a settlement with Robertson and Alphand, the economic advisor from the Quai d'Orsay, that entailed a sliding scale for coal exports to France. Starting at 18 percent, it would rise to 25 percent of production as output increased. Draper and Clay agreed that it was a temporary compromise at best and that French complaints would continue as long as coal production continued to lag.

The Military Governor was therefore pleased when early in June he learned of plans for a broad American-British program to increase coal production and was asked for his recommendations. "It is clear from the record," he wrote Patterson, "that the curve of coal production goes up and down with the availability of food." He nevertheless opposed special and costly incentive schedules—in the form of CARE packages, for instance—

because they would bring only spurts of increased output; once the incentive was earned, production would quickly drop off again.[30] In his judgment, the basic problem in the Ruhr came from the uncertainty about the coal fields' future status and the absence of an incentive for mine management. He therefore recommended that the mines be placed immediately under a German trusteeship and this move accompanied by a public announcement that the trusteeship would continue "until there is a central German government and the German people can freely determine under stable conditions the future of mine ownership." He said the question of nationalization was a formidable barrier to increased production and that a trusteeship arrangement offered the logical interim solution. "If the British government will accept such an arrangement we can do much here to see that coal production leads the upward swing of the German economy."[31]

Moreover, never willing to postpone till tomorrow what could be done today, he instructed Draper to submit the trusteeship plan at the next meeting of the Bipartite Economic Panel.[32] The initial negative British reaction revealed Bevin's plans for early nationalization of the industry and gave Clay the opportunity to ask his government for advice and instructions. Reiterating his own position, he pointed out that he had no quarrel with socialization approved by the electorate as long as the enterprise involved was not of national significance. But if it was, socialization in his judgment should wait until normal conditions had returned, with a central German government in charge, and the German people given an opportunity to decide. "We must reject or accept socialization now," Clay cabled to Petersen.[33] He had the satisfaction within a day or two of having Robertson accept the trusteeship idea "in princple." On the other hand, as so often in the past, the State Department reply was dilatory. It has been decided, the Military Governor was advised, "to invite the British government to send a delegation to Washington as soon as possible for purpose of discussing the German coal problem."[34] In other words, negotiations were again taken out of his hands, a practice he had protested against only a week earlier. "I do not believe it is helpful for discussions on German problems to be undertaken at other places while these problems are also under discussion in Berlin," he told the War Department.

> If the same problem is being discussed in several places it is much more difficult to secure full coordination of the American position. I recognize that German problems which cannot be resolved in Germany must be resolved at governmental level. I would like to suggest however that coal problems not be discussed in detail elsewhere until discussions have proved fruitless in Germany.[35]

It became increasingly clear to Clay that his objections had little impact and that he would have to live with the State Department's modus operandi or get out. He could not foresee that a dramatic clash between the War and State departments would bring the issue of policy coordination to an early head. It was Kenneth Royall, the Secretary of War, who triggered the dispute during a Berlin press conference on August 1 with the remark that he "knew of no agreement to consult with France before promulgation of the plan to raise the level of industry in Germany.[36] Royall had a right to assume that he was on safe ground, because only three days earlier Marshall had advised Murphy that no other country would have any say regarding a new bizonal level-of-industry plan.

In France, however, his remark—coming closely after the withdrawal of JCS #1067—had the effect of a bombshell. "No matter what Washington pretended it to mean," reported David Schoenbrun from Paris,

> it meant only one thing in France—priority for the reconstruction of Germany over the reconstruction of France. Foreign Minister Georges Bidault and company almost keeled over with shock while Maurice Thorez and the Communists chortle those famous last words, 'We told you so.' It is now an open secret . . . that France probably would walk out on the Marshall Plan, if America implemented to the full the apparent German program.[37]

Bob Lovett, the Undersecretary of State, advised Marshall that the French government interpreted Royall's remarks as a disavowal of the assurances the Secretary had in fact given Bidault only ten days earlier. "We are," he wrote, "exposing the United States in its relations with France to a justified charge of duplicity and dishonest dealings."[38]

The Military Governor was apprised of this development five days later in a teleconference with Kenneth Royall and William Draper on the Washington end. (Draper had just been made Undersecretary of Army. Nominally Clay's superior, he actually was from then on the Military Governor's spokesman at the Pentagon.) Apparently reading from a prepared text,[39] Royall informed Clay that developments since his visit to Berlin now made it virtually imperative for the United States government to agree to hold tripartite discussions concerning the level of German industry and the coal issue. "I have not agreed to these discussions yet," Royall said, "but I feel that I may have to do so."Because of the Military Governor's prestige he considered it most important for Clay to participate as the War Department's representative in the tripartite discussion. He wanted to clear up the level of industry and coal issues, Royall added, but let the French know at the same time that this was not to be taken as a precedent and that "they will have no further opportunity to interfere with bizonal matters unless and until they join their zone to ours."

Clay was stunned. The French had done it again. They had frustrated his first mission and now they opposed his substitute plan to make Bizonia a going concern. "My feeling is one of complete futility," he replied.

> I cannot attend as representative of the War Department. I am not saying this in a spirit of saying I quit because I can't get my way,

but I can see no hope for the solution of the German problem ahead and feel that my own ability to contribute to it is at an end. Vexing German problems cannot be solved elsewhere.[40]

Faced with the alternative of seriously alienating America's troublesome ally, Secretary Marshall decided to give in to the French. A three-power conference would convene in London with Ambassador Douglas heading the United States delegation, he advised the London embassy. The agreements reached by Robertson and Clay were to be vigorously defended, and only if there was "a genuine threat to the success of the European economic plan or to democracy in France" should suggestions for changes be submitted to Washington.[41] As far as Clay's attendance was concerned, Marshall showed little concern. He knew that Bedell Smith was waiting in Moscow, anxious to take over. Only Justice Byrnes' threat to go before Congress if Clay were relieved had prevented the contemplated change. Should the Military Governor resign, however, it would be a different matter. As Marshall said, this was essentially Secretary Royall's problem.[42] A problem undoubtedly it was, because, as Murphy advised the department, this was different from earlier resignations. "The General seems to have lost interest in the job."[43]

A few days later in a teleconference with Draper,[44] Clay let off some of the steam: "Even a soldier cannot continue to run a job in which he is not in harmony with those for whom he works," he said. "It is of course possible to run Germany from Washington, although what the results will be only time would show. I am not willing to accept the responsibility for military government in Germany with operation decisions being made elsewhere. No one is irreplaceable." He added, "I am glad those eminent German experts Douglas, Caffery, and Clayton have all problems solved. This actually obviates any need for participation in the London conference." He acknowledged that he was under orders to attend but he "did not sign up to work for Lew Douglas"; and while he had assured Royall that he would carry out all orders as long as he remained in Germany, he "did not say how long he would reamin in Germany." Undoubtedly his life-long guideposts—"duty, honor, and country"—played an important part in the General's ultimate decision to attend the London Conference. But even more important was Royall's assurance that he was trying "to induce State to take over military government." In the meantime every effort was being made "to get you the freest possible hand in the economic and other problems in Germany. If State does not take over promptly, I will seek approval of a bizonal directive to that end."[45]

Although Clay agreed to attend, he continued to resent having the role of advisor to Douglas forced on him. Accordingly, when he was questioned by Delbert Clark and other correspondents about the significance of the impending conference, his answers were short and noncommittal. It was different though when, the day before his departure for London, Marguerite Higgins from the *New York Herald Tribune* came to his office. His attitude toward the conference had not changed, but according to his code a Southern gentlement did not talk sharply to a lady. Miss Higgins' questions about an apparent Pentagon-State Department feud, delays in Germany's reconstruction, and the General's own role in the dispute were somewhat irritating, but Clay patiently explained that "it was better if the level-of-industry plan was accepted by three and still better if approved by four." As far as Bizonia was concerned, he added, "the plan was still a good approach," so that management could know which industrial plants would go for reparations and which would stay."[46]

The London Conference lasted five days and the results were better than Clay had expected, although the tensions within the American delegation were quite apparent. Douglas commented that Clay was a fine man for an army job but "not good in negotiations especially with foreigners," and in fact at a dinner with some of the Foreign Service officers, Clay remarked that he had had all that he could stand. Since no one had sent him any orders, he told them he had to make decisions on his own. Now they were carping at him and asking him to do things that were not in his basic instructions.[47] Mistrust and animosities were mutual. As some of the officials from the State Department saw it, the Military Governor completely distrusted any personnel not subordinate to him and even refused to be honest with them. They thought the same attitude extended to some of his subordinates. Clay's alleged refusal to take a broad view of American interests and to accept supervision from Washington was another one of their frequent complaints.[48]

The communiqué on the tripartite talks published on August 28 settled the Military Governor's principal concern: the plan for the level of industry that he and Robertson had agreed upon would be announced the following day.[49] As far as the bizonal plan for the management and control of the Ruhr mines was concerned, it was agreed that "it would not prejudge the future status of the mines." Furthermore the three delegations agreed that the measures about to be taken should not result in priority being given to the rehabilitation of Germany over that of the democratic countries of Europe. In sum, while the conference had been a diplomatic victory for France, the Anglo-American positions on the issues under discussion remained unchanged.

On his return from London, Clay could focus again on the two programs—denazification and decartelization—which had given him trouble before and which, in the light of a changed political climate, required early restructuring. Wartime passions back home had calmed down, and the economic revival of West Germany had become an official priority goal. William Griffith noted that by the summer of 1947 the majority of the leaders of American public opinion, "while fully conscious that Germany was neither denazified nor repentant," felt that German economic recovery was essential to fight Communism and that it should not be delayed by further attempts at "thorough denazification."[50]

The Military Governor had a good notion of what was in store. As recently as January, he had stated that the denazification program would be relentlessly pursued, but already the Moscow Conference had brought about a significant change. One of the few accomplishments of the Council of Foreign Ministers meeting had been a four-power agreement directing that denazification be expedited "by all appropriate measures" and that a date be fixed for its completion. The program should concentrate on active supporters of the Nazi regime, the agreement said, "without requiring the indiscriminate trial of the mass of nominal members of the Nazi Party." The Allied Control Authority was charged with putting these provisions into law. The Moscow decision made changes in America's denazification procedures inevitable, and it was soon reinforced by the new directive to Clay that was replacing JCS #1067. Whereas the six hundred words of his original denazification instruction had been all-comprehensive, JCS #1779 merely directed him "to implement in your zone the decision on denazification taken on April 23, 1947, by the Council of Foreign Ministers as may be agreed in the Allied Control Council."

At that time, there were still more than 700,000 cases requiring mandatory trials before German tribunals. With an average monthly trial rate of only 25,000, it was self-evident that two years would be required to bring the program to a close.[51] And Clay realized from discussions with influential visitors from Washington that he would not have those two years, that from one day to the next he might be faced with a cutoff of congressional appropriations. He still was pondering a face-saving retreat when the Soviets eased his dilemma. Rather than wait for a four-power implementation of the Moscow decision, the Soviet military government proceeded unilaterally on August 17 to turn over denazification to German tribunals with specific instructions to proceed rapidly and leniently with the small fry. It was essentially a propaganda move, although one in accord with the rational Soviet approach to the social and economic problems of the denazification process. Amendments to the regulations in the American zone thus had become inevitable. When urged by the War Department "to close out denazification quickly," Clay knew that prompt action was required. In a memorandum to the minister-presidents he suggested that the denazification proceedings be speeded up. He would be willing to accept some procedural changes, he wrote, as long as "the basic principles of the law were preserved." There was considerable disagreement within OMGUS about how to proceed, with the Public Safety Branch opposing and Clay's new denazification advisor, Theo Hall, urging early and substantial changes. After a few months of intramural debates in Berlin and intense American-German deliberations, an expedited system was agreed upon that also ended some of the employment restrictions. Public prosecutors, moreover, were authorized to accelerate proceedings and to reclassify the more nominally incriminated offenders as "followers." As a result, six months later only 110,000 cases remained on the tribunals' agenda.[52]

Since the decartelization program was not as much in the public eye, it was easier for the Military Governor to adjust to the swing in American public opinion. One of the most ardent supporters of the program, James Martin, who had headed the decartelization branch, tired of battling his opponents in the Economic Division and resigned in June.[53] By the time he left steps were underway to break up the I.G. Farben properties located in Bizonia into fifty-two independent operating units, each headed by a trustee. Their sale as independent enterprises was the ultimate aim.[54] In a parallel move, the British military government had launched "Operation Severance" with the objective of breaking the steel and iron cartels into smaller entities. And the six big banking systems that had controlled virtually the entire German financial operations had been broken up, their activities restricted to the individual *Länder*.

After Martin's departure, the Decartelization Branch was reorganized into working groups with the task of preparing cases for evaluation by a bizonal deconcentration review board. According to the Military Governor's instructions, the first job was to enforce the law and let the results show whether the program was workable and effective. The decartelization staff had consequently selected a number of monopolistic combines with a record of collaboration in the Nazi economy, preferably with international ties, that had made them tools of economic warfare.[55] These combines would be asked to show cause why they should not be broken up into several independent enterprises under new management.[56] Since it was going to take well into 1948 before the necessary staff studies could be completed, Clay knew that there was no need to rush a decision on other possible decartelization moves.

In the meantime he would continue to concentrate on the bizonal merger which now, in the light of Marshall's European Recovery Program, looked more promising than ever. Knowing Congress, Clay was not sanguine about the European program's actual enactment, but he gave it an even chance. When Washington asked about Germany's possible contribution to such a program, he made his position clear. All economic restrictions would have to be removed, feeding levels increased to normal standards, and sufficient coal for production left in Germany. The European nations would have to recognize that Germany could afford to buy only the most essential commodities, which generally were the key goods needed by *all* of Europe. Whenever a European nation could not pay for German exports in similar commodities, it would have to pay in dollars. Presumably those dollars would have to be provided under the proposed recovery program.

Clay cited other obstacles that had to be overcome: British efforts to reestablish European trade in sterling and the reluctance of European countries to forget about the past and do business again with Germany. The estimated annual costs for the German tranche of a European Recovery Program to pay for food, fertilizers and POL (petrol, oil and lubricants) was $750 million, he thought; about half this amount would be needed for other raw materials. In conclusion, he stressed the need to grant German representatives of military government—who would later represent a German government—full access to European conferences and trade markets. His final recommendation: "Germany must be given hope to early equality in treatment and not to be relegated indefinitely to an inferior status."[57]

Regardless of the outcome of a European plan, however, Clay told his staff Bizonia had to be made a going concern and military government quickly liquidated. "He was obsessed with this notion," James Sundquist recalled.

> When we discussed this, he frequently referred to his background in Georgia and his experiences as a boy when he heard about the carpetbaggers and how everybody hated them. The longer they stayed the more the South hated the North. He assumed the Germans would react the same way and he was determined to prevent it. This had burned itself quite deeply into his consciousness.[58]

When the CIC approached Clay with a request to increase its personnel to control the black market, he promptly turned them down. "Where do I find the agents to watch the new agents you intend to hire?" he asked. He knew that once there was a new currency the black market would disappear. In the meantime, he contained the problem by ordering the excessive inventory level of the post exchanges reduced. All PX warehouses in the American zone except one were closed and only a twenty-day stock authorized. This would prove more effective than thousands of new agents, he told the CIC.[59]

It was Sundquist's job to monitor the various divisions of the military government and come up with quarterly recommendations as to what projects could be phased out or pared down during the next period. Reduced personnel ceilings were the principal tool toward that end. But, as Sundquist commented,

> I don't think I was ever ahead of Clay on this. Long before I got around to initiating the procedure whereby we reviewed each one of these activities, Clay would call me in and give me the answers. He would say, now by the end of this quarter I want the transportation function eliminated, the religious affairs function closed, the education function cut or eliminated, whatever his decision had been. It was my job to protest and say, look you are going too fast. Would you let me look into that? So then it would be a matter of my being in the odd position of defending the operating units against the Commander in Chief, rather than being his hatchet man to do the cutting. But he was usually right. The hardest battle was

education. Reviewing textbooks and reconstructing the education system was a big and important job, but Clay maintained that no army of occupation had every succeeded in superimposing an educational and cultural pattern on a conquered people. It took some persuasion to change his mind, but Herman Wells, who had come to Berlin from the University of Indiana to advise the Military Governor on educational and cultural affairs, sided with management control. So the ax that was about to fall on that activity was restrained.[60]

The German administrative agencies in Bizonia had been organized and a new level of industry agreed upon, but the most difficult part of the program—the balancing of exports and imports—remained.[61] The War Department had promised Congress that Bizonia's foreign trade balance would be in the black within three or four years, but when the Military Governor looked at the figures in the fall of 1947, it was clear that the export target of $350 million for the year would not be reached and probably would fall $100 million short.[62] The Joint Export Import Agency, which had been established under the terms of the Bevin-Byrnes agreement, was trying to return to normal commercial practices, but (as Larry Wilkinson on occasion had to remind the impatient General) this was easier said than done. In spite of the gradual removal of travel and communications restrictions, the continued involvement of the military government was unavoidable as long as Germany had no viable currency and most producers therefore reluctant to sell. For the same reason the fixing of appropriate exchange rates had to remain a JEIA responsibility. Originally, a list of conversion factors ranging from thirty to eighty cents for the Reichsmark had been published,[63] but it soon became apparent that export pricing based on an inflexible list was impractical and pricing authority was therefore delegated to the field. Branch officers were instructed to determine the fair market value of export goods "measured by sales of comparable products on the international markets." It was obviously an emergency solution involving the difficult and highly complex task of market research in many countries regarding many hundreds of industrial products. Clay's specific instructions that "particular care was to be exercised to insure that evidence is on hand to refute possible future charges of selling below recognized market levels" demonstrated the route he was trying to go in order to balance Bizonia's foreign trade. At the same time, his concurrent and prolonged struggle to raise the ten-dollar export price of Ruhr coal—the world market price was twenty to twenty-five dollars—reflected the political environment he was obliged to operate in. The objections from the State Department to a new price for coal were identical with those raised against Clay's dollar policy, and in both cases he had to compromise. An export price of fifteen dollars was eventually agreed upon,[64] and a number of trade agreements offered at least temporary relief from the dollar problem because they provided for offset accounts in European banks in the currency of the importing country.[65] A foreign currency bonus to German exporters and processing transactions in which foreign firms supplied the raw materials were other devices used to stimulate foreign trade. Even with these remedial programs progress would clearly be slow. Only after a currency reform could a substantial increase in German exports be expected.

Trade agreements and offset accounts had eased the dollar problem for several of Germany's European trading partners. In the case of Great Britain and the sterling area, however, a more permanent solution had to be found.

The ink was hardly dry on the Bevin-Byrnes agreement when serious financial difficulties arose. Great Britain found it increasingly difficult to furnish the dollars required for the initial capital of the Joint Export-Import Agency, and for the subsequent funding of purchases of food, fertilizers and seed on world markets. Accordingly, General Robertson tried to find legal angles whereby he could substitute sterling for hard currency, an approach seriously resisted by the Finance Division at OMGUS.[66] Initially General Clay bent over backward to accommodate the British, and on several occasions actually overruled the technical reservations of his staff.[67] Nevertheless, when exports from Bizonia progressed more slowly than expected and the food situation demanded an increasing dollar outlay, it became clear that the weakness of the pound sterling would make it impossible for the British government to live up to the terms of the original agreement. In accordance with the emergency provisions of the 1946 understanding, American and British representatives therefore met in Washington in the fall of 1947 to negotiate some significant changes in the original fusion agreement. Clay participated in the first round of negotiations, but as they continued to drag on he returned to Germany, leaving behind as his representative Jack Bennett, his financial advisor.[68]

The revised agreement, signed by Robert Lovett for the United States and Sir William Strang for the United Kingdom, acknowledged the British inability to continue to pay dollars for German imports. Great Britain was therefore no longer liable to pay dollars for so-called Category A imports (food, fertilizers, and seed) into the bizonal area. For the following year Great Britain took on a very limited obligation to supply food as well as services, mainly by providing British ships to carry freight. The remainder of Category A goods, however, was to be supplied by the United States. By virtue of its increased contributions, the U.S. government obtained "a larger measure of authority" with regard to the Joint Export Import Agency and the Joint Foreign Exchange Agency. In both agencies the relative American and British voting strength would "reflect the proportion of appropriated funds made available to the bizone by the two governments." Probably the most consequential change affecting Clay's dollar policy was a new directive to JEIA "to maximize all trade between Bizonia and the sterling area and to conduct such trade in sterling." The new arrangement put a dent in Clay's fundamental approach to the appropriation problem, but Britain was broke and these were the best terms obtainable.

The revised agreement gave the American Military Governor the right of final decision in financial and economic matters. On his insistence, it left intact American-British parity in political affairs. There had been some pressure from higher levels to insist on a predominant American voice, but a politically astute Clay concluded that British and American objectives in Germany were close, and genuine cooperation with the British therefore essential. "To insist on lowering their status to that of a junior partner," he wrote, "would have damaged British prestige in Europe and was not really to our interest."[69]

The slow progress in bizonal exports was paralleled by developments in the Ruhr. Peacetime production remained the goal but all through 1947 daily production hovered around 260,000 tons—65 percent of that goal. Clay therefore viewed with skepticism the coal conference which, on Secretary Marshall's insistence, convened in Washington the second week of August. Not only did he object to negotiations on German internal affairs at "so many places and so many levels that no single person could comprehend them," but he also knew that no simple magic formula could be found to produce more coal. Food, transportation, housing for the miners, and a host of related questions had to be considered at the conference, none of which permitted an early solution. The conference, attended by unusually large American and British delegations, lasted four weeks but, as Clay had expected, the practical results were almost nil. The report and its recommendations generally confirmed Clay's agreement with Robertson to return the mines to German management. This should be done quickly in the expectation that German miners would produce more coal if they were working under German direction.[70] The new management would be supervised by a joint American-British control group acting for the military commanders, giving the United States for the first time an equal share in the administration of the Ruhr. But the report contained only the vaguest reference to the controversial issues of ownership of the Ruhr mines and British socialization schemes, which, the American government insisted, ought to be shelved as long as coal production remained a problem.[71]

The contest for a strong West Germany as a bulwark against Communism had by then captured Clay's fancy, supplanting the challenge of his earlier mission. Unification was still being discussed at the Allied Control Council in Berlin, but it was more talk than substance. In Clay's judgment the impending London Conference of Foreign Ministers would probably serve the same purpose. By November, therefore, he began to pressure the War Department for decisive action. Now that a transitional German administration for Bizonia had been set up and a new level of industry announced, the early establishment of a West German government seemed of paramount importance. "We must have the courage to proceed quickly with the government of West Germany," he told Draper. "We cannot continue successfully unless we establish a governmental machinery for Western Germany. The resentment of the Germans against colonial administration is increasing daily."[72]

There was a parallel hardening of Clay's stance vis-à-vis the Soviet Union. For more than a year he had rejected suggestions from members of Murphy's staff to protest at the Control Council the terrorist practices in the Russian zone.[73] As late as August 1946 he had opposed the establishment of Radio Liberty—which directed its transmissions from Munich to the U.S.S.R.—as "not in spirit of quadripartite government."[74] Now, one year later, acting entirely on his own volition, he announced to the press that the United States would begin a new policy of defending American principles of freedom and "of attacking those in which we do not believe." "We do propose to attack Communism and the police state before the German people," he explained to the questioning War Department, "whereas in the past we have confined our efforts to presenting the advantage of democracy." Characteristically, he could not bring himself to admit to others, and probably not to himself, that his attitude toward the Russians had changed. There is no major change in policy, he argued in a remarkable display of sophistry. "Under JCS #1067 our political objectives are to protect democracy which means to resist Communism. While it is true that no instructions have been given us to attack Communism, certainly we have not been told to refrain from such attack."[75] He knew of course that at home public opinion had begun to shift, that cooperation with Russia was being replaced by the new concept of a strong West German bulwark against Communism. "I must say with all sincerity at my command," Clay commented, that "42 million Germans in the British and American zones represent the strongest outposts against Communist penetration that exists anywhere. We can fail in Germany by doing nothing or too little to recreate German leadership of the German people. It is almost too late."[76]

As in Moscow, Clay had a ringside seat at the London Conference, where proceedings at Lancaster House were even more disappointing than expected.[77] Several meetings were needed to reach agreement even on the agenda; and when the ministers decided to form four permanent committees to study questions relating to a German peace treaty, they were unable to agree on the composition of the committees. A reception at Buckingham Palace was one of the few pleasant interludes. In Moscow some efforts had still been made to maintain the fiction of an alliance, but all pretense was dropped in London and the verbal exchanges between the delegates became increasingly abrasive. When Molotov stated in so many words that the Soviet position at Moscow stood unchanged and that unification of Germany had to go hand in hand with an agreement on reparations, the fate of the conference was sealed. From then on it became merely a jockeying for the best propaganda position at the time of the unavoidable break. "It is important to choose our ground carefully and to time it to the best possible advantage," the Secretary of State advised Washington. "We must at the same time be careful to avoid allowing ourselves to be maneuvered by the Russians into a situation where the break occurred on what would later appear to be an inconsequential point which would not carry conviction with our public opinion."[78] On December 15, three weeks after the conference had begun, the right time was at hand, and following Secretary Marshall's suggestion it adjourned sine die. There was a touch of melancholy in Lucius Clay's comment on this end to Franklin Roosevelt's dream:

> To those of us who had started quadripartite government in Germany with determination to make it work, who had believed for a few months [sic] that it might work and who had tried to make it work in the face of daily obstruction and frustration, there was a special significance in the results of the London Conference. While I recognized the inevitability of the course we had to follow, it was not with exhilaration but with sadness over the failure of a 'noble experiment' that I left Lancaster House when the final meeting adjourned.[79]

For Clay's assignment, the most significant development in London was an Anglo-American meeting after the breakup of the conference with Marshall and Bevin participating. The meeting in fact decided the future course of action in Germany. There would be one more effort to introduce a new currency for all of Germany, but unless there was a prompt result a bizonal currency reform would be undertaken. The dismantlement program would be continued and reparations delivered to the IARA countries. There would be a gradual evolution of a West German government "without dramatic declarations." Negotiations with France would continue in the hope that by the following summer the French would be prepared to join. The Americans and British also decided to stay in Berlin and to participate in the deliberations of the Allied Control Council "unless it is disrupted by Soviet representatives."[80]

At long last Clay had a clear road ahead of him. His relations to Marshall also had undergone a change for the better. The Secretary had not been happy to see Dulles take off on his own for Paris to consult with General de Gaulle. At the same time Clay's articulate presentation on the full merger of the zones, on the setting up of a constitutional assembly and the drafting of a constitution had made an impression. "From then on," Clay later recalled, "I had complete support from the Secretary." In a similar vein he advised Draper that "our week in London has brought us into a very close relationship with the State Department personnel concerned with occupation policy, and there appears to be little difference in our thinking as to the future."[81]

FOOTNOTES

1. Lucius D. Clay, *Decision in Germany*, p. 131. William Harlan Hale, "General Clay—On His Own," in *Harpers*, December 1948.
2. Author's interview with Mrs. Lucius D. Clay, McLean, Va., July 12, 1981. Colonel R. Joe Rogers interview with Lucius Clay, New York, N.Y., January 24, 1973.
3. *Foreign Relations of the United States 1947*, Vol. 2, pp. 356–358 and 474–475.
4. Clay for Draper, April 2, 1947; Clay for Draper, April 11, 1947; CC 8766. R.G. 200, N.A.
5. Clay for War Department, April 20, 1947. CC 8871, R.G. 200, N.A.
6. Author's interview with Richard Hallock, Washington, D.C., April 5, 1981.
7. Author's interview with James Sundquist, Washington, D.C., July 22, 1981.
8. Author's interview with Margaret Allen, Washington, D.C., March 3, 1981.
9. Clay, *Decision*, p. 174.
10. Clay for Noce, April 28, 1947, CC 8933, R.G. 200, N.A. *Foreign Relations . . . 1947*, Vol. 2, pp. 919–921.
11. Ibid.
12. Clay for Noce, May 12, 1947, CC 9129, R.G. 200 N.A.
13. Revised Plan for Level of Industry. OMGUS papers, N.A.
14. Reparations Report to the Military Governor, September 1945–June 1949, OMGUS papers, N.A.
15. U.S. Dept. of State Bulletin 17, No. 421 July 27, 1947, pp. 186–193. Clay, *Decision*, p. 238.
16. *Foreign Relations . . . 1947*, Vol. 2, p. 926.
17. War Department to Clay, July 3, 1947. WX-81354, R.G. 200, N.A.
18. Clay for War Department, July 6, 1947, CC 9790, R.G. 200, N.A.
19. Clay for Petersen (eyes only), July 16, 1947, CC 9906, R.G. 200, N.A.
20. Teleconference, Petersen-Clay, July 24, 1947. TT-8362, R.G. 200 N.A.
21. *Foreign Relations . . . 1947*, Vol. 2, pp. 1008–1009.
22. Eisenhower to Clay, July 25, 1947, in Jean Smith, ed., *The Papers of Lucius D. Clay*, p. 389.
23. Clay for Eisenhower (eyes only), July 28, 1947, CC 1046, R.G. 200 N.A.
24. *Foreign Relations . . . 1947*, Vol. 2, pp. 1009–1011.
25. Clay for Royall (eyes only), July 28, 1947, CC 1047, R.G. 200 N.A.
26. John Kenneth Galbraith, *A Life in Our Time*, p. 249.
27. *Tagesspiegel*, January 25, 1947, p. 1, *Frankfurter Rundschau*, January 25, 1947, OMGUS. Industry Branch. Memo. Field trip to Minden, January 30, 1947, OMGUS Box 263–2/17,N.A.
28. Nicholas Balabkins, *Germany Under Direct Controls*, p. 127. Charles Kindleberger, private papers.
29. Clay, *Decision*, p. 194.
30. Ibid., pp. 194–195.
31. Clay for Patterson, June 16, 1947. CC 9546, R.G. 200, N.A.
32. Clay for Petersen, June 24, 1947. CC 9661, R.G. 200, N.A.
33. Ibid.
34. *Foreign Relations . . . 1947*, Vol. 2, pp. 933–934.
35. Clay for Petersen, June 23, 1947. CC 9644, R.G. 200, N.A.
36. *Foreign Relations . . . 1947*, Vol. 2, pp. 1014–1016. *Tagesspiegel*, August 1, 1947, p 2. *The New York Times*, August 3, 1947, p. 31.
37. David Schoenbrun, "The French and the Ruhr," in *The New Republic*, August 4, 1947, p. 7.
38. *Foreign Relations . . . 1947*, Vol. 2, pp. 1014–1016.
39. Teleconference, Royall, Draper, Clay, August 8, 1947. TT 8404. R.G. 200, N.A.
40. Ibid.
41. *Foreign Relations . . . 1947*, Vol. 2, pp. 1024–1029.
42. Ibid., p. 1027.

43. Ibid., pp. 1026–1027.
44. Telex, Clay-Draper, August 16, 1947. TT 8429, R.G. 200, N.A.
45. Royall to Clay, August 19, 1947. W-84501 in Smith, *The Papers*, p. 405.
46. *New York Herald Tribune*, August 22, 1947.
47. George R. Jacobs, private papers.
48. Ibid.
49. U.S. Dept. of State, *Germany 1947-1949*, pp. 356–359.
50. William Griffith, "The Denazification Program in the American Zone of Germany," pp. 468–499.
51. Ibid.
52. Ibid.
53. James Stewart Martin, *All Honorable Men*, p. 245. Graham D. Taylor, "The Rise and Fall of Antitrust in Occupied Germany 1945–1948," in *Prologue*, Spring 1979, p. 33.
54. Clay, *Decision*, pp. 326–328.
55. Taylor, "The Rise and Fall of Antitrust," p. 33.
56. Martin, *All Honorable Men*, p. 246.
57. Clay to Secretaries of State, War and Navy, June 28, 1947, CC 9717, R.G. 200, N.A.
58. Author's interview with James Sundquist, Washington, D.C., July 22, 1981.
59. Author's interview with Richard Hallock, Washington, D.C., April 5, 1981.
60. Author's interview with James Sundquist, Washington, D.C., July 22, 1981.
61. John H. Backer, *Priming the German Economy*, Chapter 5.
62. Edward Hutton and Walt Robbins, "Postwar Foreign Trade," December 15, 1947, OMGUS Records, N.A.
63. Backer, *Priming*, p. 139.
64. Balabkins, *Germany*, p. 124.
65. Hutton and Robbins, "Postwar Foreign Trade," p. 10.
66. Keating to Clay (Moscow), ECC 8451. Bennett to Clay (Moscow), undated OMGUS records, 40–3/2.
67. Clay (Moscow) to Keating, March 26, 1947, MA-51145. OMGUS records 149–1/3. Clay (Moscow) to OMGUS, March 31, 1947, MA-51185. OMGUS records, 37–2/1, N.A.
68. Clay for Noce, September 28, 1947. CC 1776. Teleconference, Bennett-Clay, October 24, 1947. TT 8663. Teleconference, Bennett-Clay, November 2, 1947. TT 8692, R.G. 200, N.A.
69. Clay, *Decision*, p. 178.
70. *Foreign Relations . . . 1947*, Vol. 2, pp. 959–966.
71. Ibid.
72. Clay for Draper (eyes only), November 3, 1947, CC 2167, R.G. 200, N.A.
73. Louis A. Wiesner, "Organized Labor in Postwar Germany." Passim. National Archives.
74. Clay for War Department, August 12, 1946. CC 1697. Clay for War Department, September 2, 1946. CC 2948, R.G. 200, N.A.
75. Clay's Press Conference, October 28, 1947; Clay for Draper, October 30, 1947, CC 2134. Clay for Royall and Draper (eyes only), November 1, 1947, CC 2160. Clay for Draper (eyes only), November 6, 1947, CC 2216, R.G. 200, N.A. *Foreign Relations . . . 1947*, Vol. 2, pp. 893–895.
76. Clay for Draper (eyes only), November 3, 1947, CC 2167, R.G. 200, N.A.
77. *Foreign Relations . . . 1947*, Vol. 2, pp. 676–829.
78. Ibid.
79. Clay, *Decision*, pp. 348–349.
80. Clay for Draper, November 20, 1947, CC 2642, R.G. 200, N.A.
81. Ibid., Colonel R. Joe Rogers interview with General Clay, New York, N.Y., January 24, 1973. Dr. Richard D. Challener interview with General Clay, Princeton, N.J., November 23, 1965.

CHAPTER NINE

Fate Intervenes Again

AS THE NEW YEAR CAME AROUND AND THE MILITARY GOVERNOR LOOKED AT HIS timetable, he realized he was considerably behind schedule. He expected the State Department to take over in the spring. By that time the OMGUS apparatus had to be further reduced and a solid administrative foundation laid for the establishment of a West German government. Should the creation of a West German republic provoke a confrontation with the Soviet Union—as conceivably it could—either Clay himself or his successor would have to deal with it. In the meantime, a smooth transition to State Department rule was Clay's overriding aim.

In fact, this transfer had been under active consideration from the time Secretary Royall took matters into his own hands. He had discussed the change with Secretary Marshall in August 1947 and a few weeks later had followed up with a detailed schedule. Accordingly, a high commissioner should have been appointed in October and the transfer of operating personnel, budget balances and responsibilities completed by November.[1] Marshall had agreed in principle, but working-level officials at the State Department raised a number of objections. Several complex details had to be worked out, they said, and the dates Royall had suggested were rejected as unrealistic.

Negotiations nevertheless continued, and on October 18 Clay met with Lovett, Saltzman, Draper, and Gordon Gray to discuss the modalities of the transfer. It was also an opportunity for Clay to cite some of the problems he had encountered as Military Governor. Regardless of the nature of the new organization, he said, one important change would have to be made. The State Department had consistently interfered with the implementation of his orders, repeatedly sending instructions contrary to his basic directives. He had often been given instructions without an opportunity to make recommendations or even to state his position. Regardless of who is appointed, he said, "no self-respecting man would continue to operate with the degree of interference he had experienced."[2] He himself would not be willing to continue under those conditions. There was no substantive progress at the meeting, however, and two days later the functionaries at the State Department tried to withdraw. The department's press release announced that "it had no present intention to take over responsibility for the administration of occupied areas from the army and that the takeover had been indefinitely postponed."[3]

Royall had apparently anticipated such a development because a few days later, as promised to Clay, he submitted an alternative proposal to Marshall[4] that would have given the Military Governor a freer hand at the expense of the State Department policy control. Faced with the alternative of giving Clay carte blanche, Secretary Marshall quickly decided that preparations for the transfer would continue and that it should take place early in 1948.

Late in January, after testifying on the Hill, Clay had lunch with Justice Byrnes and the two Senators from Georgia.[5] All three urged him to continue in Germany, but Clay declined. As far as he was concerned, the die had been cast. A State Department team had arrived in Germany and preparations for the transfer were well advanced. Clay had asked to be returned to the United States by April 1 for retirement and the army—at last—had approved his request. Mrs. Clay already had started packing and sent some of their household goods home; the General had even ordered a couple of civilian suits.[6] In the meantime much remained to be done: the decartelization and denazification programs had to be brought to an end; and planning for currency reform and for the formation of a future German government had to proceed so that Clay's successor could take over. The Military Governor's schedule was so crowded these days that sometimes he had to miss "his day off,"[7] as he called the inspection of troops in the field. Accompanied only by Captain Edloe Donnan, his aide-de-camp, he liked to be at the jumping-off points before dawn to watch the maneuvers of the small American army that Clarence Huebner had whipped into shape in less than a year. "A company commander has the best job in the army,"[8] Clay commented to Donnan on such occasions, remembering his own days in the Panama Canal Zone under Preston Brown. After inspecting the troops all day he usually stopped at headquarters long enough to determine the cause of any shortcomings he might have seen and to correct them. Then he flew back to Berlin.

The food shortage continued to be a major problem. At the Pentagon, Tracy Voorhees had been put in charge of food supplies for the occupied areas, and all through 1947 there had been a steady increase in grain shipments to Germany. Concurrently, however, food collections in the bizone itself continued to lag and actually decreased in volume. By that time Clay had concluded that a currency reform was the only answer. Part of the problem, in his judgment, was the military government's effort to base food distribution on the type of work done regardless of income. This kind of regimentation has never been wholly successful even in Russia, he would say, and under the American economic system the amount of income had always been a factor in food distribution. Germans with large incomes would therefore continue to get food unavailable to the less affluent in spite of all the regulations American or German authorities might impose.[9] In a similarly pragmatic vein, Clay rejected proposals for police measures combined with drastic punishment. No one believes this can work in the long run, he told the Department of the Army. "It might temporarily, but at great expense to anti-Communism, which particularly resents Soviet collection methods. This is no time in Germany to try drastic, strongarm measures."[10] Questioned at a press conference about the wave of strikes protesting food shortages, he was equally philosophical. The reaction of the workers was understandable, he said; as long as they struck in an orderly fashion, it was actually a demonstration of democratic practices.

Confronted with a problem that was clearly beyond his control, the General resorted to familiar tactics. When addressing the issue in public, he exhorted his German listeners to do better and occasionally threatened them with enforced food collection by the U.S. Constabulary or a reduction in American food supplies.[11] At the same time, when communicating with the Department of the Army, he insisted that food collection under existing conditions was "surprisingly good," particularly in comparison with that in other European countries.[12] When Draper or others in the Department of the Army pressed too hard, he usually cut the discussions short. "I cannot pull rabbits out of hats," he said. "I have done my best in Germany, but if this is not enough the transfer to the State Department ought to be expedited."[13]

Because of the spoiling tactics of France, it had taken much longer than Clay had expected to get on with the level-of-industry plan that was to govern the final stages of dismantlement. London's initial opposition and Washington's procrastination had delayed the transfer of the coal mines to German management. In addition, a revision of the bizonal administrative setup had become imperative if it was to serve as a basis from which a German government could readily evolve. Clay had seen to it that the Economic Council and the Executive Committee would not be controlled by the same political party—from the standpoint of checks and balances a beneficial policy—but the resulting political frictions had impeded economic progress. There were conflicts within and among the departments and between the departments and the *Länder*.

By the end of 1947 these weaknesses had become all too apparent.[14] It was difficult enough to get essential legislation passed and even harder to secure *Länder* support to carry out the provisions of the laws that had been passed. The *Länder* complained, procrastinated and often attacked the authority of the bizonal administration. Some went so far as to refuse to share industrial and agricultural resources. Between this selfishness of the *Land* governments and the needs of central administration there was no arbiter. The small size of the Economic Council and the inadequate ratio of one representative for each 750,000 population were additional handicaps.[15] As a consequence, only a handful of ordinances had been passed during the first year of Bizonia's existence, and there were many who thought the states were abusing rather than using this period of relative predominance constructively.[16]

Upon his return from the Council of Foreign Ministers Conference in London, the Military Governor instructed his Civil Affairs Division to proceed with a reorganization that would eliminate all these deficiencies. Always interested in protecting the interests of the states against central authority, he suggested the creation of a full-fledged second chamber—a *Länderrat*—with powers of initiation and legislative veto. Like the U.S. Senate, it would be composed of two representatives from each *Land* appointed by the *Land* government. The bizonal *Länderrat*, it was expected, would not only influence legislation but also secure a more cooperative attitude on the part of the *Land* governments.[17]

Additional details of the reform were discussed in early January by the two Military Governors, and subsequently in several meetings with the minister-presidents and with representatives of the bizonal agencies. As it turned out, there were many points on which the Germans did not agree among themselves.[18] Some of the minister-presidents who were members of the SPD favored a more centralistic approach, whereas CDU representatives at the Economic Council supported a more federalistic structure. Often there was disagreement within each group, so that Clay and Robertson had to act as arbiter. The final emerging pattern encompassed, in addition to the Economic Council and Executive Committee, the new *Länderrat* and a number of old and new agencies. The reconstructed Economic Council was to consist of the original fifty-two members and an additional fifty-two to be elected by the *Landtage* on the basis of one for each 750,000 population. The new Executive Committee would have a chairman elected by the Economic Council, subject to confirmation by the *Länderrat*, and bizonal department directors also chosen by the Economic Council. (Roughly, the chairman corresponded to a prime minister and the committee to a cabinet.) All appointments to the Executive Committee would require the approval of the two military governors. It was in effect the machinery of government that Clay had planned for all along, although its authority for the time being was limited to fiscal and economic matters and its acts subject to Military Government approval.[19]

The bizonal reorganization plan also called for the establishment of a German high court sitting in Cologne and a central bank—the *Bank Deutscher Länder*. The court was to be independent of executive control and responsible for the interpretation and enforcement of bizonal legislation. The bank was designed to serve as financial agent for the German bizonal organization and to provide central control of the currency.

Clay and Robertson were ready to go public with the new administrative setup when they were stopped by an unexpected French aide-mèmoire presented simultaneously in Washington and London. The Quai d'Orsay protested against what it considered "a prelude to a powerful centralized government."[20] After three years of French obstructionism Clay was immune to surprise, and considering his low boiling point his reaction was relatively mild. "It seems always as if France and Communists take the same position, if for different reasons," his message to Washington read, "and we can only please the former by doing what the latter wants."[21] He and Robertson had after all only followed instructions; moreover, the French concept of a loose federation would not work because the economic and financial setup at Frankfurt was intended merely as a prelude to the creation of a bi- or trizonal government, should a unified Germany fail to materialize.

> We are in a critical position in Germany and either have to move forward to give the Germans increased responsibility in the bizonal area to insure their proper contribution to European recovery, or we must move backward to increase our own forces to run a more colonial type of government. . . . Unless we are willing to establish a working organization in which the Germans are given real responsibility, we would have to expand our organization many times to take care of additional export trade which we fully hope will materialize in the coming months.[22]

According to Clay's analysis, the French protest was not really designed to stop the bizonal organization. It was the French custom, an effective one he thought, to make their position public prior to an international conference in order to develop popular support at home. Both the American and British governments apparently saw the French protest in the same light because, after assuring the Quai d'Orsay that the contemplated provisional German administration would in no way prejudice a future German government, Washington and London told the two military governors to proceed. Accordingly, on February 9, 1948, two identical proclamations—drawn up with official German support—were published in the two zones.[23]

In the midst of these negotiations for a new administrative machinery, the Department of the Army had asked Clay to return to Washington for a brief appearance before the congressional appropriations committees. Because of French obstructionism, the difficult negotiations with the Germans, the strikes prompted by the food situation and implied Soviet threats of countermeasures, the General had been reluctant to leave Berlin.[24] Even Clay's personal staff had become aware that the General was more on edge than usual when angrily and without explanation he told his aide-de-camp to cancel the Washington flight. But the explanation in fact was simple. It was the General's practice to let returning OMGUS personnel share the use of the plane, which was equipped with only one bunk. As it turned out, somebody on the staff had made the mistake of putting a WAC sergeant on the passenger list. For a Southern gentleman—even if tired, worn out, and a four-star general—to use the bunk and let the lady sit up was well-nigh unthinkable.[25] The plane incident was straightened out, and as requested Clay briefly testified on the Hill.

Tensions in Germany, however, had been heightened by a provocative and widely publicized speech of Dr. Johann Semler, the Director of the German Economic Administration, casting doubt on the good faith of the American and British military governments.

As a side effect of the gradual transfer of governmental responsibilities to German hands, the country's latent dissatisfaction with occupation policies had come to the fore. There were valid reasons for discontent, and after three years under the military government's benevolent rule, the German people had become confident that they could speak up without undue personal risk. Many of the critical comments expressed through official channels endeavored to be constructive, but others, such as Semler's speech before his Christian Democrat Party friends at Erlangen, carried the heavy freight of reemerging political propaganda.

Semler's comments on the food prices, the deplorable conditions in the coal mines, the slow progress of the steel industry and the delayed currency reform were factual and justified. For reasons of his own, however, Semler apparently also felt that the time had come to challenge the integrity of the two military governments. He took exception to Clay's public comments on the duty of German farmers to deliver their quotas, actually suggesting this was done only to relieve American taxpayers of their burden and to satisfy "Mr. Clay's possible desire to make a good exit at our expense." He went on:

> The food imports which we could now have received, we were unfortunately not permitted to buy. Corn was sent, and chicken feed, and we were paying for it dearly. It is not a present. We pay for it in dollars gained by German work in German exports and are expected to say thank you in addition. It is high time the German politicians cease to say thank you for this supplementary food.

In another part of the speech, addressing himself to the British military governor, Semler took credit for recent increases in the German export price for coal:

> When I took office, we sold a ton of coal for ten dollars and made a present of five dollars to some interested person. That is today's recognized European price. We should act the same way in other cases. After three years we shall have to get the English out of the habit of plundering [*ausplündern*] the German economy any further.[26]

As Clay saw it, the most deplorable aspect of the Semler speech was that it came from a man in the best position to know the falsehoods it contained. Semler knew full well what was happening on the farms and on the black market; he knew that in spite of drastically increased American food shipments it was still impossible to increase food rations. He must have known too that the American Military Governor had persistently vetoed the purchase of vegetables from Holland and similar products from elsewhere because of their low caloric value; and he must have known above all that it was only Clay's long fight against "hidden reparations" that had finally induced Washington to accept a raise in the export prices of coal and scrap. The question became how to deal with this kind of behavior by a leading and competent official while everybody in Germany was watching America's democracy in action.

The General's initial move—the dismissal of Semler as bizonal Executive Director of Economics—was generally expected. The explanation that Semler had shown "malicious opposition to the occupying powers" and that economic recovery could not be promoted by such an attitude[27] was unassailable. But the letter of dismissal also said that "Because of the recognized right to free speech," no further action against Semler was going to be taken. Moderation had been Clay's intent; however, there were limits to his tolerance. When the *Landtag* in Munich countered by electing Semler as one of its representatives to the Economic Council, the Bavarian minister-president Dr. Hans Ehard was told bluntly that Semler's election had better be annulled. A draft proclamation dismissing the Bavarian *Landtage* had already been prepared and, as the General advised Murray von Wagoner in Munich, "He [von Wagoner] was apt to wind up as *Land* Director with no government if he didn't get things straightened out." This settled the matter—even under a benevolent military regime there were some limits to democracy; the Germans nullified the election.[28]

At the same time, however—always sensitive to public reaction—Clay ordered a press release to explain in detail the bizonal pricing policies for exports. "It has to make clear," he instructed his Public Information Officer, "that it was indeed in the interest of American and British taxpayers to collect the highest possible export prices."[29] In a similar vein William Logan, the director general of the Joint Export-Import Agency, was asked to go on the air with a major statement in defense of his agency's export policies.[30] And Clay himself, at a meeting with members of the newly appointed Economic Council and Executive Committee, took up the subject of his alleged unwillingness to buy food with export proceeds. "Actually there are a few low caloric luxury foods that could be bought with export proceeds," he said. "The Dutch want to sell their cabbages for dollars. They will advertise to the German population that cabbages are available. The whole total lot of them wouldn't add five calories a day to the German diet. But the several million dollars would bring in raw materials that could be converted into a good many millions of dollars in exports. . . ."[31] Regardless of where the opposition came from, he was going to be firm in his economic policy: caloric value alone was to govern the selection of food imports and the balancing of Germany's foreign trade would remain a fundamental goal.

While on the Spree the bizonal administrative machinery was being overhauled, on the Potomac and on the Seine the European Recovery Program had been making good progress. In December the American President had submitted his "Program for U.S. Support to European Recovery" to Congress, and thanks to an unprecedented public relations effort, the initial reaction on the Hill had been quite favorable. In Paris, a Committee of

European Cooperation had begun to analyze the economic resources and capabilities of its sixteen members to determine what each country should accomplish and what external aid it could expect. Still an issue, however, was whether the three western zones of Germany should be included in the program. As far as the Military Governor was concerned, Marshall aid would relieve him of the constant worry about a sudden cutoff of funds, and would certainly contribute to the revival of the German economy. With his course now firmly set on the creation of a strong West Germany, he was determined to take maximum advantage of the program. The initial reaction of the Americans in charge of the Marshall Plan, however, was that they would be the ones to say what Germany would get. Germany was not going to be allowed to express a voice. "My contention was," Clay later told McKinzie, "that we as military government had to speak as a government and eventually transfer that right to the Germans." As a consequence, he soon found himself in the midst of bitter controversies with some ERP officials in Paris, who resisted Germany's accession to the program. The French opposed the appearance of Germans at the Committee for European Economic Cooperation (CEEC) meetings,[32] and a representative of Norway even remarked that he personally still favored the Morgenthau Plan.[33]

Having overcome these initial difficulties, Clay had to cope next with a disappointing European Cooperation Agency (ECA) allocation of merely $364 million to the bizone, less than the initial aid given to countries with much smaller populations like the Netherlands and Belgium.[34] With a four-year record of successful supply battles on the Potomac, Clay was the last one to yield to such discrimination. "Failure in prompt German recovery would have farreaching effects on the recovery of its neighbors," he warned, urging the Department of the Army to protest the unfair allocation of ERP aid. "I know such action might well bring much international criticism of me," he said, "but I have had to resist selfish motivation by others in the relation to our support of Germany for so long that my skin is thick." Clay eventually won that battle, but lost another: the German Economic Recovery Program allocation was substantially increased, but Germany alone of all the recipient countries had to agree that all ERP aid was subject to repayment.[35] His plea to avoid deliberate discrimination against the Germans "even before ECA gets underway"[36] was eloquent but ineffective.

Clay's determined fight for an economically strong Germany soon became so notorious in Europe that he was charged with being pro-German. Clearly stung by such remarks, he insisted that nothing could be further from the truth. Such criticism, he felt, came from a confusion over short-term and long-term aims. A prostrate Germany "must be restored in some measure if there is to be a stable Europe," he said. This short-range goal was being confused, he thought, with long-range policy of preventing a repetition of German aggression. And in keeping with his by now firm anti-Soviet stance, he added that the "well-justified fear of German aggression blinds Germany's neighbors to the immediate and overshadowing menace of the Red Army externally and planned revolution internally."[37]

Characteristically, Clay insisted from the very beginning that the German part of the Marshall Plan had to be under his direct control. As early as January 1948 he had told the Department of the Army that he would be very much opposed to the assignment of an ECA representative as advisor to the Military Governor with a "separate communication channel." "It seems to me," he wrote, "that with the economy of bizonal area practically in American hands, the American representative in Germany for ECA should be the Military Governor with authority delegated to the economic · advisor on his staff."[38] The concept was not easily sold to Washington, but Clay as always remained adamant.

Four months later—the issue was still in abeyance—he mentioned to Draper his concern about the relationship with ECA. "We now have a predominant voice in German finance and economy," he wrote.

> My own hands would be strengthened if our relations with ECA were through my office, as under any other arrangements [the] British will be in appeal position. Thus, I think it extremely important that proper terms of reference be worked out which would not wreck the commanding position in Germany which we now hold and for which we have paid heavily." . . . This is not an effort on my part to retain power, because I do not expect to stay in Germany much longer.[39]

However, the American position should not be weakened and—his clinching argument—"Congress would want us to maintain in full our present control." The question was still not settled when Averell Harriman, the Special Representative of the European Cooperation Administration, visited beleaguered Berlin one month later. His proposal to accredit a representative of ECA to the Bipartite Board was equally unpalatable to the Military Governor because, as he contended, this would enhance the British position and weaken America's predominant voice in German foreign trade. The two men argued inconclusively until late at night, but the following morning Harriman yielded. "I am not sure I persuaded him with logic," the General later commented. "I think he rather accepted my view because of our mutual support over many months of a firm policy to check Communist expansion and penetration."[40]

Norman Collisson, Harriman's deputy, was appointed to work with the Military Governor's staff. An Economic Cooperation Agreement between the United States and Bizonia was signed by the two military governors, and ERP offices were set up in the German Bizonal Organization and in the Joint Export Import Agency to secure the necessary coordination. With $400 million of JEIA's export proceeds concurrently released for the purchase of industrial raw materials, the foundation for Germany's economic recovery had been laid. One contentious issue, however, remained to be settled—the dismantlement process.

Confronted on the one hand with the contradictory demands of French, British, and German political leaders and on the other with equally disparate objections by the European Cooperation Administration, the American Congress and the Inter-Allied Reparation Agency (IARA), Clay had some difficulty steering a steady course. Allocations and deliveries of dismantled industries had been insignificant all along, and repeated attempts by the IARA to present its grievances to the Council of Foreign Ministers had been unsuccessful.[41] When Russell Dorr, the U.S. delegate to the IARA in Brussels, appeared in Berlin in the summer of 1947 expecting to get information from Clay about the still confidential new level of industry, he got short shrift instead. He could not have come at a worse time. France's protests in Washington and London had interrupted the General's schedule, and Clay had just been obligated to tell the Department of State that making the bizone self-sufficient and providing an adequate reparation schedule for the IARA countries "could not be accomplished at the same time." Instead of simply telling Dorr that the two military governors had promised each other not to release any information and letting it go at that, Clay engaged in a bitter dispute that brought out the authoritarian side of his personality.

According to Dorr's report of the meeting, the General acknowledged receiving instructions from Washington to acquaint Dorr with details of the plan but said he had appealed the order and would resign rather than comply. Clay argued that the new level-of-industry plan was solely intended to reassure Germans that they no longer had to fear the threat of plant removal. He reminded Dorr that the Cabinet in Washington had voted against the resumption of reparations removals and that the Secretary of State had been the lone dissenter. When Dorr stood his ground and reminded the Military Governor in turn that as the U.S. delegate to IARA he would have to explain and, if necessary, defend the new plan, Clay's response was angry and unyielding: the projected level-of-industry plan had no implications whatever in regard to reparations, no one outside military government should have anything to do with setting that level and Clay had no interest whatever in Dorr's problems or in whether his visitor accomplished his mission or not. At this point, according to Dorr, the General then stated "with considerable emphasis and not without heat" that the question of German level of industry was the exclusive concern of Germany and therefore fully subject to his control. When Dorr took his leave a few days later, the General was more affable, although still insistent that Dorr's request was unreasonable. By way of an apology, he merely expressed the hope that when Dorr next returned to Berlin "he would find someone in his place with whom it would be easier to get along."[42]

The report on the meeting did not win Clay any friends at the State Department of course, although Dorr erred in his conclusion that "General

Clay has a strong emotional bias against the entire idea of reparations from industrial, capital equipment." John Hilldring's appraisal was more accurate:

> General Clay . . . had conducted his administration of Germany as though Germany represented the only U.S. interest in Europe. I have nothing but praise for the job Clay has done within Germany. It has been magnificent. But it is not unfair to him to say that he has been far less objective and wise in blending his administration of Germany with the equally worthy purposes of the United States in other European countries.[43]

Two of these "other European countries" in particular were pressing their claims on the reparations issue. All through 1947, the British government had continued to urge early reparations deliveries to all the participants of the IARA as well as to the Russians. A carrot in that form, it argued, might keep the Russians from creating intolerable conditions for the British, Americans, and French.[44] So insistent were the British on this score that the State Department eventually had to remind the British ambassador of a political fact of life: because the United States had recently taken over a substantial portion of the U.K. dollar commitments in the bizonal area, many members of Congress felt the United States should not continue to approve reparation deliveries. Other participating countries of the IARA, especially France, also resisted attempts to curtail dismantlement any further and—contrary to American congressional views—even wanted the deliveries to Soviet satellites continued.

In the United States, by contrast, an antireparations campaign was underway, and ex-President Hoover set the tone with his charge—erroneous though it was—that fertilizer plants were being destroyed in the American and British zones "while all of Europe is gasping for fertilizers and for food products."[45] The House of Representatives accordingly passed a Resolution which in substance would have suspended the entire dismantling process in the American zone until the economic effects could be studied. The most vocal opposition to the continuation of dismantling came of course from the German side. There were spirited protests by the political parties and trade union leaders, and the *Länderrat* issued a formal critical statement.[46]

During all the phases of the dismantlement dispute and against a background of divergent international pressures, the Military Governor nevertheless held to a steady course. In the fall of 1947, the bizonal level-of-industry plan had been finally published with a reparations list of 682 plants that included 302 usable only for the production of war materials. After several subsequent reductions, the dismantled equipment's total value of $500 million—according to a nonpartisan estimate[47]—corresponded to about 10 percent of Germany's investments in the first year after the end of reparations. The General in fact had objected to *any* reductions in the list because, as he argued, neither coal nor transport or manpower were available to Western Germany to support an industry greater than now contemplated.[48] Consequently all industrial capacity that Germany was able to use should remain, and if additional plants were left, "they would simply remain idle for a number of years."[49] Theoretically at least there was some merit in Clay's argument, but it also demonstrated once again an engineer's unwillingness to deviate from an approved blueprint.

Late in 1947, in the course of a hearing before the House Appropriations Committee, the Secretary of the Army had been reminded that the denazification program ought to be ended quickly. In spite of Royall's assurance that the much-reduced program was not impeding economic recovery, the subject came up again when Clay testified in January. He too denied any ill effects and pointed out how unfair and politically unwise it would be to end the program before the most serious cases had been tried. In any event, he promised, the program would be virtually completed by spring. Nevertheless, in February the subcommittee on foreign aid ignored Clay's advice and recommended a full amnesty for lesser offenders and followers,[50] and during some appropriations hearings in March, the Military government was again criticized for not complying with congressional wishes. The punitive stage of the occupation should be over, it was said, and people got back to work.[51] When instructed by Royall "to conclude denazification trials by the end of April, rather than in May or June as contemplated," Clay remained adamant. He had set up the program to the best of his ability, he said, and in strict compliance with his orders. There had to be an orderly conclusion without loss of face.

> I would rather lose the appropriation than what we stand for in Germany. I cannot stop denazification except by ordering Germans to stop. I think I know German reaction and stopping would not be good. It would be bowing to criticism in Germany which comes only from the Nazi element. If this is an order, please say so.[52]

A few days later he followed up by reporting that each month there was "a constantly smaller backlog which however contained increasingly the really bad actors. A general amnesty would free these men and discredit the entire program." He proposed May 1 as the earliest possible target date. Such a small number of cases would remain by then that congressional criticism would be substantially met.[53] With some hesitation, the army concurred.

As difficult as the task was, Clay delivered on his promise. In March only 23,000 trials had been completed; 109,000 cases remained for trial, and an additional 240,000 were left for processing in expedited proceedings. But Clay knew how to cut through red tape. He ordered Theo Hall, who by that time had taken over the direction of the program, to negotiate with the German authorities for the necessary amendments. Thirty thousand cases could remain after May 1, he was told, but all the others would have to be disposed of. If this goal had not been reached by then, the General would issue another amnesty; he was going to live up to his commitment to Congress.

The American-German negotiations that followed were held in an atmosphere of intense OMGUS pressure for speed. Roles were now completely reversed, Griffith wrote, with the Germans resisting efforts to break down all barriers to a speedy conclusion and insisting that the serious cases must be tried at all costs. Nevertheless, within a few weeks the *Länderrat* in Stuttgart adopted the necessary amendments. They gave prosecutors and tribunals almost complete freedom in reclassifying charged individuals and fixing sanctions. All pretrial employment restrictions, with minor exceptions, were eliminated. There was more. Acting on Clay's instructions, Hall assumed direct control of the American denazification offices in the *Länder* and for all practical purposes took over the entire program. American denazification officials visited each country; there they personally selected the cases to be left for trial, and instructed the prosecutors to process the remaining cases as "followers" under the new accelerated program. By May 1 the job was accomplished, and OMGUS could announce that only 28,065 cases remained for trial. A few weeks later the Military Governor wrote finis to America's denazification efforts, dismantled the denazification apparatus of OMGUS and discharged its personnel. By the end of the summer only a handful of individuals remained in the various headquarters offices.[54]

The General had good reasons to assume it would be less cumbersome to end the decartelization and deconcentration program. It had never enjoyed the same widespread and determined American public support that denazification had. Furthermore, early in the spring of 1948 it still was in American hands and in an exploratory stage. The repercussions the program's liquidation eventually caused could not be foreseen. Clay of course was aware of the continuous feud between the conservative pragmatists in his economic division on one side and the liberal crusaders in the decartelization branch on the other. As he planned it, however, he would let the two sides argue policy pro and con and then step in himself as final arbiter.[55] In the meantime, he kept an eagle eye on public reactions back home, mindful of Secretary Stimson's early warning that the same people who were urging punitive economic policies in Germany would be the first to turn on him if there were ill effects. When James Stewart Martin, the Branch Chief and an ardent supporter of decartelization, had resigned in June 1947, he told the press that "you can't sell democracy by putting special interests in the driver's seat."[56] American relations with Russia and France were unnecessarily complicated, he said, "because the expressed wishes of the American people are being overridden by special interest groups who have their own ideas of how Germany should be treated." Martin followed up his initial attack with a piece in *The New Republic*, warning that "a new powerful Germany is in the making."[57] Clay denied the charges that big industrial interests were exercising undue influence on the military government, and he added a sarcastic note: "I wish General Motors and others would read that charge so that I would cease being accused of not having given them an even break."[58]

In any case, Martin's accusations were clearly out of step with his government's policy. JCS #1779, which had replaced Clay's original directive in July 1947, had still stressed the need for decartelization, but nine months later the about-face in Washington's policies toward Germany had become an accomplished fact. The Russians were now the enemy, and a strong West Germany as a bulwark against Communism the official American goal. The Soviet takeover in Prague highlighted the new situation, and Clay too had begun to consider the possibility of war. The time for economic experiments in Germany was over but the message had not yet reached the trustbusters at Kronprinzen Allee. By March 1948 they had completed staff studies of the four "principal" test cases and were waiting for the green light to begin proceedings. When their new branch chief, Charles Bronson, told them instead that they were responsible for getting Germany back on its feet and that General Clay was opposed to any "uneconomical steps," "all hell broke loose."[59] A subsequent memorandum to the Military Governor, signed by nineteen rebellious staff members, asked for clarification because, as they put it, "his verbal instructions had produced a state of demoralization through the staff."

Clay confronted the group in a meeting that proved unique in military government history. He told them he had rejected deconcentration in one of the four cases because of the company's importance for the rehabilitation of Europe; a second combine had transferred part of its equipment to an independent producer, thus ending its monopoly; in the third case part of the recommended deconcentration plan had been accepted; and any decision in the fourth would be premature. From now on, he added, every case had to be examined by "a rule of reason." Since complete agreement was unlikely on the conclusions to be drawn in each individual case, the Military Governor himself would make the final determination. At first no one challenged Clay directly. However, as the discussion became more contentious, the General, his eyes flashing, banged the table. "I did not come here to be lectured on decartelization," he said, and looking around the room, he finished off in a controlled voice: "I hope that no one feels he has to leave. I hope that everyone will feel that he can remain and work under the policy that I have stated. Good night, gentlemen." He got up and left.[60] The reaction was swift. Two of the group tendered their resignations, which were accepted. The rest of the professional staff was reduced immediately and additional cuts made later. In the end, this left a handful of Americans responsible for monitoring trade practices in the American zone.

The flap in Berlin produced public repercussions in the States, however. The press, which had followed the intramural debates, reported "full reversal of a basic military government policy" and described the new approach to decartelization as a "war move." Moreover, the resignations and dismissals caused such a commotion on the Potomac that Secretary Royall had to order an investigation. A committee appointed to review the decartelization program under Garland S. Ferguson, Jr., a member of the Federal Trade Commission, submitted a report to Royall in April 1949 recommending in strong language that the decartelization program be continued.

One of the Ferguson committee members charged that several highly placed members of OMGUS had consistently worked to undermine the program.[61] The Military Governor, invited by Ferguson to refute these charges, initially informed the Department of the Army that he did not care to comply.[62] But in a personal letter to Tracy Voorhees a few weeks later he commented on the Ferguson report in some detail.[63]

After listing the accomplishments of the program, such as the breakup of the I.G. Farben enterprise and of Germany's highly centralized banking system, he cited the enactment and enforcement of laws prohibiting restraints of trade and cartel formation, and then discussed the two cases singled out in the Ferguson report. "In both of these cases," he wrote, "I made the decision and must accept the full responsibility therefore. I had opposed the breaking up of Henschel, the principal locomotive works in Germany, in a period in which transportation was almost at a standstill and because of the need for repairs to rolling stock." As far as the VKF ball-bearing plant was concerned, he had made his decision because "it was understood at that time that the production of ballbearings in Germany would be prohibited." In the meantime some limited production had been authorized, but sufficient power was vested in the Ruhr Authority to prevent the formation of cartels. "I must repeat," he concluded, "I believe we have earnestly and conscientiously executed U.S. policy. If not, those who make policy must determine if they desire further action; it has only to be directed." Not unexpectedly, the Department of the Army saw the issue in the same light as its Military Governor. Instead of complying with the Ferguson committee's recommendation, the Pentagon issued a critique of the report. Drafted by Tracy S. Voorhees, it opposed "any revival of the deconcentration program on the ground that it would endanger the recovery of the bizonal area." It also rejected the charges as being based on an inadequate understanding of the complex problems faced by the occupation authorities.

During the first months of 1948, the Military Governor was obliged to spend a great deal of time in London. In late December, when the Council of Foreign Ministers was about to adjourn, Bidault had agreed to meet again with his American and British colleagues to discuss trizonal fusion and the establishment of a West German government. The Saar had already been given to France. To satisfy the French government further, the future status of the Ruhr and security controls were put on the agenda. As on previous occasions, Clay had let it be known that he preferred not to attend. There remained much to be done, he wrote, to complete the bizonal administration and to prepare for the transfer to the State Department. "I have strong personal views relative to the Ruhr as well as to the evolution of the political and economic organization of the three Western Zones." Since the United States position would probably "tend more to the French viewpoint" and be determined before the conference began, he felt there was little he could contribute. He had no desire to "become further a controversial figure."[64] He left the final decision to the Department, where Secretary Royall held to a different view. It was essential, Royall's reply read, to continue the Army and State cooperation recently developed in London.[65] The General ought to be present.

The conference was held at India House. Ambassador Douglas chaired the meetings, in which the Benelux countries also participated. It met from February 23 to March 6 and from March 20 to June 1; the interim period was to be used by the military governors to further consider the political structure for West Germany and to try to reconcile some of the differences between the three occupying powers. Commenting on his resulting Berlin-London shuttle in his memoirs, Clay wrote that he had contributed substantially to Murphy's support. "I was unable to win a single game of gin rummy from him in the entire period of the conference."[66] There was a positive side to the shuttle, however, in the form of two birthday cakes on April 23, one in the morning from Mrs. Douglas in London and the other in the evening from Mrs. Clay upon his return to Berlin. Shuttle, gin rummy, and birthday cakes aside, Clay's presence in London turned out to be of crucial importance.

In January the French had protested the organizational changes in the bizonal administration. It was clear by then that the Quai d'Orsay aimed at the establishment of a federation of German states with only a modicum of power left to a central government. To promote this concept in London the French delegates suggested a single German chamber rather than the bicameral legislature proposed by their Anglo-American colleagues. If there had to be two chambers, however, they wanted the upper body chosen by the *Land* governments and the lower one by the *Land* legislatures. A lower chamber directly elected by the German people would tend to dominate the *Land* governments, they said. For the same reason, the central government should not have the power of taxation, but the individual states should collect and allocate taxes to the central government. Except for foreign affairs, customs, and the railroads, no central administrative apparatus should be created, and civil servants from the *Länder* ought to be seconded to run the contemplated small central administration. As far as the future of the Ruhr was concerned, the French government had finally given up on its complete separation from Germany, but the French wanted foreign ownership and management of the Ruhr's industry—both unacceptable in Clay's eyes.[67]

Clay's views on the structure of a future German government were in accord with the American South's traditional emphasis on states' rights. Cultural, educational, and religious affairs should be the prerogatives of the

Länder, he thought, and their financial independence should be safeguarded. On the other hand, the central government had to have the authority to raise the revenues it needed directly, and also had to have clearly defined but limited police authority. The official United States position was similar. It stressed that a German central government required sufficient power to enforce essential policies on a national basis and had to be more than an instrument for coordinating quasisovereign states.[68] Its powers had to be clearly defined and—analogous to the American example—the residual powers reserved to the *Länder*. Whereas the differences between the American and British positions were minor, the views of the Benelux countries were generally in line with those of France.

When the conference recessed on March 6, the gap between the various positions had been narrowed, but some fundamental differences remained. Accordingly, the three military governors were instructed to study the London discussions and come up with recommendations on how to reconcile the divergent viewpoints. Not much progress was made in Berlin, however, until the Soviet delegation walked out of the Allied Control Council on March 20. As Clay liked to say, there was never a bad wind that did not also bring something good. The Russian action convinced the French that they were at the crossroads. Their hope of preserving four-power control by blocking the plans for Bizonia now had to be abandoned;[69] there was no longer any doubt that the Anglo-Americans would carry on, with or without French participation. As the Military Governor put it, "they knew that we were ready to proceed in the three zones but otherwise were determined to go ahead in two. We are no longer willing to have a political and economic void in Central Europe which would interfere with the recovery of the European countries participating in the Marshall Plan."[70]

From here on things moved with unprecedented speed. French sources hinted that Couve de Murville, the Quai d'Orsay's German expert, was vacationing on the Riviera and had expressed interest in an informal exchange of views. This was followed by the prompt dispatch of the General's plane to pick up the French diplomat, "the most knowledgeable and intelligent French representative"[71] he had dealings with. De Murville stayed several days at the General's house at Im Dol. In the course of some intensive discussions between the two men, the emerging fundamental understanding that neither the United States nor France wanted a powerful central control in Germany pointed the way to an early breakthrough. As Clay's imaginative mind quickly recognized, a new approach was needed. All divisive and unnecessary details should be tossed aside and left for the German people to decide. Instead, the London Conference should concentrate on the broad principles to be given to the Germans for drafting a constitution. The conference also was to give the military governors general guideposts to help them determine whether the German constitution conformed to these broad principles.[72] With this concept in mind, the General drafted an eight-point memorandum. Accepted by Couve de Murville as a basis for a three-power agreement, Clay's new blueprint provided for the election of a constitutional assembly by the German people under procedures adopted by the German states. September 1, 1948, was set as a target date. The constitutional assembly would then draft a democratic constitution establishing a federal governmental structure, protective of the rights of both the participating states and the individual citizens. Once approved by the occupying powers, the constitution would be submitted for ratification to the individual states and procedures established for the federal election. The authority of the federal government would be defined by the constitution except in the field of foreign relations and in the control of war potential, where responsibilities remained in the occupiers' hands. The Clay-de-Murville agreement further specified that France would join a trizonal control authority only after a German government had been established; in the meantime, a common currency reform would be undertaken, a tripartite Allied Export-Import Agency set up, and a common customs policy determined.

Endorsed by the three military governors, the memorandum was sent to London where it became the basis for an eventual agreement, although it took five more weeks to reach a full accord that gave the French a great deal.[73] They emerged with a voice in the control of the Ruhr, the retention of level of industry control, and the assurance of a long occupation and of inspections by a military security commission. There were several snags in the negotiations, the chief one being the French delegates' concern about the reactions of the National Assembly in Paris. They feared that the proposed charter for the International Ruhr Authority—with ownership and management of the mines in German hands—might be rejected. Some British proposals regarding the Ruhr also caused delays.[74]

On June 1, 1948, the London Conference—in Clay's judgment "the most important one since Potsdam"—came finally to an end. Its agreements were promptly endorsed by the British and United States governments, but French approval was delayed. Only after a long debate and making it known that France had reserved the right to reopen the Ruhr agreement could the French parliament's concurrence be secured, and then by a majority of six.[75] A West German republic was about to become a reality.

At the Allied Control Council in Berlin, meanwhile, the onus-shifting tactics already in evidence at the December Council of Foreign Ministers Conference continued. A bizonal currency had been printed in the U.S. and shipped to Germany, and every effort made to keep "Operation Bird Dog" secret. But the Soviets, with Donald MacLean as their agent in Britain's embassy in Washington, were fully aware of what was going on.[76] For months they had insisted that a quadripartite currency would have to be printed in Leipzig, but early in February this demand was suddenly dropped. In an unexpected about-face aimed at placing the responsibility for Germany's partition at the doorstep of the Western powers, they agreed to have the currency printed in Berlin—contingent however on the establishment of a Central German Finance Department and of a Central Bank of Issue. But Clay, always an astute negotiator, played his cards right. Without economic unity in the four zones, he told Sokolovsky, these financial agencies could not function. At the same time he advised Washington of his game plan. If the Soviets insisted on their new terms, he would stand fast; if, on the other hand, they dropped their condition he would have to accept. Otherwise, "he would be forced into a position before the German people of making the next step toward partition without specific cause." This was apparently precisely what Marshall Sokolovsky had in mind, because on February 11, he agreed to the printing of a new currency in Berlin under quadripartite control without the establishment of a Central Finance Administration as a precondition, he said. "There was no need to worry," a confident Clay cabled to Draper. Within sixty days, the technical details had to be fully agreed upon. If, as he expected, there would be no agreement, he would not have lost any time because he was going to "proceed concurrently with the bizonal plans."[77]

As it turned out, this scapegoating game did not fit into the Soviet overall plan and may have been too subtle for their liking anyway. The Communist takeover in Prague on February 23 had alerted the world that a powerful Soviet move was in the making, and there were few who doubted that it would come in Berlin. If the Pentagon needed any confirmation that trouble was ahead, it came in the form of a message from Clay who for several weeks had noticed a definite change in the attitude of his Russian colleagues. From Sokolovsky on down, he reported, they had become faintly contemptuous, slightly arrogant, and certainly self-assured. Throughout his stay in Germany he had scoffed at the possibility of war with Russia, but now he felt obliged to warn the army that it might come with dramatic suddenness. "I cannot support this change in my own thinking with any data or outward evidence," he added, "but my feeling is real."[78]*

Two weeks later "the new Russian attitude" became official with the Kremlin's decision to bring the work of the Control Council to an end. At its last session on March 20, with Sokolovsky in the chair, there was the customary exchange of charges and countercharges, each side blaming the other for its unilateral actions. This had gone on for a while when the Soviet marshal launched into the reading of a prepared statement of de-

---

* To Clay's annoyance this top secret message was leaked, giving cause to critical comments that the General was an alarmist. On the other hand, Jean E. Smith, the editor of *The Papers of General Lucius D. Clay* (see Bibliography), later asserted that the cable had been dispatched in response to a visit to Berlin by General Stephen Chamberlin, Chief of Army Intelligence. Since major appropriation bills were pending, "its principal purpose was to assist the military chiefs in their congressional testimony." Smith therefore stressed that "it was sent directly to Chamberlin and not through normal command channels." (*Smith, J.,* p. 568) However, General Clay's special assistant for intelligence, Captain Richard Hallock, who personally had dispatched the cable in question, categorically rejected this interpretation. He also insisted that a direct cable to Chamberlin was the "only proper channel" for a message of this kind. (Author's interview with Richard Hallock, Washington, D.C. April 5, 1981.)

nunciation at such rapid speed that the interpreter could not keep up with him. At the end he swept up his papers, rose and announced, "I see no sense in continuing this meeting and I declare it adjourned."[79] Whereupon he and the Soviet delegation left the room. There was nothing the three Western governors could do but remain in their seats to invalidate the Soviet move, although it was clear the Control Council was dead. A note from Soviet headquarters at Karlshorst listing "supplementary provisions" to govern East-West traffic, moreover, put the West on notice of the policy of increased harassments that the Russians had decided to apply.

Three days later Clay was called to a teleconference with the Secretary of the Army and the Chief of Staff. The President had decided, he was told, that the State Department would not take over. Both Royall and Bradley expressed the hope that Clay would stay on the job, at least through the present calendar year. "You are urgently needed in Germany," they said, confident of the General's answer. "I am an army officer as long as the department feels I am needed," Clay replied. "I do want to retire as soon as I can. However, I owe too much to the army not to remain with it if it feels I am needed."[80] As he walked back to his office, he knew that fate had decided again—but it was different from previous disappointments. A scrap with the Russians was clearly in the offing; it was a challenge the fighter in Clay would have hated to miss.

Once the Allied Control Council had become inoperative, Clay had no difficulty in reaching agreement with Robertson on the terms of the currency reform. German monetary experts were subsequently taken into confidence and quarantined in a secret working place near Kassel in order to make the American draft conform with German law. But there were more snags to come. After indicating in London their willingness to participate, the French now raised new objections to a tax reduction that was to accompany the new currency. Right up to the last minute it was uncertain whether there would be a bizonal or a trizonal currency.[81]

Even more exasperating from Clay's point of view was a sudden shift in the U.S. Treasury's position regarding the terms to govern a currency reform. The so-called Colm-Dodge-Goldsmith Report, approved in August 1946, had become the basis for the Control Council's deliberations. In the intervening period the American government had directed OMGUS to leave the originally suggested and controversial equalization (burden-sharing) measures for future German determination; otherwise the original plan stood unchanged. Clay was therefore thunderstruck when suddenly advised that the Treasury had second thoughts about the wisdom of cancelling the Reich's debt, a primary necessity if the reform was to succeed.[82] After some transatlantic debates, Clay had been able to make his viewpoint prevail, when shortly before promulgating the reform he was jolted by yet another Washington move—a joint State-Treasury-Army decision that the "ten-cent military conversion rate should continue in effect."[83] "Your message has hit us like a bombshell," he cabled back, "and if it is an order it may necessitate a complete postponement of the currency reform." Since a thirty-cent con-version factor for the new mark had been agreed on, retaining a ten-cent military conversion rate would be exploiting the German economy and would undoubtedly generate similar requests from the British and French military. Moreover—and this was the clinching argument that settled the issue in Clay's favor—it would be impossible "to use a ten-cent conversion factor for the occupation forces and a thirty-cent factor for the increasing number of businessmen and business enterprises operating in Germany."

With these obstacles out of the way, the Military Governor once more reviewed the details of the contemplated reform. As a first step, all currency and savings, including both time and demand deposits, would have to be registered. The old Reichsmarks would have to be surrendered and become valueless. A six-day moratorium would be declared, but authorization would be given for the prompt exchange of sixty Reichsmarks per person on a one-to-one basis for new Deutsch Marks. The terms under which the remainder of the Reichsmarks turned in would be converted would be published one week later.[84] (Experience with currency reforms in other countries had shown that when the full terms of the conversion were made known from the start, holders of illegal funds would evade confiscation by dividing their holdings among families and friends.) As a second step, announced after one week, the registered Reichsmark would be converted into the new currency on a ten-to-one basis. Half of the balances were to be blocked and 70 percent of the blocked amount was eventually to be cancelled. The final result of the reform was a radical contraction of the money supply, since it actually entailed a conversion of 6.5 Deutsch Marks for 100 old Reichs-marks. All debts would also be simultaneously devalued at the rate of ten-to-one. The debts of the Reich, of the Wehrmacht, and of the Reichsbank would be cancelled. Finally, the *Bank Deutscher Länder* would be authorized to issue and control the new currency while establishing an upper limit of 10 billion Deutsch Marks.

While these provisions seemed satisfactory enough, the question of whether the French would come in was still open. Just forty-eight hours before the currency reform was to be announced, Clay still found himself in a teleconference with Draper discussing the latest French ultimatum: the French tax proposals had to be accepted; otherwise France would not join in the reform. "There is nothing we can do," a desolate Military Governor pointed out. "The money is en route to last stations, key officials are notified, all is in motion, already sales are stopped everywhere in large volume. The stopping of a reform now that is in motion would be an absolute disaster and is unthinkable."[85] The two men were still debating whether the Sec-retary of State or even the President should try to talk to Bidault on the phone when Clay got word that Roger Jean Charles Noiret, the French deputy military governor, was on his way to see him. "Perhaps settlement is now possible," he told Draper, and rushed home. As Clay described it, "a fantastic midnight negotiation" followed. "Noiret would call Koenig who was at home in Baden while others of his party were telephoning Paris to find out the decision of the Assembly." Finally, in the small hours of the morning, when Clay had made his last concession on the tax measure, he learned that the French Assembly had supported its government. Koenig accepted the final offer of compromise and, to Clay's immense satisfaction, they could now proceed trizonally.[86]

In the afternoon of June 18 Clay was sitting in his office in the Frankfurt I.G. Farben Building when Dr. Ludwig Erhard, the director of the Bizonal Economic Department, was announced. Clay had been about to call and tell him, as the first to know on the German side, what was in store. At this point only ten or twenty technicians actually knew the details of the currency reform. Like most Germans, Erhard was of course aware that such plans were in the air, but he did not know the terms or the day or the hour. As Jim O'Donnell reconstructed Clay's account of the meeting,[87] before the General could say anything, his visitor brought up the rumors about a reform. If a new currency was being introduced, and he, the *Wirtchaftsminister*, did not know anything about it, then he had been betrayed. What was actually going on? "I am sorry," Clay said, "but the rumor you heard is true. I had to conceal it from you, but I will gladly talk to you now." Erhard, who had a temper, nevertheless managed to remain calm. "This is really a question of honor and dignity," he said. "I must resign, Herr General. I have been made a fool of before my own people—*Dem Deutschen Volke*." "Well, Professor Erhard, I am awfully sorry to hear that," Clay replied. "But if you are going to resign, you had better do it within the next hour—it will be announced at eight o'clock."

It was Friday afternoon and the weekend was about to start, O'Donnell went on. Erhard stamped out of the I.G. Farben Building and had his chauffeur drive him to the *Hessische Rundfunk* where he had a talk program every week. He reached for the microphone and he himself announced the currency reform as if it were his own brilliant step. "Thank God for that," Clay remarked years later when he told Jim O'Donnell the story. "I could not have planned it any better." For if Erhard had come out against the currency reform, he would have destroyed it. "I called Erhard up the next day," Clay continued, "and promised I would never reveal the truth of the matter if he didn't." Erhard remained mum, and Clay told his story only years after Erhard had died.*

The Soviets had followed up their walkout from the Allied Control Council on March 20 by stopping all military traffic between Berlin and the West.[88] On April 1, when the American duty train on its daily run from Frankfurt to Berlin arrived at Marienborn, the first station inside the Soviet zone, it was halted by Russian soldiers. They demanded to see the travel orders of each passenger; unless they were checked and cleared, the train would not be permitted to proceed to Berlin. The American train

---

* *The author has not been able to confirm this story through research in the Deutsche Rundfunk Archiv.*

commander firmly rejected the Soviet demand and stressed that his men had orders to shoot if the Russians tried to get on board. The train then was moved to a siding. There it stood for twelve hours, when orders came to return to Frankfurt. Thus movement by air became the only answer.

The weakness of the Western position in Berlin had been discussed at the State Department for many months, but when the first Soviet action came, the documents governing access to Berlin were still not at hand. Questioned by Royall on this point, the Military Governor had little encouragement to offer. "The right to occupy Berlin was in an agreement reached in London by the European Advisory Commission," he said. For access rights there was only an oral agreement with Zhukov (which Clay himself had refused to accept in writing). Three years of application furthermore implied these rights.[89]

When Clay had sent his warning signal to the Pentagon on March 5, he not only had complied with an army request for support of additional appropriations, but he also had expressed his sincere concern that something serious was in the wind. The stopping of military traffic by the Russians merely confirmed his suspicions. Presumably the introduction of a Western currency would bring the crisis to a head and Berlin would be the battleground. He could not know what lay ahead, but while he waited for the other shoe to drop, he knew there was no choice but to stand firm.

He had faithfully tried to implement his government's earlier policy that envisaged a postwar cooperation with the Soviet Union. Now another policy had been handed down to him, and he was going to execute it with equal vigor. But whereas formerly there was the fall-back concept of a West German state, now no viable alternative existed. As he more clearly than many of his contemporaries recognized, a withdrawal from Berlin would provide no solution. At best, it would be the first step in an unthinkable retreat to fortress America. It was this conviction emanating from a far-sighted, perceptive mind and supported by the indomitable will of a born fighter that made the General the natural leader in one of the critical struggles in his nation's history. During the trying year that followed, his conviction never wavered in the slightest, whether he faced his superiors in Washington, his subordinates in Germany, his British and French allies, or his Soviet opponents.

When warned early in April that the American people might not be willing to start a war in order to maintain the American position in Berlin, Clay laid down his estimate of the situation in a teleconference with Omar Bradley:

There can be no question but that our departure would represent a tremendous loss of prestige and I would greatly deplore incurring such a loss of prestige unless it were forced by military action. Of course, I realize that this final decision is a matter of high government policy. Nevertheless I cannot believe that the Soviets will apply force in Berlin unless they have determined war to be inevitable within a comparatively short period of time.

You will understand of course that our separate currency reform in the near future followed by partial German government in Frankfurt will develop the real crisis. The present show is probably designed by Soviets to scare us away from these moves. Why are we in Europe? We have lost Czechoslavakia. We have lost Finland. Norway is threatened. We retreat from Berlin. We can take it by reducing our personnel with only airlift until we are moved out by force. There is no saving of prestige by setting up at Frankfurt that is not already discounted. After Berlin will come Western Germany and our strength there relatively is not greater and our position no more tenable than Berlin.

If we mean that we are to hold Europe against Communism we must not budge. We can take humiliation and pressure short of war in Berlin without losing face. If we move out our position in Europe is threatened. If America does not know this, does not believe the issue is cast now, then it never will and Communism will run rampant. I believe the future of democracy requires us to stay here until forced out. God knows this is not heroic pose, because there will be nothing heroic in having to take humiliation without retaliation.[90]

In accordance with this appraisal, Clay opposed the suggestion of nervous officials back home to evacuate dependents from Berlin. "From a strictly military point of view, a gradual evacuation would be logical," he said. But it would be politically disastrous and create mass hysteria among Germans in Berlin "who would rush to communism." "I propose to let dependents who are nervous go home," he suggested a few days later, "and I expect gradually to move inessential employees." In a parallel statement, he told his staff that it was unbecoming of an American to show any signs of nervousness. Those who were uneasy could go home, and a request to that effect would not discredit the applicant; however, he wanted no one in Berlin who had sent his family home, and a request to go home would therefore apply to all members of the family.[91]

As the day of the currency reform approached, Clay remained confident and calm. At his Saturday staff meeting in the latter part of June, he was confronted with three reports.[92] The Russians had stopped all German interzonal traffic; a bridge near Magdeburg on the principal highway connecting Berlin and the Western zone had been closed for repairs by the Soviets and all traffic forced to make a long detour; and third, the Russians had stopped the switching of rail cars among various stations in the American sector, with the result that traffic was held up. Clay's immediate and firm reply to the first incident was that in view of the persistent rumors of imminent currency reform the Russians could hardly be blamed for closing the borders as a temporary protective measure, and that if the circumstances had been reversed, the United States would probably have done the same thing. To the second, he said the Americans would have to take the detour. To the third, after making sure the cars were in the American sector, he promptly ordered them to be moved under guard within twenty-four hours to wherever they were wanted despite the fact that the control tower was in Soviet hands.

Clay had anticipated the blockade and neither overestimated nor underestimated its seriousness. So when the day was at hand and the introduction of a Western currency triggered the total blockade of Berlin, he calmly settled down for a long siege.

FOOTNOTES

1. Royall to Lovett, September 3, 1947. War Dept. papers. FILE SAOUS 014.1 Germany/ State N.A. Royal to Lovett, September 9, 1947, R.G. 59 File 110.721/9-947 N.A.
2. Memorandum of Lovett-Saltzman-Draper-Clay-Gordon Gray conversation, October 18, 1947. R.G. 59 File 740.00119 Control (Germany) /10-1847 N.A.
3. State Department Press Release, October 20, 1947.
4. Royall to Marshall, November 1947, R.G. 59 File 110.721/11-1047.
5. Lucius D. Clay, *Decision in Germany*, p. 239.
6. Ibid.
7. Teleconference, Clay-Draper, June 2, 1948. TT 9558, R.G. 200 N.A.
8. Interview with Edloe Donnan, Manchester, Mo., October 27, 1980.
9. Clay to Draper, January 13, 1948, CC 2852, R.G. 200 N.A.
10. Teleconference, Clay-Draper, January 9, 1948. TT 8950. R.G. 200 N.A.
11. *The New York Times*, January 30, 1948, p. 6.
12. Clay for Draper, January 13, 1948. CC 2852. R.G. 200 N.A.
13. Ibid.
14. *The Evolution of Bizonal Organization* prepared by OMGUS Civil Affairs Division, pp. 6–7.
15. Ibid.
16. Edward H. Litchfield, *Governing Postwar Germany*, p. 31.
17. *The Evolution*, p. 8.
18. Ibid.
19. Clay, *Decision*, pp. 180–181.
20. Ibid., p. 178.
21. Teleconference, Clay-Royall, Draper, January 12, 1948. TT 8960. R.G. 200 N.A.
22. Clay, *Decision*, pp. 179–180.
23. Ibid., p. 181.
24. Clay for Draper, January 13, 1948. CC 2852. R.G. 200 N.A.
25. Author's interview with Margaret Allen, Washington, D.C., October 25, 1980.
26. Johannes Semler, Speech at Erlangen, January 4, 1948. OMGUS records 150-3/3 N.A.
27. *Tagesspiegel*, January 19, 21, 28.
28. Diary by Murray V. Wagoner. OMGUS records 102-2/15.
29. Statement by F. Taylor Ostrander. Chief Price Control Section OMGUS. Public Information Office. (OMGUS-C-55) January 29, 1948. OMGUS records. 148-2/15.
30. William J. Logan. "Streamlining the German Export Program," Radio address on the German network in the U.S. zone, February 5, 1948. OMGUS records 108-3/11.
31. Meeting of Military Governor with President of Economic Council and Chairman of Executive Committee, February 16, 1948, OMGUS records 11-1/1.
32. Clay for Noce, April 7, 1948, CC 3752. R.G. 200 N.A. Dr. Richard McKinzie interview with General Clay, New York, N.Y., July 16, 1974.
33. HICOG, March 17, 1950, quoted in Hubert G. Schmidt, "The Liberalization of West German Foreign Trade," p. 10. Office of the High Commissioner for Germany, Historical Division, 1952.
34. Clay, *Decision*, p. 217.
35. Clay for Draper, May 5, 1948. CC 4178. R.G. 200 N.A.
36. Ibid.
37. Clay for Baruch, March 2, 1948, in Jean Smith, *The Papers of General Lucius D. Clay*.
38. Clay for Draper, January 11, 1948. CC 2839. R.G. 200 N.A.
39. Clay for Draper, May 15, 1948. CC 4308. R.G. 200 N.A.
40. Clay, *Decision*, p. 218. When Harriman arrived in Vienna on his way from Berlin, he appeared "pulverized" by the debate with Clay, according to Eleanor Dulles, (Author's interview, Washington, D.C. December 9, 1981.)
41. *Foreign Relations of the United States 1947*, Vol. 2, pp. 258–263.
42. Ibid., pp. 1109–1116.
43. Hilldring to Saltzman, November 10, 1947, R.G. 59. File 110.271/11-1047, N.A.
44. *Foreign Relations 1947*, Vol. 2, p. 904.

45. Ibid., pp. 1137–1142.
46. *Frankfurter Rundschau*, October 30, 1947, p. 1.
47. *Foreign Relations 1947*, Vol. 2, p. 1127. Henry Wallich, *The Mainsprings of the German Revival*, p. 370.
48. Clay for Draper, November 1, 1947. CC 2164. R.G. 200 N.A.
49. Clay for Draper, July 1, 1948. FMPC-274. R.G. 200 N.A.
50. Clay, *Decision*, p. 259.
51. Teleconference, Clay-Draper, Gordon Gray, March 12, 1948, TT 9205, R.G. 200 N.A.
52. Ibid.
53. Clay for Draper, March 14, 1948. CC 3499. R.G. 200. N.A.
54. William E. Griffith, "The Denazification Program in the U.S. Zone of Germany," Ph.D. Thesis, Harvard University, pp. 500–552.
55. Clay, *Decision*, p. 331.
56. *The New York Times*, July 26, 1947, p. 5.
57. James S. Martin, "German Cartels are at it Again," in *The New Republic*, October 6, 1947.
58. J. F. J. Gillen, *Deconcentration and Decartelization in West Germany*, p. 49.
59. Ibid., p. 52.
60. James Martin, *All Honorable Men*, pp. 361–362.
61. Federal Trade Commission, "U.S. Committee to Review the Decartelization Program in Germany," April 15, 1949.
62. Clay for Voorhees, CC 8245, April 4, 1949. R.G. 200 N.A.
63. Clay for Voorhees, CC 8419, April 24, 1949. R.G. 200 N.A.
64. Clay for Draper, January 30, 1948. CC 3032. R.G. 200 N.A.
65. W 95293 in Smith, *The Papers*, p. 549.
66. Clay, *Decision*, p. 401.
67. John Ford Golay, *The Founding of the Federal Republic of Germany*, pp. 6–12.
68. Ibid.
69. Ibid.
70. Clay, *Decision*, p. 397.
71. Jean Smith interview with General Clay, March 13, 1971.
72. Clay, *Decision*, pp. 397–400.
73. Ibid.
74. Golay, *The Founding*, p. 13. Clay, *Decision*, p. 336; Clay for Draper, May 11, 1948, CC 73282, R.G. 200 N.A. Clay for Draper, May 11, 1948, CC 73287, R.G. 200 N.A. Teleconference, Clay, Draper, Wilkinson, May 14, 1948, TT 9495. R.G. 200 N.A. Clay for Draper, May 19, 1948. CC 73327 R.G. 200 N.A.
75. Golay, *The Founding*, p. 13.
76. Andrea Boyle, *The Fourth Man: A Climate of Treason*, passim.
77. Clay for Dept. of the Army, February 5, 1948, CC 3095. R.G. 200 N.A.; Teleconference, Clay-Draper, February 15, 1948. TT-9079. R.G. 200 N.A.
78. Clay for Draper, February 12, 1948. CC 3178, R.G. 200 N.A.; Clay, *Decision*, p. 354.
79. Ibid., pp. 355–357.
80. Teleconference, Clay-Royall, Bradley, Noce, March 23, 1948. TT 9247. R.G. 200 N.A.
81. Clay, *Decision*, pp. 212–213.
82. W-97929 in Smith, *The Papers*, p. 354.
83. Clay for Draper, June 6, 1948; CC 4593. R.G. 200 N.A.
84. Jack Bennett, "The German Currency Reform," in *The Annals of the American Academy of Political and Social Sciences*, 1950, p. 51.
85. Teleconference, Clay-Draper, June 16, 1948. TT-9623, R.G. 200 N.A.
86. Clay, *Decision*, p. 213.
87. Author's interview with James O'Donnell, Washington, D.C., March 8, 1980.
88. Clay, *Decision*, pp. 358–360.
89. Teleconference, Clay-Royall, Bradley, Collins, Wedemeyer, March 31, 1948. TT-9286. R.G. 200 N.A.
90. Clay, *Decision*, p. 361. Teleconference, Clay-Bradley, April 10, 1948. TT 9341. R.G. 200 N.A.
91. Teleconference, Clay, Huebner, Collins, Chamberlin, March 17, 1948. TT-9218. R.G. 200 N.A. Clay for Wedemeyer, April 2, 1948, CC 36 88, R.G. 200 N.A. Clay, *Decision*, p. 360.
92. Don Humphrey, private papers.

CHAPTER TEN

Defending Berlin

THE LONDON AGREEMENT THAT SET THE STAGE FOR THE ESTABLISHMENT OF A
West German state had prompted the Soviet walkout from the Allied Control Authority. Similarly, the introduction of a West German currency had triggered the Russian blockade of Berlin. Clay, having masterminded the framework of the London Agreement, had no illusions about the difficulties it would entail. The confrontation with the Soviet Union, while dramatic and fraught with dangers, was only part of it. The key elements of his concept of a strong West German state as a bulwark against Communism—the creation of an Interntional Ruhr Authority, a trizonal fusion, and the drafting of an occupation statute—still had to be negotiated. Judging from the Quai d'Orsay's past performance, it would be an arduous task at best. Setting up a German constitutional assembly and drafting a constitution, on the other hand, would be primarily a German responsibility. But since his own constitutional views were rigid, the extent of German cooperation seemed uncertain.

Clay had assumed he would be gone by now, leaving the State Department the responsibility for implementing his grand design for a West German republic. That fate had decided otherwise at least gave him an opportunity to make sure the right building blocks got put in the right places. Indeed, as he considered the formidable array of obstacles still ahead of him, the task of defending Berlin seemed almost minor in comparison.

The currency reform had been announced in West Germany on Friday, June 18, shortly after the banks had closed for the weekend. A few hours earlier, each of the Western military governors had notified Marshal Sokolovsky of the impending step and, for the record, expressed the hope that an agreement for a new all-German currency would soon be reached. The Soviets also were informed that the Western sectors of Berlin would not be affected by this action.[1] Two days later the Soviet military governor replied that the new bank notes would not be admitted for circulation in the Soviet zone or in Berlin, "which is part of the Soviet occupation zone." It seemed to him, he wrote, "that the Western practical action" had destroyed the hopes of the German people for a uniform currency. Sokolovsky was satisfied with Clay's statement that the announced currency reform would not be introduced in the United States sector of Berlin. "I believe that this goes without saying," he concluded, "since there can be only one currency in circulation in Berlin."[2] Synchronized with his response was the issue of a new set of traffic regulations imposed, as the Russians explained, to protect the Eastern zone from a flood of devalued Reichsmarks. The American reaction, in the form of a press release, was to reject the Soviet position, stressing that Berlin was an international city.[3] American forces would stay in Berlin, even if land access were denied them. It was perfectly possible to supply the 10,000 Americans in the city by air for an indefinite length of time, the statement said. Clay followed this up with a letter to the Soviet military governor suggesting a quadripartite discussion of the currency situation in Berlin.[4]

Two days after the new currency had been introduced in the Western zone, the financial experts of the four powers met in an effort to find a solution to the problem.[5] Jack Bennett, Clay's financial adviser, represented the United States. On the Western side, there was little hope that the Soviets would agree to what Bennett termed a "reasonable solution for the Berlin money." Because it was a foregone conclusion that the Soviets would respond by trying to make an Eastern currency the city's legal tender, Clay had taken some precautions. Ten planeloads of the new Western currency had been flown into Berlin disguised as military cargo; altogether a fund of DM 250 million was ready for distribution. A dozen carefully screened German financial experts had been recruited to study the problem of extending the currency reform to the Western sectors of Berlin. At York House, a military government building in the British sector, a "cage" had been established where the German experts worked, ate, and slept. They were allowed no outside contacts and were instructed to tell their families they were going to Frankfurt to work on a military government job. To strengthen this alibi, they had even been picked up at their homes, driven in the direction of the Tempelhof airport, then brought back to York House. As Frank Howley, the colorful head of the military government detachment in Berlin, put it, "no key physicists with the dark secrets of the atom bomb locked in their brains were guarded and shrouded more carefully."[6]

Although Soviet intentions were anticipated, no Western position for the meeting of financial experts had yet crystallized. According to an official French announcement, France's delegate had actually convinced his American and British colleagues that the Soviet-sponsored currency should be legal tender for Berlin.[7] Clay, reporting the same development somewhat differently, merely advised the Department of the Army that "the discussion did allow this hypothesis of a Soviet zone currency in Berlin to be presented."[8] Considering the farreaching effects of the exclusive use of Russian-printed money in Berlin, it was clear the Russians—as so often—had overplayed their hand. Their additional demand was unacceptable to the West: that the Soviet authorities alone and not the quadripartite *Kommandatura* would be responsible for the issuance of money and the control of banking and finances throughout the entire city. As Bennett and his two colleagues pointed out, the Russians had no jurisdiction in the Western sectors, and the Western military governors were not prepared to abdicate their sovereignty in favor of the Soviet military government. After inconclusive discussions until late in the evening the meeting broke up.[9] Just before adjournment a Soviet courier arrived to inform the Soviet delegate that everything was set for a Soviet currency reform to become effective immediately. A makeshift new currency did indeed appear in the Soviet sector[10] on June 24, a total blockade of Berlin was simultaneously declared, and the Western powers proceeded with their own reform. As Clay reported to Washington, French cooperation had again been most difficult to secure. It came in the last moment and was accompanied by a warning about "the incalculable consequences" of such action. Since they undoubtedly would "extend beyond the frame of Berlin the French government was obliged to disassociate itself from all responsibility."[11]

Berlin's city fathers—whose assembly hall was located in the Soviet sector—thus found themselves in a serious predicament. Marshall Sokolovsky had proclaimed that Berlin was economically part of the Soviet zone and therefore had ordered the *Magistrat* to adopt the East Mark. At the same time the three Western powers had ordered the city government not to obey this unilateral order because it violated the city constitution and the four-power agreements at the Allied *Kommandatura* and at the Control Authority. On June 23, in a dramatic four-hour session,[12] a majority of the city fathers—courageously disregarding the threats of communist mobs inside and outside the building—formally restated that Berlin's constitution prescribed four-power rule; consequently, two currencies would circulate in Berlin side by side and the city administration continue as before. The following afternoon a mass meeting called by the SPD showed that Berlin's Socialist leaders were far from willing to yield to Communist terror tactics. Some 80,000 Berliners jammed the Hertha Stadium to hear their party leaders delcare that the eyes of the world were focused on Berlin. As the chairman of the local SPD told the crowd, the Communists, "following the model of Hitler and the example of Prague, tried to seize power in Berlin by terror. But they miscalculated. . . . Berlin will remain free, it will never become Communist." And he exhorted "the Western powers and free men everywhere to come to the assistance of Berlin."[13]

The meeting at the stadium was still in progress when the Military Governor, accompanied by Murphy and Donnan, returned from Heidelberg. He had told the press in Frankfurt that nothing but war would drive the United States out of Berlin. And in Heidelberg he had spent the day at army headquarters with Clarence Huebner, his military deputy, and Arthur Trudeau—who commanded the First Constabulary Brigade in Wiesbaden—where they discussed the organization of an armored convoy to Berlin.[14] In Clay's estimate, given a determined Western effort the convoy would get through to Berlin. There would be no hostilities, he believed, unless the Soviet Union was committed to war,[15] and in that case, pressures would continue elsewhere even if the Western powers were willing to give up the city. Clay accordingly directed the two generals to plan for a task force to proceed on the autobahn to Berlin. It would deliver about 500 tons of food and fuel supplies and thereby open up the main access route. A total force of about 5,000 to 6,000 men would be involved, and, in addition to American units, would include British and French forces.[16] Until he had Washington's approval, however, he would take no action beyond the planning stage.

Upon his return to Kronprinzen Allee, Clay found his staff divided. Some thought the sensible policy for the United States was to withdraw. "If your hand is in the fire," one official was quoted as saying, "why not pull it out." Others believed the Soviets were bluffing and the United States had to stay. With his own staff divided,[17] the French opposed, and the support from Washington hesitant, the report about the courageous actions of Berlin's city fathers came as welcome news. The Germans, it seemed, were resolved to see this situation through. It was an impression strongly confirmed the following day in a meeting with Ernst Reuter and Willy Brandt, Kurt Schumacher's liaison at the Berlin *Magistrat*. Reuter, a prominent member of the Communist Party in his younger years and now a bitter enemy of Communism, had been elected lord mayor in 1947, although a Soviet veto had prevented his taking office and his deputy, Louise Schroeder, had been acting mayor ever since.

As Clay later recalled, he told Reuter:

> Before I go ahead now with my final recommendations, I want you to know this, that no matter what we do, Berliners are going to be short of fuel and short of electricity. I don't believe they'll be short of food, but I'm sure there will be times when they are going to be very cold and feel very miserable. Unless they are willing to take this and stay with us, we can't run this. If we are subjecting them to a type and kind of treatment which they are unwilling to stand, and they break on us, our whole airlift will fail. I don't want to go into it unless you understand that fully. Unless you are convinced that the Berliners will take it.

Reuter replied without hesitation, "General, I can assure you, I do assure you, that the Berliners will take it." According to Brandt, "Reuter did not quite believe the city could be supplied by air, but his answer was firm: 'We shall do what we feel to be our duty.'"[18] Visibly impressed, the Military Governor then called Curtis LeMay in Wiesbaden, ordering him to drop promptly all other uses of military aircraft so the entire fleet of C-47s could be put on the Berlin run. Having thus completed his three-pronged muster, Clay was now sure of the resources he had on hand. The "Task Force Trudeau," commanded by its eponym, would be composed of one constabulary regiment supported by the First Division's field artillery and an engineer battalion. A British tank battalion and a French battalion from the 3rd Spahi's regiment would probably be added once the plan had been approved. There was insufficient bridging equipment on hand, but this could be gotten quickly from the States.[19] The resilience of the Berlin population was really amazing, Clay thought, but this also entailed certain risks. It might drive Sokolovsky and the SED to extreme measures.[20] The available transport fleet of C-47s was small but LeMay's prompt response that he could fly in coal as well as other supplies was reassuring.[21] Finally, Albert Wedemeyer—the chief of Plans and Operations in the Pentagon, whose troops during the war had been supplied via the airbridge over the HUMP in South Asia—was equally positive. "There is no question," he said, "of our being able to support your position in Berlin by air if enough airplanes are made available."[22]

Clay covered the events of the last days in a June 25 cable to the department. The decision to extend the new currency to Berlin, he said, was made in view of Sokolvsky's announcement that a Soviet zone currency under complete Soviet control would be introduced in Berlin. "We were prepared to compromise on a special currency for Berlin," Clay explained, "or on a Soviet currency under four-power supervision. However, the British and ourselves feel strongly that the placing of currency control in Berlin completely in Russian hands was a recognition of Soviet sovereignty in Berlin. It could defer the real issues for a few weeks only."[23] The General was handing the final draft of the cable to Captain Allen when word came in that the Secretary of the Army wanted an immediate teleconference. As Royall's opening comment indicated, Washington was worried. "I would not want any action taken in Berlin which might lead to possible armed conflict," he said, "Maybe the issue of the new currency should be delayed or slowed up?" There was no possible way now to suspend the issue or to slow it down, Clay replied, He did not expect an armed conflict; the only danger came from German Communist groups causing trouble under Soviet direction. When asked for his recommendations, he suggested a sharp protest in Moscow for the record and "the development of external pressures in case the Soviets—as expected—" . . . reject the protest." The United States would have to make a decision now, he said, about how far it wanted to go. "We here think," he added, "it is extremely important to stay and we are prepared to stay unless German suffering drives us out."

Royall's reply that the limited question of a Berlin currency was not a good reason to go to war got a firm response. "We are not trying to provoke war," Clay said. "If the Soviets go to war, it will not be because of Berlin currency issue, but only because they believe it is the right time. In such a case they would use the currency issue as an excuse. "I can only say," he concluded, "that our remaining in Berlin means much to our prestige in Germany, in Europe, and in keeping high the courage of Western Europe. To retreat now is to imply we are prepared to retreat further." The teleconference ended inconclusively with Clay's comment that his "British colleague had been splendid throughout" but there was "not any support even moral from the French."[24]

The General had second thoughts as he walked up the stairs to his office from the teleconference room; maybe a compromise proposal on the currency issue ought to be made after all. The conference with the secretary convinced him that "Washington did not want to have an issue now."[25] Nor did the French want any part of an issue, while the British were still firm, but most unhappy. Accordingly in a second cable to the department he outlined two courses of action. "I am convinced," he said, "that a determined movement of convoys with troop protection would reach Berlin and that such a showing might well prevent rather than build up Soviet pressures which could lead to war. Nevertheless I realize fully the inherent danger in this proposal since, once committed, we could not withdraw." As an alternative he suggested another meeting with Marshal Sokolovsky. He was not sanguine about the outcome, he cabled, but if the department agreed he would suggest to the Russians a trade agreement whereby the DM would be used in interzonal trade, but not in general circulation. This would "maintain the principle that Western currency is being used in Berlin but obviate the difficulties of two currencies in circulation. We have now asserted our right to issue and can probably afford to compromise to prevent the severe punishment of Berlin without serious loss of prestige."[26] As he later admitted, he himself did not like the proposal, but if Washington wanted an alternative suggestion he ought to make it.

Clay reviewed the situation with Frank Howley and others at a staff meeting the following afternoon.[27] The Russians had stopped all rail and road traffic to Berlin and curtailed the supply of electric current normally reaching the Western sectors from the Soviet zone. Sokolovsky, moreover, had ordered that any food trucked into Berlin from the Russian zone could be distributed only in the Soviet sector. The Russians whipped up a vicious propaganda campaign synchronized with the blockade to break the morale of the Berliners. Rumors were spread about the return of the Mongolian army units that had savagely sacked the city in May and June 1945. The Soviet radio reported riots in the Western sectors. American troops had fired on demonstrating Germans, causing hundreds of casualties. The Western parts of the city were reportedly in chaos and the occupying powers were preparing to leave the city. As directed by Clay, Howley had gone on the air to explain American intentions to the German people. "We are not getting out of Berlin," he had promised. "We are going to stay. I don't know the answer to the present problem—not yet—but this much I do know. The American people will not stand by and allow the German people to starve."[28]

There were more difficult problems than Soviet propaganda to contend with, however. It normally took 20,000 tons of supplies per day to keep the three Western sectors running. Under an emergency plan developed several months earlier, the barest minimum to support the occupation authorities on any austerity basis and maintain stockpiles for the German population was 4,000 tons a day. This included food, coal, medicine, and all essentials to feed the people, keep vital industries intact, and maintain public services. "We have thirty-six days food and forty-six days coal on hand," Howley announced.[29] Some planes will be coming in tomorrow, Clay said. "There won't be many but there will be planes. How fast can you get ready to accept them and what do you want brought in first?" "We'll accept cargoes as fast as they come in," was Howley's reply, "and we'll have flour first, please."[30]

The next day wartime twin-engined C-47 transports brought in 200 tons of flour. It was the first effort to supply a city of two and a half million by air, a feat nobody thought possible at the time.

As a minor counterirritant to the Soviet blockade, the Military Governor ordered the strict enforcement of traffic safety orders. He knew it would mean arresting a substantial number of Russians for speeding as they drove their confiscated German cars through the American sector en route from their homes in Potsdam.[31] He did not expect that one of the first victims of the order would be the Soviet military governor himself. When Sokolovsky refused to stop for a jeep patrol, his car was intercepted and stopped by one of the patrolling U.S. armored cars. Armed Russian bodyguards, following in a second car, made the mistake of jumping out with guns in hand. The American patrol quickly put a gun in the pit of Sokolovsky's stomach and, as Clay described it, "his bodyguards calmed down." He was held for almost one hour before an American officer arrived to identify and release him. General Clay felt bad about the incident, and two days later he called on Sokolovsky at Karlshorst to express his personal regrets: "I did not want this incident," he advised the Department, "to develop into any possible excuse to delay or defer further meetings between us."[32] He expected Sokolovsky to treat the matter in his usual humorous way, but not so. The Marshall received Clay with marked official politeness but with evident restraint and a complete lack of his normal cordiality. "For the first time in the history of our meetings," the General reported, "no refreshments were offered." Nevertheless, while claiming "half-heartedly" that the arrest was deliberate, Sokolovsky expressed his disapproval of the arrests now occurring on both sides. The two generals thereupon agreed that such incidents did not offer a solution to the Berlin problem, and both promised to issue instructions that they be avoided in the future. "I was under the impression that he is set on his present course," Clay continued in his report, "but is by no manner of means happy or confident. I was also of the definite impression that he had hoped I was bringing some proposal with me and that he kept waiting for me to offer such proposal."[32]

The same weekend saw important developments taking place in Washington. At a Pentagon meeting on Sunday, June 27, Forrestal, Royall, Lovett, Bradley and Norstad concluded that there were three possible courses of action: to withdraw from Berlin before September 1, by which time a constituent assembly for a West German government would presumably have met; to retain the Allied position in Berlin by all means, possibly including supplying the city by convoy; or, third, to look for a diplomatic solution while maintaining a firm stand in Berlin and postponing an ultimate decision. They also weighed the possibility of a show of force—sending to Europe two B-29 groups widely known as the carriers of the atomic bomb. The upshot of the deliberation was to leave the crucial decision for a conference in the Oval Office the following noon.[33]

As Forrestal described the meeting with the President, when the specific question of America remaining in Berlin was raised, Truman replied there would be no discussion on that point. "We were going to stay, period." And when Secretary Royall expressed some concern that the problem might not have been fully thought through, the President said that "we would have to deal with the situation as it developed," but the essential decision was "that we were in Berlin by terms of an agreement and that the Russians had no right to get us out by either direct or indirect pressure."[34] The President, moreover, approved sending the B-29s to Europe.

Only four days after the beginning of the blockade, then, the crucial decision to hold Berlin thus had been made even if it still was not clear how to do it. Clay had cabled to Draper the preceding day that an additional fifty C-54s, each capable of carrying ten tons, would be needed. But illustrative of the incremental nature of most political decisions, neither in Berlin nor in Washington had the "airlift" yet become a conscious program. ("Within ten days I felt we could do it," Clay later said.)[35]

On July 3, when the three military governors met with their Russian counterpart for the second time, the Soviet position concerning the blockade was clarified. Clay and his colleagues had gone to Karlshorst expecting to discuss the transport situation and a possible compromise. Sokolovksy, however, maintained the pretext of technical difficulties, never once mentioning the currency issue. Instead he referred to "economic disorder" in the Soviet zone which the Allies allegedly had created and which made it impossible to provide alternative routes to Berlin.[36] Finally, letting the cat out of the bag, he remarked that "these economic disorders have been created by the London Conference." He was not prepared to answer any questions on the resumption of traffic, he said, unless the results of the London Conference were also included in the discussion. In other words, Robertson inquired, the question of transport was related to the German problem? Without directly answering, Sokolvsky let this interpretation stand.[37]

As far as Clay was concerned, it had been a useful meeting because it proved, as he had surmised all along, that currency reform was not the real issue. Evidently the Soviet government had a maximum and a minimum objective: either the Western powers would have to abandon their plans for a West German government, or they would have to get out of Berlin. In any event the issue was now out of Clay's hands and would have to be resolved on the governmental level.

The very next day Secretary Marshall handed the Soviet ambassador a note that opened up the diplomatic dialogue. It mentioned the "extremely serious international situation" caused by the Soviet action. Berlin was not part of the Soviet zone but an international city, it said. American forces had been withdrawn in 1945 from Saxony and Thuringia in exchange for the Western occupation of Berlin and free access to the city, and several notes between Truman and Stalin had confirmed this agreement. The United States, the note continued, therefore insisted that freight and passenger traffic between the Western zones and Berlin had to be fully restored. Any disagreement between the Allied powers ought to be settled by negotiations or by other peaceful means as provided in Article 33 of the Charter of the United Nations, but prerequisite was the full restoration of the movement of goods and persons from the West to Berlin.[58]

Clay entertained no illusions about an early solution to the crisis on the diplomatic level. It would be a long siege, and plans had to be made to maintain the Western position. An armored column was still his preference, but a stepped-up airlift as the alternative was now entering the planning stage. "Present American airlift into Berlin has had a peak delivery of about 1,000 tons in twenty-four hours," he cabled to Bradley on July 10.

> LeMay has asked for fifty additional C-54s. I request that this request be approved and the additional C-54s dispatched immediately. In good weather we should come very close to 2,000 tons a day with American lift. I believe the British will reach at least 1,000 tons per day. Three thousand tons per day would provide us with food, essential coal, and even raw materials to maintain some industrial activity in Western sectors.[39]

In a second cable to Bradley dispatched a few hours later, Clay addressed the issue of a conference at governmental level to consider the entire German question. There should be no negotiations under duress, he stressed; in other words, the blockade would have to be lifted first. On the other hand, if the Russians complied, a flat refusal to discuss the German problem as a whole "would adversely affect our moral position. It would be exploited to show that we do not desire to reach an agreement."[10] Because he was sure such a meeting "would not record any real accomplishment," Clay warned that it should not be permitted to "delay our plans for Western Germany." He again raised the subject of a convoy "to make our right of way into Berlin usable," and reiterated his belief that "if the Soviet Union does intend war, it is because of a fixed plan." If the Russians had not such a plan, he said, there would be no hostilities whatever action the Allies took to relieve the blockade. Finally, he recommended the development of economic embargoes or other countermeasures to support the Berlin position.[41]

The proposal to send an armored column to Berlin was apparently being given careful consideration at the Pentagon because two teleconferences with Berlin on the Plans and Operations level dealt with numerous technical questions concerning the dispatch of convoys. Although Clay always maintained that a convoy would have gotten through and Robert Murphy was of the same opinion, the Joint Chiefs of Staff, Secretary Acheson,[42] Royall, and also Frank Howley,[43] held to a different view. But even if Clay's prediction had proved correct and the safe arrival of the convoy had given his fighting spirit the desired triumph, the question remains unanswered—what would have happened then? The exchange of some incisive questions and hesitant answers in the Plans and Operations teleconferences cast some interesting light on this crucial aspect.

Washington: Are you prepared to occupy the autobahn in its entirety? It is foreseen that once convoy has proceeded across zonal frontiers sabotage could destroy bridges in front of and behind convoy thereby effectively bottling convoy without use of force.
Berlin: Do not contemplate occupation of autobahn. [125 miles long]
Washington: In the event the Soviets permit the passage of the convoy of 200 trucks without forcible resistance but continue to impede rail and barge traffic, . . . What would be your plan to continue to supply Berlin? Motor transportation available to the combined English, French and United States troops apparently *not sufficient* (emphasis added) to supply Berlin indefinitely at a level sufficient to provide basic economic support and concurrently carry on essential administrative requirements in Trizonia.
Berlin: Since your question is more policy than operational, we will pass it on to General Clay for his action.[44]

There is no evidence in dispatches that the General ever faced up to these critical questions himself. In a cable to Draper on July 19, he again recommended the convoy,[45] and two days later, during dinner with the Secretary of Defense in Washington, the subject came up again.[46] Clay's comment that "three weeks earlier it would have been easier to put an armored convoy through" is a possible indiction that he too had some second thoughts on the question. In a 1971 interview with Jean Smith, he confirmed this interpretation: "I still wish we had tried. I wanted to do so for pride. I don't know what we would have done, if we had gone through and the Russians just let us go through and then had stopped the next group of German trucks that moved in and out." In any case, when he met with President Truman the following day he was able to settle the question of supplying Berlin by air. By that time he had asked for 160 C-54s, but the Air Force was unwilling to denude American strength in other areas and had hesitated to comply with this request. It was the President himself who overruled his advisers and decided in Clay's favor. (Truman told Clay that he also would have approved the armed convoy, but all the military chiefs were against it.)[47] When Clay returned to Berlin a few days later, he told the press he had been promised a considerable increase in Skymaster aircraft and that with their help the airlift could be built up to handle 4,000 tons a day.[48] The expanded airlift would give the Western powers time to tackle the problem through diplomatic channels.

The Soviet government, meanwhile, citing Yalta and Potsdam as well as the four-power agreement on the control machinery in Germany, had replied to the American note on July 14. The agreement concerning the quadripartite administration of Berlin was an integral part of the agreement for the four-power administration of Germany as a whole, the Soviet note declared. Because the latter had been destroyed by Western actions "the legal basis which assured their right to participate in Berlin also had been undermined."[49] While not objecting to negotiations, the Soviet government made it clear that the discussion could not be confined to Berlin but would have to cover the entire issue of quadripartite control of Germany. In his comments on the Soviet note the following day, General Clay thought it very shrewdly drafted. It placed the Western Allies in a position to negotiate only at their specific request, thus permitting the Soviet government to establish the conditions of the meeting. He therefore believed that aside from the convoy the only recourse was to throw the matter of the blockade into the International Court or into the United Nations. The three Western governments thought otherwise, however, and instructed their ambassadors in Moscow to raise this issue at the very highest Soviet level.

As it turned out, the Soviets were in no hurry to accommodate their former allies, and it was not until the evening of August 2 that the three envoys were able to get through to Premier Stalin. It was a long meeting with Bedell Smith, as the senior representative, acting as a spokesman for the ambassadors. From Stalin's vantage point it seemed that the three Western powers were faced with the unpleasant alternatives of either withdrawing from Berlin in ignominious defeat or staying there under sufferance and abandoning the plans for a West German government. Although Smith and his two colleagues strongly doubted the possibility of supplying Berlin by air during the winter, they nevertheless stood their ground, refusing to yield to Stalin's demands for a stay in the implementation of the London Agreement. They also rejected his assertion that the Western powers by their actions had forfeited the legal right to remain in Berlin. After a lengthy debate and probably persuaded that he could not break the impasse with a frontal attack, the Soviet Premier moderated his demands and came up with a new proposal. The Western DM would be withdrawn from Berlin and replaced by the Soviet-zone mark as the only legal tender in Berlin, and all transport restrictions would simultaneously be removed. The Soviets would not insist any longer on a postponement of the London decisions. It should be on the agenda of the next Council of Foreign Ministers meeting or other four-power conference, but in the meantime the insistent Soviet request to that end would have to be recorded in the document to be drawn up by the four powers.[50]

In a teleconference with Royall on August 3, Clay promptly questioned whether the withdrawal of the Western currency was meant to take place without conditions. This could be disastrous, he pointed out, unless the

Western powers had a voice in the issue of the currency and in the extension of credits in Berlin. He did not see, however, how Washington could refuse a Council of Foreign Ministers meeting but recommended that "we renew our determination to proceed in Western Germany."[51]

The following day, after having read Bedell Smith's second and more detailed report on the Kremlin meeting, Clay followed up his teleconference with an additional warning to Royall.[52] He considered the ambassador's second message far less optimistic, he cabled, because it mentioned nothing about a quadripartite control of the Berlin currency, and without it "we would in fact in short order have no real say in Berlin government." The Soviets were currently taking measures that "clearly indicated their determination to obtain full control of Berlin's banking and credit system. German political leaders who visited us last night," he added, "believe that the acceptance of such measures would in fact destroy the present city government." Obviously, no other course of action was left open but to accept in principle the Soviet proposal, Clay said, but "we should do so with our eyes open. . . ."[53]

Just as Clay expected, the negotiations in Moscow soon hit a snag. Instead of drawing up an agreement incorporating Stalin's proposal, Molotov resorted to the initial Soviet negotiating position and repeatedly tried to make postponement of a West German government a precondition; he also insisted on defining "all transport restriction—the ones Stalin had agreed to remove—as only those imposed after June 18. As Ambassador Smith concluded, Molotov's draft would have enabled the Soviets to control the life of Berlin whether Western troops remained there or not; it would have delayed the establishment of a West German government; and it would have permitted the Soviets to reimpose the blockade at their discretion. To exchange these concessions for a partial lifting of the blockade seemed a dubious bargain at best."[54]

Unable to make any progress with Molotov, the three ambassadors asked for another meeting with "the Chief." It took place on August 23 and its results were hardly more encouraging. The Soviet premier agreed to four-power control over the Berlin currency and the bank of emission, but he remained vague on the lifting of traffic restrictions. His proposal whereby only the restrictions recently imposed would be lifted left the door open for further disagreements. As far as the London agreements were concerned, he made it clear that the impending meeting of the Parliamentary Council in Bonn was his principal concern. He was not appeased by Ambassador Smith's explanation that a government at Frankfurt had not been contemplated as a central German government and that "the agency to be set up now would in no way hamper eventual understanding on a central government for United Germany." Instead, he cunningly suggested a four-power communiqué that would say "the question of the London decisions was also discussed including the formation of a Western German government," and that the discussion took place "in an atmosphere of understanding." Smith could not fail to recognize the "dynamite" in these harmless-sounding words, the enormous effect they would have on the people of West Germany. But his counterproposal, to add that "no agreement was reached on this subject"—for all practical purposes ended the Western démarche. Stalin lost interest in the discussion and was unavailable for further meetings.[55]

From then on Molotov became increasingly truculent, and the lack of progress forced the diplomats to conclude that the best solution was to pass the buck. As Smith described it, the four military governors were instructed to find within a week practical ways of doing two things at the same time: lifting the blockade, and introducing Soviet currency into Berlin under effective four-power supervision. The wording of the instructions was left vague, however, and Stalin's oral commitment to a quadripartite control of the German bank of currency emission was omitted. It was clearly an agreement for agreement's sake, and Clay's frustrated conclusion "that our acceptance of ambiguous wording just to obtain an agreed directive would lead nowhere"[56] was confirmed in the following week. Sokolovsky not only demanded complete control of all trade with Berlin but also rejected supervisory power of a quadripartite finance commission over the German bank of emission. And he raised the ante by demanding restrictions on civil air traffic between Berlin and the West.[57] "My present feeling is that the Soviet position is to take their terms in full or else," Clay told Washington in the course of another teleconference.[58] "We have no intention of making any agreement," Secretary Royall advised, "that could give to the Soviets such powers over currency or trade as would make it impractical for us to remain in Berlin in a manner compatible with our prestige. State concurs in this message."[59] At least this cleared the air as far as Washington's support was concerned. Negotiations continued, but by the end of the allotted time Clay and his Western colleagues decided to concede the failure of their mission. "Marshal Sokolovsky has given ground on most subsidiary issues," their joint report to the three governments read. But three points of disagreement remained: the functions of the quadripartite financial commission, the control of trade, and the proposed restrictions on air transport.[60] As a consequence, negotiations reverted to regular diplomatic channels, prompting a declaration by the Western powers that the negotiations in Berlin had failed because of the Soviet refusal to agree on four-power control of the bank of emission.[61]

A few days later, Clay was in Paris meeting with Secretary Marshall and Ambassadors Smith, Douglas, and Murphy for a general exchange of views. It was at that point, after a meeting with the British and French ambassadors, that the decision was reached to take the Berlin issue to the United Nations.[62] The Kremlin was accordingly informed that the "illegal coercive" blockade had made further negotiations impossible, that the Soviets had created "a threat to international peace and security," and that the democracies therefore found themselves "obliged to refer the action of the Soviet government to the Security Council of the United Nations." In the course of the Paris conversations—also joined by Ambassador Caffery and Dr. Philipp Jessup, the American representative on the Security Council—Clay had an opportunity to report on the situation in Germany and Berlin. As he saw it, the results of the European Recovery Program were so far most satisfactory, and the success of the currency reform had changed the economic outlook entirely. He hoped that there soon would be an economically healthy Europe and Western Germany, "able to assert rather than absorb pressures," and that this power, when it developed, would bring the Berlin blockade to an end.[63]

While everybody at the meetings agreed that the Western powers had to remain in Berlin at least temporarily, the concept of a strong West German state as the principal dam against Communism failed to find the same unequivocal support. An alternative approach, the early four-power evacuation of Germany as a first step toward neutralization of the country, was still an active State Department option. Marshall as well as Bedell Smith felt that time was on the side of the Russians and that Berlin was a liability to be disposed of at the first auspicious moment.[64]

Clay had brought with him some impressive data on the performance of the airlift. It had started out in June, he said, with 110 airplanes, all twin-engined C-47s with an individual load capacity of under three tons, providing a maximum lift of 700 tons a day. Since then most of the C-47s had been replaced by C-54s with a ten-ton load capacity, and the daily delivery was now 4,000 tons. Moreover, an additional seventy C-54s, on order or en route, would increase the daily air delivery to 8,000 tons, he predicted. Operating day and night, airplanes were taking off or landing every forty-eight seconds at each of the two airfields in Berlin.[65] The problem was no longer planes, but adequate landing space. After the imposition of the blockade, two new and heavier runways at Tempelhof and one at Gatow had been constructed, and a third airport at Tegel in the French sector was in the planning stage. On an inspection trip to China in 1945, Clay had seen what could be done with manual labor, and he was confident the Berlin workers would respond to his call. Graders, bulldozers, and other pieces of heavy machinery were coming in from the States; they were cut up in Frankfurt with oxyacetylene torches, packed, and shipped by airplane to Tempelhof, where the individual pieces were welded together again. The army engineers had reported that the Tegel airport would be ready in March, but Clay said he was confident it would be completed by the end of the year. Clay's audience listened with interest as he described the intricate elements of this wholly new logistical world, but the underlying skepticism remained. True, the Berlin airlift was opening up a new perspective of American air power—the capacity to move anything, anywhere, anytime[66]—but for old soldiers like Marshall and Smith the strategic concepts of a passing age were still dominant.

Clay was confident the airlift would succeed, although the acid test was still to come in November and December when the weather was really bad. Nevertheless, it seemed to him that an important benchmark had been reached with the Berlin issue before the United Nations. The economic revival of West Germany was the strongest factor in the equation. Encouraged by the currency reform and ERP support, the Germans were back at work and production was steadily rising. The moratorium on foreign investments in occupied Germany was still on the books, but Clay planned to have this impediment to economic growth quickly removed.[67] The political outlook, on the other hand, was uncertain at best. German leaders remained doubtful of the Western resolve to proceed with their announced policies, and negotiations for an occupation statute and trizonal fusion dragged on with no end in sight.

The city of Berlin had been virtually split after the Soviets, unable to win on the diplomatic front, had reverted to their usual terror tactics. Four-power negotiations in Berlin and Moscow were still in progress when they unleashed their local stooges. Communist thugs roamed the streets of East Berlin, threatening the democratic members of the city government.[68] A scheduled meeting at city hall had to be called off because of Communist threats and the declared unwillingness of the Soviet commandant to protect the city fathers. A second session of the city assembly on September 6 was broken up by Communist-led gangs, causing the non-Communist deputies to flee to West Berlin. A few days later they resumed their sessions in a makeshift assembly hall in the British sector and scheduled elections for a Western sector parliament.

After the riots the leaders of the democratic parties called a protest meeting in the Reichstag square, located in the British sector just across the line from the Soviet sector. It was an impressive rally, with 300,000 Berliners demonstrating their dislike of Communism and listening to speeches by Ernst Reuter and other political leaders. On the whole the demonstration was orderly, but as it broke up a small group of German teenagers rushed to the Brandenburg Gate, and one of them climbed up and removed the Soviet flag flying from the top. Soviet police and soldiers opened fire on the participants and several Germans were killed.[69]

The valiant support of the Berliners was comforting to Clay in these days of stress, but he did not really approve of mass demonstrations. "We are in the midst of a dangerous game," he wrote to Draper. "Mass meetings directed against Soviet military government can easily turn into mass meetings against other occupying powers and can develop into the type of mob government which Hitler played so well to get in power. Robertson and I will probably have a quiet talk with the responsible Germans. . . ."[70] The point the General made was well taken; only a few weeks later he was confronted with another out-of-hand demonstration in the American zone, forcing him to slap a curfew on the city of Stuttgart.

While still in a contemplative mood, Clay summarized his views in a letter to Justice Byrnes. "The situation in Berlin is tense," he wrote,[71] "although by no manner of means as tense as it is written up in the United States. The German political leaders have shown outstanding courage in resisting Soviet terrorist tactics and the Communists have been unable to gain Berlin politically. The airlift has been a magnificent success and can keep us in Berlin through the winter." As for the attitude of German political leaders, he thought they were apprehensive about Western resolve in the face of Soviet opposition. They apparently feared that the next Council of Foreign Ministers meeting would result in a unified Germany, leaving them branded as the sole exponents of a separatist West German government, and they were proceeding "very cautiously." Clay, however, expected no agreement with the Russians, and remained convinced "that a strong Western government reoriented toward Western Europe would do much to restore a political and economic balance in Europe in our favor." Playing up to his friend's ego, he mentioned Byrnes' Stuttgart speech, which Clay himself had actually masterminded. "It continues to govern us," he wrote, "in a way which all of us here firmly believe to be wise and sound." As for his personal plans, he had intended to be gone by now but "while Berlin is under siege I cannot ask for retirement. Marjorie is still with me," he concluded the letter, "although she feels really that she is being cheated in being so far away from our grandson."[72]

John Foster Dulles, the presumptive Secretary of State in a Dewey Cabinet, flew into Berlin on October 17 to look over the situation. Frank Howley, who saw him at a luncheon in the Military governor's residence in Im Dol, thought that "despite the cheerful leaping flames, the climate around the fireplace was anything but warm. Ice divided Dulles and Clay. . . . The only subject on which they appeared to agree was Rhine wine. On that theme they were in perfect accord."[73] Ernst Reuter, the unseated mayor of Berlin, was brought in after lunch, and Dulles—who was very lukewarm about the airlift—asked whether the Germans would stand fast during the winter, "or will they give up, accept Russian aid, and get us out of Berlin rather than take more suffering?" Reuter's reply could not have been more emphatic: "The people of Berlin were accustomed to suffering. We are willing to suffer a great deal more to escape Russian domination." This was not exactly what Dulles had expected to hear, but he left town seemingly impressed. A statement released at the time of his departure reaffirmed the American resolve to remain in Berlin. The same evening Dulles had dinner with his sister in Paris. He then was convinced of the success of the airlift, she recalled.[74]

A few weeks later Clay was in New York as one of the principal speakers at the Alfred E. Smith Memorial Foundation Dinner. "In a moment of weakness," as he put it, he had accepted Cardinal Spellman's invitation to speak, and found it difficult to get out of the commitment.[75] Sharing the rostrum with Cardinal Spellman, Governor Thomas E. Dewey and Mayor William O'Dwyer, he gave his listeners a review of the historial circumstances that led to the present problems in occupied Germany. "What we are doing in Germany," he said, "was indeed an experiment in history, an effort to establish a democratic government under occupation," but "it is an experiment which must succeed." Communist influence in Europe had reached its high tide and was declining. The only way the Russians could stop that decline was to rekindle the fear of Soviet armed might, and they had deliberately picked Berlin as the place to do it. Clay described the accomplishments of the airlift in some detail, admitting that it was a costly operation. But the costs he said were "insignificant when compared with its contribution to the spirit of freedom-loving people. . . . Certainly never in the past and perhaps never again in the future will the responsibility of America to preserve the beliefs it holds most dear be as great and as difficult to exercise as today."[76]

Because of the critical situation in Berlin, he spent only twenty-four hours in Washington and New York, returning to Germany immediately after the Smith dinner. As soon as he was back in Berlin, Dr. Jessup arrived to see for himself whether the city could be held and to bring Clay up to date on developments at the United Nations. To no one's surprise, the Soviet representative at the Security Council, Andrei Vishinsky, had denied the existence of a blockade, insisting that defensive countermeasures had to be taken to protect the Soviet zone from being flooded by the new currency; moreover, he had insisted that the Council of Foreign Ministers was the proper forum for settling the German problem, not the United Nations.[77] When the Security Council nevertheless decided to include the Berlin dispute on its agenda, Vishinsky announced that the Soviet Union would not participate in the discussion. The six "neutral" members of the Security Council under the leadership of the Argentine foreign minister, who chaired the Security Council, attempted to work out a compromise they hoped would provide a basis for ending the blockade. The resolution finally presented to the Security Council on October 22 called for an immediate removal of the traffic regulations, for a simultaneous meeting of the four military governors to arrange for a unified East Mark currency in Berlin in accordance with the Moscow directive of August 30, and finally for a Council of Foreign Ministers meeting to discuss the German problem.[78] The resolution was clearly less advantageous to the Soviet Union than the Moscow directive and Vishinsky, who referred to it as "an agreement," emphasized this discrepancy before casting a negative vote.[79] Jessup told Clay that Trygve Lie, the Secretary General of the United Nations, was an unusually energetic man, who thought it was his duty as Secretary General to try to resolve the conflict through mediation. He doubted Lie would succeed, but before charting his further course of action at the U.N. Jessup had come for a first-hand look at the situation.

Clay anticipated a result from the Jessup visit much like the one following the Dulles luncheon a few weeks earlier. In both cases the impressions gained on the scene of action would tend to strengthen the American resolve.

General William Tunner, the head of the Combined Airlift Task Force, talked with Jessup in Frankfurt and suggested that the United States was close to "something new and revolutionary and universally important."[80] It was no exaggeration to say that in four months the lift had taught American airmen more about the possibilities of mass movement of goods by air than they probably would have learned in a decade of normal development.[81] The daily capacity of the lift had just been increased by 1,000 tons, he said, and although November and December, with its treacherous flying conditions, was still ahead, he had no doubt the difficulties would be overcome.

At Clay's urging, Jessup spoke over the German radio network on October 31, informing the Berliners of the recent developments at the United Nations while assuring them that the United States was determined to remain in Berlin as a matter of right.[82] For Jessup the conversation with Tunner had been reassuring, but it was a piece of news provided by Clay that removed the last vestiges of doubt that Berlin could be held. The Military Governor announced that on the following day, November 1, food rations would be increased by about 20 percent, with particular emphasis on fats and sugar. The new average ration for the population would be nearly 2,000 calories, or about 220 more than before the blockade.[83] Convinced that time was now on the side of the West, Jessup returned to the United Nations, where Trygve Lie quickly noticed a hardening in the American stance.[84]

When Clay, in the course of a teleconference with Draper, had discussed the Cardinal Spellman invitation, the undersecretary brought up the subject of General MacArthur's age and possible retirement. To Draper's mind, Clay's assignment to Japan "would represent an ideal solution from the point of view of the army and the American people when General MacArthur retires." In view of the impending elections, Draper also suggested that Clay should submit another request for retirement by the end of the year; the thought being that the new Administration would have its own ideas regarding commanders as well as Cabinet members. Clay's request would be kept on file by Secretary Royall until after the election to avoid "possible future embarrassment" for the Military Governor.[85] The positions were now reversed; Clay rejected the idea of such a letter. "I cannot now voluntarily leave with Berlin still in blockade" because this would mean "running out." "No soldier can request retirement," he added, "and be consistent with his lifetime principles under present conditions." Should the proper authorities determine otherwise, "that is something the soldier always faces." As to the Japan suggestion, he appreciated the thought behind it, "but it calls for a fresher person," he thought.[86]

Clay's stay in America in connection with the Al Smith Memorial Dinner had been brief, but the pickets in front of the Waldorf-Astoria, clamoring for his removal, had driven home the fact that his popularity back home was in rapid decline. Only a few weeks earlier, the caption "I shall not be bluffed" under the General's picture on *Time's* cover had been applauded from coast to coast as the reflection of a proud nation's will.[87] There had even been admiring references to Clay as the "General Patton of the cold war,"[88] as aggressive in defense as his predecessor was in chasing the enemy through France. Now suddenly his commutation of certain war crime sentences had aroused public ire. Almost overnight the image of the hero had given way to that of the villain, although—needless to say—there was nothing in the world that could have left Clay less concerned.

The war crime trials in Dachau had been completed in December 1947. Since there were no courts of appeal, it was the Military Governor's responsibility to act as a reviewing and clemency officer for more than 1,400 sentences, including 400 death sentences. After his legal staff had gone over the transcripts, he personally reviewed every sentence that involved either life imprisonment or death. "There was no other responsibility," he wrote, "which weighed more heavily on me."[89] By the fall of 1948 he had approved some death sentences, commuted others, and still had many under review. Then came the case of the infamous Ilse Koch and this description by *Harpers*:

American Judge-Advocate Officers may go on arguing, whether this putty-faced, dumpy ex-mistress of Buchenwald was really as deadly as charged. But deadly or not, she managed this fall by the mere fact of winning a commutation of her jail sentence for major crimes to do something which even the massive strength of Soviet Russia had failed to accomplish, namely to undermine the position of the American Military Governor in Germany, General Lucius D. Clay. Europeans cry out at the spectacle of America solicitously returning a hated Nazi to early freedom. Soviet propagandists make use of it as a beautiful barbed weapon with which to puncture American claims to democratic leadership, and at home the Senate investigation subcommittee demands an explanation and calls the red-faced Army on the carpet—something the Senate hasn't dreamed of doing since the days of the Pearl Harbor investigation.[90]

"As I examined the record," Clay wrote, "I could not find her a major participant in the crimes of Buchenwald. A sordid, disreputable character, she had delighted in flaunting her sex, emphasized by tight sweaters and short skirts, before the long-confined male prisoners, and had developed their bitter hatred. Nevertheless these were not the offenses for which she was being tried."[91] "There was absolutely no evidence in the transcript," Clay told an interviewer, to warrant her being given the death sentence. Some reporters had called her "Bitch of Buchenwald" and written that she had lampshades made out of human skin in her home. It was even introduced in court, although it was absolutely proven that the lampshades were made out of goat skin. So I reduced her sentence expecting the reaction which came. I suppose I received more abuse for that than for anything else I did in Germany.[92]

In the face of an aroused public opinion it became even more difficult for Clay to explain several cases of clemency in the Malmédy trial, which dealt with the cold-blooded murder of captured American troops in the Battle of the Bulge. After months of searching among German prisoners, the members of the unit responsible for the massacre were finally identified, but it was found that they had been sworn to silence and their silence was difficult to break.[93] "They were the tough, hardbitten fanatics of Nazism, and to break them in the first instance we had brought in as their jailers American troops who had witnessed the results after the Malmédy murder. And these troops used very rough methods to get the first breaks," Clay explained. "After the first breaks we got plenty of breaks so that we did not have to use this first evidence for the conviction but whether you could ever have gotten the conviction without this first evidence was very doubtful. But anyway that bothered me enough so that I cut the death sentence to life imprisonment." Possibly he had erred in judgment, he admitted, but nobody could share his responsibility as a reviewing officer.[94]

The Ilse Koch and Malmédy cases inevitably became prime subjects for Communist propaganda. But as far as the German public was concerned, the dramatic spectacle of the highest-ranking American official in Germany exercising his responsibilities in the bright light of public opinion—adverse public opinion at that—provided an unforgettable lesson. "This truly unloved but just man!" wrote the *Frankfurter Neue Presse*, expressing a widely held German view.[95]

FOOTNOTES

1. *Berliner Schicksal* 1945–1952, p. 52. Phillips Walter Davison, *The Berlin Blockade*, p. 9.
2. *The Soviet Union and the Berlin Question.* Ministry of Foreign Affairs, U.S.S.R., pp. 25–27.
3. *Tagesspiegel*, June 22, 1948.
4. Phillips W. Davison, *The Berlin Blockade*, p. 93, Frank Howley, *Berlin Command*, p. 97.
5. *The New York Times*, June 22, 1948, pp. 1 and 18, and June 25, 1948 p. 19. Clay for Draper, June 23, 1948, CC 4845 R.G. 200, N.A.
6. Howley, *Berlin*, pp. 186–187.
7. Davison, *Berlin Blockade*, p. 93.
8. Clay for Draper, June 23, 1948, CC 4845, R.G. 200, N.A.
9. Jack Bennett, "The German Currency Reform" in the *Annals of the American Academy of Political and Social Science*, p. 267.
10. Howley, *Berlin*, p. 188.
11. Clay for Draper, June 23, 1948, CC 4834, R.G. 200, N.A.
12. Davison, *Berlin Blockade*, p. 95–97; Howley, *Berlin*, pp. 190–192.
13. Davison, *Berlin Blockade*, pp. 100–101, *Tagesspiegel*, June 25, 1948.
14. Author's interview with General Arthur Trudeau, Washington, D.C., August 14, 1978.
15. Lucius D. Clay, *Decision in Germany*, p. 374; Clay for Bradley, July 10, 1948, CC 5188, R.G. 200, N.A.
16. Author's interview with General Trudeau.
17. Davison, *Berlin Blockade*, p. 104.
18. Jean Smith interview with General Clay, March 9, 1971. Willy Brandt, *My Road to Berlin*, pp. 193–194.
19. Author's interview with General Trudeau.
20. Clay, *Decision*, p. 442.
21. Ibid., p. 366.
22. Charles J. F. Murphy, "The Berlin Airlift," *Fortune*, November 1948.
23. Clay for Royall, June 25, 1948, CC 4880, R.G. 200, N.A.
24. Teleconference Clay-Royall-Collins, June 25, 1948, TT-9667, R.G. 200, N.A.
25. Teleconference Clay-Noce, June 26, 1948, TT-9677, R.G. 200, N.A.
26. Clay for Draper, June 25, 1948, CC 4875, R.G. 200, N.A.
27. Howley, *Berlin*, p. 204.
28. Ibid., p. 200
29. Ibid., p. 201.
30. Ibid., p. 204.
31. Clay, *Decision*, p 372.
32. Ibid., p. 373; Clay for Royall, June 28, 1948, CC 4924, R.G. 200, N.A.
33. James F. Forrestal, *Diaries*, pp. 452–453.
34. Ibid., pp. 454–455.
35. Clay for Draper, June 27, 1948, CC 4910, R.G. 200, N.A. Jean Smith interview with General Clay, March 9, 1971
36. Clay for Royall and Bradley, July 3, 1948, CC 5027, R.G. 200, N.A.
37. Ibid.
38. *Foreign Relations of the United States 1948*, II, pp. 950–953.
39. Clay for Bradley, July 10, 1948, CC 5109, R.G. 200, N.A.
40. Clay for Bradley, July 10, 1948, CC 5118, R.G. 200, N.A.
41. Ibid.
42. Dean Acheson, *Present at the Creation*, pp. 262–263.
43. Interview with General Frank Howley. New York, N.Y. April 15, 1980.
44. Teleconference Attention Gailey from Pritchard, July 12, 1948, TT-9766; Teleconference Mayo-Pritchard TT-9768, R.G. 200, N.A.
45. Clay for Draper, July 19, 1948, CC 5222, R.G. 200, N.A.
46. Forrestall, *Diaries*, p. 459.
47. *Foreign Relations . . . 1948*, II, p. 997. The dates given in FRUS are in error. Clay was in Berlin on July 19 and departed on July 20 for U.S. *See* Clay for Bradley and Royall,

July 19, 1948, CC 5217, R.G. 200, N.A. Richard McKinzie interview with Clay, New York, N.Y., July 16, 1974. Jean Smith interview with Clay, March 9, 1971.

48. Davison, *The Berlin Blockade*, p. 154.
49. *The Soviet Union and the Berlin Question*, Ministry of Foreign Affairs of the U.S.S.R., pp. 42–46.
50. Davison, *The Berlin Blockade*, pp. 158–159; Walter B. Smith, *My Three Years in Moscow*, pp. 239–260, *Foreign Relations . . .*, 1948, II, pp. 995–1176.
51. Teleconference Clay-Royall, Bohlen, August 3, 1948, TT-9890, R.G. 200, N.A.
52. Clay for Bradley and Royall, August 4, 1948, CC 5432, R.G. 200, N.A.
53. Ibid.
54. Davison, *The Berlin Blockade*, p. 139; Smith *My Three*, p. 247.
55. Smith, *My Three*, p. 252.
56. Clay, *Decision*, p. 370.
57. Clay for Draper, September 1, 1948, CC 5777, R.G. 200, N.A.
58. Teleconference Clay-Royall, Draper, Southard (Treasury), Reber (State), September 2, 1948, TT-1131, R.G. 200, N.A.
59. Royall to Clay, September 3, 1948, TT-1136, in Smith, *The Papers*, p. 815.
60. Teleconference, September 8, 1948, TT-1173, R.G. 200, N.A.
61. Clay, *Decision*, pp. 375–376.
62. Davison, *Berlin Blockade*, p. 241.
63. Clay, *Decision*, pp. 375–376.
64. Ibid., p. 376; Harry Truman, *Years of Trial and Hope*, p. 126.
65. Murphy, "Berlin Airlift"; Clay, *Decision*, pp. 381–382.
66. Ibid.
67. Clay for Department of Army, November 7, 1948, CC 6651, R.G. 200, N.A.
68. Davison, *Berlin Blockade*, p. 179.
69. Clay, *Decision*, p. 179.
70. Clay for Draper, September 11, 1948, CC 5909. R.G. 200, N.A.
71. Clay for Byrnes, September 18, 1948, in Jean Smith, ed., *The Papers of Lucius D. Clay*, pp. 858–860.
72. Ibid.
73. Howley, *Berlin*, pp. 223–224. Jean Smith interview with General Clay, March 13, 1971.
74. Interview with Eleanor Lansing Dulles, Washington D.C., December 9, 1981.
75. Clay for Draper, August 28, 1948, CC-5733, R.G. 200, N.A.
76. *The New York Times*, October 22, 1948, pp. 1 and 4.
77. *Official Records of the Security Council*, Third Year, No. 113.
78. Trygve Lie, *In the Cause of Peace*, p. 202.
79. Ibid.
80. Murphy, "Berlin Airlift."
81. Ibid.
82. Clay, *Decision*, p. 387. *Tagesspiegel*, October 31, 1948.
83. Howley, *Berlin*, p. 230.
84. Lie, *In the Cause*, p. 210.
85. Teleconference, October 13, 1948, Clay-Draper, TT-1406, R.G. 200, N.A.
86. Ibid.
87. *Time*, July 12, 1948.
88. William Harlan Hale, "General Clay—On His Own" *Harpers*, December 1948.
89. Clay, *Decision*, pp. 253–254. Jean Smith interview with General Clay, February 9, 1971.
90. Hale, "General Clay," ibid.
91. Clay, *Decision*, pp. 253–254. Jean Smith interview with General Clay, February 9, 1971.
92. Ibid.
93. Ibid.
94. Ibid.
95. Don Humphrey, private papers.

CHAPTER ELEVEN

And Engineering the Ramparts

POLITICAL CIRCUMSTANCES HAD DELAYED THE ESSENTIAL MONETARY REFORM in West Germany for three years. When finally, on June 18, 1948, a new currency was introduced, its instantaneous effects were electric. Clay's comment to Justice Byrnes that they were "unbelievable" tends to illustrate the perceptive confines under which he and his economic advisers operated.[1] Three years earlier the astonishing fact had already been brought out that important components of Germany's advanced industrial economy were still intact. The Strategic Bombing Survey conducted by the U.S. Air Force had revealed that despite constant bombing, Germany's industry managed to operate at nearly full peacetime capacity until December 1944, and it was only the destruction of the German transportation system in the following months that actually paralyzed industrial production. The survey also showed that the economy apparently had not suffered from shortages of machine tools, general machinery, or even plant facilities except temporarily in a few isolated cases. The air force was forced to conclude that the air war had only slowed down the economy, that indeed by the end of the war 80 to 85 percent of Western-controlled Germany's economic potential was still intact.[2]

During the three years preceding reform, the absence of a viable currency had forced the greater part of agricultural and industrial production into hidden barter channels, obscuring the real status of the country's prostrate economy. Moreover, even though some manufacturers and traders had built additional warehouses to store their hoarded goods, the actual extent of hoarding had escaped public notice. Most Americans, innocent of memories of a runaway inflation, were flabbergasted to see the changes that took place literally overnight. On June 19, a Saturday, scarcely a single article could be seen or had in the retail shops; two days later shop windows and shelves were full of consumer goods not seen in Germany for years. The scarcity of money in the first weeks forced the hidden inventories into the market and the dramatic change in the supply of goods was one of the principal reasons the reform found general acceptance. But public critics were not lacking. One of the most eloquent was Kurt Schumacher who, in the course of an SPD Convention in September 1948, pointed out that the German possessors of goods had selfishly and shamelessly withheld

255

them from their suffering compatriots while foreign countries, some of them almost as poor as Germany, had poured relief commodities into Germany with scant hope of recompense.[3]

Ludwig Erhard, the director of the Bizonal Economic Administration, had a better grasp of the economic realities of the country than his American and British colleagues, and he promptly abolished rationing and price controls on some 400 different commodities—with impressive results. Monthly steel production, which had been 324,000 tons in May, jumped to 599,000 tons in December and to over 700,000 tons by the spring of 1949. Hard-coal production in the Ruhr had been running at a daily average of 266,000 tons before the currency reform, and rose to over 330,000 tons in the spring of 1949. By that time overall production already had climbed to 89 percent of the 1936 level.[4]

A number of concurrent developments enhanced the impact of the currency reform. The Military Governor ordered the release of JEIA's accumulated export proceeds for the import of industrial raw materials, and in his usual hard-driving manner saw to it that ECA shipments were not unduly delayed. "Unless procedures are simplified," he warned Royall, "the pipeline will dry up and the present favorable basis for increases in production . . . may be stopped in its tracks. . . ." The simplification of trade procedures by JEIA, the extension of its operations to the French zone, and the gradual transfer of foreign trade to the private sector increased the general feeling of optimism. Accordingly within a few months West German export figures quadrupled and the share of finished and semifinished products rose from 12 percent to 35 percent.[5] For Clay, who was duly impressed with the speed of the country's recovery, it was gratifying to report to his friend Byrnes that "Germany is going back to work and in West Germany particularly the people on the streets visibly have taken a new hold on life."[6] With the food supply also better than at any time since the war, the Military Governor could now focus on the formation of a West German government in accord with the London decision.

As it soon turned out, however, the country's quick economic recovery also generated a number of domestic conflicts. Whereas Clay's political and economic instructions had been specific, those dealing with labor were couched in general terms. Thus given a free hand, Clay developed his own basic policy of introducing an orthodox American free-enterprise system to Germany. Since the concept did not correspond with German tradition or with the social forces at work in postwar Germany, a number of clashes inevitably arose. Clay's comment in his memoirs that his relations with labor leaders "were always pleasant even though we did not always agree" ought therefore to be taken with a grain of salt.[7] His subsequent observation—"it was difficult for the United States military government to be as popular with the rank and file of union members as British military government which represented a Labor Government"—came closer to the truth.[8] In actuality his personality—possibly even more so than in any other area—determined the nature of military government relations with organized labor.

Like most military men, Clay was cool toward unions and the concept of trade unionism, although he did not let this attitude affect his personal relations with labor leaders or the conduct of his policies. He did not care for Kurt Schumacher and his kind of uncompromising advocacy, but he was on excellent terms with men like Ernst Reuter, the Socialist Mayor of Berlin, and Sidney Hillman, from the Congress of Industrial Relations. Joe Keenan of the American Federation of Labor was his principal labor adviser. The two men had worked closely together on the War Production Board and a deep friendship had developed.[9] In fact in 1974, when Keenan celebrated his sixtieth year in the International Brotherhood of Electrical Workers, Clay—a dying man then—traveled to Chicago to honor his friend as the banquet's principal speaker.

As far as the labor policies of the military government were concerned, Clay insisted on neutrality toward the German political parties that advocated different patterns of economic life.[10] He recognized the trade unions' influence on the development of democratic processes and their sincere support of the denazification program.[11] At the same time, however, he ignored the recommendations of some of his advisers to give special aid to what they called "the democratic elements in the labor movement."[12] In the first place, Clay said, a policy of neutrality was the only democratic way to give the Germans freedom of choice, and he was not going to imitate Soviet methods of favoritism. In the second place, he maintained, the only way to undermine Communist strength was to raise the economic level of Western Germany. This attitude plus his stubborn refusal to allow national labor organizations a controlling role over local unions alienated the labor leaders more than anything else. In accordance with the General's somewhat abstract and doctrinaire belief that democracy had to start at the grass roots, early elections of shop stewards and the formation of work councils had to be promoted so the unions could be formed from the bottom up. Clay was unmoved by the argument that this approach was contrary to German tradition, and moveover disregarded the palpable fact that Communist influence was greatest at the grass-roots level.

Prior to the currency reform, workers and management alike had had little interest in money and in producing for the legal market, but they had great interest in compensation deals—in effect, barter and payment in kind. From this situation arose a considerable degree of "codetermination" of workers with regard to production and marketing. A producer would have to negotiate such compensation deals not only with his suppliers but also with his and the supplier's workers. The practice developed of conducting such transactions with the work council's participation, because if the workers did not get their cut in the goods they wanted, production went down, absenteeism went up, and skilled workers would wander off to better jobs.[13] The pattern to make the right of worker codetermination a permanent feature of German industrial life was thus set. Once the currency reform had set the stage for the return of normal conditions, labor leaders began to press for codetermination and socialization by law. A number of bitter conflicts with the Military Governor was the consequence.

In March 1947, General Clay had begun what was to become a regular practice of holding periodic formal conferences with the trade union leaders in the U.S. zone to discuss any problems the unions cared to raise.[14] From the standpoint of the labor leaders, these meetings were not altogether satisfactory. They were able to obtain the release of all union property that had been blocked at the beginning of the occupation. On the other hand, with regard to most of their political demands Clay remained adamant. The Military Governor indicated that in principle he favored the right of unions to organize throughout Germany; all-German trade unions nevertheless would have to wait, he declared, until there was a quadripartite agreement on fundamentals such as freedom of movement throughout the country, freedom of speech, press and radio, as well as freedom of action for all political parties.[15] He subsequently encouraged the creation of a bizonal union but again objected to its extension to the French zone before Trizonia had become an established fact. Clay remained equally firm in his opposition to socialization and to codetermination. As he interpreted political neutrality, such fundamental political decisions had to await a freely elected West German government. He had already objected in 1946 to the inclusion of a socialization section in the constitution of Hesse, insisting that a separate popular vote be taken on this issue; and when the provision was confirmed by the electorate, he had prevented enactment until an all-German vote could be taken. Through similar skillful political maneuvers, he had also blocked socialization in the Ruhr.

By the summer of 1948, the SPD and the unions had begun to press hard for the works councils' broad right of codetermination in business management.[16] Disregarding the advice of the labor officers at OMGUS, they continued to use legislative methods to achieve their aim. After almost two years of preparation, the *Landtag* of Hesse passed a farreaching works council law in May 1948 with the votes of both the SPD and CDU and sent it to the Military Governor for review.[17] It not only made the establishment of works councils mandatory but also gave them extensive codetermination rights. Württemberg-Baden and the *Land* Bremen followed suit in August, but Clay was not about to yield to such pressures.[18]

It remains uncertain if he was influenced—as sometimes asserted—by the fact of a new Republican majority in Congress and the wish to protect his appropriation, or whether the rigid interpretation of neutrality was the principal reason for his position. In any event, he could not help recognizing that his labor policies de facto helped the return of the old management class to power. He implicitly conceded that much in his reaction to a State Department message urging approval of the Hessian law. He informed Draper:

It is my view that the Hesse proposal is the most extreme measure of this type that I have seen. While it is true that it was adopted by both political parties, it seems clear to me that the action was based in large part on the desire to get this legislation on the books prior to the adoption of a German Constitution and the formation of a central government. I propose to approve these portions of the law dealing with the rights of works councils in other than economic matters but to suspend the economic provisions. . . .[19]

To the State Department contention that disapproval would mean an end to democratic and trade-union forces, he merely replied that "trade union forces seem to survive in America very well indeed without the benefit of such a law. Such a change in German economic patterns at this time," he added,

would defeat our efforts of recovery. The trade unions are trying desperately—and no one can blame them—to obtain a foothold in management. Their strength is relatively great now since they have been encouraged in every way by military government whereas management associations have in fact been discouraged. Hence the influence of management in public opinion is probably at its lowest point in German history.

If the State Department wanted the Hessian law approved, he should, Clay maintained, be so instructed through the customary army channels.[20]

For three years Washington had drawn back from difficult decisions, leaving it up to the Military Governor to chart his own course—so Clay could hardly have been surprised when no such instructions were forthcoming and he was left to enforce his policies. As a consequence some labor leaders—the highly vocal Kurt Schumacher among them—began to conclude that the Military Governor was antilabor and said so rather bluntly in an "anything but friendly"[21] meeting with Clay on July 29. Meanwhile, the SPD decided to go public with numerous demonstrations and attacks in the press against high prices, Erhard's removal of economic controls, and Clay's imminent suspension of the Hessian codetermination law.[22] The impression that the American military government was throwing its weight on the side of capital against labor was reinforced by OMGUS's tolerating the return of some business leaders whom the leftists considered prime supporters of Nazism. Gradually most businessmen charged with being Nazis had been tried by German tribunals and the overwhelming majority acquitted or classified as "followers." By 1948 many of them had resumed their former positions. "German industrialists, once outlawed for backing Nazis, have made a comeback and are ready for a showdown with labor unions," a perceptive American reporter confirmed.[23]

Labor's codetermination gains and a continuing upward trend of prices finally provoked some unions into drastic action. On October 28, largely under works councils and Communist pressure, the unions in Stuttgart held a big demonstration against these grievances. According to Louis Wiesner,[24] the labor officer on Murphy's staff, the only speaker was the SPD member Hans Stetter, chairman of the local union federation. Stetter's speech to more than 40,000 demonstrators was militantly anti-Erhard and anti-military government. He attacked the military government's concept of democracy, challenged the high occupation costs, opposed further plant dismantlings, and advocated continued struggle against Clay's suspension of the economic codetermination paragraphs in the works council law. But Stetter did not invite violence, and immediately upon closing the demonstration had the loudspeaker system disconnected to prevent the Communists from using it. Nevertheless, after the demonstration a small group of rowdies, including some Communists, attacked a few shops notorious for their high prices. When German and American military police attempted to disperse the crowd, a regular riot ensued, during which police of both nationalities were injured. According to Wiesner, "the incident was not serious," but General Clay immediately had Stetter escorted to his Frankfurt office and blamed him "in the most abusive language for the trouble." Clay then ordered a 9 P.M. to 4 A.M. curfew imposed on Stuttgart until further notice. Charles LaFollette, director of the military government for Württemberg-Baden, the minister-president, the lord mayor of Stuttgart, the political parties and the unions all protested the curfew, which Clay removed only a few days later.[25]

Clay himself saw the incident in the light of law and order.

> I was unwilling to accept such actions, as acceptance might well lead to further and more serious incidents in which bloodshed could occur. Therefore, I asked Mr. LaFollette the director of the state government to impose a curfew on the city. He did so reluctantly since he did not share my view that failure to do so might lead to other and similar incidents. The speech of the German labor leader had been inflammatory and directed against military government; so I sent for him to advise him that when such speeches were followed by disorderly conduct directed against American personnel the speaker would have to accept responsibility. I blamed neither unions nor labor for this act of the individual but my responsibility for the safety of the occupation personnel would not permit me to let a demonstration turn into acts of force against our personnel without warning of the strong measures which would result if there was repetition.[26]

The General's stern measure nevertheless had some beneficial effects. When the trade unions in Bizonia called a 24-hour work stoppage two weeks later and more than nine million workers protested against the prevailing economic policies, the day passed quietly with no serious disorders anywhere. Clay, who had strongly denied that the Stuttgart curfew was "a blow at labor," later referred to the bizonal work stoppage as "an impressive demonstration of labor solidarity and strength."[27]

Unable to change military government policies in Germany, the union leaders went one step further by trying to enlist the support of their friends in the United States. As a result, the foreign policy resolutions at both the AFL and CIO annual conventions in 1948 condemned the "antilabor policies" of the American military government. This was followed by a number of letters to Clay, which he answered with explicit justification of his policy. The AFL's final act, the publication of the correspondence and a request to the White House for Clay's recall, came too late to have any effect. By then a German government had been formed and the trade unions had to use the route that Clay had recommended all along. The right of codetermination for works councils then became the law of the land and socialization measures were shelved.[28]

In the course of his conversations with Couve de Murville in April, Clay had drafted the outline of a six-power compromise that had become the framework of the London Agreement, the most important event since Potsdam, as he liked to say. It gave him the directives he needed for the engineering project he had in mind—the establishment of a Western rampart against the dangers threatening from the East. The essential elements of the task, as he saw it, were the convocation of a constitutional assembly, the drafting of a democratic federal constitution, its enactment through a popular referendum, the creation of an International Ruhr Authority, the election of a parliament, the formation of a West German government, the merger of the three Western zones and the drawing up of an occupation statute. With responsibilities partly in German and partly in the Military Governor's hands, it would be at the least a time-consuming job, especially since French obstructionism could be expected to continue.

Clay was therefore doubly shocked when it turned out that the Germans too were reluctant to follow the path laid out for them by the Anglo-Americans. In a meeting on July 1 the minister-presidents were handed four documents containing the essentials of the London Agreement. The documents authorized the convocation of a constituent assembly, the drafting of a constitution and some modifications of the *Land* boundaries. In addition they were informed that the powers reserved for the military government would be expressed in an occupation statute to be released to them as soon as completed.[29] In short, they were now being told, on the initiative of the three Allied powers, to proceed independently toward the creation of a Western state. As the minister-presidents could not fail to recognize, however, they were being asked to share the historical responsibility for a permanent division of the Reich. Moreover, they were left uncertain about the extent of their authority and the final policy aims of the Western powers.[30]

The eleven minister-presidents conferred in Koblenz from July 8 to July 10. Their first unofficial reaction came in the form of a comment by Dr. Reinhold Maier, minister-president of Württemberg-Baden, who told the *Landtag* on July 7 that "we would rather continue without legal statute, dangerous though it may be, than accept a statute of this kind."[31] The communiqué published at the end of the Koblenz deliberations as well as the comments and recommendations submitted to the military government confirmed this negative response. It was obvious that none of the Germans wanted to be identified with the contemplated division of the German nation. The minister-presidents welcomed a unification of the three Western zones, their reply said, and they also agreed on the creation of an executive body through general elections; but the unified area should serve administrative purposes only and any appearance of conferring the character of a state on the governmental structure thus created ought to be avoided. It was necessary, the minister-presidents said, to refrain from using such terms as "constitution" and "government," but to adopt instead the concept of a "united economic and administrative area." The drafting of a German constitution should therefore be postponed until an all-German government was formed. However, the German leaders were prepared to recommend to their respective *Landtage* the setting up of a parliamentary council to draft a *Grundgesetz*, or Basic Law.[32] In order to maintain a clear distinction between it and a constitution, the *Grundgesetz* should not be submitted to a vote by popular referendum.

In his memoirs—aware of their historic significance—Clay described the German response in a positive light.

> Unfortunately, that part of the letter expressing doubt as to the advisability of calling the new organization a government was widely interpreted as an evidence of their unwillingness to accept responsibility for a separate Western government. However, their letter had not refused to accept responsibility and I was confident that they would go ahead. I knew from talks with them that the minister-presidents from our zone were eager to do so.[33]

The General's immediate reaction, however, had been very different from this benign interpretation. He had correctly assumed that Kurt Schumacher—merely a party boss in his eyes[34]—had directed the actions of the SPD minister-presidents at the Koblenz meeting and evidently had been able to persuade the rest to go along. He was outraged that the chiefs of popularly elected state governments had shirked what he believed to be their duty and had yielded to the "illegitimate" dictate of a party leader without a popular mandate. "At the frostiest conference of the last twelve months," he told the minister-presidents of the American zone that "he felt deserted in his struggle with the Russians for Berlin and for the development of Western Germany."[35] And when talking to the press, he expressed surprise that the Germans wanted to accept less authority and responsibility than the Allies were willing to concede. "In the light of history this was a unique development," he said.[36]

At a meeting with his French and British colleagues a few days later to discuss the German recommendation, Clay was not surprised when

General Koenig took advantage of the new development. The London decisions ought to be modified to accommodate German wishes, the Frenchman suggested, an occupation statute drawn up first, and what functions the Germans should assume determined later. As a consequence, "the military governors had difficulty in agreeing on the reply," Clay wrote, "but Robertson and I held him to the London Agreement."[37] At the next meetings with the Germans on July 20 and July 25, the Allies laid down the law: the London decisions were governmental and any changes would require renegotiations; this would cause unavoidable delays and the German leaders would have to accept responsibility for failure to return government to German hands promptly.[38] The minister-presidents' resistance crumpled in the face of this ultimatum. They unhappily recognized that in the game of contending international forces, West and East Germans alike were merely pawns, who—for the time being at least—had no choice but to yield to the demands of the victors.

In their two meetings with the military governors, the minister-presidents retreated on most substantive points, but they persuaded the miliatry governors to accept the term "Parliamentary Council" instead of "Constituent Assembly" and the term "Basic Law" followed in parentheses by the words "Provisional Constitution."[39] They also agreed to recommend ratification by the *Landtage* rather than by popular referendum. After the fundamentals had been settled, the minister-presidents convened a committee of experts on constitutional law at Herrenchiemsee to draft the guiding principles for the Basic Law. Its accomplishments were unique in the history of constitutional conventions, Golay wrote, because within two weeks it produced not only "guiding principles" but the complete draft of a constitution together with a detailed analytical report.[40] The Parliamentary Council subsequently elected by the *Landtage* had sixty-five members, including CDU and SPD delegations of twenty-seven each, an FDP delegation of five, and six delegates representing the splinter parties. After electing Konrad Adenauer as president and establishing the necessary committees, the council promptly went to work.

With German cooperation secured, General Clay could turn his attention to the charter for an International Ruhr Authority, the drafting of an occupation statute and the preparations for a trizonal fusion—all issues involving Allied responsibility. Aware that agreements with France would be difficult to achieve, he was not surprised when a London conference on the Ruhr under the chairmanship of Ambassador Douglas promptly ran into difficulties. Even before it convened on November 11, France challenged a bizonal reorganization of the coal and steel industries that placed them under German supervision. As the Quai D'Orsay saw it, the contemplated control of coal and steel allocations for export was not sufficient. In addition there ought to be international ownership of the mines and tight controls over a German management. It was extremely dangerous, Premier Robert Schuman argued in Paris, to give a central German government the ultimate authority to determine ownership of the mines.[41] Never in the past had any German government had such power which it was now proposed to bestow on a wholly unknown government.

Clay had no doubt that a Ruhr agreement was a precondition for a trizonal fusion as well as for the setting up of a West German government. He also saw clearly the dilemma he faced: on the one hand to avoid any action that might have a depressing effect on German production and morale; on the other to prevent a negative French reaction that might affect future three-power cooperation.[42] At the same time there were some essentials to be preserved at all costs: the predominant position of the Allied military government vis-à-vis an International Ruhr Authority had to be maintained; the size of the individual coal and steel industries had to be large enough to make them viable enterprises, credit worthy enough to attract foreign investments; moreover, foreign control over management would have to be opposed because in the long run it would be galling to German pride and would provoke charges that its purpose was to secure industrial information and to prevent German competition. Taking a statesmanlike long-range view, Clay feared this might become "the cancerous sore which would lead to passive or even active resistance and would prevent any rapprochement between Germany and the Western European countries."[43]

With regard to the security issue so constantly invoked by France, he thought that the Military Security Board provided by the London Agreement—with its inspection and enforcement powers in addition to its authority to limit productive capacity—should be sufficient to alleviate the fears of Germany's neighbors. Clay himself was too involved with the problems caused by the blockade of Berlin to spend any time in London. He was represented at the conference by his economic advisor, Larry Wilkinson, but he himself was also in frequent contact with Ambassador Douglas. "I did not feel free, however, to make specific recommendations directly to him," he wrote, "which I know made him think that I was 'jurisdictionally' minded, but I had no mandate from the army." It was a significant comment because it illustrated one of the General's principal problems with the State Department—his rigid adherence to proper army channels as opposed to the freewheeling communications methods of the department. Although he insisted on Pentagon clearances, he could feel certain that the ultimate impact in London would not be affected by the delay.[44]

As Clay interpreted France's motives, it was not the Ruhr itself but the rapid recovery of Germany as a whole that was at the root of the problem. General Koenig repeatedly referred to the tendency to make Germany the strongest power in Europe again and the center of the continent's economy. Such comments were clearly a consequence of the remarkable upturn in the German economy, which made its recovery no longer academic. Clay liked to argue, however, that there were forty million people living in West Germany who had to import at least half of their food requirements; they could survive only with a substantial industry and a surplus available for export. A strong industrial base of course constituted a war potential, and, as a consequence, security for Germany's neighbors could only be obtained by rigidly enforced disarmament agreements.[45]

The General's messsages to the Department of the Army followed the same line of reasoning. The United States would be asked to support a large annual deficit in Germany's foreign trade for at least two more years and probably longer, one of his telegrams said.[46]

> Our efforts to reduce this period to the minimum are in direct conflict with the French efforts to retard Germany's recovery as much as possible. The restoration of good management in the Ruhr, steel and coal properties is essential . . . to further progress. . . . The Germans have become accustomed to the thought of international control as envisaged in the London Agreement. If we go beyond this I think we may expect a rapid growth of political unrest in the Ruhr area which will be fermented by the Communists into work stoppages and strikes, which will interfere seriously with both German and European recovery. We must remember that we are no longer dealing with an inarticulate people and that forty million Germans have their eyes and ears on the Ruhr conference now underway in London.[47]

As usual, he was particularly sensitive to French efforts in London to impinge on the dominant role of the United States in the person of the Military Governor.

> The United States because of its large financial support of Germany now exercises through its Military Government the controlling voice in the German economy. If during the period of Military Government it agrees to give to the Ruhr authority power which negates this control then it has not only made it possible for others to control the German economy but it will also have sacrificed its position of financial and economic control which the Congress demanded. . . . In my own case, I shall in all probability not be here when the Ruhr Authority is operating, Therefore, I can say in all earnestness that for three and a half years effort after effort has been made to destroy this effectiveness of a single United States administrative agency in Germany by adding additional agencies. It is obvious that this would be inefficient. It is of course desired by the European powers who recognize the weakness of division of authority. . . .[48]

Negotiations in London dragged on for weeks while pressures for an early settlement at Pennsylvania Avenue and Downing Street mounted. Rather than yield to French demands, Clay at first suggested indefinite postponement; then—realizing the adverse effects this might have on his plans for early establishment of a West German government—he came up with a compromise proposal. It provided for French acceptance of the Anglo-American plan for the International Ruhr Authority (IRA) with the proviso that prior to the end of military government rule a study would be made to determine which of the currently existing control responsibilities should be transferred to the Authority.[49] Somewhat earlier he had already softened French resistance by suggesting prompt French participation in the bizonal steel and coal control groups.[50] As a consequence, Clay's formula was quickly accepted.[51]

The final agreement stipulated that the IRA, composed of representatives of the six participating countries, would be established before a West German government was formed. It would allocate coal and steel from the Ruhr for exports, consider the minimum needs of a self-sustaining German economy, prevent discriminatory trade practices, and protect foreign interests in the Ruhr enterprises. Eventually the IRA would take on all or part of the security responsibilities currently in the hands of the military government. Although Clay himself had proposed this formula, he had reservations about the last provision. With the final goal of a strong free enterprise economy always in mind, he feared this lack of finality might discourage the capital investments he considered essential to Ruhr industry.[52]

With one building block at last in place and others still in German hands, there remained two others—Trizonia and the occupation statute— for which the three military governors had the primary responsibility. French opposition not only impeded progress on both issues but General Koenig also actually warned his colleagues that France might be unwilling to accept a West German government "because of the present climate." The Parliamentary Council ought to be reminded of the limitation on its authority, he said, and it should be made crystal clear, too, that France would not accept a strong centralized government.[53] An aide-mèmoire from the military governors to the Parliamentary Council, drafted by Clay, accordingly stressed the necessity of protecting the powers of *Länder*. An upper chamber had to have sufficient authority and the taxing power of the central government limited, it said. Although this step should have alleviated French concern, Koenig was still dragging his feet on a trizonal merger, as well as on the drafting of an occupation statute.

In an early comment,[54] Clay had suggested to Draper that the statute should be kept as short as possible. It should mention the broad objectives of the occupation and list the reserved powers of the military governors, such as the conduct of foreign relations, foreign trade and the Ruhr. The military governors should also retain the authority to block amendments to the constitution and, in the case of an emergency, to resume the full powers of government. Characteristically, for Clay's sense of justice, he also suggested the establishment of a high court composed of representatives of the occupying powers and German jurists. "I believe it is only fair that there should be an independent judicial review," he wrote. "It seems to me that the time has come to establish a real check on the powers of the military governors. I rather expect that this particular provision may not be liked by some of our colleagues. To my mind, it is essential to insure the success of our program."[55]

The military governors had promised to keep the minister-presidents informed of their progress in drafting the occupation statute. But there were so many disagreements and the positions of the three generals were so far apart that they were unable to keep their promise.[56] After four months of fruitless negotiations they decided instead to submit to the three governments a joint report listing their different positions. Nor had any progress toward a trizonal fusion been made; inconclusive conferences with the Parliamentary Council, convened at Adenauer's request, also revealed fundamental differences among the German political parties. The Christian Democrats favored a federal government of limited power, while the Socialists insisted on a more centralized government. Accordingly, when the new year came around the outlook was bleak, and Clay recognized that his progress toward a West German government was stymied until they could resolve matters with the Parliamentary Council and the three governments.

On January 5, in a letter to Omar Bradley, Clay therefore broached the subject of retirement once again. Because of the Berlin situation he had agreed last year to stay on in Germany, he wrote. Understandably, he had become associated in the German mind with the American determination to remain in Berlin, but now that the airlift had proved its capability a reassessment was in order. A new Administration with a new Secretary of State was about to take office in Washington and he was uncertain whether he would be able to administer a changed policy. Moreover, all major negotiations were now conducted at various governmental levels and no longer the Military Governor's direct responsibility. He did not want to run out on the job, he wrote, and continued to be at General Bradley's orders, but he definitely felt his retirement would be in the best interests of the army.[57] In a teleconference a few days later, however, Secretary Royall indicated that Clay's retirement at this particular moment (when the second Truman Administration was being formed) could be harmful. "It might lend some color to propaganda that we are relaxing our firm policy toward Russia." In view of Secretary Marshall's resignation it might be appropriate to wait until his successor, Dean Acheson, had had an opportunity to "express his confidence and support of our administration in Germany."[58]

There were several causes of dissatisfaction that Clay's letter to Bradley suggested but did not spell out. He was clearly unhappy about the lack of progress toward his concept of a strong West Germany integrated into Western Europe as a bulwark against Communism. The Allies had so far failed to implement the London Agreement and the German leaders, who sensed this lack of resolve, seemed uncertain how to proceed. On the day the Berlin blockage was imposed, the foreign ministers of the Soviet satellite countries assembled in Warsaw had come out with a lengthy communiqué strongly criticizing the London Agreement and offering a number of policy recommendations, among them an end to the occupation, a peace treaty and the withdrawal of all occupation forces from Germany. These proposals had caught the fancy of some high-level officials at the State Department,[59] and the arrival of a new Secretary of State might mean a new policy toward Germany at odds with Clay's concept, one he would find impossible to implement.

In the meantime, since further progress toward the establishment of a West German government depended on others, he as Military Governor could do his share by consolidating the Allied position in Berlin. A number of measures to tighten the counterblockade[60] served his purpose: vehicles bound for or returning from the Soviet zone were forbidden to cross the Western zones regardless of their point of origin or their destination; controls over the zonal borders were strengthened, and the shipment of goods from West Berlin to Soviet-controlled territory severely restricted. Since the division of the city was by now extensive in most respects, Clay wanted to complete it by making the DM the only legal tender in the Western sectors. But as usual the French, who in Clay's judgment really wanted to pull out of Berlin, objected to a move that would tie the city too closely to West Germany.

Early in February the British had expressed their readiness to make the Western currency the only legal tender, but Clay was certain of a French veto. "It seems difficult to let the French whose contribution to support of Berlin is negative block this measure," Clay cabled the department, "it is a policy which plays into Communist hands."[61] Encouraged by Washington's support, Clay maintained his pressure on General Koenig, but only after the United Nations committee of six neutrals had reported the failure of its mission to solve the problem of Berlin's currency did the French finally yield. "The arrangement of two currencies accepted side by side had become inconsistent with the smooth ordering of economic and financial life in Berlin," a tripartite announcement said, "and grave economic and social injustices have resulted. Accordingly as of March 20, the East Mark shall cease to be legal tender in the Western sectors of Berlin." It was a development of historical proportions and promptly recognized by the Berliners as such. "This step is more important than a whole sheaf of declarations that the Western powers were going to stay here," Mayor Reuter declared. "It means the definite recognition that Berlin belongs to the West ideologically and politically—now it must be bound to the West economically."[62]

A trizonal conference that opened in London in January was supposed to solve the problems of the occupation statute and the trizonal fusion,[63] but disagreements on the military government level were not eased by the change in negotiators and locale. The political stalemate made Clay increasingly irritable and tense and was reflected in his messages to the department. He resented not being consulted;[64] was bitter that the French government had finally succeeded "in that apparent anatomical impossibility of making the tail wag the dog";[65] complained that "we sought so anxiously for compromise that we have accepted United Kingdom and French proposals without having a single U.S. position upheld";[66] and castigated a London draft of the occupation statute as "a maze of language which would make the effect of soundly administrating Germany almost ridiculous."[67] At the same time he declined to send a representative to London[68] and refused to continue trizonal fusion negotiations on his level because of "his sad experience that negotiations in two places concurrently are impossible."[69] He suggested instead that the London Conference should adjourn so that a foreign ministers meeting in Washington could straighten out the difficulties and come out with a package deal.[70]

Clay was equally critical of the German draft of the Basic Law during a joint review session with Robertson and Koenig. The relations between the federal government and the *Länder* were poorly defined and too much power was centered in the federal government, he said. Only the Bundesrat (the upper house) was left to protect the rights of the states; the *Länder* retained almost no rights in the fields of finance, health and welfare.[71] Moreover, the inclusion of Berlin in the German draft as one of the federal states was inconsistent with the Western position that Berlin was under quadripartite control by international agreement. At the time of the aide-mèmoire there were only a few articles that did not conform to the London Agreement, but since November the council, it seemed, had made deep inroads into the power of the *Länder*. Clay's concluding negative comment that "in view of this unsatisfactory outcome we can probably only get what we want by dictating it" was probably more an indication of the General's nervous tension than of the objective situation. (One year later, describing the meeting in his memoirs, he mentioned by contrast "the excellent provisions for the protection of democratic rights and processes" in the draft and mainly took exception to "an administrative structure which might prove less than adequate for this purpose."[72])

General Koenig announced his agreement with Clay's criticisms in their entirety, adding that the French government would never authorize the inclusion of Berlin in the Basic Law. General Robertson argued that it would probably be a mistake to compel the Parliamentary Council to make major changes. For his part, he considered the provisions on civil service unacceptable but felt that an attempt had been made to balance concentration of powers in the federal government by giving the Bundesrat a wide latitude for control. The draft of the Basic Law as it stood represented a compromise among the German parties, and Robertson was concerned about the reaction should amendments be imposed by fiat.[73] After further discussion, the three military governors agreed that outright disapproval of the law would be undesirable, and therefore decided to have their political advisers study the document and report any deviations from the provisions of the London Agreement. At the same time the Committee of Five (consisting of two members of the CDU, two of the SPD and one of the FDP) representing the Parliamentary Council was asked to defer placing it before the plenary session until the military governors could comment in detail.[74]

When the three generals resumed their discussion with the report of their political advisers in hand, it became clear they could not achieve a united front. Robertson was prepared to accept the Basic Law as drafted except for the provisions on the civil service and Berlin. The fact that the proposed powers for the central government might strengthen the position of the SPD and thereby increase the chances for farreaching socialization was apparently of no concern to the Labor government in London. For Koenig and Clay, on the other hand, the centralization of authority was unacceptable. When they met with the leaders of the Parliamentary Council on March 2, the military governors stated their respective positions and asked for acceptance of the amendments they proposed. The exact wording was not so important, Clay remarked, as long as the spirit of the amendments was met. The Parliamentary Council responded by enlarging the Committee of Five to seven by including representatives of the Center and German parties. This new body was instructed to see what changes could be made to meet the military governors' wishes. Although the status of Berlin as not covered by Basic Law was clarified, two sets of counterproposals submitted on March 10 and March 17 still proved unsatisfactory.[75]

As far as the French desire for security was concerned, a confederation of German states would have been the ideal solution. Since this was clearly no longer in the cards, they were willing to settle for the American position. As they correctly perceived, the bottom line would be determined not in Washington but by the General from Georgia, whose views on states' rights and a federal structure of government were by then well known. Accordingly, Clay was told that "Foreign Minister Robert Schuman had expressed the view informally" that his and the General's ideas on Germany were not unalike, and a meeting of the two men was arranged. With the State Department's concurrence and accompanied only by Riddleberger, Clay—in civilian clothes—slipped into Paris on March 20. Schuman, who had grown up and studied law in Metz under German rule and whose first language was German, aimed at an early Franco-German reconciliation, an endeavor not fully shared by the Quai d'Orsay. At a three-hour luncheon in Schuman's apartment, with Clay apparently doing most of the talking, the two men achieved a meeting of the minds in important respects. "I gave him a report on what we were doing and trying to do," Clay later recalled. "He said, that's what I suspect. This isn't the way I've been told but this is the way I suspected it was." The two men agreed as a common aim to re-establish a peaceful, self-sufficient West Germany that would be attracted to Western Europe and included some day in a West European union. They also concurred on the need for an early tripartite agreement, a short occupation statute, and French leadership in the rapprochement with West Germany. There were other points raised by Clay to which Schuman assented "in principle," leaving some areas of disagreement and later discussion.[76]

All in all, it was a worthwhile meeting because it assured the General of some French support. But the concluding point in Clay's report that "his [Schuman's] subordinates in France and Germany may be expected to try to defeat his efforts" was well taken, because discord on the military government and London diplomatic levels continued. Washington, moreover, still seemed confused as no definite German policy had emerged; Acheson wondered whether the decision to establish a West German state "had not rather been the brainchild of General Clay and not a governmental decision." And plans for withdrawing all occupation troops and extending the authority of a West German government to all of Germany were still under active consideration.[77]

Meanwhile there was little progress on the German side, and the Soviets were renewing their efforts to prevent a consolidation in the West. On March 13, a group of leading Germans had a six-hour conference with Rudolph Nadolny, a former German ambassador to the Soviet Union, now referred to by the press as "confidential man of the Soviet military administration." The meeting took place in Bad Godesberg in the home of Dr. Andreas Hermes, a former German foreign minister. Professor Erhard, Herman Abs (the director of the *Bank Deutscher Länder*), Dr. Fritz von Twardovsky (former counsellor of the German legation in Moscow), and Franz Blücher (a former minister of finance of North Rhine Westphalia) were among those present at the meeting. Nadolny had reportedly stated that "Germany and Russia must come to an agreement." A few weeks earlier, the head of the CDU in the Soviet zone had visited Dr. Adenauer repeatedly in order to "discuss a peace plan." As Riddleberger consequently summarized the situation to the department, "If present differences over the Bonn constitution, the occupation statute, trizonal fusion and the other stumbling blocks to creation of a viable West German state are not speedily resolved, we may be faced with a very different political and psychological situation in Western Germany."[78] It is hardly surprising that Clay's messages to the department were equally alarming. ". . . at the present, tripartite meetings of military governors are a duplicate of quadripartite meetings with Koenig taking the place of Sokolovsky," he told Assistant Secretary Voorhees in a teleconference, and he added, "It is difficult to expect West Germans to move ahead vigorously when the three governments which have authorized their constitution appear hopelessly deadlocked."[79] He repeatedly urged a cancellation of the London talks, protested against "piecemeal solutions which are defeating our German objectives," and finally in despair warned "there will be no West German government" and "that we have lost Germany politically."[80] In his judgment only a comprehensive agreement could save the situation.

It was the gradual but fundamental change in the attitude of the United States toward Europe that finally helped remove the remaining obstacles to a West German state. The reorientation of American foreign policy to a system of defensive alliances had been signaled by the bipartisan Vandenberg Resolution in June 1948, which pledged the United States to as-

sociate itself with "regional and other collective arrangement" for individual
or collective defense in case of an "armed attack." Backed by this resolution,
Secretary Marshall had begun the negotiations for a defensive military alliance, the North Atlantic Treaty, which were brought to a successful
conclusion by Dean Acheson in April 1949. Somewhat earlier, the new
Secretary had come to the same negative evaluation of the London talks as
Clay:

> My first impression on going over the material prepared in London
> by British, French and American 'experts' in anticipation of the
> April meetings was one of despair. The papers were tremendously
> complex and totally incomprehensible. Nearly two-hundred ques-
> tions had been "reserved" for decisions of the ministers because of
> disagreement among the experts. . . . The chances of the three
> ministers even understanding to say nothing of disentangling this
> mess seemed small. . . . It was literally 'unthinkable' to them [the
> 'experts'] to discard the whole substance of their expertise. But this
> had to be done. Two weeks before the April meetings I did it,
> telling them to take their papers away and start over again.[81]

The signing of the North Atlantic Treaty—it greatly eased France's latent
fears—was followed by a number of quiet meetings with Acheson, Bevin,
and Schuman. Inspired by the prevailing optimism, the three foreign ministers managed to settle most of the outstanding questions concerning Germany within one week. The key documents they signed were: a memorandum regarding the principles governing the rights and responsibilities
of the three powers following the establishment of a German Federal Republic; an occupational statute; and a trizonal fusion agreement. There were
also two tripartite messages, one addressed to the Parliamentary Council
and the other to the military governors. As Dean Acheson concluded, "the
first week of April 1949 was one for which none of us ever needed to feel
apologetic."[82]

When Stalin's interview two months earlier with Kingsbury Smith of
the International News Service was followed by press reports suggesting
an early end of the blockade, Clay had pushed them aside as mere spec-
ulation. Unaware that the interview had produced the Jessup-Malik conversations at the UN, the General also refused to see any significance in
the March 29 announcement of Sokolovsky's replacement. "I do not believe
the blockade will be lifted," he told the department the following day.[83]
Negotiations with the Parliamentary Council had made him equally pes-
simistic about the early passage of an acceptable constitution, and he again
asked for retirement. "Political situation is now very uncertain," he cabled
to Bradley and Royall, "and this condition may last indefinitely."[84] He
suggested the announcement of his departure for April 15, but Bradley
replied that "the announcement of your departure will have to wait until
the name of your replacement is decided."[85] So by the end of March, with

the end of the blockade, the formation of a German government, and Clay's retirement all in abeyance, the outlook was still uncertain.

In Bonn, meanwhile, political positions had hardened. The SPD had declared it was not prepared to go beyond its proposals and demanded that a plenary session of the Parliamentary Council take a vote on the last drafts of the controversial articles. The CDU/CSU announced that it expected to present fresh proposals on the financial issues, whereas the Free Democrats, who held the balance of power, did not declare themselves.[86] Clay, tenacious as ever, was resolved not to give way. As he advised the War Department his objections were "principally in financial fields where virtually no tax powers are left to the states and even the federal government may transfer tax revenues from a prosperous state to a poor state. Of course this right to transfer funds would completely destroy any state power and therefore make a highly centralized government." Another feature he opposed was what he called "the priority legislative right given to the federal government. . . . The objection to our comments comes from the SPD," he explained, ". . . I believe SPD feels that professed decentralization would interfere with socialization. . . ."[87]

The crisis over the Basic Law reached its climax on April 5 when one of the two messages from the foreign ministers was handed to the Parliamentary Council, urging "due consideration to the recommendations of the military governors which conform with the provisions of the London Agreement."[88] It had the intended effect on the German parliamentarians, and the Free Democrats decided to yield to Allied pressures. Five days later the situation changed dramatically for the better when the liaison officers of the three powers communicated to the Committee of Seven the results of the Washington conference. The occupation statute, reduced to two and a half pages, required no changes in the Basic Law. And the promise of a prompt replacement of the military government by a civilian high commission once the new Federal Republic was established was a powerful incentive to complete the work of the Parliamentary Council.

After ten months of frustration, Lucius Clay was delighted to see the organizational elements of his project now fall into place. Once the Basic Law had been voted on and approved by the military government, his mission would come to an end. But anxious as he was to see this happen, he refused to compromise. Instead he remained determined as ever to make his concepts of federalism prevail in the end.

The three military governors had received a letter from their foreign ministers promising "that in the financial field any provision put forward . . . in the direction of securing financial independence and adequate strength for both the *Länder* and federal government . . . will receive sympathetic understanding." With regard to concurrent legislative jurisdiction, any solution was acceptable that did not violate the London Agreement, would ensure *Länder* autonomy and assure "to the federal government sufficient powers in the important fields of government to enable it to deal effectively with these fields in which the interests of more than one *Land* are substantially necessarily involved." The foreign ministers left it to the military governors "to determine the time they may consider it appropriate to communicate these views to the Parliamentary Council." As far as Clay was concerned, that time had not yet come. In his judgment the letter would strengthen the hand of Kurt Schumacher, the leader of the SPD, who had publicly announced his intention to resist the changes in the Basic Law demanded by the military governors and to force its adoption without amendment. Schumacher apparently believed that financial control had to be centered in the federal government if socialization was to follow. Clay described his opponent as

> fanatical, strong-minded and of integrity. He had lost an arm in World War I and had just lost a leg through amputation and was confined to his home most of the time though this did not appear to interfere with his political leadership. . . . If he and his party could defy the occupying powers and get away with it, they could go to the polls triumphantly proclaiming their success as defenders of the German people against the Allies.

Whatever his British and French colleagues or his own superiors in Washington might think or do, he Lucius Clay was going to see to it that this did not happen.[89]

On April 14 he and his colleagues met with the Committee of Seven, once again under the chairmanship of Dr. Adenauer. The atmosphere of the meeting was favorable because the military governors had reached agreement on a definition of federal police power that was in accord with German wishes. The original plan had been to have the electoral law drafted by the minister-presidents, but the military governors yielded to German suggestions that this responsibility be left to the Parliamentary Council. Clay again stressed the need for a speedy completion of the Basic Law and suggested there was "no precedent for three military governors trying so hard to divest themselves of authority and with so little success." He noted that the last German proposals on the controversial points had not been a promising basis for further discussions, but said he would welcome any new proposal that would facilitate negotiation of an agreement "across the table." The Germans thereupon asked for another meeting, with April 25 as the earliest date in view of the SPD congress scheduled for April 20.[90]

Schumacher was playing for big stakes. At the SPD meeting of April 20 he announced dramatically that the Social Democrats would not endorse the Basic Law unless the powers of the upper house (representing the *Länder*) were drastically curtailed and the federal government given clear financial supremacy. The SPD, he declared, refused to be a tool of foreign or particularist interests or to yield to Allied pressure as the Christian Democrats had. As Dr. Lewis Edinger, Schumacher's biographer, told it, "He asserted that his party's determination to defend the national interest was inflexible, that its patriotic principles were immutable, and that its record of militant opposition to Western and Soviet designs against Germany contrasted sharply with the action of Christian Democrats and Communist collaborationists."[91]

In contrast to the American military governor, the Labor government in London had no qualms about triumphant Social Democrats. Robertson, therefore, tried to persuade Clay to release the foreign ministers' letter, and when he failed Bevin intervened through diplomatic channels. The General nevertheless stood his ground. "Our instructions leave timing to discretion of the military government," he told Voorhees; "Koening and I do not believe it is timely yet, while Robertson does. If you have no confidence in the discretion of the military governors please issue instructions." A second cable read: "The issue today is whether or not Schumacher and his small group of party bureaucrats sitting around him in Hannover are to succeed in their policy of defying the occupation authorities." It was the Military Governor's emphatic opinion, the message concluded, that the present time "is not only inappropriate but would actually destroy the chances of a final agreement."[92]

On April 21, one day after the SPD congress, the controversy came to a head. During a teleconference with Voorhees and Murphy at the Washington end, Clay was told that Acheson shared the British opinion that the message should be delivered promptly. "In offering compromise now," Clay replied, "we bow to the arrogance and defiance of Schumacher and make him the top hero in Germany for his defiance. If you want that, go ahead. Don't ask me to do it." And when Murphy countered that it was "his and Clay's function to carry out a government agreement as our Secretary of State understands it," Clay blew up. Unless it was an order he would instruct his deputy General Hays to deliver the message; he himself would request immediate retirement.[93] The conference ended inconclusively and, after some deliberations, Washington decided on a two-pronged approach: First, Murphy would promptly fly to Berlin to bring the recalcitrant General back to reason, and also to check on whether his health was failing, as some of Clay's friends in the Pentagon had begun to fear; second, at the same time, the Chief of Staff would issue direct instructions.

But even General Bradley's carefully worded order, "We as soldiers in our long careers have often had to carry out orders with which we did not entirely agree,"[96] still met resistance. "Your message has added to my difficulties because of very real respect to you and your good opinion," Clay replied. He expressed doubt whether the duties of the military governor were strictly those of a soldier and suggested that "any occupant of an office which exercises civil responsibility has the right to ask to be relieved when political decisions were made he could not agree with." He even referred to the American philosophy expressed at Nuremberg "which found no excuse for a soldier carrying out political orders which he professed not to believe in."[95] Clay nevertheless decided the time had come to yield, and on April 23 the foreign ministers' letter was delivered to the Parliamentary Council. Murphy arrived the following day and could report to Bradley and Voorhees that there was "no reason for immediate concern over Clay's condition. Physically he looks well," his message said, "and he seemed cheerful at the end of today's talk."[96]

Describing the conflict in his memoirs, Clay insisted that his political neutrality had not changed and that "in this instance the CDU favored federal government which was also tripartite policy."[97] In defense of his tactics he also suggested that by the time the letter was released not one of the parties could use it to support its position and the letter therefore had lost much of its political significance. Be that as it may, it is only fair to point out that the General's own personal concept of states' rights was in line with the views of the CDU and that the German conservatives were clearly the beneficiary of the Military Governor's stubborn opposition. One of Clay's critics, John F. Golay, accordingly accused Clay of partisan bias and considered his explanation a lame one. "Any concession agreed upon by the Allied governments," Golay wrote, "should have been extended in a spirit of neutrality . . . fall as they might."[98]

When the military governors met again with the Germans—the group now included representatives from Berlin as observers—they found a greatly improved atmosphere. The German compromise proposals now in effect conceded the administration of major taxes by the Länder to the Allies and a restoration of Bundesrat powers to the Social Democrats. At the same time, they retained for the federal government the power to legislate in the concurrent fields "to maintain economic and legal unity." In the course of a six-hour meeting in the U.S. headquarters building in Frankfurt, the Germans declined to make any further changes. Since Robertson urged acceptance and General Koenig was willing to settle for whatever was satisfactory to the American delegation, Clay found himself in a difficult position, the decision on the extent of federalization now in his hands. "If my decision was one which could not be accepted by the Germans," he wrote, "I would be responsible for delaying the formation of the West German government." The awareness of this responsibility, combined with Clay's superior drafting talents, produced the meeting's successful end. After several hours of inconclusive debates, with the three military governors on one side of the table and the Parliamentary Council on the other, Clay came forth with his own formula. It authorized the federal legislature to establish taxes in order to raise funds for education, health, and welfare and to make grants to those states unable to manage those responsibilities with their own funds.[99] After a brief discussion the Germans accepted the Clay formula, and the last building block for a West German government—the Basic Law—could be moved into place.

It was in a teleconference with Voorhees the following day that Clay learned for the first time of the Jessup-Malik negotiations on the unconditional lifting of the blockade. When asked for his comments, Clay cabled back: "I would urge that now matters have gotten this far we insist on prompt reply from the Soviets with immediate and complete lifting of the blockade." At the same time he pointed out that the Soviet move represented a complete change in the Soviet tactics to win Germany. They will accept a solution of the German problem very largely on Western terms, he suggested, including acceptance of the occupation statute and perhaps even the Bonn constitution. He concluded:

> Their purpose will be however to prevent the new Germany from being oriented toward the West and integrated into an association of Western European states. Thus they would create a buffer state which if we tended to lessen our present efforts they could exploit by promises and other means. The inherent danger was the well-known tendency of democracies to rest on their laurels.[100]

Twenty-five years later he could point out that his comment about "resting on one's laurels" had been well justified. "I have never understood," he told Richard McKinzie,

> why they had to keep the blockade negotiations quite as close as they did, because I think at that stage of the game we had bargaining power: world opinion, opinion at home, and the fact that we were being successful. It was obvious the blockade wasn't working; it had lost the Russians all of Germany and caused a great deal of sympathy in East Germany for Berlin. . . . That was the time when we should have renegotiated the Berlin status and the access rights to the roads. . . . We had a bargaining power then that we didn't use. . . .[101]

On May 4, it was announced that the four powers had agreed to lift the Berlin blockade, and Clay could at last be sure that his agreed-upon departure date of May 15 would be firm. With the siege lifted and a West German government about to be installed, he had reason to believe that at long last his task had been brought to a successful end—that is, until a message from his government seemed to tell him otherwise. With victory in the struggle for Germany in sight, George Kennan's planning staff had come up with a new scenario calling for all occupying forces to withdraw to the German periphery, leaving the German people to form a government for all of Germany. The plan did not consider the all-important relationship of West Germany to the European Recovery Program or to Western Europe, and, of course, it meant abandoning Western efforts to set up a West German government.[102] When the paper detailing these proposals for the forthcoming Council of Foreign Ministers meeting was discussed in the course of a teleconference, the Military Governor reacted with unusual restraint. He knew that neither the British nor the French would accept such a plan, which seemed to demonstrate once again why his country had never won a peace. "If you really want to turn Germany over to the Soviets," he said, "then this is the way to do it. . . . The withdrawal in fact makes Germany a buffer state immediately."[103] And in a cable dispatched the following day he added: "We have won the battle but under the State Department proposal are writing an armistice as if we had lost the battle. It would place us in a disadvantageous position in the unending and continuing struggle between Communism and freedom."[104] When a cable from Murphy advised the Military Governor the following day that the plan was not in accord with Secretary Acheson's view, Clay knew he now could leave without undue concern.[105]

On May 12 the West German constitution was formally approved by the military governors—the same day the blockade of Berlin was lifted. Three days later, the General was finally on his way back to the States, looking forward, as he used to say, "to a tour of catfishing on the Chattahoochee River."

FOOTNOTES

1. Clay for Byrnes, September 18, 1948, in Jean Smith, ed., *The Papers of General Lucius D. Clay.* pp. 858–860.
2. U.S. Strategic Bombing Survey. *The Effects of Strategic Bombing on the German War Economy.*
3. Louis Wiesner, "Organized Labor in Postwar Germany," p. 344.
4. Lucius D. Clay; *Decision in Germany*, p. 214, John H. Backer, *Priming the German Economy*, Ch. 6; F. A. Lutz, "The German Currency Reform and the Revival of the German Economy" in *Economica*, May 1949, pp. 131–138.
5. Ibid.
6. Clay for Byrnes, September 18, 1948, in Smith, *The Papers*, pp. 858–860.
7. Clay, *Decision*, p. 292.
8. Ibid., p. 293.
9. Author's interview with Joe Keenan, Washington, D.C., June 26, 1980.
10. Clay, *Decision*, p. 293.
11. Ibid., p. 291.
12. Wiesner, "Organized," pp. 269–270.
13. Ibid., p. 270.
14. Ibid., p. 273.
15. Ibid., p. 322.
16. Ibid.
17. Ibid., p. 348.
18. Ibid., p. 350.
19. Clay for Draper, June 19, 1948, CC 4775, R.G. 200, N.A.
20. Ibid.
21. Wiesner, "Organized," p. 353.
22. Ibid., pp. 353–354.
23. Ibid., p. 357, Marguerite Higgins in *New York Herald Tribune*, European edition, March 1, 1949.
24. Ibid., p. 362.
25. Ibid.
26. Clay, *Decision*, pp. 296–297.
27. Ibid.
28. Wiesner, "Organized," pp. 364–365.
29. Clay, *Decision*, p. 409.
30. Hans Peter Schwarz, *Vom Reich zur Bundesrepublik*, p. 607.
31. John F. Golay, *The Founding of the Federal Republic of Germany*, p. 14.
32. Tagesspiegel, July 10, 1948; *The New York Times*, July 10, 1948, pp. 1 and 4. Golay, *The Founding*, pp. 14–15.
33. Clay, *Decision*, p. 410.
34. Lewis J. Edinger, *Kurt Schumacher*, p. 167.
35. Golay, *The Founding*, p. 15.
36. *Tagesspiegel*, July 15, 1948.
37. Clay, *Decision*, p. 410.
38. Ibid.
39. Ibid., p. 411.
40. Golay, *The Founding*, p. 19.
41. *Foreign Relations of the United States 1948*, Vol. II, p. 418.
42. Clay, *Decision*, p. 338.
43. Ibid.
44. Ibid.
45. Clay for Department of Army, November 22, 1948, CC 6839, R.G. 200, N.A.
46. Ibid.
47. *Foreign Relations . . . 1948*, Vol. II, p. 496.
48. Clay for Lincoln, November 18, 1948, CC 6772, R.G. 200, N.A.
49. Clay for Draper, December 5, 1948, CC 6977.
50. Clay, *Decision*, p. 333.
51. Ibid., p. 339.
52. Ibid.

53. Ibid., p. 413.
54. Clay for Draper, August 19, 1948, CC 5604 in R.G. 200, N.A.
55. Ibid., p. 413.
56. Golay, The *Founding*, p. 24.
57. Clay for Bradley, January 5, 1949, CC 7304, R.G. 200, N.A.
58. Teleconference Clay-Royall, January 8, 1949, TT-1803, R.G. 200, N.A.
59. *Foreign Relations . . . 1948*, Vol. II, pp. 1325–1337.
60. Phillips W. Davison, *The Berlin Blockade*, p. 264.
61. Clay for Department of Army, February 11, 1949, CC 7716, R.G. 200, N.A.
62. Davison, *The Berlin*, p. 263.
63. Clay, *Decision*, p. 418.
64. Clay for Draper, January 18, 1949, CC 7462, R.G. 200, N.A.
65. Clay for Draper, January 23, 1949, CC 7529, R.G. 200, N.A.
66. Clay for Department of Army, February 3, 1949, CC 7624, R.G. 200, N.A.
67. Clay for Voorhees, February 11, 1949, CC 7725, R.G. 200, N.A.
68. Clay for Draper, February 1, 1949, FMPC-287, R.G. 200, N.A.
69. Clay for Draper, January 31, 1949, FMPC-279, R.G. 200, N.A.
70. Clay for Draper, January 30, 1949, CC 7600, R.G. 200, N.A.
71. Golay, *The Founding*, pp. 96–102.
72. Clay, *Decision*, p. 421.
73. Golay, *The Founding*, p. 97.
74. *Foreign Relations . . . 1949*, Vol. III, pp. 217–220; Golay, *The Founding*, p. 161–162; Clay, *Decision*, p. 424.
75. Clay, *Decision*, p. 425.
76. Clay, *Decision*, pp. 425–427; Clay for Voorhees, March 21, 1949, CC 8086, R.G. 200, N.A.; *Foreign Relations . . . 1949*, III, pp. 115–118, Jean Smith interview with General Clay, February 25, 1971.
77. *Foreign Relations . . . 1949*, Vol. III, pp. 82–84, 102.
78. Ibid, pp. 224–225.
79. Clay, *Decision*, 424; Golay, *The Founding*, 102; Teleconference, Clay-Voorhees, Goldwaithe Dorr, TT-2012, March 17, 1949.
80. Ibid. Clay for Voorhees, March 24, 1949, CC 8121, R.G. 200, N.A.
81. Dean Acheson, *Present at the Creation*, pp. 286–287.
82. Acheson, *Present*, p. 290. Foreign *Relations . . . 1949*, Vol. III, pp. 175–186.
83. Teleconference Clay-Haislip, March 30, 1949, TT-2066, R.G. 200, N.A.
84. Clay for Bradley and Royall, March 26, 1949, CC 8154, R.G. 200, N.A.
85. W-86283, March 29, 1949, in Smith, *The Papers*, p. 1062.
86. Golay, *The Founding*, pp. 102–104.
87. Clay for Voorhees, March 31, 1949, FMPC-697, R.G. 200, N.A.
88. Golay, *The Founding*, p. 103; *Foreign Relations . . . 1949*, Vol. III, p. 185.
89. Clay, *Decision*, p. 431.
90. Clay, *Decision*, pp. 430–431; Riddleberger to Acheson, April 14, 1949; *Foreign Relations . . . 1949*, Vol. III, pp. 237–244.
91. Edinger, *Schumacher*, pp. 160–161.
92. Clay for Department of Army, April 19, 1949, CC 8358; Clay for Department of Army, CC 8363, April 19, 1949, R.G. 200, N.A.
93. Clay-Voorhees-Murphy Teleconference, TT-2150, April 21, 1949, R.G. 200, N.A.
94. W-87548, April 22, 1949, in Smith, *The Papers*, p. 1124.
95. Teleconference Clay-Voorhees, Bradley, TT-2154, April 22, 1949, R.G. 200, N.A.
96. *Foreign Relations . . . 1949*, Vol. III, p. 251.
97. Clay, *Decision*, pp. 431–433.
98. Golay, *The Founding*, pp. 108–109.
99. Clay, *Decision*, pp. 433–435.
100. Clay for Voorhees, May 1, 1949, CC 8467, R.G. 200. N.A.
101. Richard McKinzie interview with Lucius Clay, New York, N.Y. July 16, 1974.
102. Teleconference Clay-Voorhees, Dorr, May 5, 1949, TT-2185, R.G. 200, N.A.; *Foreign Relations . . . 1948*, II, pp. 1325–1337.
103. Ibid.
104. Clay for Voorhees, May 7, 1949, CC 8519, R.G. 200, N.A.
105. Clay, *Decision*, p. 439.

CHAPTER TWELVE

An End and a Beginning

LEAVETAKING BEGAN APRIL 23 AT IM DOL, CLAY'S BERLIN RESIDENCE, ON THE occasion of his fifty-second birthday. Margaret Allen, Edna Shelley, Edloe Donnan, and other members of his small personal staff watched with some feeling of nostalgia as the General cut his birthday cake. Four exciting years, possibly the best ones in their individual lives, were about to end. All that would remain were memories, the knowledge of having served with one of their country's great men, and Clay's final toast: "To those who made me happiest."[1]

Ten days later, the day after the President had accepted the Military Governor's resignation, 10,000 men from the First Division and Constabulary assembled at Grafenwoehr, Bavaria, for the farewell parade before their retiring Commander in Chief. To Clay they seemed as valiant a group of soldiers as their battle-tested predecessors, and he reminded them of their inheritance—the proud traditions of the Allied armies who had liberated Europe. They were to remain in Germany, he said, to ensure that the peace and freedom for which the war had been fought might endure. After the last of the regiments had passed in review, sixty Thunderbolt fighters of the 86th Fighter Wing forming a gigantic CLAY swept across a brilliant cloudless sky.

In an even more eloquent if less spectacular farewell tribute, thousands of Berliners who had toughed out the airlift with Clay came to watch the customary Sunday retreat ceremony before Military Government headquarters at Kronprinzen Allee—the street soon to be renamed Clay Allee by a grateful city. It was his last official act before he and Mrs. Clay boarded the plane at Tempelhof; only at a refueling stop in Newfoundland did he learn that he was to address Congress the following day and be honored by the President with the second oakleaf cluster to his distinguished service medal.

Introduced by Speaker Sam Rayburn as "a man of the many men I have seen who is able as any man I ever met in the army or out," Clay spoke to the Congress briefly and without notes.

> For two years, the United States had tried desperately to make four-power agreement work. We failed because one of the four

powers had but two objectives in Germany: the one to exact the maximum in reparations and the other to establish the type and kind of government which could be controlled or at least exploited to the full by a police state. The three Western powers therefore had to go it alone. And now the Germans too have cast their die for a government which stands for the dignity of man as an individual.

It is impossible to forget and it is difficult to forgive. We all remember that Germany started the aggressive war. But it is difficult for free people to realize the moral deterioration of a people who come under a dictatorship. A people who have been subject to such a regime cannot be returned to democracy overnight. I saw in Berlin the spirit and soul of a people reborn. Two and a half million Germans had a second opportunity to choose freedom. They had forgone their first opportunity, they did not forgo their second opportunity. . . . it may be indeed the spirit that lights the flame for freedom in Germany that may grow with the years. We must encourage that flame, and try to develop a Germany which sees Germany not alone but as a part of a new European concept devoted to a common economic effort and to a common love for freedom.[2]

There were two more official ceremonies, one the traditional New York tickertape parade, with Bob Murphy and Bill Draper sharing in the honors; the other a glorious homecoming in Marietta, where Clay addressed the welcoming crowd in the bleachers just across from his father's monument. The festivities there included a barbecue attended by 8,000 Georgians and a parade honoring Clay with one float enticingly bedecked with a pole, a pail of live bait, and a jug of corn whiskey. But a piece in *The New Yorker* describing the event reported, "He hasn't found time for any catfishing yet."[3]

The months of vacation on Cape Cod that followed were not wholly devoid of work because the General was preparing the official account of his four years in Germany. "Official" it was indeed: his *Decision in Germany*— a bureaucratic justification of military government—seems equally significant for what it omits as for what it tells. But the code of Lucius D. Clay as a public servant precluded the "now it can be told" disclosures so prevalent in our day. While the General was writing his memoir, the telephone at Cape Cod rang off the hook with job offer after job offer.[4] Clay had his own ideas about that. He turned down a financially rewarding proposal from a prominent banker on the West Coast because, as Marjorie Clay tells it, "the General would not work for anybody he could not respect." He also refused at first to work in the "canyons of New York," she said, although later when he changed his mind he actually "loved it." But at the time he wanted and eventually chose a small company in a small town, when anyone who knew the General could have predicted it was not his cup of tea. The job as chief executive officer with the Ecusta Paper Company in Brevard, North Carolina, offered little challenge and lasted about a year.

Always true to his code, he resigned when the company was purchased by Olin, a manufacturer of amunition during the war.[5]

He chose to leave on the grounds that it would be unbecoming for a retired army officer to be involved with munitions makers, particularly an officer who had handled army contracts during the war and who might conceivably some day be handling them again.[6]

In Germany he had gone out of his way to avoid suspicions of favoritism, nepotism, or carpetbagging. He refused to have his son Frank's wedding moved to England so the mothers of bride and groom could attend, because such a privilege was not available to other officers in the army of occupation.[7] When a nephew, a major working in the OMGUS secretariat, had tried to remain in the same job as a civilian at higher pay, he was ordered back into the army.[8] Clay disallowed a recommended decoration for Lucius Clay, Jr., who also served in the occupation forces.[9] And when, during the General's last days in Berlin, a German guest at his table recognized the wine served as having been requisitioned from his own cellar, an embarrassed Military Governor—overdrawing his bank account—sent him a check for seven thousand dollars.[10] In a similar vein, he refused to take advantage of a special IRS ruling that allowed Eisenhower and other generals to treat the profits from their memoirs as capital gains. He could have saved a substantial sum on taxes.

Clay had no job, no savings to speak of, and an annual retirement pay of $9,000, when a new challenge unexpectedly presented itself. He happened to be in New York City on behalf of the Crusade for Freedom, the initial financing organization for Radio Free Europe which he headed, when he received a telephone call from Sidney Weinberg, the New York financier. He suggested that the General meet with Carl Conway, chairman of the Continental Can Company. Weinberg and Clay had worked together in Washington during the war, Weinberg with the War Production Board and Clay responsible for army supplies, but the two men had not seen each other for several years; Clay had never met Conway and knew nothing about Continental Can. At tea in Conway's apartment he learned a few things about the company. It was too highly centralized, Conway said, and its operations were stifled by too much control from the top. Conway was unhappy with the way things were going and asked Clay to meet that same evening with Continental's board of directors. Later at dinner the directors questioned the General about his ideas on decentralization. "I had not prepared for the meeting," Clay later recalled, "but I always have been in favor of decentralization. I had very firm views on the necessity for decentralization of operations with centralization of budgets and controls so that you never lost control but at the same time did not interfere with the daily operations of the various parts of an organization." He expressed his views with his usual eloquence and vigor.

By the time Clay had a nightcap with the directors, answered more questions, and left for home, it was obvious that Continental Can was interested in his services. The next day he was invited to join the board of directors for lunch at the Recess Club. "I went up to lunch with them," Clay continued his story,

> and when the lunch was over, Mr. Conway and Mr. Weinberg said, 'The board meeting won't last very long, come on over and then we'll have a talk.' So I went over to the Continental Can office, which was then at Pershing Square. Mr. Conway took me to his office and said, 'just wait here for us.' About five or ten minutes later, he walked in with Mr. Weinberg. He said, 'You've just been elected chairman of the board and chief executive officer of Continental Can Company. Will you come in and preside over the meeting.' Just like that. So I presided over the meeting. About a month later, the financial vice president came in to me and he said, 'We are getting ready to make out your check, but we don't know what to make out.' I said, 'Well, I don't either.'

Fascinated by the new challenge he had not even discussed salary or pay. "Here was a company that needed a change, that needed someone to strengthen the organization. That in itself was a challenge," Clay explained many years after he had left Continental.[11] Under his direction it had grown from a middle-sized firm into the largest and most diversified packaging company in the world.

The first four years after the German Wehrmacht had surrendered were instrumental in shaping United States relations with the Soviet Union and Germany in the postwar world. When hostilities ended in Europe in May 1945, the Rooseveltian concept of continued cooperation with Russia to forestall future German aggressions was still very much alive. The war romanticism of the American-Russian brotherhood-in-arms had not yet given way to more sober considerations. Four years later, the Soviet Union had taken Germany's place as America's main adversary and a new concept of West Germany as a bulwark against Communist expansionism was about to take hold.

Soviet disregard for some of the terms of Yalta and Potsdam—as interpreted by the U.S. Department of State—had been at the roots of this dramatic development. A re-emerging anti-Communism in America and the reawakening of temporarily suppressed suspicions of the Kremlin were of equal significance. The Red Army's activities in Romania, Bulgaria, Hungary, and Poland had been the initial irritants. Later Soviet acquisitive moves toward Iran and Turkey had added to the tensions. Although the Russians were stopped by a Western display of force, it was too late to prevent a break. While hostilities were still in progress, President Roosevelt had focused almost exclusively on winning the war and refused to engage in postwar planning. "I dislike making plans for a country which we do not yet occupy," he wrote to Cordell Hull in October 1944. "Much of this is dependent on what we and the Allies find when we get into Germany—and we are not there yet."[12]

In accord with this policy of postponement, the President's views about the future were expressed in general terms. They entailed democratic governments evolving from free elections, a strong United Nations to prevent future wars, and an economic system of multilateralism to prevent economic blocs. The underlying assumption was that the American-British-Soviet alliance would continue thus safeguarding the stabilization of Europe after the war. It was this set of general and loose ideas that prevailed in America's policymaking circles at the time General Clay departed for Europe, where only a negative directive awaited him.

Viewing his German assignment like any odd engineering task, the newly appointed Deputy Military Governor quickly recognized that the early economic unification of the four zones of the occupation was the key. His immediate area of responsibility—the American zone of occupation— could not be made self-supporting and, he thought, with no end in sight congressional appropriations were eventually bound to cease. With the example of 1923—the demise of the American occupation of the Rhineland—always in the back of his mind, he feared that history would repeat itself. Accordingly Germany had to be quickly unified lest his mission end in failure.

Moreover, in view of the always present risk of cuts in appropriations, outlays for the occupation had to be held to a minimum until a merger of the four zones would relieve the burden on the American taxpayer. Having had the rare experience as a military engineer of looking at the army from the outside as well as the inside, Clay knew only too well that the occupation was not a job for soldiers. Accordingly his early conceived blueprint for the completion of his mission entailed a four-pronged approach. The military government would have to be promptly divorced from army general staff tutelage; American personnel had to be drastically reduced and administrative responsibilities soon turned over to qualified and carefully chosen Germans. Finally, at the international level of the Control Council, there had to be an incessant pressure toward unification. Unlike some of the professional diplomats at the State Department, the Deputy Military Governor was not affected by any doubts about the Yalta and Potsdam agreements as guideposts for four-power cooperation. Like Eisenhower and other American military leaders, he expected continued friendly relations with the Soviet Union. The key to getting along with the Soviets was that it was necessary to give trust in order to get trust, he told a doubting Charles Bohlen early in 1945. Facing a group of equally skeptical American journalists, he insisted that good relations with Russia were a must. "It has to work," he said. "How can you expect to succeed at the United Nations if you cannot cooperate in Berlin?"[13]

At the same time he had no illusions about the difficulties ahead. He knew that he had been handed one of the most difficult and thankless jobs his government had to offer, and he recognized the validity of his friend's warning: "The job would ruin the best man's reputation." "There was not

anyone of requisite size," Clay later told an interviewer, "who would vol-
unteer to take the job or would take it except an army officer whom you
could tell to take it. There wasn't anybody in the State Department who
wanted the job."[14]

The economic restrictions imposed by JCS #1067 initially seemed a
formidable obstacle. However, encouraged by Henry Stimson to use discretion in implementing them and mindful of his warning that "its drafters
would be the first to turn against you if things went wrong,"[15] Clay began
slowly to dismantle the economic paragraphs of the directive. "If you
couldn't restore the German economy, you could never hope to get paid
for the food that they had to have," he said. "By virtue of this sort of thing
it was modified constantly; not officially, but by allowing this deviation and
that deviation et cetera. We began slowly to wipe out JCS #1067," Clay
went on.

> When we were ordered to put in a currency reform, this was in
> direct contravention of a provision of JCS #1067 that prohibited
> us from doing anything to improve the German economy. It was
> an unworkable policy and it wasn't changed just without any dis-
> cussion or anything by those of us who were in Germany. It was
> done by gradual changes in its provisions, by an exchange of ca-
> blegrams, conferences and so on.[16]

The same latitude did not apply to denazification, however, which was
undoubtedly the least successful military government program in occupied
Germany. Drafted in the heat of wartime passions, its comprehensive provisions were stringent, without any escape clauses and—most important in
its effect—strongly supported by American public opinion during the first
postwar years. Bad orders indeed they were; the General had no choice
but to enforce them vigorously even while recognizing their many failings.
Decartelization, on the other hand, limped along—in part because Germany
was broken up into four zones and in part because decartelization meant
different things to different people. To some Americans it meant breaking
up cartel arrangements, to others it meant antitrust legislation; and to the
British (at least while under a labor government) it meant outright socialization. Faced with an ambiguous text and contradictory pressures from
home, Clay proceeded slowly until the tide of public opinion had changed.

In pursuing the educational objectives of his mission, an integral part
of developing a democracy, he had to focus for more than two years on the
mechanical processes of education—school buildings had to be restored,
new textbooks printed and new teachers selected. The task of guiding and
influencing German institutions to introduce more progressive and democratic educational methods could be only started in his last year. Nevertheless, there were some permanent results: the Free University was established in Berlin during the blockade, and educational exchanges as well as
the Amerika Häuser (the cultural information centers) survived.

Democratization obviously could not be achieved by military fiat, although, as Don Humphrey wrote, "the Military Governor's autocratic temperament and democratic convictions were well suited to the dualism inherent in that ambiguous task."[17] While personally aloof from the Germans, Clay was fully aware of the need to establish a government and of the fact that vitality in government was essential to have any chance of success. Accordingly he put up an unrelenting fight against his British and French allies—and often against his own staff—to give Germans responsibility, and thereby experience with the problems inherent in a democracy. As safeguards for the future, all he could do was to plant some legislative and constitutional measures in the hope that the seed would grow, and this he readily did.*

While Washington's policymakers vacillated, Clay maintained a steady course. There is no doubt that one-man rule despite its many drawbacks helped, and one-man rule there was. "Give me the facts," Clay used to say, "and then we'll determine policy." But it really meant, "Give me the facts and I'll give you the policy." Clay fell short in his capacity to use the perception and wisdom of others fully, Don Humphrey thought. "He makes up his mind by himself with an almost mystical belief in his rightness," another critical staff member noted.[18] And James Sundquist, the Management Control Officer in Berlin, recalls one of Clay's meetings with his top advisers in preparation of the currency reform:

> I sat there rather flabbergasted—here was his Chief Financial Advisor not giving advice at all, but taking orders and just asking to have the orders made clear. And then Clay turned to the economic officer and the same thing happened, and when it came to my turn, he gave me my directions and I was going through the same process—exactly how did you mean that, this way or that way? Well, I thought for God's sake, where does he get his advice. These are his chief advisors and none of them obviously has even known that these matters were being discussed. And they come back and the decision has been made.[19]

Despite one-man rule, however, the picture of the "Dictator General" promoted by some of Clay's adversaries is not correct.[20] Fundamentally a modest man with democratic beliefs, an autocratic temperament and a technocratic brain, he operated with a small personal staff and eschewed the trappings of high office both in his personal surroundings and also when on the move. When he traveled on inspection in the zone, he had standing orders against police escorts[21] and he tongue-lashed any self-serving official or commander who laid on a flaming police or military escort that blew sirens and scattered civilians. Hugh Baillie, the president of the United Press news agency passing through Berlin shortly after visiting Tokyo, made some invidious comparisons between the two occupations. Clay listened for a while and finally asked Baillie in what respect he thought the

---

* Among the positive aspects of JCS #1067 was also its Restitution provision. It pertained to identifiable property taken by the Nazis under duress, and was vigorously opposed.

German occupation had failed. Baillie replied that in Japan, MacArthur had dramatized the occupation: "He has given the Japanese vivid ideas about Americans. The Japanese love the show he put on for them and the Germans would love it too if you would do the same thing over here." After considering the suggestion for a moment, Clay remarked with his slow smile, "Well sir, I cannot picture Bob Murphy and myself riding up to headquarters on a pair of white horses."[22]

In what was probably the General's last interview before his death, one of his comments also provides us with some significant insight. Asked how West Point and his subsequent engineering education had prepared him for life, Clay's answer was brief but to the point:

> I think the basic program of West Point probably taught you that whatever your job was to do, you just said yes and went out and did it or tried to do it anyway. I think this is a basic and most important aspect of training for the embryonic military leader. As far as the period in the Corps of Engineers is concerned, I owe everything I have in life to the Corps of Engineers.[23]

Meticulous obedience to orders was fundamental to the General who "would have given his eyeteeth to have commanded a division in combat"[24] at the time he went to Germany, to stay on through four turbulent and trying years. But of equal significance was the engineer in the man, the engineer who had become accustomed to sizing up each new project—whether technical, political, economic, or social—as another engineering task, to develop a blueprint and to stick to it until the project's successful completion. "Clay remembers," William Harlan Hale wrote, "that he was originally assigned to Germany not only as a general but as an engineer and his job, as he sees it, is primarily an engineering job to get economic wheels turning again, to free the dammed-up energies of his German wards and thereby to make the country hum. He has gone all-out for German efficiency. . . ."[25]

It was the engineering element which predominated—but did not ever exclude—the democratic ethic in Clay's stewardship of postwar Germany. And it was the continuing and creative tension between these two facets of Clay's mind which perhaps more than any other circumstance shaped the outcome of his mission and the form of Western Germany today.

Clay went to Germany expecting to take orders, but during the first two years no orders came. He consequently made policy himself. For a man "always eager to make progress somewhere and somehow"—to quote Jim Riddleberger[26]—this became habit-forming. The result was friction and frequent controversy with the State Department. One fundamental cause was State's repeated attempts to make European policy at the expense of the War Department's German budget, which was Clay's responsibility. But more often it was the General's unrelenting and uncompromising pursuit of what he considered his government's German policy and the Pentagon's reluctance to countermand any orders given by a commander in the field.

When the unification of Germany was still the official American goal and Clay was stymied in his work at the Control Council, he unilaterally ordered the stop of reparations, masterminded the Stuttgart speech, negotiated a tentative settlement of the critical reparations problem with his Soviet counterpart, and eventually issued a final warning.

> A failure to investigate it [the German economic potential] fully means the partition of Germany. . . . Obviously this establishes the frontier of Western democracy along the Elbe, . . . We have much at stake in gaining the opportunity to fight for democratic ideals in Eastern Germany and in Eastern Europe. This opportunity would result from the true unification of Germany under quadripartite control.[27]

Only at the Moscow conference in March 1947 did Clay become aware that the winds of history had shifted and that his government had charted a new course. Looking in one direction and persisting in that direction with great physical and nervous intensity, as one astute observer had put it,[28] he did not permit himself to be distracted by any of the happenings in Eastern Europe, in France, in Iran, in Turkey, or elsewhere. Now he realized that Roosevelt's "noble experiment" had come to an end and that the unification of Germany was not any longer in the cards.

As a new concept that included an economically strong West Germany emerged, one found the American Military Governor again in the lead. 'We must have courage to proceed with the government of West Germany first provisionally and then representatively," he tells Washington once he has gotten his bearings and adjusted to his government's new policies. "Two and a half years without a government is much too long. . . . I must say with all sincerity at my command that 42 million Germans in the British and American zones represent today the strongest outposts against Communist penetration that exist anywhere."[29] He relentlessly pleaded for the establishment and publication of a new German level of industry that would drastically curtail the dismantlement process, built up a transitional German administration, insisted on the installation of a German management and trusteeship for the Ruhr industry, and developed in conjunction with Couve de Murville an American-French compromise that envisaged the establishment of a West German government. Once that was agreed upon in principle, he made sure that implementation followed swiftly. The German representatives were handed a schedule for the drafting of a constitution, and Clay not only saw to it that the schedule was kept but also that the final product was in accord with his own firm concepts of a democratic federation. While these negotiations were in progress, the East-West conflict over Berlin finds in the American Military Governor a natural leader of the

Free World. His call to arms—"If we mean that we are to hold Europe against Communism, we must not budge"—made history. When the airlift broke the blockade and a West German government was formed, Clay's job in Germany came to an end. He departed as the architect of a new German Federal Republic, which was soon to take its place in a Western anti-Soviet bloc.

Clay faced in a brief historical period the dilemma which had confronted Germany's neighbors for generations—to work with the Germans in pursuit of a mutual goal, or to work against them in fear of their vitality and aggressive spirit. He soon chose to work with them, and he pursued that vision consistently and forcefully for a critical period in modern history. He succeeded—if that is the word to use—in restoring a viable and increasingly self-confident state in the western part of the German national domain. In doing so he sought to provide a reborn German nation-state with political concepts, institutions, and associations in the international arena which would contain the negative forces so long and so rightfully feared by Germany's neighbors.

The issues encountered by Germany and the Atlantic community are a test of critical importance for the solution Clay adopted nearly forty years ago. It is a measure of the significance of the man that we can say his judgment and energies shaped the questions we and the Germanys of today now face. And it is a measure of the human dilemma that we cannot yet say what the answer will be.

FOOTNOTES

1. Author's interview with Edna Shelley (Mrs. Robert Gates), St. Louis, Missouri, October 27, 1980.
2. *Congressional Record*, May 17, 1949, House, p. 6339; Senate, p. 6313.
3. *The New York Times*, May 29, 1949; E. J. Kahn, Jr., "Soldier in Mufti," in *The New Yorker*, January 13, 1951.
4. Author's interview with Mrs. Lucius D. Clay, McLean, Va., July 12, 1981.
5. Ibid.
6. Kahn, Jr., "Soldier."
7. Author's interview with Margaret Allen, Washington, D.C., September 12, 1981.
8. Demaree Bess, "An American Viceroy in Germany," in *Saturday Evening Post*, May 10, 1947.
9. Letter, July 19, 1981, General Lucius D. Clay, Jr., to author.
10. Author's interviews with James O'Donnell, Washington, D.C., March 8, 1981; Edloe Donnan, Manchester, Missouri, October 27, 1981.
11. Mark Nackman interview with General Clay, New York, N.Y., October 16, 1973.
12. Foreign Relations of the United Nations 1945, the Conferences at Malta and Yalta, p. 158.
13. *The New York Times*, June 25, 1945.
14. Richard D. McKinzie interview with General Clay, New York, N.Y., July 16, 1974.
15. Lucius D. Clay, *Decision in Germany*, pp. 18 and 54. Jean Smith interview with General Clay, February 5, 1971.
16. Richard D. McKinzie interview with General Clay, New York, N.Y., July 16, 1974.
17. Don Humphrey, private papers.
18. William Harlan Hale, "General Clay—On His Own," in *Harpers*, December 1948.
19. Author's interview with James Sundquist, Washington, D.C., May 5, 1980.
20. Don Humphrey, private papers.
21. Author's interview with Richard Hallock, Washington, D.C., April 5, 1981.
22. Bess, "An American Viceroy in Germany."
23. Dr. Kanarek interview with General Clay, August 16, 1977.
24. McKinzie interview with General Clay, New York, N.Y., July 16, 1974.
25. Hale, "General Clay—On His Own."
26. Author's interview with James Riddleberger, Washington, D.C., August 6, 1981.
27. Clay for Byrnes. Memorandum. November 1946. In Smith, *The Papers*, pp. 274–284.
28. Author's interview with George Kennan, Princeton, N.J., March 19, 1980.
29. Clay for Draper, November 3, 1947. CC 2167, R.G. 200, N.A.

Epilogue

Don D. Humphrey

Lucius Clay is destined to remain a controversial figure. Blunt soldier and shrewd diplomat; democrat and autocrat; administrator and policy maker; world figure and citizen of Georgia. Clay defies summing up.

One remembers of Clay the aquiline features and the piercing eyes. He looks like a Roman emperor, and some have added that he acts like one. The first part is apt; the second is good enough for an aphorism. Yet it is equally misleading, for the General is the antithesis of all that is pompous and pretentious. Clay ruled by his intelligence, his energy, and the vehemence of his convictions, and not by rank. He was, in fact, a most unmilitary general, a statement that may be contradicted by those who have heard only the precision of his speech, have witnessed the speed of his decisions, and, on occasions, the hauteur of his manner. Clay lived and operated in a goldfish bowl. He never cloaked his remarks in the anonymity of the uniform or sought protection in the privilege of rank. He took responsibility, he ruled, he answered criticism, and, when necessary, slugged it out—with or without gloves. It is Clay the man, not Clay the general, who was so intimately identified with every aspect of the German occupation.

Clay's failures are mainly those of American policy—the negative objectives; the failure to reshape the German mind by encouragement and support of the constructive forces; the failure to restore Ruhr coal and European trade; the maintenance of an economic wilderness bounded by dollar rule in the heart of Europe for four critical years. I know of no one who, under the circumstances, could have done so well as Clay. But Clay was the occupation and history does not measure success and failure in the light of circumstances.

Clay gave all of himself to the job. In his selflessness, in his courage, in his devotion to his country and to peace, he was truly a great man. But more was required than the capacities of a single man. Clay fell short in his incapacity to use the perception and wisdom of others fully.

Hostile critics do not question Clay's penetrating intelligence or his extraordinary competence. He would not have claimed for himself that he was easy to get along with. The post he held for four years was among the most trying and thankless jobs in history. Lesser men would have come home under the criticism thrown at Clay. No one outside the President carried a greater load of responsibility. The support that he gained he made for himself. The people who did not like Clay, whether in Washington or among our European Allies, were mainly those who did not deal with him directly. Those who worked directly with him or faced him across the table know his irascible strength, but they feel also the warmth and wealth of his magnetism.

Whether in the counsels of the American element or at the council tables of Europe, Clay was truly a formidable opponent. Intelligent, resourceful, tough, articulate—he brought to bear on an issue a mastery of detail and, excepting money matters, a profound sense of the larger values. The quality, however, which carried the punch, and which threw people off balance in dealing with and in appraising him, was Clay's intensity. Having lived so deeply with a job so serious, he was outraged by criticism or opposition from neophytes.

The seeming contradictions in Clay were many. Humility was not his particular virtue. Yet I believe that Clay's greatest quality, and the one that enabled him to lead when there was no leadership, and to survive where generals were expendable, was his utter selflessness. The capacity for policy and the stability to administer are a unique combination. Add to this, selflessness, and there emerges something rare in public figures. General Clay is such a man.

Bibliography

I. Primary Sources

A. Memoirs and Recollections

Acheson, Dean. *Present at the Creation*. New York: Norton, 1969.

Adenauer, Konrad. *Memoirs: 1945–53*. Chicago: Regnery, 1966.

Bohlen, Charles E. *Witness to History 1929–1969*. New York: Norton, 1973.

Byrnes, James F. *Speaking Frankly*. New York: Harper, 1947.

———. *All in One Lifetime*. New York: Harper, 1958.

Catroux, Georges. *J'ai vu tomber le Rideau de fer, Moscou 1945–1948*. Paris: Hachette, 1952.

Churchill, Winston S. *The Second World War*. 6 vols. New York: Bantam, 1962.

Clay, Lucius D. *Decision in Germany*. Garden City, N.Y.: Doubleday, 1950.

Deane, John R. *The Strange Alliance: The Story of Our Efforts at Wartime Cooperation with Russia*. New York: Viking, 1947.

Djilas, Milovan. *Conversations with Stalin*. New York: Harcourt, 1962.

Dulles, John Foster. *War or Peace*. New York: Macmillan, 1950.

John Foster Dulles Papers. Seeley G. Mudd Manuscript Library. Princeton, N.J.: Princeton University.

Eden, Anthony. *The Memoirs of Anthony Eden: Full Circle*. Boston: Houghton Mifflin, 1960.

———. *The Reckoning*. Boston: Houghton Mifflin, 1965.

Fahy, Charles. "Memoirs." New York: Columbia University, Oral History Office.

Galbraith, John Kenneth. *A Life in Our Time*. Boston: Houghton Mifflin, 1981.

Harriman, Averell W. *Peace with Russia?* New York: Simon & Schuster, 1959.

Howley, Frank. *Berlin Command*. New York: Putnam's, 1950.

Hull, Cordell. *The Memoirs of Cordell Hull*. 2 vols. New York: Macmillan, 1945.

Kennan, George F. *Memoirs, 1925–1950*. Boston: Little, Brown, 1967.

Leahy, William Daniel. *I Was There*. New York: Wittlesey House, 1950.

———. Diary 1941–1946. U.S. Library of Congress.

Lie, Trygve. *In the Cause of Peace*. New York: Macmillan, 1954.

Maier, Reinhold. *Ein Grundstein Wird Gelegt*. Tuebingen: Wunderlich, 1964.

Maisky, Ivan. *Memoirs of a Soviet Ambassador*. New York: Scribner's, 1968.

Millis, Walter, ed. *The Forrestal Diaries*. New York: Viking, 1951.

Morgenthau Diary: Germany, U.S. Congress, Senate Committee on the Judiciary, Subcommittee to Investigate the Administration of the Internal Security Act and Other Security Laws, 90th Cong., 1st sess., Nov. 1967.

Murphy, Robert. *Diplomat Among Warriors*. Garden City, N.Y.: Doubleday, 1964.

Paley, William S. *As It Happened: A Memoir*. Garden City, N.Y.: Doubleday, 1979.

Puender, Hermann. *Von Preussen Nach Europa*. Stuttgart: Deutsche Verlagsanstalt, 1968.

Ratchford, B. U. and W. D. Ross. *Berlin Reparations Assignment*. Chapel Hill, N.C.: University of North Carolina Press, 1947.

Roosevelt, Elliot. *As He Saw It*. New York: Duell, Sloan and Pearce, 1946.

Sherwood, Robert E. *Roosevelt and Hopkins: An Intimate History*. New York: Harper, 1948.

Smith, Walter Bedell. *My Three Years in Moscow*. Philadelphia: Lippincott, 1950.

Standley, William H. *Admiral Ambassador to Russia*. Chicago: Regnery, 1955.

Stettinius, Edward. *Roosevelt and the Russians: The Yalta conference*. Garden City, N.Y.: Doubleday, 1949.

Stimson, Henry L. *On Active Service in Peace and War*. New York: Harper, 1947.

Strang, William Lord. *Home and Abroad*. London: Andre Deutsch, 1956.

Talbott, Strobe, ed. *Khrushchev Remembers*. Boston: Little, Brown, 1970.

Truman, Harry S. *Memoirs*. Garden City, N.Y.: Doubleday, 1955–1956.

Vandenberg, Arthur H., Jr. *The Private Papers of Senator Vandenberg*. Boston: Houghton Mifflin, 1952.

Wallace, Henry Agard. *The Price of Vision: The Diary of Henry A. Wallace 1942–1946*, edited by John Morton Blum. Boston: Houghton Mifflin, 1973.

Wells, Herman B. *Being Lucky*. Bloomington, Ind.: Indiana University Press, 1980.

Zhukov, Georgii K. *Reminiscences and Reflections*. New York: Delacorte Press, 1971.

B. Documents

"American Relations with the Soviet Union." A report to the President by the Special Council to the President. Sept. 1946, Annex. In Krock, Arthur, *Memoirs*. New York: Funk & Wagnalls, 1968.

Berliner Schicksal 1945–1952. Amtliche Berichte und Dokumente. Berlin Senat.

Civil Affairs Division (OMGUS). *The Evolution of Bizonal Organizations*. March 1948.

Clay, Lucius D. Public Papers. Record Group 200. N.A.

Cornides, W., and H. Volle. *Um den Frieden mit Deutschland*. Vol. 6 of *Dokumente und Berichte des Europa Archivs*. Oberursel, 1948.

Degras, Jane. *Soviet Documents on Foreign Policy.* 3 vols. London: Oxford University Press, 1951–1953.

Die Deutsche Frage auf der Moskauer Konferenz der Aussenminister. Europa Archiv, Sonderheft 2.1947.

Federal Trade Commission. Report of the U.S. Committee to Review the Decartelization Program in Germany (Fergusson Report). April 15, 1949.

Dr. Geiler Akten. Wiesbaden Staatskanzlei. Der Hessische Ministerpräsident.

IARA Bericht 1949 uber Deutsche Auslandsvermogen. Bremen, 1950.

Interallied Reparations Agency. *Report of the Assembly.* Brussels, 1951.

JEIA (Joint Export Import Agency).
Instructions
Monthly Reports

Memorandum H. Hilldring to Asst. Sec. of War, November 7, 1945. ASW 370.8 Germany. Control Council. National Archives.

Ministère des Affaires Etrangères. *Documents français relatifs à l'Allemagne 1945–1947.*

Office of Military Government for Germany (US) Federal Records Center, Suitland, Maryland, OMGUS records, Record Group 260. USFET records, Record Group 338.

Reparationsleistungen der Sowjetischen Besatzungszone Deutschlands. Europa Archiv 4.

Rossmann Papers. *Bundes Archiv Koblenz.*

Schmidt, Hubert G. *Food and Agriculture Programs in West Germany.* U.S. High Commissioner for Germany, Office of the Executive Secretary, Historical Division, 1952.

———. *The Liberalization of West German Foreign Trade.* U.S. High Commissioner for Germany, Office of the Executive Secretary, Historical Division, 1952.

Smith, Jean Edward, ed. *The Papers of General Lucius D. Clay.* Bloomington, Ind.: Indiana University Press, 1974.

The Soviet Union and the Berlin Question. (Documents) The Ministry of Foreign Affairs of the U.S.S.R. Moscow, 1948.

Sowjetische Reparations Politik Seit 1945. Hannover: Sopade Denksshrift no. 29, 1950.

Statistisches Jahrbuch fur das Deutsche Reich. 1936 Statistisches Reichsamt, 1937.

U.N. Security Council. Official Records. Third Year. No. 113.

U.S. Congress
Congressional Record. 78th Congress. 2nd sess. May 8, 1944.

———. 79th Congress. 1st sess. March 13, 1945.

———. 79th Congress. 1st sess. April 10, 1945.

———. 79th Congress. 1st sess. May 17, 1945.

———. 79th Congress. 1st sess. November 27, 1945.

———. 79th Congress. 2nd sess. July 19, 1946.

———. 81st Congress. 1st sess. May 17, 1949.

House. Committee on Appropriations. Hearings on *First Deficiency Appropriations Bill 1947*. 80th Cong., 1st sess.

———. Committee on Appropriations. Hearings *on Military Establishment Appropriations Bill for 1947*. 79th Cong., 2nd sess.

———. Special Committee on Post-War Economic Policy and Planning. *Economic Reconstruction in Europe*. 8th Report (Serial 10936). 79th Cong., 1st sess. 1945.

———. Committee on Appropriations. Hearings on *First Deficiency Appropriations Bill 1948*. 80th Cong., 2nd sess.

Senate. *Accessibility of Strategic and Critical Materials in Time of War*. Report of Committee on American and Insular Affairs. Appendix 4, Report no. 1627. 83rd Cong., 2nd sess.

———. Committee on Appropriations. Hearings on *European Interim Aid and GARIOA*. 80th Cong., 1st sess.

———. Committee on Appropriations. Armed Services and Banking and Currency. Hearings on *Occupation Currency Transactions*. 80th Cong., 1st sess.

———. Committee on Banking and Currency. Hearings on *President Truman's Request to Increase Lending Authority of Export-Import Bank*. 79th Cong., 1st sess. July 1945.

———. Special Senate Committee Investigating the National Defense Program. Meader Report. Nov. 22, 1946.

———. Executive Hearings. Senate Foreign Relations Committee. April 1, 1947.

U.S. Department of Commerce, Bureau of the Census, Foreign Commerce and Navigation of the U.S. Foreign Trade Statistics 1946 and 1947.

U.S. Department of State

Bulletin 13, no. 323 (September 2, 1945).

Bulletin 13, no. 338 (December 16, 1945).

Bulletin 15, no. 376 (September 15, 1946).

Bulletin 16, no. 404 (March 30, 1947).

Bulletin 16, no. 405 (April 6, 1947).

Bulletin 16, no. 406 (April 18, 1947).

Bulletin 16, no. 407 (April 20, 1947).

Bulletin 16, no. 408 (April 27, 1947).

Bulletin 16, no. 410 (May 11, 1947).

Germany 1947–1949, The Story in Documents.

Foreign Relations of the United States. Diplomatic Papers.

1933. vol. 2. The British Commonwealth; Europe.

1935. The British Commonwealth; Europe.

1943. The Conferences at Cairo and Teheran.

1944. vol. 1. General.

1944. vol. 4. Europe.

1945. The Conferences at Malta and Yalta.

1945. vol. 2. General; Political and Economic Matters.

1945. vol. 3. European Advisory Commission; Austria; Germany.

1945. vol. 4. Europe.

1945. The Conference of Berlin (Potsdam). 2 vols.

1945. vol. 5. Europe.

1946. vol. 2. Council of Foreign Ministers.

1946. vol. 5. The British Commonwealth; Western and Central Europe.

1946. vol. 6. Eastern Europe; the Soviet Union.

1947. vol. 2. Council of Foreign Ministers; Germany and Austria.

1948. vol. 2. Germany; Austria Council of Foreign Ministers.

1949. vol. 3. Germany and Austria.

State Department Files. National Archives.

Record Group 43. Records of Council of Foreign Ministers.

Record Group 59. 740.00119 European War.

Record Group 59. Notter Files

Record Group 59. 740.00119 Control (Germany).

U.S Office of Strategic Services. National Archives.

Research and Analysis Report 2350. "Problems of German Reparations."

Research and Analysis Report 1899. "Russian War Damage and Possible Reparations Claims."

U.S. Strategic Bombing Survey. Rare Books Collection. Library of Congress.

"A Brief Study of the Effects of the Area Bombing on Berlin, Augsburg, Bochum and Leipzig."

"The Effects of Strategic Bombing on the German War Economy."

"The German Machine Tool Industry."

U.S.S.R. "Documents: The Crimea and Potsdam Conferences of the Leaders of the Three Great Powers." *International Affairs, nos. 6–10.* Moscow: June-October 1965.

von Oppen, B. R., ed. *Documents on Germany under Occupation.* New York: Oxford University Press, 1955.

C. Speeches

Dulles, John Foster. "Europe Must Federate or Perish." *Vital Speeches of the Day.* January 17, 1947.

Faingar, Isakhar Moiseevich. "Germaniia i Reparatsii" [Germany and Reparations]. April 24, 1947. Moscow: Ministry of Higher Education, 1947.

Molotov, V. M. *Speeches and Statements at the Moscow Session of the Council of Foreign Ministers 1947.* London: Soviet News, 1947.

————. *Problems of Foreign Policy*. Moscow: Foreign Languages Publishing House, 1949.

Stalin, J. Election Speech of February 9, 1946. *The New York Times*. February 10, 1946.

D. Newspapers, Magazines, Public Opinion Polls
Cantril Hadley and Mildred Strunk, *Public Opinion 1935–1945*.

Current Digest of Soviet Press 3, no. 20.

Business Week

Economist (London)

Frankfurter Rundschau

Life

New York Herald Tribune

The New York Times

Newsweek

Tagesspiegel (Berlin)

Time

U.S. News and World Report

Wall Street Journal

Washington Post

E. Unpublished Papers
Joseph Dodge Papers. Detroit Public Library, Detroit, Mich.

John F. Dulles Papers. Princeton University, Princeton, N.J.

Dwight D. Eisenhower Papers, Eisenhower Library, Abilene, Kansas.

William Leahy Diary, Library of Congress, Washington, D.C.

Isador Lubin Papers, Roosevelt Library, Hyde Park, New York.

J. Anthony Panuch Papers, Truman Library, Independence, Mo.

Richard Scandrett Papers, Cornell University, Ithaca, N.Y.

Henry Stimson Diary, Yale University, New Haven, Conn.

Harry S Truman Papers, Truman Library, Independence, Mo.

Note: I also would like to express my appreciation to Don Humphrey, George R. Jacobs and Charles Kindleberger for their permission to do research in papers in their private possession.

F. Interviews and Correspondence
Margaret Allen

George Ball

Colonel John L. Bates

Ambassador Jacob Beam

A. Jackson Bennett

Franz Bierman

Ambassador Charles Bohlen

Robert Bowie

James Boyd

Lieutenant General A. J. Boyle

Major General Hugh Casey

Major General Frank Clay

General Lucius D. Clay

Mrs. Lucius D. Clay

General Lucius D. Clay, Jr.

Dr. Lucius D. Clay, III

Benjamin Cohen

Edloe Donnan

Eleanor Lansing Dulles

David Ginsburg

Bill Graever

Richard Hallock

Ambassador W. Averell Harriman

John Hazard

Russell Hill

Brigadier General Frank Howley

Donald Humphrey

George R. Jacobs

Joseph Keenan

Ambassador George Kennan

Colonel Thomas Lancer

John J. McCloy

Donald McLean

Oliver Margolin

Edward Mason

Ben Narvid

James O'Donnell

Major General Ralph M. Osborne

Ambassador James Riddleberger

Seymour Rubin

Charles Saltzman

Edna Shelley (Mrs. R. S. Gates)

Joe Slater

Brigadier General James F. Stratton

John McHugh Stuart, Jr.

James Sundquist

Sylvia Tint (Mrs. Charles O'Connor)

Lieutenant General Arthur Trudeau

Major General Robert Walsh

General Alfred C. Wedemeyer

Leo Werts

Louis Wiesner

Lawrence Wilkinson

G. *Interviews with General Lucius D. Clay by Others*
Dr. Richard D. Challener, Princeton University, Princeton, N.J.

Dr. Harold Kanarek, Historical Division of the Office of the Chief of Engineers, Washington, D.C.

Dr. Richard McKinzie, Truman Library, Independence, Mo.

Mark Nackman, Continental Can Corporation, New York.

Colonel R. Joe Rogers, U.S. Army, Military History Institute, Carlyle Barracks, Pennsylvania.

Dr. Jean E. Smith, University of Toronto, Toronto, Canada.

II. Secondary Sources

Abeken, Gerhard. *Geld und Bankwesen in Der Soviet Besatzungszone Seit Der Waehrungs Reform*. Bonn: Bundes Ministerium Für Gesamtdeutsche Fragen, 1951.

Adler, Hans A. "The Postwar Reorganization." *Quarterly Journal of Economics 63*, no. 3 (August 1949).

Alexandrov, Vladimir. "The Dismantling of German Industry." In *Soviet Economic Policy in Post-War Germany*, edited by Robert Slusser. New York: Research Program on the U.S.S.R., 1953.

Allen, T. Henry. *The Rhineland Occupation*. Indianapolis: Bobbs-Merrill, 1927.

Almond, Gabriel. *The Struggle for Democracy in Germany*. Chapel Hill, N.C.: University of North Carolina Press, 1949.

Alsop, Joseph and Stewart. "Why We Changed Our Policy in Germany." *Saturday Evening Post*, December 7, 1946.

Alt, Franz, *Der Prozess Der Ersten Regierungs Bildung Unter Konrad Adenauer*. Eichholz: Politische Akademie, 1970.

Armstrong, Ann. *Unconditional Surrender*. New Brunswick, N.J.: Rutgers University Press, 1961.

Backer, John H. *Priming the German Economy: American Occupational Policies 1945–1948.* Durham, N.C.: Duke University Press, 1971.

———. *The Decision to Divide Germany, American Foreign Policy in Transition.* Durham, N.C.: Duke University Press, 1978.

Bagratuni, A. "Reparations From Germany's Current Production." *New Times,* April 18, 1947.

Bailey, Thomas A. *The Man in the Street: The Impact of American Public Opinion on Foreign Policy.* Gloucester, Mass.: Smith, 1964.

———. *Probing America's Past: A Critical Examination of Major Myths and Misconceptions.* Lexington, Mass.: Heath, 1973.

———. *A Diplomatic History of the American People.* Third Edition. New York: Crofts, 1946.

Balabkins, Nicholas. *Germany Under Direct Controls: Economic Aspects of the Industrial Disarmament 1945–1948.* New Brunswick, N.J.: Rutgers University Press, 1964.

Balfour, Michael, and John Mair. *Four Power Control in Germany and Austria, 1945–1946.* London: Royal Institute of International Affairs, 1956.

Bemis, Samuel Flagg. *A Diplomatic History of the United States.* New York: Holt, Rinehart, 1964.

Bennett, Jack. "The German Currency Reform." *Annals of the American Academy of Political and Social Science* 267 (January 1950).

Berkes, Ross N. "Germany: Test Tube of Peace." *American Scholar,* 1946–47.

Berry, Lelah. "An Army Wife Lives Very Soft—in Germany." *Saturday Evening Post,* February 15, 1947.

Bess, Demaree. "American Viceroy in Germany." *Saturday Evening Post,* May 3 and 10, 1947.

———. "Will We Be Pushed Out of Berlin?" *Saturday Evening Post,* July 31, 1948.

Bidault, Georges. "Agreement on Germany: Key to World Peace." *Foreign Affairs,* Vol. 24, No. 4, July 1946.

Bishop, Donald. *The Roosevelt-Litvinov Agreements.* Syracuse, N.Y.: Syracuse University Press, 1965.

Blum, John Morton. *Roosevelt and Morgenthau.* Boston: Houghton Mifflin, 1972.

Bolton, Seymour. "Military Government and the German Political Parties." *Annals of the American Academy of Political and Social Science* 267 (January 1950).

Boorsten, Dan. *The Image.* New York: Atheneum, 1971.

Boyle, Andrea. *The Fourth Man: A Climate of Treason.* New York: Dial, 1979.

Bungenstab, Karl Ernst. *Umerziehung Zur Demokratie? Re-Education Politik im Bildungswesen Der U.S.-Zone 1945–49.* Düsseldorf: Bertelsmann Universitätsverlag, 1970.

Burks, R. V. "Eastern Europe." In *Communism and Revolution,* edited by Cyril E. Black and Thomas P. Thornton. Princeton, N.J.: Princeton University Press, 1964.

Carman, Harry J., and Harold C. Syrett. *A History of the American People.* New York: Knopf, 1952.

Carr, Albert Z. *Truman, Stalin and Peace.* Garden City, N.Y.: Doubleday, 1950.

Caute, David. *Communism and the French Intellectuals, 1914–1960.* New York: Macmillan, 1964.

Cecil, Robert. "Potsdam and Its Legends." *International Affairs* (July 1970).

Chamberlin, William H. *America's Second Crusade.* Chicago: Regnery, 1950.

Chambers, S. P. "Post-War German Finances." *International Affairs* 25, no. 3 (July 1948).

Clark, Delbert. *Again the Goose Step.* Indianapolis: Bobbs-Merrill, 1949.

———. "He Knows Germans." *The New York Times,* November 17, 1946.

Clay, Lucius D. *Germany and the Fight For Freedom.* Cambridge, Mass.: Harvard University Press, 1950.

Clemens, Diana Shaver. *Yalta.* New York: Oxford University Press, 1970.

Coles, Harry, and Albert Weinberg. *Civil Affairs: Soldiers Become Governors.* Washington: Office of the Chief of Military History, 1964.

Collier, Richard. *Bridge Across the Sky.* New York: McGraw-Hill, 1978.

Council on Foreign Relations. *The United States in World Affairs 1947/48: An Account of American Foreign Relations.* New York: Harper, 1948.

Croan, Melvin, and Carl J. Friedrich. "The East German Regime and Soviet Policy in Germany." *The Journal of Politics,* Vol. 20, No. 1, February 1958.

Curry, George. *James F. Byrnes,* vol. 14, pt. 1, of *The American Secretaries of State and Their Diplomacy.* New York: Cooper Square, 1965.

Dahl, Robert. *Congressional Foreign Policy.* New York: Harcourt, 1950.

Dallek, Robert. *Franklin D. Roosevelt and American Foreign Policy 1932–1945.* New York: Oxford University Press, 1979.

Davison, Walter Phillips. *The Berlin Blockade. A Study in Cold War Politics.* Princeton, N.J.: Princeton University, 1958.

Dennett, Raymond, and Joseph E. Johnson, eds. *Negotiating with the Russians.* Boston: World Peace Foundation, 1951.

Detzer, Karl. "Clay of Berlin." *The Reader's Digest,* October 1948.

Deuer, Wallace R. "The Army in Power." *Survey,* February 1950.

Deuerlein, Ernst. *Die Einheit Deutschlands, 1941–49.* Frankfurt: Metzner, 1957.

Divine, Robert A. *Roosevelt and World War II.* Baltimore, Md.: Johns Hopkins University Press, 1969.

Dobb, Maurice. *Soviet Economic Development Since 1917.* New York: International Publishers, 1948.

Donovan, Frank. *Bridge in the Sky.* New York: McKay, 1968.

Dorn, Walter L. *Inspektionsreisen in Der U.S. Zone.* Stuttgart: Deutsche Verlagsanstalt, 1975.

Dulles, Eleanor. "The Evolution of Reparation Ideas." In *Facts and Factors in Economic History.* New York: Russell, 1967.

Edinger, Lewis J. *Kurt Schumacher.* Stanford, Cal.: Stanford University Press, 1965.

————. "Post-Totalitarian Leadership: Elites in the German Federal Republic." *The American Political Science Review* LIV 1960.

Elliott, W. Y. "The Control of Foreign Policy in the United States." *The Political Quarterly*, vol. XX, no. 4. October–December 1949.

Farnsworth, C. Beatrice. *William Bullitt and the Soviet Union.* Bloomington: Indiana University Press, 1967.

Feis, Herbert. *Between War and Peace: The Potsdam Conference.* Princeton, N.J.: Princeton University Press, 1960.

————. *Churchill, Roosevelt, Stalin: The War They Waged and the Peace They Sought.* Princeton, N.J.: Princeton University Press, 1957.

————. *The Diplomacy of the Dollar: First Era, 1919–1932.* Hamden, Conn.: Archon, 1965.

————. *From Trust to Terror: The Onset of the Cold War, 1945–1950.* New York: Norton, 1970.

Ferrell, Robert H. *George Marshall*, vol. 15 of *The American Secretaries of State and Their Diplomacy.* New York: Cooper Square, 1966.

Festinger, Leon. *A Theory of Cognitive Dissonance.* Stanford, Cal.: Stanford University Press, 1957.

Fitzgibbon, Constantine. *Denazification.* London: Joseph, 1969.

Fredericksen, Oliver. *American Military Government of Germany 1945–53.* Darmstadt: HICOG, 1953.

Friedman, William. *The Allied Military Government of Germany.* London: Stevens, 1947.

Friedrich, Carl J. *American Experiences in Military Government in World War II.* New York: Rinehart, 1948.

Gaddis, John Lewis. *The United States and the Origins of the Cold War, 1941–1947.* New York: Columbia University Press, 1972.

Galbraith, John Kenneth. "Is There A German Policy?" *Fortune*, January 1947.

Gardner, Lloyd C. *Architects of Illusion: Men and Ideas in American Foreign Policy, 1941–1949.* Chicago: Quadrangle, 1970.

Gervasi, Frank. "Watchdog in the White House." *Colliers*, October 9, 1948.

Gillen, J. F. J. *Deconcentration and Decartelization in West Germany 1945–1953.* HICOG: Historical Division, 1953.

————. *State and Local Governments in West Germany 1945–1953.* HICOG: Historical Division, 1953.

Gimbel, John. *The American Occupation of Germany: Politics and the Military, 1945–1949.* Stanford, Cal.: Stanford University Press, 1968.

————. *The Origins of the Marshall Plan.* Stanford, Cal.: Stanford University Press, 1976.

————. "American Military Government and the Education of a New German Leadership." *Political Science Quarterly*, vol. LXXXIII, no. 2. June 1968.

————. "U.S. Post-War German Policy." *Political Science Quarterly* 87, no. 2 (June 1972).

Ginsburg, David. *The Future of German Reparations.* Washington, D.C.: National Planning Association, February 18, 1947.

Golay, John Ford. *The Founding of the Federal Republic of Germany.* Chicago: University of Chicago Press, 1958.

Gottlieb, Manuel. "Failure of Quadripartite Monetary Reform, 1945–47." *Finanzarchiv* 17 (1957).

———. "The German Economic Potential." *Social Research* 17 (March 1950).

———. *The German Peace Settlement and the Berlin Crisis.* New York: Paine-Whitman, 1960.

———. "The Reparations Problem Again." *Canadian Journal of Economic and Political Science* 16 (February 1950).

Gräfrath, Bernard. *Zur Geschichte der Reparationen.* Ost-Berlin: Deutscher Zentralverlag, 1954.

Graupner, R. *Inter-Alliierte Reparations Abkommen uber die Liquidation des Deutschen Auslandsvermogens.* Bremen: Studiengesellschaft fur Privatrechtliche Auslandsinteressen, 1950.

Greer, Thomas H. *What Roosevelt Thought: The Social and Political Ideas of Franklin D. Roosevelt.* East Lansing, Mich.: Michigan State University Press, 1958.

Griffith, William E. "Denazification in the United States Zone of Germany." *The Annals* (January 1950).

———. "The Denazification Program in the U.S. Zone of Germany." Doctoral dissertation, Harvard University, 1950.

Grosser, Alfred. *The Colossus Again: West Germany From Defeat to Rearmament.* New York: Praeger, 1955.

Guradze, Heinz. "The Laenderrat: Landmark of German Reconstruction." *Western Political Quarterly* (June 1950).

Hacker, Jens. *Sovietunion und DDR zum Potsdamer Abkommen.* Köln: Wissenschaft und Politik, 1968.

Härtel, Lia. *Der Länderrat des Amerikanischen Besatzungsgebietes.* Stuttgart: Kohlhammer, 1951.

Hale, William Harlan. "General Clay—On His Own." New York: *Harpers*, December 1948.

Halperin, Morton H., and Arnold Kanter, eds. *Readings in American Foreign Policy: A Bureaucratic Perspective.* Boston: Little, Brown, 1973.

Hammond, Paul V. "Directives for the Occupation of Germany: The Washington Controversy." In *American Civil-Military Decisions*, edited by Harold Stein. University, Ala.: University of Alabama Press, 1963.

Harmssen, G. W. *Am Abend der Demontage.* Bremen: F. Truejen Verlag, 1951.

———. *Reparationen, Sozialprodukt, Lebensstandard: Versuch einer Wirtschaftsbilanz.* Bremen: F. Truejen, 1947.

Hayter, William. *The Diplomacy of the Great Powers.* London: Baylis, 1960.

Herring, George C., Jr. "Lend Lease to Russia and the Origins of the Cold War." *Journal of American History* 56, no. 1 (June 1969).

Herz, John H. "The Fiasco of Denazification in Germany." *Political Science Quarterly*, vol. LXIII (December 1948).

Herz, Martin. *Beginnings of the Cold War*. Bloomington: Indiana University Press, 1966.

Hill, Russell. *The Struggle for Germany*. New York: Harper, 1947.

Hofstadter, Richard. *The Paranoid Style in American Politics*. New York: Knopf, 1965.

Holborn, Hajo. *A History of Modern Germany*. 3 vols. New York: Knopf, 1959.

Hughes, Richard D. "Soviet Foreign Policy and Germany, 1945–1948." Doctoral dissertation, Claremont College Graduate School, Berkeley, Cal. 1964.

Jervis, Robert. *Perception and Misperception in International Politics*. Princeton, N.J.: Princeton University Press, 1976.

Joesten, Joachim. *Germany—What Now?* Chicago: Ziff-Davis, 1948.

Johnson, Alvin. "Denazification." *Social Research*, vol. 14 (1947).

Jonas, Manfred. *Isolationism in America, 1935–1941*. Ithaca, N.Y.: Cornell University Press, 1966.

Jones, Joseph. *The Fifteen Weeks*. New York: Viking, 1955.

Kahn, E. J., Jr. "Soldier in Mufti." *The New Yorker*, January 13, 1951.

Kecskemeti, Paul. *Strategic Surrender: The Politics of Victory and Defeat*. New York: Atheneum, 1964.

Kennan, George F. "A Rebuttal and an Apology." In *Containment and the Cold War: American Foreign Policy Since 1945*, edited by Thomas G. Paterson. Reading, Mass.: Addison-Wesley, 1973.

———. *Russia and the West under Lenin and Stalin*. Boston: Little, Brown, 1960.

———. *Russia Leaves the War*. New York: Atheneum, 1967.

Kimball, Warren F. *Swords or Ploughshares: The Morgenthau Plan for Defeated Nazi Germany 1943–1946*. Philadelphia: Lippincott, 1976.

Klein, Burton H. *Germany's Economic Preparations for War*. Cambridge, Mass.: Harvard University Press, 1959.

Knappstein, Karl Heinrich. "Die Versaeumte Revolution." *Die Wandlung*, Jahrgang II, Heft 8, November 1947.

Kogon, Eugen. "Das Recht Auf Politischen Irrtum." *Frankfurter Hefte*. Heft 7, July 1947.

Kolko, Gabriel. *The Politics of War: The World and United States Foreign Policy, 1943–1945*. New York: Vintage, 1968.

Krieger, Leonard. "The Inter-Regnum in Germany: March–August 1945." *Political Science Quarterly*, vol. LXIV, no. 4 (December 1949).

Kuklick, Bruce. *American Policy and the Division of Germany: The Clash with Russia over Reparations*. Ithaca, N.Y.: Cornell University Press, 1972.

Lefever, Ernest. *Moralism and U.S. Foreign Policy*. Washington, D.C.: Brookings Institute, 1973.

Levering, Ralph S. *American Opinion and the Russian Alliance 1939–1945*. Chapel Hill, N.C.: University of North Carolina Press, 1976.

Lippmann, Walter. *The Cold War: A Study in U.S. Foreign Policy*. New York: Harper, 1947.

———. "A Defective Policy." In *Containment and the Cold War: American Foreign Policy Since 1945*, edited by Thomas G. Paterson. Reading, Mass.: Addison-Wesley, 1973.

———. *Public Opinion*. New York: Free Press, 1965.

———. *Public Opinion and Foreign Policy in the United States: Lectures*. London: Allen and Unwin, 1952.

———. *U.S. Foreign Policy: Shield of the Republic*. New York: Johnson Reprint, 1971.

Litchfield, E. H. *Governing Postwar Germany*. Ithaca: Cornell University Press, 1948.

Lochner, Louis. *Herbert Hoover and Germany*. New York: Macmillan, 1961.

———. "The Idiocy of Our De-Nazification Policy." *The Reader's Digest* (June 1948).

Loewenfeld, Philipp. "The Bavarian Scandal." *The New Republic*, June 18, 1945.

Lubell, Samuel. "The Untold Tragedy of Potsdam." *Saturday Evening Post*, December 8, 1945.

Lundestad, Geir. *The American Non-Policy Towards Eastern Europe 1943–1947*. Oslo: Universitetsforlaget, 1978.

Lutz, F. A. "The German Currency Reform and the Revival of the German Economy." *Economica*, vol. XVI, no. 62, May 1949.

McCloy, John H. *Bericht Uber Deutschland*. Bonn: HICOG, 1951.

Macridis, Roy C. "French Foreign Policy." In *Foreign Policy in World Politics*, edited by Roy C. Macridis. Englewood Cliffs, N.J.: Prentice-Hall, 1958.

Maier, Charles S. *The Origins of the Cold War and Contemporary Europe*. New York: Watts, 1978.

Martin, James Stewart. *All Honorable Men*. Boston: Little, Brown, 1950.

———. "Germany's Cartels Are At It Again." *New Republic*, vol. 117, October 6, 1947.

Mason, E. S. "Reflections on the Moscow Conference." *International Organization* 1, no. 2 (May 1947).

Mayer, Arthur L. "Winter of Discontent." *The New Republic*, March 10, 1947.

Merkl, Peter H. *The Origins of the West German Republic*. New York: Oxford University Press, 1963.

Meurer, Hubert. "U.S. Military Government in Germany: Policy and Functioning in Trade and Commerce." Manuscript, OCMH, U.S. Military Government, European Command. Karlsruhe, Germany, 1950.

Middleton, Drew. "Uncommon Clay." *The New York Times*, July 15, 1945.

———. *The Struggle for Germany*. Indianapolis: Bobbs-Merrill, 1949.

Milekovsky, A. G., ed. *Meshdunarodnoe Otnosheniya posle Vtoroi Mirovoi Voini* [International Relations After the Second World War]. Vol. 1 (1945–1949). Moscow, 1962.

Mills, Judson, E. Aronson, and Hal Tobinson. "Selectivity in Exposure to Information." *Journal of Abnormal and Social Psychology* 54 (1959).

Montgomery, John D. *Forced To Be Free. The Artificial Revolution in Germany and Japan.* Chicago: University of Chicago Press, 1957.

Morgenthau, Hans. "John Foster Dulles." In *An Uncertain Tradition: American Secretaries of State in the Twentieth Century,* edited by N. A. Graebner. New York: McGraw-Hill, 1961.

Morgenthau, Henry. *Germany Is Our Problem.* New York: Harper, 1945.

―――. "Our Policy Toward Germany." *New York Post,* November 26 and 28, 1947.

Mosely, Philip E. "Dismemberment of Germany." *Foreign Affairs* 28, no. 3 (April 1950).

―――. "The Occupation of Germany: New Light on How the Zones Were Drawn." *Foreign Affairs* 28, no. 4 (July 1950).

―――. "Soviet-American Relations since the War." *Annals of the American Academy of Political and Social Science* (May 1949).

―――. "The Treaty with Austria." *International Organization* 4, no. 2 (May 1950).

Moskowitz, Moses. "The Political Re-Education of the Germans: The Emergence of Parties and Politics in Württemberg-Baden (May 45–June 46). *Political Science Quarterly,* vol. LXI, no. 4.

Murphy, Charles J. V. "The Berlin Airlift." *Fortune* (November 1948).

Nettl, J. Peter. *The Eastern Zone and Soviet Policy in Germany, 1945–1950.* London: Oxford University Press, 1951.

―――. "German Reparations in the Soviet Empire." *Foreign Affairs* 29, no. 2 (January 1951).

Niethammer, Lutz. *Entnazifizierung in Bayern.* Frankfurt am Main: S. Fischer, 1972.

Notter, Harley. *Postwar Foreign Policy Preparation: 1939–1945.* Washington, D.C.: U.S. Government Printing Office, 1949.

O'Connor, Raymond C. *Diplomacy for Victory: Franklin Delano Roosevelt and Unconditional Surrender.* New York: Norton, 1971.

Opie, Redvers, et al. *The Search for Peace Settlements.* Washington, D.C.: Brookings Institute, 1951.

Osgood, Robert Endicott. *Ideals and Self-Interest in America's Foreign Relations.* Chicago: University of Chicago Press, 1953.

Padover, Saul. *Experiment in Germany.* New York: Duell, Sloan and Pearce, 1946.

Paterson, Thomas G. "The Abortive American Loan to Russia and the Origins of the Cold War, 1943–1946." *Journal of American History* 56, no. 1 (June 1969).

―――. *Soviet-American Confrontation: Postwar Reconstruction and the Origins of the Cold War.* Baltimore, Md.: Johns Hopkins University Press, 1973.

―――, ed. *Cold War Critics.* Chicago: Quadrangle, 1971.

―――. *Containment and the Cold War: American Foreign Policy Since 1945.* Reading, Mass.: Addison-Wesley, 1973.

Penrose, E. F. *Economic Planning for the Peace.* Princeton, N.J.: Princeton University Press, 1953.

Peterson, Edward N. *The American Occupation of Germany.* Detroit: Wayne State University Press, 1977.

Plischke, Elmer. "Denazification Law and Procedure." *The American Journal of International Law* (October 1947).

———. "Denazifying the Reich." *Review of Politics* (April 1947).

Pratt, Julius W. *A History of United States Foreign Policy.* Englewood Cliffs, N.J.: Prentice-Hall, 1972.

Price, Harry Bayard. *The Marshall Plan and Its Meaning.* Ithaca, N.Y.: Cornell University Press, 1955.

Range, Willard. *Franklin D. Roosevelt's World Order.* Athens, Ga.: University of Georgia Press, 1959.

Rheinstein, Max. "Renazifying Germany." *University of Chicago Magazine* (April 1947).

Rosenau, James N. *Public Opinion and Foreign Policy.* New York: Random House, 1961.

Rostow, Eugene V. "The Partition of Germany and the Unity of Europe." *Virginia Quarterly Review* 23, no. 1 (Winter 1947).

Rudolph, Vladimir. "The Administrative Organization of Soviet Control." In *Soviet Economic Policy in Post-War Germany*, edited by Robert Slusser. New York: Research Program on the U.S.S.R., 1953.

Ruland, Bernd. *Geld Wie Heu Und Nichts Zu Fressen.* Bayreuth: Hestia, 1968.

Salomon, Ernst Von. *Fragebogen.* Garden City, N.Y.: Doubleday, 1955.

Schaffer, Gordon. *Russian Zone.* London: Allen and Unwin, 1947.

Scharf, Claus, and Hans-Joergen Schroeder. *Die Deutschland Politik Gross Britanniens und Die Britische Zone 1945–1949.* Wiesbaden: Franz Steiner, 1979.

Schlange-Schöningen, Hans. *Im Schatten Des Hungers.* Hamburg: P. Parey, 1955.

Schmid, Richard. "Denazification." *American Perspective*, vol. II, no. 5 (October 1948).

Schmitt, Hans A. *U.S. Occupation in Europe After World War II.* Lawrence: Regents Press of Kansas, 1978.

Schoenbrun, David. "The French and the Ruhr." *The New Republic*, August 4, 1947.

Schrenck-Notzing, Caspar von. *Charakterwäsche.* Stuttgart: Seewald, 1965.

Schwarz, Hans Peter. *Vom Reich zur Bundesrepublik.* Neuwied: Luchter Hand, 1966.

Sharp, Toni, *The Wartime Alliance and the Zonal Division of Germany.* Oxford: Clarendon Press, 1975.

Shulman, Marshal D. *Stalin's Foreign Policy Reappraised.* New York: Atheneum, 1969.

Smith, Jean E. *The Defense of Berlin.* Baltimore, Md.: Johns Hopkins University Press, 1963.

———, ed. *The Papers of General Lucius D. Clay: Germany 1945–1949.* Bloomington, Ind.: Indiana University Press, 1975.

———. "Selection of a Proconsul for Germany: The Appointment of General Lucius D. Clay, 1945." *Military Affairs*, vol. 40 (October 1976).

Snell, John L. *The War-Time Origins of the East-West Dilemma over Germany.* New Orleans: Hauser 1959.

Stettinius, Edward R. *Roosevelt and the Russians.* New York: Macmillan, 1949.

Stolper, Gustav. *The German Economy, 1870–1940.* New York: Reynal, 1940.

———. *German Realities.* New York: Reynal, 1948.

Stolper, Toni. *Ein Leben in Brennpunkten Unserer Zeit.* Tuebingen: Wunderlich, 1950.

Strauss, Harold. *The Division and Dismemberment of Germany from the Casablanca Conference to the Establishment of the East German Republic.* These, Ambilly, 1952.

Sylvester, Harold J. "American Public Reaction to Communist Expansion From Yalta to NATO." Doctoral dissertation, University of Kansas, 1970.

Taylor, Graham T. "The Rise and Fall of Antitrust in Occupied Germany." *Prologue* (Spring 1979).

Taylor, Telford. *Sword and Swastika.* New York: Simon & Schuster, 1952.

Toynbee, Arnold Joseph, and Veronica M. Toynbee, eds. *The Realignment of Europe.* 2 vols. London: Oxford University Press, 1962.

Ulam, Adam B. *Expansion and Coexistence: The History of Soviet Foreign Policy, 1917–1967.* New York: Praeger, 1968.

Varga, E. "Vosmeshchenije ushcherba gitlerovskoi germaniyei i yeyo soobshchnikami" [Reparations by Hitler's Germany and Its Accomplices]. *Voina i Rabochi Klass,* no. 10 (15 October 1943).

Voznesensky, Nikolai A. *The Economy of the USSR during World War II.* Washington, D.C.: Public Affairs Press, 1948.

Wallich, Henry. *Mainsprings of the German Revival.* New Haven: Yale University Press, 1955.

Warburg, James P. *Germany: Bridge or Battleground?* New York: Harcourt, 1947.

———. *Germany Key to Peace.* Cambridge: Harvard University Press, 1953.

Wegener, Hertha. "Economic Relations between Soviet Russia and Eastern Germany." Master's thesis, Columbia University, 1951.

Weir, Sir Cecil. "Economic Developments in Western Germany." *International Affairs,* vol. 25, no 3 (July 1949).

Welles, Sumner. *Seven Decisions That Shaped History.* New York: Harper, 1951.

———. *The Time for Decision.* New York: Harper, 1944.

———. *Where Are We Heading?* New York: Harper, 1946.

Wiesner, Louis. "Organized Labor in Post-War Germany." Manuscript N.A.

Williams, Benjamin H. *The Economic Foreign Policy of the United States.* New York: Fertig, 1967.

Williams, William Appleman. *The Tragedy of American Diplomacy.* New York: Dell, 1972.

Willis, F. Roy. *The French in Germany, 1945–1949.* Stanford, Cal.: Stanford University Press, 1962.

Wolfers, Arnold. "United States Policy Toward Germany." Memorandum Number Twenty. Yale Institute of International Studies. New Haven, February 21, 1947.

Wolfson, Irving. "The AMG Mess in Germany." *New Republic*, March 4, 1946.

Yergin, Daniel. *Shattered Peace: The Origins of the Cold War and the National Security State*. Boston: Houghton Mifflin, 1977.

Yershov, Vassily. "Confiscation and Plunder by the Army of Occupation." In *Soviet Economic Policy in Post-War Germany*, edited by Robert Slusser. New York: Research Program on the U.S.S.R., 1953.

Young, Roland. *Congressional Politics in the Second World War*. New York: Columbia University Press, 1956.

Ziemke, Earl. *The U.S. Army in the Occupation of Germany*. Washington, D.C.: Office of Military History, 1975.

Zink, Harold. *American Military Government in Germany*. New York: Macmillan, 1947.

———. *The United States in Germany 1944–1955*. New York: Van Nostrand, 1957.

———. "The American Denazification Program in Germany." *Journal of Central European Affairs*, vol. VI, no. 3, (October 1946).

Index

Aachen, 9, 61
Abs, Herman, 271
Acheson, Dean, 38, 124, 132, 142, 267, 271, 272, 278
Adcock, Clarence L., 28, 80
Adenauer, Konrad, 263, 271, 274
Agarts, Victor, 186
Allen, Margaret, 117, 136, 182, 185, 237, 281
Allied Control Authority (ACA)
  composition, 13, 26; activation, 22–27 *passim;* and reparations, 65, 68 (*see also* Level of Industry Committee); and decartelization, 69, 70; and German foreign trade, 39, 84; tentative agenda, 76, 77; and French policies, 88, 89, 188; acts on German external assets, 108; decides steel production, 96–98 *passim;* prepares for Moscow CFM conference, 169, 170; McNarney at, 124; lack of progress, 109, 181; and currency reform, 162; denazification, 196; and German unification, 201, 285; break-up, 222–25 *passim;* 233
Alphand, Hervé, 176
Angell, Walter, 94
Atlee, Clement, 27

Baillie, Hugo, 287
Bennett, Jack, 200, 234
Berlin Airlift. *See* Blockade of Berlin
Bernstein, Bernard, 11
Bernstorff Albrecht, Graf von, 157
Bevin, Ernest, 27, 40, 183, 199, 203, 272
Bidault, Georges, 111, 189, 193, 220, 226
Bizonia
  Bipartite Board established, 148; and Länderrat, 149; supported by Hoover, 159; problems of merger, 166–68 *passim;* acceleration of merger, 186–88 *passim;* transitional administration established, 201; reorganization, 208, 209; and Clay, 100, 124, 129, 147–49 *passim*, 183, 195

Black market, 112–15, 140, 141, 160, 166, 255 (*see also* Inflation)
Blockade of Berlin
  stoppage of military traffic, 227–30 *passim;* triggered by currency reform, 233; total blockade declared, 235; Clay proposes convoy, 235–42 *passim;* and Truman, 240–42; Moscow negotiations, 243–45; before Security Council, 246, 249; and performance of airlift, 246; and split of Berlin, 247; Jessup-Malik negotiations, 272, 276, 277
Blücher, Franz, 271
Bohlen, Charles F., 172, 182, 285
Bowie, Robert
  personal assistant to Clay, 7, 8; comments on Clay, 44, 46, 56, 106; and denazification policy, 53, 116; member of Denazification Policy Board, 117; negotiates law of liberation, 118; mentioned, 78
Boyd, James, 7
Boyle, Jack, 107
Bradley, Omar, 4, 225, 228, 239, 241, 267, 272, 275, 276
Brandt, Willy, 236
Bullit, William C., 33
Bullock, Roy, 84
Bülow, Bernhard von, 157
Byrnes, James
  endorses selection of Clay, 5; assists in finding financial advisor, 7; at Potsdam, 39; in Stuttgart, 40, 133–36 *passim;* with Clay in Office of War Production, 51; quoted, 3; and impasse at ACA, 109; suggests cautious policy toward France, 111; intervenes at Clay's resignation, 128; proposes zonal merger, 130; pacifies Clay, 133; and Bevin-Byrnes agreement, 151, 199; resignation, 171; mentioned, 147, 149, 151, 182, 207, 248, 255, 256

Caffery, Jefferson, 111, 194, 246

Casey, Hugh (Pat)
refuses to swap position with Clay,
7; Clay's best man, 47; quoted,
46, 49; at Frank Clay's wedding,
104
Churchill, Winston, 21, 23, 27, 35, 36
CINCEUR (Commander in Chief, Europe), 166
Civil Affairs Division (War Department), 8
Clark, Delbert, 57, 87, 136, 165, 194
Clay, Alexander Stevens (father of Lucius D. Clay), 44, 45
Clay, Frank (son of Lucius D. Clay),
104
Clay, Lucius D.
Appointed Deputy Military Governor: 4, 5, 52; and Military Governor, 137, 165
Background and Childhood: 44, 45,
46
Character and Attributes: 3, 4, 6,
21, 22, 31–59 *passim*, 76, 78, 103–
11 *passim*, 121, 136, 157, 158, 164,
165, 170, 182, 184, 190, 207, 210,
215, 251, 252, 282, 283, 287–293
passim
Early Career: 3, 5, 6, 46–51, 76,
288
Marriage: 47
Personal relations: with Sokolovsky,
87, 88, 128, 129; and retirement,
124, 133, 165, 190, 194, 250, 267,
272; and press, 15, 16, 61, 64, 68,
118, 121, 195, 285; and Congress,
49, 50, 76, 77, 83, 155, 156, 160,
162, 175, 216, 217, 281, 282; and
SHAEF, 8, 9, 10, 13, 14, 15, 17,
21; at conference of Supreme
Commanders, 22, 23; with Zhukov (Berlin access), 23, 24; and
economic unification of Germany,
76, 77, 83, 89, 99, 100, 109, 123,
131, 150, 151, 160, 166, 181, 202,
203, 285; and France (*see* French
obstructionism); and Kennan,
George, 91, 148; at State Department meeting, 92, 93; reviews
German problem, 23, 124, 150;

drafts U.S. policy statement, 131;
suggests provisional German government, 131; rebuked by State,
132; and Stuttgart speech (of Secretary Byrnes), 133–36, 289; and
Army of Occupation, 166, 184,
185, 207, 281; at Moscow CFM
Conference, 173–77, 289; at London CFM Conference, 202–203; at
London Six-Power Conference,
221–22; and Labor, 256–61 *passim;*
and imminence of war, 224; and
Berlin Airlift (*see* Blockade of Berlin); and defense of Berlin, 228–
30, 289; and establishment of
German government (*see* German
Federal Republic); with Ecusta Paper and Continental Can Company, 282–84 *passim*
Physical Appearance and Condition:
3, 103, 104, 136, 137, 210
Relations with Superiors and Fellow
Officers: 3, 5, 7, 10, 15, 21, 28,
46–54 *passim*, 57, 63, 65, 67, 68,
77, 90, 100, 104, 105, 110, 124,
128, 132, 133, 137, 143, 165,
171–77 *passim*, 194, 195, 203, 216;
staff, 105, 106 (*see also* Byrnes,
James; Casey, Hugh; Draper, William; Hilldring, John; Eisenhower,
Dwight; McCloy, John J.; McNarney, Joseph; Marshall, George
C.; Smith, Walter Bedell)
Speeches: 15, 16, 80, 81, 249, 281,
282
Views and Opinions: on JCS #1067,
12, 52, 55, 57, 90, 98–100 *passim*,
117, 202, 286; on Allied Control
Authority, 23, 57, 99, 100, 170,
182; on denazification, 54, 55, 59,
72, 117–19, 143–44, 164, 165,
217, 286; on transfer of responsibility to Germans, 76, 79, 80, 81,
166, 201, 207, 210, 285, 286, 289;
on democratization, 58, 79; on end
of Rhineland occupation (after
WW I), 76; on Lend-Lease to
Russia, 87; on IARA, 94; on dollar policy, 85, 161, 199 (*see also*

Humphrey, Don); on anti-fraternization policy, 54; on need for central administrative machinery, 100; on currency reform, 116; on lagging coal production, 191, 192, 201; on internationalization of Ruhr, 171; on Länder constitutions, 147; on war crimes, 138, 139, 251, 252; on barter markets, 140, 141; on political neutrality, 145–47, 187, 257, 258; on Byrnes resignation, 171; on end of military government, 198; on reparations compromise, 150, 151, 289; on communism, 202; on food shortages, 137, 138, 157, 207, 208; on socialization, 187, 192, 258, 259; on West German government, 202; on takeover by State Department, 206, 207, 208, 225

Clay, Lucius D., Jr. (son of Lucius D. Clay), 283

Clay, Lucius D., III (grandson of Lucius D. Clay), 47, 48

Clay, Marjorie (wife of Lucius D. Clay), 7, 47, 50, 51, 104, 133, 182, 221, 282

Clayton, William L., 194

Clifford, Clark, 151

Coal production, 84, 112, 191, 201, 256

Cohen, Ben, 134, 151, 172, 174–76

Collisson, Norman, 214

Colm, Gerhard, 147

Congressional elections, 155

Connally, Tom, 129, 133, 134

Control Council. *See* Allied Control Authority

Conway, Carl, 283

Couve de Murville, Maurice, and Clay, 222–23, 261, 289

Currency reform
plans for, 114, 115; and Länderrat, 117; and German food production, 157; and foreign trade, 162; printing of, 162, 167, 223, 224; and French opposition, 225–26; and blockade, 223–30 *passim;* impact of, 255; and Clay, 114–16 *passim,* 131, 186, 223–30 *passim;* one currency for Berlin, 268

Dawson, William W., 71

Deane, John R., 34

Decartelization
at ACA, 69; British opposition, 70, 145; at Länderrat, 80; headed by Martin, 120; opposed by Draper, 120, 144, 145; unilateral American proposal, 144; law #56, 163; reorganization, 197; termination, 219–20; and Clay, 68–70, 141, 162, 163, 218–20 *passim,* 286

De Gaulle, Charles, 41, 47, 88, 89, 111, 203

Deindustrialization of Germany
Morgenthau's plan for, 35, 37, 65; and media, 64; Calvin Hoover Report on, 67, 68; and Level of Industry Committee, 76; explained to Länderrat, 80; re-defined by State Department, 96; termination recommended by Hoover, 159; denounced by Soviets, 174 (*see also* Reparations)

Demilitarization, 58, 80, 173, 181

Democratization and Clay, 58, 59, 79, 181

Denazification
in JCS #1067, 52, 53; Stimson on, 55; implementation, 58–61 *passim;* press criticism, 62–64 *passim;* and Länderrat, 80; objective of, 117–18; German views, 117, 118, 141; quadripartite directive on, 118; law of liberation, 119, 141, 142; amnesties, 143, 164, 165; at Moscow CFM Conference, 173, 196; and JCS #1779, 196; changing American public opinion, 195, 196; termination, 197, 217, 218; and Clay, 59–64 *passim,* 70–72 *passim,* 99, 116–19 *passim,* 131, 141–44, 164, 165, 181, 196

Denazification Policy Board, formed, 99; task of, 117, 168

Dewey, Thomas E., 249

Dirksen, Herbert von, 157

Dismantlement. *See* Deindustrialization of Germany
Displaced Persons (DPs), 28, 159
and Clay, 20, 21, 22
Dodge, Joseph, 105, 114, 147
Donnan, Edloe, 106, 207, 235, 281
Dorn, Walter, 60, 99, 164
Dorr, Russell, 215
Douglas, Lewis, 7, 12, 16, 52, 194, 195, 221, 245, 263
Draper, William
appointed economic advisor, 1; and reparations, 65; and decartelization, 69, 70, 120, 144; requests funds for imports, 112; and Meader Report, 163; at Moscow Conference, 183, 191; appointed Undersecretary of Army, 193; and Clay, 194, 202, 203, 206, 224, 226, 240, 242, 247, 250, 258, 266, 287
Dratvin, Mikhail, 121, 122, 123
Dulles, John Foster, 35, 172–77 *passim,* 203, 248

ECA (European Cooperation Administration). *See* Marshall Plan
Echols, Oliver P., 16, 108, 131
Ehard, Hans, 212
Eisenhower, Dwight
learns of deputy, 3; and McCloy, 4, 8; and Bedell Smith, 5; and Wickersham, 12; as Military Governor, 13; meets with Zhukov, 22, 23; attitude toward USSR, 35, 87, 285; directive on German parties, 42; promises combat assignment, 50, 51; and denazification, 54, 62; and Clay, 21, 28, 50, 90, 104, 165, 190; leaves Germany, 104; mentioned, 159, 170, 184
European Advisory Commission, 11, 12, 13, 21, 24, 228
Erhard, Ludwig, 227, 256, 259
EUCOM (European Command), 166

Fahy, Charles, 63, 70, 99, 116
Ferguson, Garland S., Jr., 220

FIAT (Field Information Agency, Technical), and Clay, 106–108
Food rations, 82, 110, 111, 113, 156, 159, 160
Forrestal, James, 136, 239, 242
Fragebogen (questionnaire), 60, 62, 117
Freisler, Roland, 26
French obstructionism, 89, 90, 109–11 *passim,* 121, 124, 188–95 *passim,* 208–10 *passim,* 210, 222–27 *passim,* 261–68 *passim*
Friedrich, Carl, 72

Galbraith, John Kenneth, 191
Geiler, Karl, 80
German elections, 79, 120, 145, 146, 166
German external assets, and Clay, 108, 109
German Federal Republic
French concept, 221; and Clay's views, 222; at London six-power conference, 223; building blocks, 261; German opposition, 261–63; constitution (basic law), 263, 269–74 *passim;* power of Länder, 266, 269, 273, 274; occupation statute, 267, 268, 272, 273; and Clay, 261–78 *passim,* 289, 290
German foreign trade, 84, 85, 112, 121, 122, 161, 162, 199
and export promotion, 86, 162; and export-import offices, 84, 86, 162; and food imports, 83, 84, 155, 161; and export pricing, 199; and sterling area, 200, 201; and Clay, 200, 212
German Standard of Living Board
establishment of, 65; and Calvin Hoover Report, 67
German steel production, 183, 188, 256
and Clay, 96–98, 121
Golay, John F., 276
Goldsmith, Raymond W., 114, 115
Gouin, Felix, heads three party cabinet, 111
Gray, Gordon, 206

Griffith, William, 63, 195

Haislip, Wade H., 58
Hale, William Harlan, 288
Hall, Theo, 196, 218
Hallock, Dick, 184, 224
Handbook for Military Government, 11, 12, 19, 59
Harding, Warren G., 76
Harmon, Ernest, 134
Harriman, Averell, 34, 38, 106, 214
Hawkins, Philip, 163
Hazard, John, 87
Hermes, Andreas, 271
Hester, Hughes, 82
Higging, Marguerite, 195
Hilldring, John, 5, 8, 61, 78
  and Clay, 7, 10, 15, 67, 100, 105, 110, 132, 216
Hillman, Sidney, 257
Hoegner, Wilhelm, 71, 80
Hoesch, Leopold von, 157
Hoover, Calvin, 66–68 *passim*, 86
Hoover, Herbert, and Clay, 155–59 *passim*, 161–65 *passim*, 216
Hopkins, Harry, 34, 35, 87
Hougland, Peter, 68
Howley, Frank, 24–26, 234, 238, 239, 242, 248
Huebner, Clarence, 166, 184, 207, 235
Hull, Cordell, 284
Humphrey, Don D.
  assists Calvin Hoover, 66; quotes Clay on "Bad Orders," 72; opposes export policy, 85; on steel settlement, 97, 98; on Clay's use of staff, 106, 287; on Clay's nervous tension, 136; drafts reparations compromise, 149–51 *passim*, 171; at Moscow conference, 176; and on democratization, 286

IARA (Interallied Reparations Agency), 93, 189, 203, 215, 216
I.G. Farben industry, 69, 107, 197, 220
Inflation, 84, 113–18 *passim*

Soviet approaches, 113–14 (*see also* Black market)

JCS #1067
  efforts to modify, 12; date of effectiveness, 27; drafting of, 37; on displaced persons, 20; on denazification, 52, 53, 62, 143; on fraternization, 54; on concentration of economic power, 69; Stimson's comments on, 55; and Potsdam agreement, 57; and M.G. Law #8, 64; and disease and unrest formula, 37, 52, 83, 98; neutralization of, 90, 114, 158; and quadripartite denazification directive, 118; attacked by Herbert Hoover, 158; replaced by JCS #1779, 188, 193
JEIA (Joint Export Import Agency), 162, 199, 212, 214, 216
Jessup, Philipp, 246, 249, 250, 272, 276
Jodl, Alfred, 139

Keenan, Joseph B., 116, 257
Keitel, Wilhelm, 139
Kennan, George, 91, 136, 148, 277
Keynes, John Maynard, 38, 40
Kindleberger, Charles, 175
Koeltz, Louis Marie, 89, 90, 97, 123
Koenig, Pierre, 89, 90, 109, 188, 226, 227, 263, 264, 266, 268, 269, 270, 271, 275, 276
Kolpakov, Boris T., 149
Kommandatura, 13, 24–26 *passim*, 146, 234, 235
Koster, Adolf, 157
Koval, Konstantin Ivanovich, 149

LaFollette, Charles, 260
Länderrat
  organization of, 80, 81, 120; and currency reform, 117; and denazification, 117, 118, 143; as model, 124; problems of bizonal merger, 148; and reparations, 216; and Clay, 120–24 *passim*, 166, 168

Lattre de Tassigny, Jean de, 22
Leahy, William, 92, 151
Lee, John, 4
LeMay, Curtis, 236, 237, 241
Lend-Lease for Soviet Union, 33, 34, 87
Lenin, Vladimir, 31, 33, 172
Level of Industry Committee (of Control Council)
   establishment, 76; Calvin Hoover report, 86; staffs, 95; disagreements on data, 95, 96; final plan, 122; and Clay, 94, 121
Lie, Trygve, 249, 250
Litchfield, Edward, 105
Litvinov, Maxim, 32
Lochner, Louis, 156
Loewenfeld, Philipp, 62
Logan, William, 212
Lovett, Robert, 193, 200, 206, 239

MacArthur, Douglas, 7, 49, 250, 287
MacLean, Donald, 223
Marshall, George C.
   and Eisenhower, 5, 8, 13, 51; Secretary of State, 171; and Clay, 172–77 passim, 182, 183, 186, 193, 194, 203, 207, 245; at Harvard, 189; and blockade, 240, 245, 246; resignation, 267
Marshall Plan (European recovery program), 158, 189, 193, 212, 272
   and Clay, 194, 195, 213, 214, 246
Martin, James Stewart, 120, 144, 162, 163, 197, 218
McCloy, John J.
   considered for Deputy Military Governor, 4, 5; at SHAEF, 8; disease and unrest formula, 37, 90; and Lewis Douglas, 52; quoted, 56; and Clay, 18, 52, 54, 57, 63, 65, 68, 77, 80
McKinzie, Richard, 213
McLean, Donald S., 7, 78, 99
McNarney, Joseph T., 147, 159, 164–66
   and Clay, 104, 124, 133, 134
McSherry, Frank, 8–10, 15
Maier, Reinhold, 80, 118, 119, 261

Margolin, Oliver, 157, 158
Matthews, Freeman, 27, 93, 148, 172, 176
Meader, George, 162, 163
Middleton, Drew, 17, 47
Military Government Law #8 (on denazification)
   drafting of, 63, 116; content, 63, 64; impact, 70, 71, 99; as an interim solution, 116
Mills, Sir Henry Percy, 70
Molotov, Vyacheslav M., 33, 129, 130, 174, 175, 202, 203, 244, 245
Montgomery, Sir Bernard, 22
Morgenthau, Henry, 4, 11, 32, 35, 36, 37, 65, 68, 113
Murphy, Robert D.
   in Africa, 8; at press conference, 15; at meeting of Supreme Commanders, 22; at conference with Zhukov, 24; quoted, 31, 42; explains French policy, 94; opposes Clay, 106; intervenes at Clay's resignations, 128, 190, 194; at Stuttgart, 134; supports reparations compromise, 149; mentioned, 7, 144, 176, 193, 221, 235, 245, 275, 278, 282

Nadolny, Rudolph, 271
Noce, Daniel, 172
Noiret, Roger Jean Charles, 226
Norstad, Lauris, 239

O'Donnell, James, 24, 138, 227
O'Dwyer, William, 249
Office of Military Government (U.S.)
   formation, 28; criticized by N.Y.T., 67; and reparations, 68; a "one man show," 78; as part of the executive machinery, 80; and foreign trade policy, 86, 162, 200; and German food production, 138; and decartelization, 144, 145, 163, 218; licenses political parties, 146; staff reduction, 160; and denazification, 165, 196, 218; relation to EUCOM, 166; and coal production, 191; to be replaced by State Department, 206

OMGUS. *See* Office of Military Government (U.S.)
Oppenheimer, Fritz, 164
Osborne, Ralph, 106, 107

Paley, William S., 59
Parks, Floyd L., 24
Patterson, Robert P., 4, 5, 68, 156, 171, 191
Patton, George S., 58, 61, 63, 67
Pauley, Edwin, 38, 65
Petersen, Howard, 147, 165, 189
Pollock, James, 60, 120
Potsdam Agreement
    supersedes JCS #1067, 27, 98; in Clay's hands, 55; as guidepost for Clay, 57, 68; and Morgenthau plan, 65; N.Y.T. claims misinterpretation, 67; on dismantlement, 69; and Level of Industry committee, 76; on central agencies, 80; on foreign trade, 84, 122; French rejection of, 85; re-interpreted by State Department, 96, 98; and Soviets, 243
Potsdam Conference, 26, 35, 39
Price, Byron, 92, 98

Raeder, Erich, 139
Ratchford, Benjamin, 66
Rayburn, Sam, 281
Regional Coordinating Office (in Stuttgart), 120
Reparations
    controversy after W.W.I, 36; opposition to, 37, 38; Potsdam agreement, 39; and Pauley, 65; lack of progress in 1945, 68; and export-import plan, 122; in Soviet zone, 128; compromise on, 149–51, 171; at Moscow CFM conference, 174–76; and effects of revised level of industry, 188; final list, 216; and Clay, 64–66 *passim*, 122, 123, 149–51, 170–77 *passim*, 216–17
Reuter, Ernst, 236, 247, 248, 257, 268
Revised Level of Industry plan, 183, 188, 189, 190, 201, 208, 289

Rhineland occupation (after W.W.I), 76
Riddleberger, James, 27, 51, 56, 93, 172, 176, 270, 271, 288
Robertson, Sir Brian
    background, 97; offended by Clay, 56, 57; opposes steel decision, 97, 98; opposes law on German external assets, 109; on bipartite board, 148; and revised level of industry, 189; and coal production, 191, 192, 201; and foreign trade, 200; and blockade, 240, 247; and German constitution, 269–76 *passim*; mentioned, 176, 209, 263
Roosevelt, Franklin
    recognizes Soviet government, 32; preference for Military Governor, 4; rejects handbook 11; lend-lease, 33, 34; and Morgenthau, 35; at Yalta, 36; postwar planning, 37, 284, 285; and war romanticism, 92, 284; and postwar design, 181; and failure of "noble experiment," 203
Royall, Kenneth, 4, 190, 193, 194, 206, 207, 217, 220, 221, 225, 228, 237–45 *passim*, 250, 267, 272
Ruhr industries, 112, 171, 192, 201, 221, 261, 263; and Clay, 264–66 *passim*, 289

Saltzman, Charles, 206
Schacht, Hjalmar, 69
Schäffer, Friedrich, 62, 63, 71, 80
Schoenbrun, David, 193
Schumacher, Kurt, 236, 255, 259, 262, 274, 275
Schuman, Robert, 263, 270, 271
Semler, Johann, 210, 211
SHAEF (Supreme Headquarters Allied Expeditionary Force)
    Clay's arrival at, 8; and U.S. Group Control Council, 3, 13–18 *passim*; organization, 8–10; civilianization of, 18; disbanded, 27; wheat shipments by, 19, 110; and German P.O.W., 19, 20; and supply of

Berlin, 25; handbook, 59; and denazification, 53, 60, 62; and food situation, 82, 137
Shelley, Edna, 136, 281
Smith, Jean E., 24, 224, 242
Smith, Kingsbury, 272
Smith, Walter Bedell
aspires to be Deputy Military Governor, 3, 5, 194; and command channels, 9, 14, 28; and Clay, 8, 133, 173; comments on cooperation with Soviets, 182; negotiates lifting of blockade, 241–46 passim
Socialization of German industry, 41, 187, 201, 258
Sokolovsky, Vassily Danilovich
at Tempelhof, 22; and Control Council agenda, 22; background, 87; personal relations with Clay, 87, 88, 128, 129; opposes steel decision, 97; at Frank Clay's wedding, 104; suggests reparations compromise, 149; opposes Bizonia, 169; and ACA report, 170; and currency reform, 223, 224; and walk-out at ACA, 224, 225; and blockade, 237–40 passim, 245; mentioned, 177
Somervell, Brehon, 3, 6, 7, 171
Spellman, Francis, 249, 250
Stalin, Josef, 23, 33, 34, 241–44 passim, 272
Stayer, Morrison, 83
Stetter, Hans, 260
Stimson, Henry
and McCloy, 4; on role of Deputy Military Governor, 5; at Bad Homburg, 54; on denazification, 55; on JCS #1067, 55, 90, 218, 286; mentioned, 181
Stolper, Gustav, 157, 158
Strang, Sir William, 200
Stratton, James, 47, 51, 52
Stuttgart speech (of Secretary James Byrnes), 40, 133–36, 141
Sundquist, James, 166, 185, 198, 287
Symington, Stuart, 148

Taylor, Telford, 139
Thorez, Maurice, 111
Trudeau, Arthur, 48, 49, 235
Truman, Harry
withdrawal from Saxony and Thuringia, 21, 23, 241; anti-Russian statements, 33, 92; cancels lend-lease, 34; at Potsdam, 39, with deGaulle, 88; and Byron Price, 91; "no appeasement" policy, 92; and German external assets, 108; and doctrine, 173; blockade of Berlin, 240–42; second administration, 267
Tunner, William, 250
Twardovsky, Fritz von, 271

U.S. demobilization, 18, 19, 21, 23, 28
U.S. expeditionary force in USSR (after W.W.I), 31, 32
USFET (U.S. Forces in European Theater), 16, 17, 70
U.S. Group Control Council
at Versailles, 3; performance, 4; and Wickersham, 10; succeeds German country unit, 11; friction with SHAEF, 14; Clay's appraisal of, 15; at Hochst, 17; and Army channels, 18; and access to Berlin, 21; advance party of, 23; drafts denazification directive, 62; prepares brief on agricultural situation, 81
U.S. Strategic Bombing Survey, 112, 255

Vandenberg, Arthur H., 129, 133, 134, 136, 271
Vishinsky, Andrei Y., 176, 249
Voorhees, Tracy L., 156, 207, 220, 271, 275, 276

Wagoner, Murray van, 212
War criminals, 59, 60
Wedemeyer, Albert, 237
Weeks, Ronald, 23, 26
Weighing program, 98, 137, 138, 157

Weinberg, Sidney J., 46, 283
Weir, Sir Cecil, 120
Wells, Herman, 199
Wheeler, Burton K., 68
Wickersham, Cornelius W., 10–13
Wiesner, Louis, 260
Wilkinson, Lawrence, 144, 199, 264
Winant, John, 21, 28, 70

Wysor, Rufus, 68

Yalta Conference, 5, 35, 36, 37, 65, 88, 243

Zhukov, Grigori K., 22–26 *passim*, 86, 145, 228
Zink, Harold, 119